1421

www.**booksattransworld**.co.uk

1421

THE YEAR
CHINA
DISCOVERED
THE
WORLD

GAVIN MENZIES

BANTAM PRESS

LONDON · NEW YORK · TORONTO · SYDNEY · AUCKLAND

TRANSWORLD PUBLISHERS
61–63 Uxbridge Road, London W5 5SA
a division of The Random House Group Ltd

RANDOM HOUSE AUSTRALIA (PTY) LTD
20 Alfred Street, Milsons Point, Sydney,
New South Wales 2061, Australia

RANDOM HOUSE NEW ZEALAND LTD
18 Poland Road, Glenfield, Auckland 10, New Zealand

RANDOM HOUSE SOUTH AFRICA (PTY) LTD
Endulini, 5a Jubilee Road, Parktown 2193, South Africa

Published 2002 by Bantam Press
a division of Transworld Publishers

A catalogue record for this book is available from the British Library
ISBN 0593 050789

Typeset in 12/15pt Granjon by
Falcon Oast Graphic Art Ltd.

Printed in Great Britain by
Mackays of Chatham, Chatham, Kent

1 3 5 7 9 10 8 6 4 2

This book is dedicated to my beloved wife Marcella, who has travelled with me on the journeys related in this book and through life.

CONTENTS

LIST OF MAPS AND DIAGRAMS

Diagrams

LIST OF PLATES

Kangnido map by Ch'uan Chin and Li Hui. 1402. Ryukoku University Library; the Cape of Good Hope on a stormy day. © *Nik Wheeler/Corbis*.

Galle stele. *Dominic Sansoni*; straits of Malacca, Malaysia. *Chris Caldicott*; Chinese fishing nets at Cochin, Kerala, India. *Ancient Art & Architecture Collection*; coast of Zanzibar. *Chris Caldicott*; the fort at Kilwa, Tanzania. *Werner Forman Archive*; pillar tomb at Kunduchi, Tanzania. *Werner Forman Archive*.

The Piri Reis map, 1513. Topkapi Museum, Istanbul.

View of the South Orkney Islands, Antarctica. *John Noble/Wilderness Photographic Library*; a tabular iceberg, South Ocean, Antarctica. *John Noble/Wilderness Photographic Library*.

between pages 296 and 297

Fourteenth-century blue and white porcelain bowl with a phoenix and a quilin cavorting between lotus scrolls, recovered from the Pandanan wreck, Palawan, Philippines. Courtesy of the National Museum of the Philippines.

The Jean Rotz map, 1542. British Library, Department of Maps.

Lacquer chest by Dámaso Ayala Jiménez, 1997, from the collection of Fomento Cultural Banamex, A.C.; *Rosa laevigata*. © *Dr Koonlin Tan*; bronze cannon; Chinese bronze mirror; coin of Zhu Di (1403–24); two Central American grinding stones. All recovered from the Pandanan wreck, Palawan, Philippines. Courtesy of the National Museum of the Philippines.

The Waldseemüller map, 1507. *Library of Congress, Washington, D.C.*

The Pizzigano chart, 1424. James Ford Bell Library, University of Minnesota, Minneapolis.

between pages 360 and 361

Guadeloupe: La Souffrière, Basse Terre, and Les Saintes from the sea. *Both courtesy Gérard Lafleur*.

The Vinland map. Beinecke Rare Book and Manuscript Library, New Haven;

diver above the Bimini Road. *Lynne Sladky/Associated Press*; underwater view of the Bimini Road. *Wade Pemberton*; pyramid, Guímar, Tenerife, Canary Islands. *Courtesy Casa Chacona Museum.*

Cantino world chart, 1502. Biblioteca Estense, Modena.

Sixteenth-century engraved view of Calicut. *Ancient Art & Architecture Collection*; detail of a 14th-century Catalan atlas, Bibliothèque Nationale, Paris; Christopher Columbus by Ridolfo Ghirlandaio (1483–1561), Museo Navale di Pegli, Genoa. *Photo Scala*; Vasco da Gama, from a Portuguese manuscript, c. 1558, the Pierpont Morgan Library, New York. *Photo Pierpont Morgan Library/Art Resource/Scala*; contemporary anonymous portrait of Ferdinand Magellan. *Photo Scala*; *Captain James Cook, Sir Joseph Banks, Lord Sandwich and two others* by John Hamilton Mortimer, c. 1771, National Library of Australia, Canberra. © *Bridgeman Art Library*; *A View of the 'Endeavour's' Watering Place in the Bay of Good Success*, 1769, British Library. © *Bridgeman Art Library.*

Henry the Navigator, from *The Monument to the Discoveries*, Belèm, Lisbon. © *Dave G. Houser/Corbis*

The line illustrations appearing on the opening pages of the chapters are taken from *The Illustrated Record of Strange Countries* (*I Yü Thu Chih*), c. 1420, and are reproduced by courtesy of the Cambridge University Library.

Sources of other line illustrations are as follows: 120: Bridgeman Art Library; 168: from *Science and Civilisation in China*, Joseph Needham, 1971, Cambridge University Press; 245: from *Nova typis transacta navigatio* by Honorius Philoponus, 1621; 286: The Newport Historical Society (P2278); 323: Mark Horton/Debbie Fulford, from *Shanga, the archaeology of a Muslim trading community on the coast of East Africa* by Mark Horton, 1996, British Institute in East Africa; 360: Heritage-Images/© the British Library; 389: the British Library, Department of Manuscripts.

The endpaper illustration and the maps on xxii–xxiii and 14–15 were drawn by Neil Gower; the remaining maps were compiled by Jerry Fowler and Julia Lloyd.

CHINESE NOMENCLATURE

MOST NAMES ARE RENDERED IN PINYIN, WHICH IS NOW STANDARD in China – for example, Mao Zedong is the modern spelling, not Mao Tse-tung. For simplicity, however, I have retained the older form of romanization known as Wade-Giles for names that have long been familiar to Western readers. The *Wu Pei Chi*, for instance, is more readily recognized than the *Wu Bei Zhi*. I have also kept the more established spellings of Cantonese place names, writing of Hong Kong and Canton rather than Xianggang and Guangdong. Inscriptions on navigational charts have been left in the older form, as have academic texts in the bibliography.

ACKNOWLEDGEMENTS

A BRIEF OUTLINE OF SOME OF THE MORE IMPORTANT MAPS, documents and other pieces of evidence I have used to form the conclusions presented in this book has been included in the Appendices, and the primary and secondary sources I have used are cited in the Bibliography. However, this is a book for the general reader, not the academic; three-quarters of the evidence has had to be omitted for lack of space. For that reason much of the detail of my proofs and calculations and a large amount of other supporting material have been placed on the internet at www.1421.tv. In addition, I am happy to answer any specific queries and to make my research notes available to any bona fide researcher. Contact should be made in writing, via my publisher in the first instance.

Although my name appears on the cover, this book is a collective endeavour and would not have been possible without the dedicated efforts of many more people than I can possibly name in the limited space available. My sincere thanks to all those who have helped me with advice, guidance and support, and to those who have been inadvertently omitted my sincere apologies – corrections will follow in the next edition.

I am indebted first to those in the Royal Navy who educated me in seamanship, cartography and astro-navigation. The discoveries on which the book is based could never have come about without that knowledge. I visited over nine hundred museums in the course of my researches, but must single out the wonderful collections of the British Museum, the Shaanxi Historical Museum in Xian, China, and Lima's Museum of History. I am also grateful to the Biblioteca Marciana and the Museo Correr in Venice; Barcelona's Museu Marítim; the Fornsals Museum, Visby, on the island of

Gottland; the National Maritime Museum, Greenwich; the Smithsonian Institution; the James Cook Museum in northern Australia; the Waikato Museum of Art and History, Auckland, New Zealand; the Tillamook County Pioneer Museum, Oregon; the Natural History Museum of North California; the Zihuantanejo Museum, Michoacán, Mexico; the National Museum of Australia; and the Warrnambool Art Gallery.

In England, my sincere thanks go to the British Library, particularly the staff of the Map Library and Humanities I, with its matchless collection and superb service. The School of Oriental and African Studies, the School of Slavonic Studies, and the School of Islamic Studies of the University of London; the Royal Asiatic Society; the Public Record Office; the Hakluyt Society; the Science Museum and the Natural History Museum; the Bodleian Library, Oxford; the Cambridge University Library and the Eastern Art Library, Oxford, have also been very helpful.

All the distinguished experts I asked to read and comment on my draft have generously given of their time. I am grateful for their help but must stress that responsibility for the opinions expressed in this book and for any errors and omissions rests with me alone. First and foremost, my thanks go to Professor Carol Urness, curator of the James Ford Bell Library at the University of Minnesota, Minneapolis; and also to Dr Joseph McDermott, Faculty of Oriental Studies, University of Cambridge; Professor John E. Wills Jr, Professor of History at the University of Southern California; Professor G. R. Hawting, Professor of Medieval and Islamic History at the School of Oriental and African Studies, London; Dr Konrad Hirschler; John Julius Norwich; Dr Taylor Terlecki of the Faculty of Medieval and Modern Languages and Literature, University of Oxford; Dr Ilenya Schiavon of the Venice State Archive; Dr Marjorie Grice-Hutchinson; Professor Sir John Elliott, Regius Professor of Modern History, University of Oxford; and Admiral Sir John Woodward GBE KCB.

Among other individuals, I must mention Dr Linda Clark at the

History of Parliament Offices; Professor Mike Baillie of the Palaeoecology Centre of the School of Archaeology and Palaeoecology, Queen's University, Belfast; Dr Robert Massey of the Royal Observatory, Greenwich; Ms Helen Stafford and Professor Philip Woodworth of the Proudman Oceanographic Laboratory, Birkenhead; Bob Headland of the Scott Polar Research Institute, Cambridge; Shane Winser of the Royal Geographical Society (with the Institute of British Geographers); Brian Thynne of the Caird Library of the National Maritime Museum, Greenwich; Dr Piero Falchetta, librarian of the Biblioteca Marciana, Venice; Chris Stringer of London's Natural History Museum; Professor Bryan Sykes, Professor of Human Genetics at the University of Oxford; Vice-Admiral Sir Ian McIntosh KBE CB DSO DSC; Dr Fernanda Allen; and Ron Hughes.

My thanks also go to Dr Johan de Zoete, curator of the Museum Enschede, Haarlem; Dr Muhammad Waley, curator of the Persian and Turkish Collection at the British Museum; Stuart Stirling; Professor Timothy Laughton, Department of Art History, University of Essex; Professor Sue Povey, a human geneticist at the Department of Biology, University College, London; the late Dr Josie Hicks; Professor Christie G. Turner II, Regent's Professor of Anthropology, Arizona State University; Professor John Oliver, Department of Astronomy, University of Florida; Marshall Payn; Alan Stimson, formerly Keeper of Navigation, Royal Observatory, Greenwich; and Dr K. Tan.

Professor João Camilo dos Santos of the Portuguese Embassy, London; the curator of the Torre do Tombo in Lisbon; Daphne Horne, curator of the Gympie Historical Society Museum, Queensland; Brett Green; Vanessa Collingridge; Michael Fitzgerald, curator of the Tepapa Museum, Tongarewa; Catherine Mercer, librarian at the Waikato Museum; Robin J. Watt; and Professor Roderich Ptak of Munich University have all been very helpful to me too, and my thanks must also go to Steven Hallett of Xanadu Productions; Professor Yingsheng Liu, Nanjing; Dr Eusebio Dizon,

Director of Underwater Research, Museum of Manila, Philippines; Madam Wenlan Peng, formerly Head of English Language Broadcasting for Central China Television; Captain Richard Channon; Commander Mike Tuohy; Christine Handte, the captain of the sailing junk *RV Heraclitus*; the curator of the Macao Maritime Museum; Dr Wang Tao of the School of Oriental and African Studies; Miss Viviana Wong; Professor Kenneth Hsu; Dr John Furry; David Stewart and the Reed and St Louis families; Robert Metcalf; Commodore Bill Swinley, former Chief of the Bermudan Armed Forces; Monsieur Gérard Lafleur; David Borden; Kirsten and Professor Paul Seaver; Professor George Maul, Florida Institute of Technology; Professor Maude Phipps; and Dr K.K. Tan.

I must also express my gratitude to Voyages Jules Verne, which provides wonderful tours with extremely knowledgeable guides; Anthony Simonds-Gooding; Wendi and Mike Watson and their team; Steven Williams and Sophie Ransom of Midas Public Relations; Jack Pizzey; Pearson Broadband and Paladin Invision and their teams. I'm also grateful to Dr Joseph McDermott, Elizabeth Hay, Dr Hubert Lal, Dr Taylor Terlecki, Dr Marjorie Grice-Hutchinson, Ian Hudson, Amy Crocker, my wife Marcella Menzies and our elder daughter, Vanessa Gilodi-Johnson, all of whom have provided translations from a variety of foreign languages.

Luigi Bonomi of Sheil Land Associates has been a wonderful literary agent, and at my publishers, Transworld, my heartfelt thanks go to Larry Finlay, Sally Gaminara, publishing director of Bantam Press, Simon Thorogood, Deborah Adams, Julia Lloyd, Alison Martin, Rebecca Winfield, Helen Edwards, Sheila Lee, Neil Hanson, Garry Prior, John Blake, Ed Christie and their teams. I'm also grateful to Gillian Bromley, Daniel Balado, Elizabeth Dobson, Joanne Hill and Sarah Ereira for their work on the text.

Finally, my appreciation to those who have stood by me and the book for fourteen long years. My special thanks to Frank Hopkins, an old friend and an Oxford history scholar, and to Laura Tatham –

no writer could have had a more skilful, loyal and dedicated assistant. Last of all, Marcella, my wife, has provided enduring love and support and the finances to pay for my researches. I and this book owe everything to her.

Gavin Menzies
London
July 2002

The countries beyond the horizon and at the ends of the earth have all become subjects and to the most western of the western or the most northern of the northern countries, however far away they may be.

– part of an inscription on a memorial stone erected by Admiral Zheng He at Ch'ang Lo on the banks of the Yangtze estuary in 1431

Voyages of the Treasure

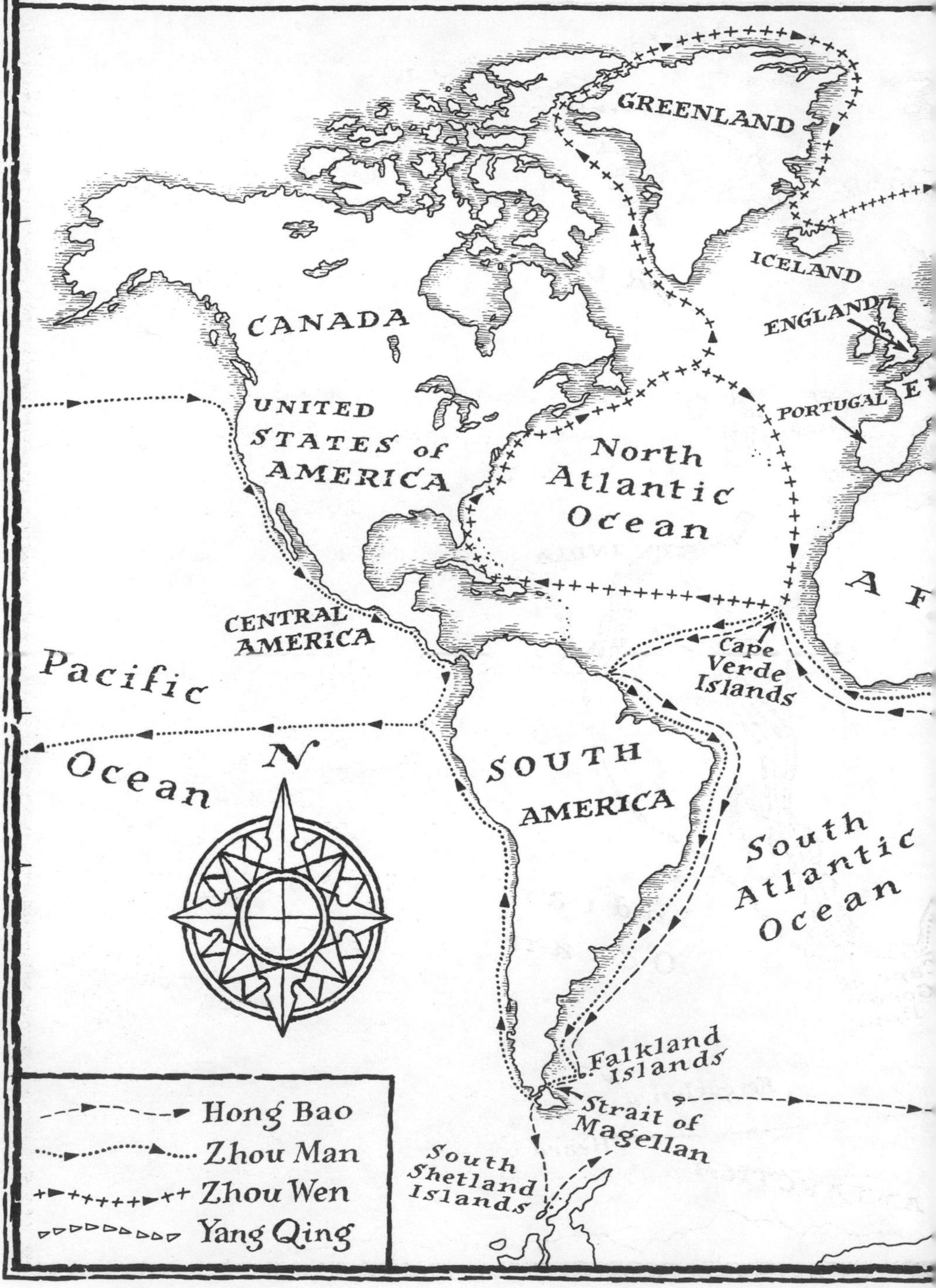

GREENLAND

ICELAND

ENGLAND

CANADA

PORTUGAL

UNITED STATES of AMERICA

North Atlantic Ocean

A F

Pacific

CENTRAL AMERICA

Cape Verde Islands

Ocean

N

SOUTH AMERICA

South Atlantic Ocean

Falkland Islands

Strait of Magellan

South Shetland Islands

- - -►------► Hong Bao
· · · · ·►· · · · ·►· · · Zhou Man
+ ►+ + + + +►+ + Zhou Wen
▷▷▷▷▷▷▷▷▷▷ Yang Qing

Fleets, 1421~3

Gower

Arctic Ocean

RUSSIA

...OPE

...ICA

Beijing
CHINA

JAPAN

INDIA

Spice
Islands

AUSTRALIA

NEW
ZEALAND

Indian
Ocean

Campbell
Island

Cape of
Good
Hope

Kerguelen

Heard Island

ANTARCTICA

INTRODUCTION

OVER TEN YEARS AGO I STUMBLED UPON AN INCREDIBLE discovery, a clue hidden in an ancient map which, though it did not lead to buried treasure, suggested that the history of the world as it has been known and handed down for centuries would have to be radically revised.

I was pursuing an interest that had become a consuming passion for me: medieval history, and in particular the maps and charts of early explorers. I loved to examine these old charts, tracing contours, coastlines, the shifting shapes of shoals and sandbars, the menace of rocks and reefs. I followed the ebb and flow of tides, the pull of unseen currents and the track of prevailing winds, peeling back the layers of meaning contained within the charts.

The wintry plains of Minnesota started me on my research. It was not necessarily the first place you would think of to discover a document with such profound implications, but the James Ford Bell Library at the University of Minnesota has a remarkable collection of early maps and charts, and one in particular had attracted my attention. It had been in the collection of Sir Thomas Phillips, a wealthy British collector born in the late eighteenth century, but its existence had remained virtually unknown until the collection was rediscovered half a century ago.

The chart was dated 1424 and signed by a Venetian cartographer by the name of Zuane Pizzigano. It showed Europe and parts of Africa, and as I compared it with a modern map, I realized that the cartographer had drawn the coastlines of Europe accurately. It was an extraordinary cartographic achievement for that era, but not one of earth-shattering significance in itself. However, my eye was then drawn to the most curious feature of the map. The cartographer had also drawn a group of four islands far out in the western Atlantic. The names he gave them – Satanazes, Antilia, Saya and Ymana – did not correspond to any modern place-names and there are no large islands in the area where he had positioned them. That could have been a simple error in calculating longitude, for Europeans did not master that difficult art until well into the eighteenth century, but my first, troubling thought was that the islands were imaginary and had existed only in the mind of the man who drew the chart.

I looked again. The two biggest islands were painted in bold colours, Antilia in dark blue, Satanazes in pillar-box red. The rest of the chart was uncoloured, and it seemed certain that Pizzigano wished to emphasize that these were important, recently discovered islands. All the names marked on the chart appeared to be in medieval Portuguese. Antilia – *anti* 'on the opposite side of' and *ilha* 'island' – meant an island on the opposite side of the Atlantic to Portugal; other than that, there was nothing in the name to help me identify it. Satanazes, 'Satan's or Devil's Island', was a very distinctive name. A greater number of towns were marked on the largest island, Antilia, indicating that it was better known. Satanazes had only five names, and featured the enigmatic words *con* and *ymana*.

My interest was now thoroughly aroused. What were these islands? Did they really exist? The date of the map, its provenance and authenticity were unimpeachable, yet if it was genuine, it marked lands in places where, according to the accepted history, no Europeans had ventured for another seven decades. After several months of examining charts and documents in map rooms and archives, I became convinced that Antilia and Satanazes were actually the Caribbean islands of Puerto Rico and Guadeloupe. There were far too many points of similarity between them for it to be a coincidence, but that meant that somebody had accurately surveyed the islands some seventy years before Columbus reached the Caribbean. This seemed an incredible revelation – Columbus had not discovered the New World, yet his voyage had always been regarded as an absolutely defining moment. It marked the point when, led by the Portuguese, Europeans had begun to embark on the great voyages of discovery, the long, restless expansion over the face of the globe that was to characterize the next five hundred years.

I needed further evidence to support my discovery and I sought the help of an expert in medieval Portuguese, Professor João Camilo dos Santos, who was then at the Portuguese Embassy in London. He examined the Pizzigano chart and corrected my translation of *con/ymana* to 'volcano erupts there'. The words had been placed in the southern part of Satanazes, just where there are three volcanoes on Guadeloupe today. Did they erupt before 1424? In high excitement I rang the Smithsonian Institution in Washington DC. The volcanoes had erupted twice between 1400 and 1440 but had otherwise been dormant during the previous hundred years and the succeeding two and a half centuries. Moreover, there were no other volcanic eruptions in the Caribbean at that time. I felt I was home and dry; I believed I had found solid evidence that someone had reached the Caribbean and established a secret colony there sixty-eight years before Columbus.

Professor Camilo dos Santos gave me an introduction to the curator of the State Archives in the Torre do Tombo in Lisbon, and on a beautiful early autumn afternoon I began further research there, hoping for corroboration of my hunch about Portuguese landings in the Caribbean. To my astonishment, I came across something entirely different: far from the Portuguese having discovered those Caribbean islands, they were completely unknown to them at the time Pizzigano was drawing his chart. They were, however, shown on another, slightly later chart – drawn by some other, unknown cartographer – that had not come into Portuguese hands until 1428. In addition, I found a command issued by the Portuguese prince Henry the Navigator to his sea-captains in 1431, ordering them to go and find the islands of Antilia shown on the 1428 chart; had the Portuguese discovered them, Henry's edict would scarcely have been necessary. But if the Portuguese had not discovered and surveyed Antilia and Satanazes, who on earth had? Who had provided Pizzigano and the other cartographers with their information?

I began more research, tracing the rise and fall of medieval civilizations that had long since crumbled into dust. In turn, I eliminated virtually every navy in the world that could feasibly have undertaken such an ambitious voyage in the early decades of the fifteenth century. Venice, the oldest and most powerful naval power in Europe, was in disarray. The old Doge was ill, his powers waning, and his successor was waiting in the wings, determined that Venice should abandon its maritime tradition and become a land power. Northern European powers barely had the ships to cross the English Channel, let alone explore new worlds. The Egyptian rulers were mired in civil wars – there were no fewer than five sultans in 1421 alone. The Islamic world was also disintegrating: the Portuguese had invaded its North African heartlands and the once-mighty Asian empire of the Mongol emperor Tamerlane was in pieces.

Who else could have explored the Caribbean? I decided to see if there were other charts like the 1424 map, showing continents that had been surveyed before the European voyages of discovery. The deeper I dug, the more bombshells I uncovered. I was astonished to find that Patagonia and the Andes had been mapped a century before the first European sighted them, and Antarctica had been accurately drawn some four centuries before Europeans reached the continent. The east coast of Africa was shown on another chart, with longitudes that were perfectly correct – something Europeans did not manage to achieve for another three centuries. Australia appeared on another map, three centuries before Cook, and other charts showed the Caribbean, Greenland, the Arctic and the Pacific and Atlantic coasts of both North and South America long before Europeans arrived.

To have drawn maps of the entire world with such accuracy, these explorers, whoever they were, must have circumnavigated the globe. They must have been skilled in astro-navigation and must have found a method of determining longitude to draw maps with negligible longitude errors. To cover the enormous distances involved, they must have been able to sail the oceans for months at a time and that would have meant desalinating sea-water. As I was later to discover, they also prospected and mined for metals, and they were skilled horticulturalists, transplanting animals and plants right across the globe. In short, they had changed the face of the medieval world. I seemed to be looking at a series of the most incredible journeys in the history of mankind, but one that had been completely expunged from human memory, the majority of records destroyed, the achievements ignored and finally forgotten.

These revelations were both astounding and horrifying. If I was to pursue them I would be challenging some of the most basic assumptions about the history of the exploration of the world. Every schoolchild knows the names of the great European explorers and navigators whose exploits have resounded down the ages. Bartolomeu Dias (c. 1450–1500) left Portugal in 1487 and became the first man to round the Cape of Good Hope, the southern tip of Africa. He was driven to the south of the Cape by a storm and when he found no land he turned north, rounding the Cape and making landfall on the east coast of Africa. Vasco da Gama (c. 1469–1525) followed in Dias's wake ten years later. He sailed up the east coast of Africa and crossed the Indian Ocean to India, opening up the first sea route for the spice trade. On 12 October 1492, Christopher Columbus (1451–1506) sighted land in the modern Bahamas. He has gone down in history as the first European to glimpse the New World, though Columbus himself never appreciated this, believing that he had actually reached Asia. He made three further voyages, discovering many of the Caribbean islands and the mainland of Central America. Ferdinand Magellan (c. 1480–1521) followed Columbus and is credited with the discovery of the strait between the Atlantic and the Pacific that bears his name to this day. His ship continued west to complete the first circumnavigation of the world, though Magellan did not survive to see the expedition's triumphant return to Spain, having been killed in the Philippines on 27 April 1521.

All these men owed a huge debt to the great figure of Henry the Navigator (1394–1460), the Portuguese prince whose base in southwest Portugal became an academy for explorers, cartographers, shipwrights and instrument makers. There, the design of European ships was revolutionized, navigational instruments and techniques developed and improved, and impetus given to the great voyages of exploration and colonization.

As I ended my researches in the Torre do Tombo, a mood of utter confusion engulfed me. I spent a misty evening sitting in a bar on Lisbon's waterfront, looking out at Henry the Navigator's statue. His enigmatic smile was one I now understood. We both shared a secret: he had followed others to the New World. The more I brooded, the more intrigued I became. Who were these master mariners who had discovered and charted these new lands and oceans without leaving any trace of having done so, other than these enigmatic maps?

The identity of the master hand was revealed in a curious way. The coasts of Patagonia, the Andes mountains, the Antarctic mainland and the South Shetland Islands had all been drawn with remarkable accuracy on one chart. The distances covered, from Ecuador in the north to the Antarctic peninsula in the south, were immense; a huge fleet must have been required. There was only one nation at that time with the material resources, the scientific knowledge, the ships and the seafaring experience to mount such an epic voyage of discovery. That nation was China, but the thought of searching for incontestable proof that a Chinese fleet had explored the world long before the Europeans filled me with dread. An attempt to uncover the details of any event from nearly six centuries ago would have been daunting enough, but this one was made even more difficult by one massive, perhaps insurmountable, obstacle. In the mid-fifteenth century almost every Chinese map and document of the period was deliberately destroyed by officials of the Chinese court, following an abrupt reversal of its foreign policy. Far from embracing the outside world, after these momentous discoveries China turned in on itself. Anything commemorating its expansionist past was expunged from the record.

If I was to piece together the remarkable story of the Chinese voyages of discovery, I would have to look elsewhere for proof, but I feared almost to begin. It seemed arrogance bordering on hubris to believe that a retired submarine captain could reveal a story many great minds had failed to unearth, but though I was a mere amateur compared to the distinguished academics in the field, I started with one crucial advantage. In 1953, when I joined the Royal Navy at the age of fifteen, Britain was still a world power with great fleets and bases to support them strung right across the globe. During my seventeen years in the Navy I sailed the world in the wake of the great European explorers. Between 1968 and 1970, for example, I was in command of HMS *Rorqual* and took her from China to Australasia, the Pacific and the Americas.

The coasts, cliffs and mountains early explorers had viewed from their quarterdecks were those I saw through a submarine periscope, with roughly the same perspective. I quickly learned that what is seen from sea level is not necessarily what is actually there. In those days satellite navigation was unknown; we had to find our way by the stars. I saw the same stars those great European explorers had seen and calculated my position by measuring the height and direction of the sun, just as they had attempted to do. The mariner's guiding stars in the southern hemisphere are Canopus and the Southern Cross. These stars played a vital role in the extraordinary story I was to uncover, and without the experience of astro-navigation I had gained in the Navy, this book would never have been written and the discoveries I made might have remained unrecognized for many more years.

A layman, no matter how distinguished in other fields, looks at a map or a chart and sees only a series of outlines that may or may not be the misshapen representations of familiar lands. An experienced navigator looking at the same map can deduce far more: where the cartographer who had first charted it had sailed, in what direction, how fast or slow, how near to or far from the land he had been, the state of his knowledge of latitude and longitude, even whether it was night or day. Given sufficient knowledge of the lands and oceans depicted on the chart, a navigator can also explain why what the chart shows as islands could be mountain peaks, why what was then an extensive body of land might now be shoals, reefs and islands, and hence why some lands might have been depicted with curiously distended forms.

I had seen the maps, dating from the fifteenth and early sixteenth centuries, that show parts of the world then unknown to European explorers. There are inaccuracies – some of the lands depicted are unrecognizable, or misshapen, or in locations where no land exists – and because the picture they offer of the world contradicts the accepted history of exploration they have long been dismissed as fables, forgeries or, at best, puzzling anomalies. But I found myself returning to those early maps and charts again and again, and as I studied them and evaluated them, a new picture of the medieval world began to emerge.

My research confirmed that several Chinese fleets had indeed made voyages of exploration in the early years of the fifteenth century. The last and greatest of them all – four fleets combining in one vast armada – set sail in early 1421. The last surviving ships returned to China in the summer and autumn of 1423. There was no extant record of where they had voyaged in the intervening years, but the maps showed that they had not merely rounded the Cape of Good Hope and traversed the Atlantic to chart the islands I had seen on the Pizzigano map of 1424, they had then gone on to explore Antarctica and the Arctic, North and South America, and had crossed the Pacific to Australia. They had solved the problems of calculating latitude and longitude and had mapped the earth and the heavens with equal accuracy.

I was educated by a Chinese *amah* for the first five years of my life – I remember to this day my sorrow at our parting – and I had made a number of visits to China over the years, but despite my interest in that great country, my knowledge of its history was by no means deep. Before I could follow the incredible course of these Chinese voyages of discovery, I would first have to immerse myself in the unfamiliar world of medieval China. That was a voyage of discovery in itself, and my ignorance of those remarkable people was shared, I suspect, by many in the West. The more I learned, the more I was awe-struck by the glory of that ancient, learned and incredibly sophisticated civilization. Their science and technology and their knowledge of the world around them were so far in advance of our own in that era that it was to be three, four and in some cases five centuries before European know-how matched that of the medieval Chinese.

Having learned something of that great civilization, I spent years travelling the globe on the track of the Chinese voyages of exploration. I researched in archives, museums and libraries, visited ancient monuments, castles, palaces and the major sea-ports of the late Middle Ages, explored rocky headlands, coral reefs, lonely beaches and remote islands. Everywhere I went I discovered more and more evidence to support the thesis. It turned out that a tiny handful of Chinese documents and sailing directions had escaped the wholesale destruction of records, and there were several first-person accounts: two by Chinese historians, another by a European merchant, and others by the first European explorers to follow in the Chinese wake, who discovered evidence and artefacts left by their predecessors.

There was also a wealth of physical evidence: Chinese porcelain, silk, votive offerings, artefacts, carved stones left by the Chinese admirals as monuments to their achievements, the wrecks of Chinese junks on the coasts of Africa, America, Australia and New Zealand, and the flora and fauna transplanted far from their places of origin and thriving when the first Europeans appeared. Everything I found was confirmation of the accuracy of the maps that had first captured my imagination. The remarkable information that those maps contain is, and always has been, there for all to see, but it has eluded many eminent historians of China, not for want of any diligence on their part but simply because of their lack of knowledge of astro-navigation and the world's oceans. If I have found information that escaped them, it is only because I knew how to interpret the extraordinary maps and charts that reveal the course and the extent of the voyages of the great Chinese fleets between 1421 and 1423.

Columbus, da Gama, Magellan and Cook were later to make the same 'discoveries' but they all knew they were following in the footsteps of others, for they were carrying copies of the Chinese maps with them when they set off on their own journeys into the 'unknown'. To misuse a famous quotation: if they could see further than others, it was because they were standing on the shoulders of giants.

I

Imperial China

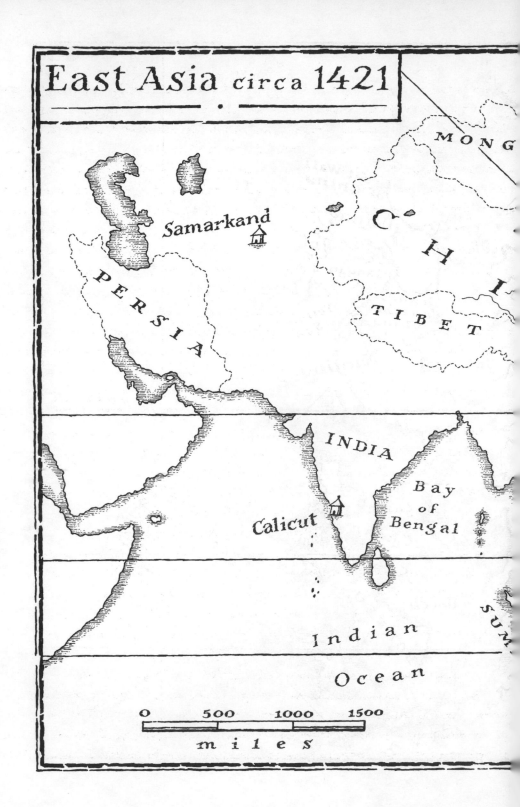

East Asia circa 1421

MONG

C H I

TIBET

PERSIA

Samarkand

INDIA

Calicut

Bay
of
Bengal

Indian

Ocean

SUM

0   500   1000   1500

m i l e s

1

THE
EMPEROR'S
GRAND
PLAN

ON 2 FEBRUARY 1421, CHINA DWARFED EVERY NATION ON earth. On that Chinese New Year's Day, kings and envoys from the length and breadth of Asia, Arabia, Africa and the Indian Ocean assembled amid the splendours of Beijing to pay homage to the Emperor Zhu Di, the Son of Heaven. A fleet of leviathan ships, navigating the oceans with pinpoint accuracy, had brought the rulers and their envoys to pay tribute to the emperor and bear witness to the inauguration of his majestic and mysterious walled capital, the Forbidden City. No fewer than twenty-eight heads of state were present, but the Holy Roman Emperor, the Emperor of Byzantium, the Doge of Venice and the kings of England, France, Spain and Portugal were not among them. They had not been invited, for such backward states, lacking trade goods or any worthwhile scientific knowledge, ranked low on the Chinese emperor's scale of priorities.

Zhu Di was the fourth son of Zhu Yuanzhang, who had risen to become the first Ming emperor despite his lowly birth as the son of a hired labourer from one of the poorest parts of China.[1] In 1352, eight years before Zhu Di's birth, a terrible flood had struck parts of China. The Yellow River had burst its banks, submerging vast areas of farmland, washing away villages and leaving famine and disease in its wake. The country was still in the throes of a terrible epidemic. The Mongols had ruled China since its conquest in 1279 by the great Kublai Khan, grandson of the greatest warlord of them all, Genghis Khan. But in 1352, plagued by famine and disease and desperately poor as a result of the depredations of their Mongol overlords, the peasants around Guangzhou on the Pearl River delta rose in revolt. Zhu Yuanzhang joined the rebels and rapidly emerged as their leader, rallying soldiers and farmers to his cause. During the next three years the revolt spread throughout China. Over decades of peace, the once ferocious Mongol warriors, the scourge of all Asia, had grown idle and complacent. Riven by internal dissension, they proved no match for the army raised by Zhu Di's father. In 1356, his forces captured Nanjing and cut off corn supplies to the Mongols' northern capital, Ta-tu (Beijing).

Zhu Di was eight years old when his father's army entered Ta-tu itself. The last Mongol Emperor of China, Toghon Temur, fled the country, retreating north to the steppe, the Mongol heartland. Zhu Yuanzhang pronounced a new dynasty, the Ming, and proclaimed himself the first emperor, taking the dynastic title Hong Wu.[2] Zhu Di joined the Chinese cavalry and proved himself a brave and skilful officer. At the age of twenty-one he was sent to join the campaign against the Mongol forces still occupying the mountainous south-western province of Yunnan, bordering modern Tibet and Laos, and in 1382 he was ordered to destroy Kun Ming, to the south of the Cloud Mountains, the remaining Mongol stronghold in the province. After the city was taken, the Chinese butchered the adult defenders and castrated those prisoners who had not reached puberty. Thousands of young Mongol boys had their penises and testicles severed. Many perished of shock and disease; the surviving eunuchs were conscripted into the imperial armies or kept as servants or retainers.

Eunuchs served as 'palace menials, harem watch dogs and spies'[3] for rulers throughout the ancient world, in Rome, Greece, North Africa and much of Asia, and they had played an important role throughout Chinese history.[4] Surprisingly, they were intensely loyal to the emperors who had authorized their mutilation. There had been eunuchs at the imperial court since at least the eighth century BC and as many as seventy thousand were employed in and around the capital. Only sexless males were permitted to act as personal servants to the emperor and to guard the women of his family and the quarters occupied by his concubines in the 'Great Within', inside the palace doors. Emperors retained thousands of concubines both as a symbol of their power and to ensure a number of male heirs at a time of high infant mortality; guaranteeing the continuity of the dynasty and the worship of ancestors was a vital part of Chinese cultural rites. Non-eunuchs, even relatives of the emperor and his consorts, were barred from the vicinity of the women's quarters on pain of death. The absence of potent males ensured that any children born to the concubines had been sired by the emperor alone.

Eunuchs also helped to preserve the aura of sanctity and secrecy that surrounded the imperial throne. While the gods granted a 'Mandate of Heaven' to legitimize the emperor's rule, they could rescind it if he proved guilty of human failings, misgovernment or misconduct. It was forbidden to look upon the emperor: even senior officials kept their eyes downcast in the imperial presence, and when he passed through the streets, screens were erected to shield him from public gaze. Only the 'effeminate, cringing eunuchs', slavishly dependent upon the emperor for their very lives, were considered cowed enough to be silent witnesses to his private foibles and weaknesses.[5]

Ma He, one of the boys castrated at Kun Ming, was billeted in the household of Zhu Di, where his name was changed to Zheng He. Many of the Mongols whom Zhu Di and his father expelled had adopted the Muslim faith. Zheng He was a devout Muslim besides being a formidable soldier, and he became Zhu Di's closest adviser. He was a powerful figure, towering above Zhu Di; some accounts say he was over two metres tall and weighed over a hundred kilograms, with 'a stride like a tiger's'.[6] When Zhu Di was elevated to Prince of Yen – a region centred on Beijing – and given the new and more important responsibility of guarding China's northern provinces, Zheng He went with him. Zhu Di based himself in the former Mongol capital, Ta-tu, and renamed it Beijing. By 1387, after over thirty years of fighting, the last vestiges of Mongol rule had been purged from China. Zhu Di's father, the ageing and increasingly paranoid Emperor Hong Wu, systematically purged his military command, eliminating anyone who might offer even the most remote challenge to his authority. Many senior commanders committed suicide rather than bring dishonour and disgrace to their families and their ancestors by being dismissed or executed, but nonetheless, tens of thousands of civil and military officers were put to the sword.

After the death of his first-born son, Hong Wu had chosen his grandson, Zhu Yunwen – Zhu Di's nephew – to succeed him. He distrusted Zhu Di, believing he was a Mongol. Hong Wu had married a Mongol princess but had not been told she was already pregnant (with Zhu Di). When the old emperor died six years later in 1398, Zhu Yunwen duly continued his policy of eliminating potential rivals. In the summer of the following year, assassins were sent north to kill Zhu Di. To escape execution, he abandoned his fine house and for several months became a vagrant on the streets of Beijing, sleeping in gutters at night and wandering the streets by day. He feigned madness, growing filthy and unkempt, unrecognizable as a prince of the imperial line, and the execution squad passed by this apparently harmless vagrant. Then Zhu Di turned on his pursuers. Aided by his loyal eunuch bodyguard, headed by Zheng He, Zhu Di gathered his forces in secret to strike against his would-be killers. He assembled eight hundred men in a park in Beijing, having previously filled it with honking geese to muffle the clanking of their armour and weapons. Taken by surprise, the assassins were themselves butchered. The victorious Zhu Di at once began to raise and train an army.

When he received the news of his men's failure, Zhu Yunwen immediately despatched an army of half a million men to crush Zhu Di, but the seasons were turning, and his troops were sent north from Nanjing wearing only their summer uniforms and straw sandals. Many men froze as the pitiless winter advanced. Zhu Di's army was on manoeuvres outside Beijing when the demoralized troops of Zhu Yunwen began their advance on the city. They were routed in a battle in which even the women of Beijing took part, hurling pots down on their attackers from the city walls.

In 1402, Zhu Di marched south on Nanjing at the head of a great army. The imperial capital was a divided city. The mandarins, the educated elite in Nanjing, loathed the court eunuchs. Their antipathy was deep-seated and almost as old as imperial China itself. As his personal attendants, the eunuchs had the emperor's ear; like

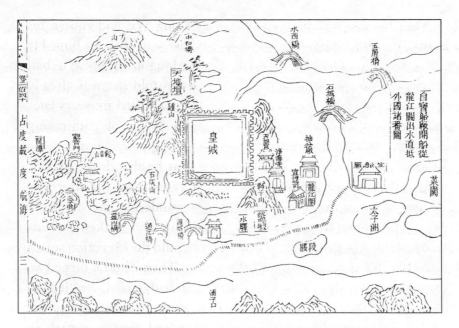

A plan of imperial Nanjing from the *Wu Pei Chi* (*Wu Bei Zhi*). This seventeenth-century treatise on armaments drew on illustrations from earlier manuals; the shipyards are on the right across the bridge.

the courtiers of European rulers, they grew wealthy through their imperial connections. But while the eunuchs held sway in the 'Great Within', mandarins alone were entitled to hold office in the 'Great Without' beyond the palace walls.

Men became mandarins and holders of exalted official positions only after years of intensive study and examinations based exclusively upon the teaching of Confucius (551–479 BC), the 'Great Sage' who had expressed his own disapproval of eunuchs holding positions of power. Eunuchs received no Confucian education and relied solely upon the emperor for advancement. Mandarins were steeped in Confucian ethics and a code of moral values intended to maintain order and hierarchy in society by eliminating the opportunity for people to disturb the *tao* (interaction of natural forces). It determined everyone's life, their rank, their rites and the position allocated to them in the social hierarchy. The Confucian definition of good government required that 'a prince be a prince ... the subject a subject, the father a father, the son a son'.[7] Orderly, well-mannered continuity was at the heart of Confucianism and of mandarin government, and the mandarins saw rural farmers, not foreigners or merchants, as the backbone of society. The farmers represented stability, whereas merchants and foreigners continually upset the *tao*.

The mandarins surrounding Zhu Yunwen had succeeded in marginalizing the court eunuchs, stripping them of much of the power and influence they had previously possessed, and when Zhu Di's army appeared before the walls of Nanjing, the eunuchs threw open the city gates to them. Zhu Di seized the Dragon Throne[8] and pronounced himself emperor, taking the dynastic title Yong Le. Zhu Yunwen was never found. It was believed he had escaped, dressed as a monk. Zheng He remained at the new emperor's side, one of a group of eunuchs who formed an inner circle within Zhu Di's staff. They had personal knowledge of and gained influence in affairs of state, saw the emperor frequently and became familiar with his moods and wishes. As they were permitted to enter the concubines' quarters, they also became conversant with the intrigues among the two thousand women sequestered there.

The eunuchs were once more a political force. In recognition of his service to the emperor, the most powerful figure of all was the Grand Eunuch, Zheng He. In the folds of his white silk cloak he carried a jewelled casket containing the shrunken remnants of his severed penis and testicles, a fact which earned him the nickname San Bao, 'The Three-Jewelled Eunuch'. The casket containing his *pao* – 'manhood treasures' – would accompany him to the next world, where once again he could become a whole man. But in this earthly life, he was sworn to serve and do the bidding of his patron and ruler, the third Ming emperor, Zhu Di.

Within twelve months, despite never having been to sea, Zheng He had been appointed Commander-in-Chief of one of the largest fleets ever built. One of Zhu Di's first orders had been to double the

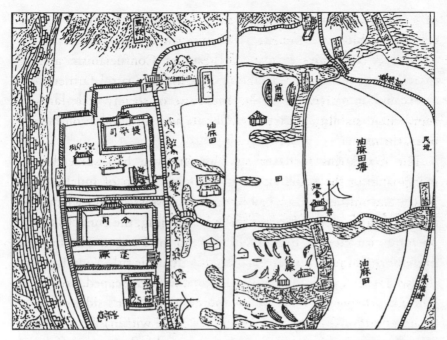

A plan of the Longjiang shipyards from the *Lung Chiang Chhang Chih*, a history
of the yards at the time of Zheng He, published in 1553. The administrative
offices are on the left, the slipways and docks on the right.

size of the Longjiang shipyards, near Nanjing. Already the principal
shipyards in China, they were now vastly expanded, covering several
square miles on the banks of the Yangtze beyond the eastern gate
of Nanjing. Seven vast dry-docks were built, connected by a series of
locks to the river, and each one could be subdivided to permit three
ships to be built simultaneously. They remain there to this day.[9] Zhu
Di's aim was to create what even Kublai Khan had failed to achieve:
a maritime empire spanning the oceans.

Prior to the ninth century, ships voyaging beyond coastal waters
were almost always foreign-owned, but from the ninth century
onwards China developed its own ocean-going fleet. The Song and
Yuan (Mongol) dynasties had maintained large fleets, sent emissaries
overseas and built a substantial foreign trade, gradually wresting
control of the spice trade from the Arabs who had once dominated

it. Zhu Di now embarked on an incredible expansion of the Chinese fleet. In addition to the warships and the merchant fleet he had inherited, Zhu Di commissioned 1,681 new ships, among them many gigantic nine-masted 'treasure ships', named after the huge value and quantity of goods they could carry in their vast holds. Tens of thousands of carpenters, sailmakers and shipwrights from the southern provinces around the shipyards were put to work to build them. In addition to 250 treasure ships, the fleet contained more than 3,500 other vessels. There were 1,350 patrol ships and the same number of combat vessels based at guard stations or island bases, 400 larger warships and another 400 freighters for transporting grain, water and horses for the fleet. The emperor's ships were to sail the oceans of the world and chart them, impressing and intimidating foreign rulers, bringing the entire world into China's 'tribute system'. Rulers paid tribute to China in return for trading privileges and protection against their enemies, but China always gave its trading partners a greater value of goods – silks and porcelain at discounted prices, often funded by soft loans – than was received from them. They were thus in perpetual debt to China. These ships were also tasked with hunting down the fugitive Zhu Yunwen: 'There are some who say he is abroad. The emperor ordered Zheng He to seek out traces of him.'[10] All should know who was the rightful occupant of the Dragon Throne: the Emperor on Horseback, Son of Heaven – Zhu Di.

As soon as he had claimed the imperial throne, Zhu Di decided to relocate the capital to his former stronghold of Beijing. The ageing Tamerlane had decided to seize his last and greatest prize of all, China, and Zhu Di resolved to meet the threat head on. Tamerlane (the anglicized form of Timur-i-Lang, or 'Timur the Lame', a nickname he received as a result of arrow wounds sustained in battle) had proved a worthy successor to his forebears Genghis Khan and Kublai Khan. 'He loved bold and valiant soldiers, by whose aid he opened the locks of terror, tore men to pieces like lions and overturned mountains.'[11] From his capital at Samarkand, straddling the

Silk Road, the great trading route through central Asia, Tamerlane had waged relentless campaigns across Asia, conquering northern India, Persia and Syria, and defeating the Ottomans at Ankara in 1402. Now his gaze had turned eastwards, his aim to destroy the Chinese armies, overthrow Zhu Di and restore China to Mongol rule.

To counter this potent threat, the new emperor took with him to Beijing his court, guarded by a million-strong army, but his vision for the new imperial capital encompassed far more than its being a defensive stronghold to thwart Tamerlane. Kublai Khan had built Ta-tu to a traditional Chinese design and diverted rivers to encircle the city. Zhu Di incorporated the basic elements of Kublai Khan's capital, but he demolished the royal enclosure and replaced it with a classic imperial complex, the Forbidden City, with far more perfect proportions than its former design. The walled capital surrounding it was to be built on an awesome scale: fifteen hundred times the area of walled London at that time and housing fifty times the population.

Yet building the world's greatest city to dazzle his people and intimidate his enemies and all the rulers of the world was only one part of Zhu Di's master plan. He would also repair the Great Wall, built by the first Chinese emperor, Qin Shi Huangdi, during the Qin dynasty (221–206 BC). Qin Shi Huangdi had united the warring provinces of China and was the first man to rule the entire country. The wall was erected at ruinous expense to protect China's northern frontiers from attack, but over the following 1,600 years it had been allowed to crumble into disrepair. Zhu Di began a programme of rebuilding and strengthening, adding watchtowers and turrets along the wall's existing 5,000 kilometres and extending it by a further 1,400. It ran from the Pacific as far west as the Heavenly Mountains in central Asia.

Still Zhu Di's aims were higher. He despatched expeditions to China's eastern neighbours and along the Silk Road across central Asia to recreate the trading empire China had possessed in the golden age of the Tang dynasty over five centuries earlier. All this in addition to his fleet-expansion programme.

Zhu Di intended to achieve all these stupendous goals within two decades. Running through all his policies was his determination that the Chinese should once again believe in themselves and their illustrious history. The Mongols had been expelled, China was Chinese again. Zhu Di was always concerned by the fact that he was not his father's designated heir, and he constantly sought to demonstrate that the gods had bestowed legitimacy on his ascent to the Dragon Throne. Hence the first buildings he commissioned were those of the great ceremonial complex, the Temple of Heaven, at the centre of the new Forbidden City. It was to be not only the stage for the annual ceremonies the emperor, the Son of Heaven, was required to perform, but the very heart of the new Chinese empire. A new observatory, in turn, would be at the epicentre of Beijing. Zhu Di took a personal interest in astronomy, and in the means by which he could build on the wonderful legacy he had inherited in this field. Chinese astronomers had well over two thousand years' experience of recording events in the night sky. They had noted the appearance of a new star in 1300 BC, had charted every arrival of Halley's comet since 240 BC, and by 1054 were describing the supernovas of the Crab Nebula with their attendant pulsars, quasars and neutron stars.

During more than a century of rule over China, the Mongol emperors had neglected this priceless inheritance; in the first year of his reign, Zhu Di restored the nightly practice of recording the stars. His astronomers charted no fewer than 1,400 of them as they traversed the sky, and they were able to predict both solar and lunar eclipses with considerable accuracy. Zhu Di also set up a committee of distinguished astronomers to 'compare and correct the drawings of the guiding stars'[12] and eventually persuaded the Shogun of Japan, the King of Korea, and Prince Ulugh Begh, grandson of Tamerlane, to do the same. The emperor's interest in astronomy was practical, not theoretical. He was determined that his astronomers should perfect new methods of using these guiding stars, enabling his admirals to navigate accurately at sea and correctly locate the new territories they would find on their journeys of discovery. His aim was to ensure that Beijing's great observatory was the reference point from which the entire world would be explored and charted, and all new discoveries located – in short, the centre of the known universe.

The relocation of the capital from Nanjing to Beijing was by far the most complex and far-reaching project undertaken during the Ming dynasty. The move started in 1404, when ten thousand households were forcibly moved north to increase Beijing's population. A vast army of workers was also required to accomplish Zhu Di's vision and hundreds of thousands of Chinese labourers were force-marched to the north; some 335 army divisions were re-deployed to guard them, even though the threat from Tamerlane's Mongol hordes had quickly evaporated. The great warlord had left Samarkand at the head of a vast army in January 1405, his aim to march eastwards through the mountains, set up encampments near the Chinese border, and await the first sign of the approach of spring before striking deep into China, catching the emperor's forces unprepared. Sick and old, Tamerlane was too weak to march and was carried in a litter – a couch carried by bearers – but even so, the privations of the journey over such bleak terrain in the depths of winter were too much for him. He died on 18 February without even sighting the Chinese frontier. His army broke up into rival factions and dispersed.

Zhu Di's plans for Beijing remained unaltered by the news of Tamerlane's death, but feeding the first construction workers soon began to prove difficult. The growing season in the north was short; millet could be grown, but not rice, and corn and barley produced poor yields. There was nowhere near enough grain to feed the tidal waves of workers continuing to arrive. Zhu Di delegated his third son, Zhu Gaozhi, to assume military command of Beijing, and tax rebates were granted to anyone who could grow grain around the city. When this measure failed to produce enough to feed the growing armies of workmen, the emperor decided that the Grand Canal must be repaired and enlarged to carry shipments of grain northwards.

Begun in 486 BC under the Wu dynasty, the canal was one of the wonders of the ancient world. From AD 584 onwards it was extended and the individual sections linked together to form a system stretching for 1,800 kilometres – to this day the longest man-made waterway in the world. However, it was built at a horrific human cost: it is estimated that half of the six million labour force perished at their work. The financial stresses and domestic up-heavals caused by the building of the canal were also one of the principal causes of the rapid collapse of the short-lived Sui dynasty (AD 589–618).

The Grand Canal was the main artery of commerce between north and south China, but its capacity was no longer equal to the demands being placed upon it. The work to enlarge it was carried out in two stages. In 1411, dredging and reconstruction of the northern section began to clear 130 miles of channel, and thirty-six new locks were built, for Beijing was over a hundred feet higher than the Yellow River. Three hundred thousand labourers were employed on the task. The southern section from the Yellow River to the Yangtze was opened in 1415. The completed canal stretched from Beijing in the north to Hangzhou on the coast, south of Shanghai. Grain was transported in no fewer than three thousand flat-bottomed barges, and shipments rose from 2.8 million piculs (approximately 170 million kilograms) in 1416 to five million (300 million kilograms) by the following year.

The insatiable demand for grain to feed the workforce in Beijing led to shortages and famine elsewhere in China, and the timber required for Zhu Di's great schemes stripped the forests of hard-wood. Quite apart from the timber needed to build the Forbidden City, each treasure ship in the emperor's huge fleet consumed the wood of three hundred acres of prime teak forest. The imperial navy was supported by a new fleet of auxiliary store ships, and hundreds of smaller merchant ships were also built to trade between Chinese,

An early Ming grain freighter from the *Thien Kung Kai Wu*
(*Tian Gong Kai Wu*), 'The Exploitation of the Works of Nature', 1637.

Indian and African ports. Yet more hardwood was used in the construction of the thousands of grain barges plying the Grand Canal.
Hundreds of thousands, if not millions, of acres of forest were felled.
Annam (the northern part of modern Vietnam) and Vietnam were
also denuded of trees, sparking off the first of a series of uprisings
against Chinese rule.

Zhu Di also faced domestic problems. The scale and cost of his
grandiose schemes provoked increasingly ferocious opposition from
the mandarins, and even an emperor could not undertake a massive
project like the building of the Forbidden City without their co-
operation. The mandarins were responsible for raising the tax
revenues to fund Zhu Di's projects, and, as with officials of any court
in any country, there were a thousand ways for them to delay or
hinder schemes they did not favour. Zhu Di continued to pursue his
dreams with a customary mixture of guile and ruthlessness, even

going so far as to exploit the arrival of a 'quilin' – in reality a common giraffe obtained by Admiral Zheng He on one of the epic expeditions that began in 1405, when his fleet visited East Africa – to bamboozle and outmanoeuvre his opponents.

The quilin was an important animal in Chinese mythology, said to have the body of a musk deer, the tail of an ox, the forehead of a wolf, the hoofs of a horse, and a fleshy horn like a unicorn. In legend, a quilin had appeared before a young woman, Yen Tschen-tsaii, in the sixth century BC. It dropped a piece of jade into her hand on which was engraved a message: she would bear a son, 'a king without a throne'.[13] The son she bore was Confucius, whose philosophy of system and order was to dominate Chinese thought for over two millennia.

The 'quilin' was presented to Zhu Di by Zheng He on 16 November 1416. Proclaiming its arrival as a sign of heavenly approval for his rule, Zhu Di immediately convened a council to confirm once and for all the merits of transferring the capital from Nanjing to Beijing. The court poet wrote a eulogy to the emperor and, astounded by the appearance of the celestial animal, the mandarins duly obliged him.

The whole of China was now mobilized to achieve the completion of the imperial design. Gangs were sent to fell yet more teak in the forests of the Chinese provinces of Jiangxi, Shanxi and Sichuan, and in Annam and Vietnam. Kilns were built to manufacture enormous quantities of bricks. A workforce of artisans, soldiers and labourers was recruited from all over the Chinese empire. In all, one million men were employed directly on constructing the Forbidden City, three and a half million indirectly. A further one million soldiers stood guard over them.

Once barges could carry food along the Grand Canal to this multitude of workmen, the rate of progress on the Forbidden City accelerated. Improvements were made to the moats, walls and bridges of the former Ta-tu and a start was made on the emperor's residence, the western palace in the Forbidden City. In March 1417, the emperor left Nanjing for the last time, and by the end of that year most of the palace buildings had been completed. In 1420, sections of the southern city wall that had fallen into disrepair under the Mongols were restored, and later that year the Temple of Heaven was completed. Sufficient buildings had also been erected to enable the court permanently to move north, and on Chinese New Year's Day, 2 February 1421, the magnificent new capital was inaugurated. To emphasize the importance of the occasion, the envoys of all visiting heads of state were required to bow and kow-tow – prostrate themselves and press their foreheads to the ground – at Zhu Di's feet. China's absolute dominance was further highlighted by the humiliation imposed on two of the most powerful men in the world: the son and grandson of the mighty Tamerlane. Their first attempt at kow-towing before Zhu Di was deemed unsatisfactory and one of Zhu Di's eunuchs, Haji Maulana, made them repeat it. Their second attempt was also inadequate. Only after their third prostration at his feet did the emperor pronounce himself satisfied.

This array of foreign heads of state kow-towing before the emperor was the culmination of fifteen years' assiduous diplomacy. Chinese foreign policy was quite different from that of the Europeans who followed them to the Indian Ocean many years later. The Chinese preferred to pursue their aims by trade, influence and bribery rather than by open conflict and direct colonization. Zhu Di's policy was to despatch huge armadas every few years throughout the known world, bearing gifts and trade goods; the massive treasure ships carrying a huge array of guns and a travelling army of soldiers were also a potent reminder of his imperial might: China alone had the necessary firepower to protect friendly countries from invasion and quash insurrections against their rulers. The treasure ships returned to China with all manner of exotic items: 'dragon saliva [ambergris], incense and golden amber' and 'lions, gold spotted leopards and camel-birds [ostriches] which are six or seven feet tall' from Africa; gold cloth from Calicut in south-west India, studded with pearls and precious stones; elephants, parrots, sandalwood, peacocks, hardwood, incense, tin and cardamom from Siam (modern Thailand).

Those rulers who accepted the emperor's overlordship were rewarded with titles, protection and trade missions. In south-east Asia, Malacca was rewarded for its loyalty by being promoted as a trading port at the expense of Java and Sumatra; the emperor even personally composed a poem for the Malaccan sultan. The sub-servient Siamese were also extended trading privileges to the detriment of the truculent Cambodians. Korea was especially important to China: Zhu Di lost no time in despatching an envoy to the King of Korea, Yi Pang-Won, granting him an honorary Chinese title. The Koreans needed Chinese medicine, books and astronomical instruments, and in return they agreed to set up an observatory to co-operate with Zhu Di in charting the world. They traded leopards, seals, gold, silver and horses – one thousand of them in 1403, ten thousand the next year. Despite some reluctance, they also found it expedient to comply with Chinese requests to fill Zhu Di's harem with virgins.

As soon as he had expelled the last Mongols from China in 1382, Zhu Di had despatched his eunuch Isiha to the perennially trouble-some region of Manchuria in the far north-east, and in 1413 the Jurchen people of Manchuria responded by sending a prestigious mission to Beijing, where its members were showered with titles, gifts and trading rights. Japan was also assiduously courted. The third Ashikaga Shogun Yoshimitsu was a Sinophile; he lost no time in kow-towing as 'your subject, the King of Japan'.[14] His reward was a string of special ports opened to promote trade with Japan, at Ningbo, Quanzhou and Guangdong (Canton). Like Korea, Japan also set up an observatory to aid Zhu Di's astronomical research.

Having pacified Manchuria and brought Korea and Japan into the Chinese tribute system, Zhu Di next turned his attention to Tibet. Another court eunuch, Hau-Xian, led a mission to court the famous holy man the Karmapa, leader of one of the four sects of Tibetan Buddhism, and bring him to China. When he arrived, a procession of Buddhist monks met him outside the city and Zhu Di bestowed upon him the title 'Divine Son of India Below the Sky and Upon the Earth, Inventor of the Alphabet, Incarnated Buddha, Maintainer of the Kingdom's Prosperity, Source of Rhetoric'. The emperor then presented the Karmapa with a square black hat bearing a diamond-studded emblem. It has been worn by successive incarnations of the Karmapa ever since.

Joining China's tribute system also gave rulers and their envoys the opportunity to visit the capital of the oldest and finest civilization in the world. The traditional imperial capital of Nanjing had received dignitaries from around the world, and now the new capital of Beijing began to welcome the latest arrivals. Although the emperor's main concern was to awe all countries into becoming tribute-bearing states, great efforts were also made to learn about their history, geography, manners and customs. Beijing was to be not only the world's greatest city but its intellectual capital, with encyclopedias and libraries covering every subject known to man. In December 1404, Zhu Di had appointed two long-time advisers, Yao Guang Xiao and Liu Chi, assisted by 2,180 scholars, to take charge of a project, the Yong-le-Dadian, to preserve all known literature and knowledge. It was the largest scholarly enterprise ever undertaken. The result, a massive encyclopedia of four thousand volumes containing some fifty million characters, was completed just before the Forbidden City was inaugurated.

In parallel with this great endeavour, Zhu Di ordered the opinions of 120 philosophers and sages of the Song dynasty to be collated and stored in the Forbidden City together with the complete commentaries of thinkers from the eleventh to the thirteenth centuries. In addition to this wealth of academic knowledge, hundreds of printed novels could be bought from Beijing market stalls. There was nothing remotely comparable anywhere in the world. Printing was unknown in Europe – Gutenberg did not complete his printed Bible for another thirty years – and though Europe was on the eve of the Renaissance that was to transform its culture and scientific knowledge, it lagged far behind China. The library of Henry V (1387–1422) comprised six handwritten books, three of which were on loan to him from a nunnery, and the Florentine Francesco Datini, the wealthiest European merchant of the same era, possessed twelve books, eight of which were on religious subjects.

The voyage to the intellectual paradise of Beijing also offered foreign potentates and envoys many earthly delights. Carried in sumptuous comfort aboard the leviathan ships, they consumed the finest foods and wines, and pleasured themselves with the concubines whose only role was to please these foreign dignitaries. The formal inauguration of the Forbidden City was followed by a sumptuous banquet. Its scale and opulence emphasized China's position at the summit of the civilized world. In comparison, Europe was backward, crude and barbaric. Henry V's marriage to Catherine of Valois took place in London just three weeks after the inauguration of the Forbidden City. Twenty-six thousand guests were entertained in Beijing, where they ate a ten-course banquet served on dishes of the finest porcelain; a mere six hundred guests attended Henry's nuptials and they were served stockfish (salted cod) on rounds of stale bread that acted as plates. Catherine de Valois wore neither knickers nor stockings at her wedding; Zhu Di's favourite concubine was clad in the finest silks and her jewellery included cornelians from Persia, rubies from Sri Lanka, Indian diamonds and jade from Kotan (in Chinese Turkestan). Her perfume contained ambergris from the Pacific, myrrh from Arabia and sandalwood from the Spice Islands. China's army numbered one million men, armed with guns; Henry V could put five thousand men in the field, armed only with longbows, swords and pikes. The fleet that would carry Zhu Di's guests home numbered over a hundred ships with a complement of thirty thousand men; when Henry went to war against France in June of that year, he ferried his army across the Channel in four fishing boats, carrying a hundred men on each crossing and sailing only in daylight hours.

For a further month after the inauguration of the Forbidden City, the rulers and envoys in Beijing were provided with lavish imperial hospitality – the finest foods and wines, the most splendid entertainments and the most beautiful concubines, skilled in the arts of love. Finally, on 3 March 1421, a great ceremony was mounted to commemorate the departure of the envoys for their native lands. A vast honour guard was assembled: 'First came commanders of ten thousands, next commanders of thousands, all numbering about one hundred thousand men . . . Behind them stood troops in serried ranks, two hundred thousand strong . . . The whole body . . . stood so silent it seemed there was not a breathing soul there.'[15] At noon precisely, cymbals clashed, elephants lowered their trunks, and clouds of smoke wafted from incense-holders in the shape of tortoises and cranes. The emperor appeared, striding through the smoke to present the departing ambassadors with their farewell gifts – crates of blue and white porcelain, rolls of silk, bundles of cotton cloth and bamboo cases of jade. His great fleets stood ready to carry them back to Hormuz, Aden, La'Sa and Dhofar in Arabia; to Mogadishu, Brava, Malindi and Mombasa in Africa; to Sri Lanka, Calicut, Cochin and Cambay in India; to Japan, Vietnam, Java, Sumatra, Malacca and Borneo in south-east Asia, and elsewhere.

Admiral Zheng He, dressed in his formal uniform, a long red robe, presented the emperor with his compliments and reported that an armada comprising four of the emperor's great fleets was ready to set sail; the fifth, commanded by Grand Eunuch Yang Qing, had put to sea the previous month. The return of the envoys to their homelands was only the first part of this armada's overall mission. It was then to 'proceed all the way to the end of the earth to collect tribute from the barbarians beyond the seas . . . to attract all under heaven to be civilised in Confucian harmony'.[16] Zheng He's reward for his lifelong, devoted service to his emperor had been the command of five[17] previous treasure fleets tasked with promoting Chinese trade and influence in Asia, India, Africa and the Middle East. Now he was to lead one of the largest armadas the world had ever seen. Zhu

Di had also rewarded other eunuchs for their part in helping him to liberate China. Many of the army commanders in the war against the Mongols were now admirals and captains of his treasure fleets. Zheng He had become a master of delegation. By the fourth voyage fleets were sailing separately. On this great sixth voyage loyal eunuchs would command separate fleets. Zheng He would lead them to the Indian Ocean then return home confident that they would handle their fleets as he had taught them.

The envoys' parting gifts were packed into their carriages, the emperor made a short speech, and then, after kow-towing one last time, the envoys embarked and the procession moved off. Servants ran behind the carriages as they rumbled down to the Grand Canal a mile to the east of the city. There, a fleet of barges decked with silk awnings awaited them. Teams of horses, ten to twelve for each barge, stood on the banks, bamboo poles tied to their harnesses. When the envoys were aboard, whips cracked and the sturdy animals began to drag the barges on their slow journey down to the coast.

Two days and thirty-six locks later, they arrived at Tanggu (near the modern city of Tianjin) on the Yellow Sea. The sight that greeted the envoys at Tanggu was one that must have lingered long in their minds. More than one hundred huge junks rode at anchor, towering above the watchers on the quayside – the ships were taller by far than the thatched houses lining the bay. Surrounding them was a fleet of smaller merchant ships. Each capital ship was about 480 feet in length (444 *chi*, the standard Chinese unit of measurement, equivalent to about 12.5 inches or 32 centimetres) and 180 feet across – big enough to swallow fifty fishing boats. On the prow, glaring serpents' eyes served to frighten away evil spirits. Pennants streamed from the tips of a forest of a thousand masts; below them great sails of red silk, light but immensely strong, were furled on each ship's nine masts. 'When their sails are spread, they are like great clouds in the sky.'[18]

The armada was composed very much like a Second World War convoy. At the centre were the great leviathan flagships, surrounded by a host of merchant junks, most 90 feet long and 30 feet wide. Around the perimeters were squadrons of fast, manoeuvrable warships. As the voyage progressed, trading ships of several other nations, especially Vietnam and India, joined the convoy, taking advantage of the protection afforded by the warships and the opportunities offered as the magnificent armada, almost a trading country in its own right, swept over the oceans. Each treasure ship had sixteen internal watertight compartments, any two of which could be flooded without sinking the ship. Some internal compartments could also be partially flooded to act as tanks for the trained sea-otters used in fishing, or for use by divers entering and leaving the sea. The otters, held on long cords, were employed to herd shoals of fish into nets, a method still practised in parts of China, Malaysia and Bengal today. The admiral's sea cabin was above the stern of his flagship. Below were sixty staterooms for foreign ambassadors, envoys and their entourages. Their concubines were housed in adjacent cabins and most had balconies overlooking the sea. Chinese ambassadors, one for each country to be visited, were housed in less grand but nonetheless spacious apartments. Each ambassador had ten assistants as *chefs de protocol* and a further fifty-two eunuchs served as secretaries. The crewmen's quarters were on the lower decks.

In 1407, Zheng He had established a language school in Nanjing, the Ssu-i-Quan (Si Yi Guan), to train interpreters, and sixteen of its finest graduates travelled with the fleets, enabling the admirals to communicate with rulers from India to Africa in Arabic, Persian, Swahili, Hindi, Tamil and many other languages. Religious tolerance was one of Zhu Di's great virtues, and the junks also habitually carried Islamic, Hindu and Buddhist savants to provide advice and guidance. Buddhism, with its teachings of universal compassion and tolerance, had been the religion of the majority of the Chinese people for centuries. Buddhism in no way conflicted with Confucianism, which could be said to be a code of civic values rather than a religion. On this sixth and final voyage of the treasure fleets which would last until 1423, the Buddhist monk Sheng Hui and the religious leaders Ha San and Pu He Ri were aboard.[19] After the inauguration of the Forbidden City and the dedication of the awesome encyclopedia the Yong-le-Dadian, thousands of scholars found themselves without an obvious role. It would have been natural for Zhu Di to send them overseas on the great voyages of exploration. Through interpreters, Chinese mathematicians, astronomers, engineers and architects would have been able to converse with and learn from their counterparts throughout the Indian Ocean. Once the ambassadors and their entourages had disembarked, the vast ships with their labyrinths of cabins would have been well suited to use as laboratories for scientific experiments. Metallurgists could prospect for minerals in the countries the Chinese visited, physicians could search out new healing plants, medicines and treatments that might help to combat plagues and epidemics, and botanists could propagate valuable food plants. Chinese agricultural scientists and farmers had millennia of experience of developing and propagating hybrids.

The native Chinese flora is perhaps the richest in the world: 'In wealth of its endemic species and in the extent of the genus and species potential of its cultivated plants, China is conspicuous among other centres of origin of plant forms. Moreover the species are usually represented by enormous numbers of botanical varieties and hereditary forms.'[20] In Europe, a long period of economic and agricultural decline followed the fall of the Roman Empire. The plant forms known to the Western world from Theophrastus to the German fathers of botany show that European knowledge had slumped, but there was no corresponding 'dark age' in Chinese scientific history. Botanical knowledge, and the number of plant species recorded by the Chinese, grew steadily as the centuries passed. The contrast between the voyages of discovery of the Chinese and those of the Europeans cannot be overestimated. The only interest of the Spanish and Portuguese was in gathering sustenance, gold and spices, while warding off attacks from the natives. The great Chinese fleets undertook scientific expeditions the

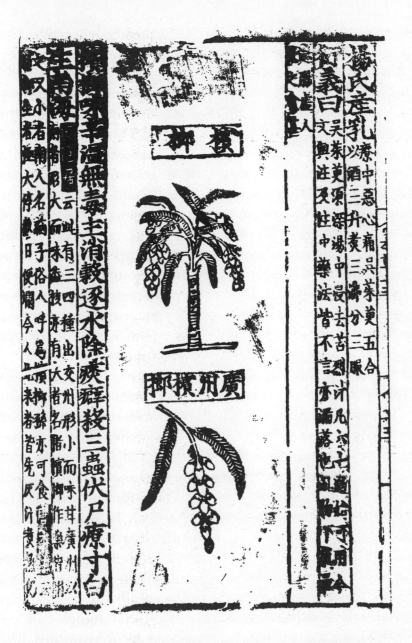

The betel-nut tree from the *Chêng Lei Pên Tshao* (*Cheng Lei Ben Cao*),
'Classified Pharmaceutical Natural History', 1468. Above is the whole palm,
below the fruit. The description to the left of the drawings states that it grows
in the South Seas.

Europeans could not even begin to equal in scale or scope until Captain Cook set sail three and a half centuries later.

As the admirals and envoys embarked, and the armada was readied for sea, the water around the great ships was still black with smaller craft shuttling from ship to shore. For days the port had been in turmoil as cartloads of vegetables and dried fish and hundreds of tons of water were hauled aboard to provision this armada of thirty thousand men for their voyage. Even at this late hour, barges were still bringing final supplies of fresh water and rice. The great armada's ships could remain at sea for over three months and cover at least 4,500 miles without making landfall to replenish food or water, for separate grain ships and water tankers sailed with them. The grain ships also carried an array of flora the Chinese intended to plant in foreign lands, some as further benefits of the tribute system and others to provide food for the Chinese colonies that would be created in new lands. Dogs were also taken aboard as pets, others to be bred for food and to hunt rats, and there were coops of Asiatic chickens as valuable presents for foreign dignitaries. Separate horse-ships carried the mounts for the cavalry.

The staggering size of the individual ships, not to mention the armada itself, can only be understood in comparison with other navies of the same era. In 1421, the next most powerful fleet afloat was that of Venice. The Venetians possessed around three hundred galleys – fast, light, thin-skinned ships built with softwood planking, rowed by oarsmen and only suitable for island-hopping in the calm of a Mediterranean summer. The biggest Venetian galleys were some 150 feet long and 20 feet wide and carried at best 50 tons of cargo. In comparison, Zhu Di's treasure ships were ocean-going monsters built of teak. The rudder of one of these great ships stood 36 feet high – almost as long as the whole of the flagship the *Niña* in which Columbus was later to set sail for the New World. Each treasure ship could carry more than two thousand tons of cargo and reach Malacca in five weeks, Hormuz in the Persian Gulf in twelve. They were capable of sailing the wildest oceans of the world, in voyages lasting years at a time. That so many ships were lost on the Chinese voyages of discovery testifies not to any lack of strength in their construction but rather to the perilous, uncharted waters they explored, from rocky coasts and razor-sharp coral reefs to the ice-strewn oceans of the far north and far south. Venetian galleys were protected by archers; Chinese ships were armed with gunpowder weapons, brass and iron cannon, mortars, flaming arrows and exploding shells that sprayed excrement over their adversaries. In every single respect – construction, cargo capacity, damage control, armament, range, communications, the ability to navigate in the trackless ocean and to repair and maintain their ships at sea for months on end – the Chinese were centuries ahead of Europe. Admiral Zheng He would have had no difficulty in destroying any fleet that crossed his path. A battle between this Chinese armada and the other navies of the world combined would have resembled one between a pack of sharks and a shoal of sprats.

By the end of the middle watch – four in the morning – the last provisions had been lashed down and the armada weighed anchor. A prayer was said to Shao Lin, Taoist goddess of the sea, and then, as their red silk sails slowly filled, the ships, resembling great houses, gathered way before the winds of the north-east monsoon. As they sailed out across the Yellow Sea, the last flickering lights of Tanggu faded into the darkness while the sailors clustered at the rails, strain-ing for a last sight of their homeland. In the long months they would spend travelling the oceans, their only remaining links to the land would be memories, keepsakes and the scented roses many brought with them, growing them in pots and even sharing their water rations with them. The majority of those seamen at the rails would never see China again. Many would die, many others would be ship-wrecked or left behind to set up colonies on foreign shores. Those who eventually returned after two and a half years at sea would find their country convulsed and transformed beyond all recognition.

2

A
THUNDERBOLT
STRIKES

O N THE NIGHT OF 9 MAY 1421, TWO MONTHS AFTER ZHENG
He's armada had set sail, a violent storm broke over the
Forbidden City.

On this night by chance a conflagration started . . . lightning struck the top of
the palace that had been newly constructed by the Emperor. The fire that
started in that building enveloped it in such a manner that it seemed as if
100,000 torches provided with oil and wicks had been lit up therein . . . so
much so that the whole city was set ablaze with the light of that conflagration
and the fire spreading . . . it burnt down the Ladies' Apartments behind the
Hall of Audience . . . about 250 quarters were consumed to ashes, burning a
large number of men and women. It continued burning like that until it was
day and in spite of all efforts, the fire could not be brought under control until
it was afternoon prayer time.[1]

Balls of fire appeared to travel down the Imperial Way itself, along
the very axis of the Forbidden City, destroying the Hall of Great
Harmony, the Hall of Central Harmony and the Hall of Preserving
Harmony – the magnificent palaces where Zhu Di had received
leaders of the world three months earlier. The emperor's throne was
burned to cinders. 'In his anguish he repaired to the temple and
prayed with great importunity, saying, "The God of Heaven is angry
with me, and, therefore, has burnt my palace; although I have done
no evil act. I have neither offended my father, nor mother, nor have
I acted tyrannically." '[2]

The shock killed the emperor's favourite concubine. Zhu Di was
so distraught that he was unable to make proper arrangements for
her burial in the imperial mausoleum.

He fell ill owing to his anguish and on account of this it could not be
ascertained as to in what manner the dead personage was buried . . . The
private horses of the deceased lady were let loose to graze freely . . . on the
mountain where the sepulchre was situated. They had also posted about that
sepulchre a number of maidens and eunuchs . . . leaving for them provisions

to last five years so that after that period when their food got exhausted, they might likewise die there.[3]

Chinese emperors believed they ruled with the mandate of heaven. The manner in which the lightning struck and the severity of the fire that followed could hardly have been more ominous for Zhu Di. An event of this terrible nature could only signal the gods' demand for a change of emperor. Zhu Di temporarily handed power to his son, Zhu Gaozhi. 'The illness of the Emperor having increased, his son used to come and sit in the audience hall.'[4] Struggling to comprehend the nature of the calamity that had befallen him, the emperor then issued an edict to his people:

> My heart is full of trepidation, I do not know how to handle it. It seems that there has been some laxness in the rituals of honouring heaven and serving the spirits. Perhaps there has been some transgression of the ancestral law or some perversion of government affairs. Perhaps mean men hold rank while good men flee and hide themselves, and the good and evil are not distinguished. Perhaps punishments and jailings have been excessive and unjustly applied to the innocent, and the straight and the crooked not discriminated . . . Is this what brought about [the fire]? Harshness to the people below and above, going against heaven. I cannot find the reason in my confusion . . . If our actions have in fact been improper, you should lay these out one by one, hiding nothing, so that we may try to reform ourselves and regain the favour of heaven.[5]

The edict unleashed a predictable storm of criticism from the mandarins. Most of it was targeted on Zhu Di's grandiose plans and projects, notably the Forbidden City that the gods had destroyed. Vast areas had been denuded of trees to build the enormous halls, tens of thousands of artisans had laboured for years on the fabulous rooms, huge sums had been invested in marble and jade, the Grand Canal had been rebuilt using a million teaspoons to ferry grain, and the treasury drained to such an extent that peasants had even been reduced to eating grass. And all this toil, suffering and sacrifice had led only to a carpet of ashes and cinders. The fires also coincided with a terrible epidemic of some unknown disease that had been raging in the south for two years. More than 174,000 people had died in the province of Fujian alone and their bodies lay rotting in the fields, for there was no-one to bury them. The epidemic seemed yet another sign of the gods' anger.

The mandarin Minister of Revenue, Xia Yuanji, who had managed to find the funds for the Forbidden City and for Zheng He's great armada, bravely stepped forward to accept personal responsibility for the catastrophe, but to no avail. Frantic efforts were made to pacify the people. Twenty-six high-ranking mandarin court officials were sent on 'calming and soothing' missions[6] and, in an attempt to save his throne, Zhu Di issued a series of ill-conceived decrees. A halt was placed on future voyages of the treasure fleets and foreign travel was prohibited.

Zhu Di had been plagued by other indignities and misfortunes. He had suffered a series of strokes during the previous four years and was being treated with an elixir containing arsenic and mercury that was probably poisoning him. Shortly before the great fire, he had also been thrown from his charger, Tamerlane's former steed and a present from one of the Mongol conqueror's sons, King Shah Rukh of Persia. Zhu Di was so furious that he was determined to put Shah Rukh's ambassador to death.

Thereafter the Qazi, coming forward, said to the ambassadors: 'Dismount and when the Emperor arrives prostrate yourselves on the ground!' They did so.

When the Emperor came near he asked them to mount again. The ambassadors mounted and proceeded along with him. The Emperor began to make complaint saying to Shadi Khwaja: 'I mounted for chase one of the horses which you brought me, and it being extremely old and feeble fell down throwing me off. Ever since that day my hand is giving me pain and has become black and blue. It is only by applying gold a good deal that the pain has abated a little.'[7]

A mandarin replied on behalf of the Persians:

> The ambassadors are in no way to blame, for if their sovereign had sent good horses or bad as presents, those persons had no choice in the matter . . . Moreover, even if your Majesty has the envoys cut in pieces it shall make no difference to their sovereign. On the other hand . . . the whole world would say that the Emperor of China had acted contrary to all convention by imprisoning the envoys.[8]

Slurs on Zhu Di's manhood were even more humiliating. He had fathered no children after 1404, and had probably been impotent since the Empress Xiu's death in 1407. Two imperial concubines had been found trying to assuage their sexual frustration by attempting intercourse with one of the eunuchs who guarded them. In the subsequent witch hunt, 2,800 concubines and eunuchs were alleged to have been involved in treasonable activity; Zhu Di personally executed many of them, but before they died a number of Korean concubines flung insults at him, taunting him for his impotence: 'You have lost your yang power and that is why your concubines resorted to relationship with a young eunuch.'[9]

Apparently abandoned by heaven, the humiliated, ill and distraught old emperor also faced mounting political problems. The construction of the Forbidden City, the Grand Canal, the fleet of treasure ships and the repair of hundreds of miles of the Great Wall had placed enormous strains on China's economy, and the felling of the vast hardwood forests had provoked rebellions in Annam and Vietnam. The first rebellion, in 1407, was led by Le Qui Ly, a former minister of the Vietnamese court who usurped the throne and introduced reforms that won him wide support. Taxation was simplified, ports were opened to foreigners and trade boomed. Restrictions were placed on the acquisition of land by the wealthy at the expense of peasants, a system of health care was introduced, and the army and civil service were reorganized; ability was henceforth to be the key word. His ultimate aim was to end his country's subjugation by

China. Vietnam would no longer be a colony, but a proud and united sovereign nation. Zhu Di had sent an army southwards to crush the rebellion, depose Le Qui Ly and begin the systematic obliteration of Vietnamese national identity. Native literature was burnt and works of art destroyed. Chinese classics became required reading in schools and Chinese dress and hairstyle were imposed on Vietnamese women. Local religious rites were outlawed and private fortunes confiscated, while the pillage of the forests continued.

Another uprising began in 1418, this time led by an aristocratic landowner, Le L'oi, the founder of the dynasty that was to rule Vietnam for 360 years. Although twice defeated by the Chinese armies, each time he managed to escape to the jungle and continue the war. Despite a massive commitment of combat troops, the Chinese could neither find Le L'oi nor suppress his guerrilla army.

Insurrection spread throughout Annam and Vietnam; the entire coastal region south of the Red River delta (near modern Hanoi) was in revolt. Enormous numbers of Chinese troops were now tied down in the jungle at vast cost to the treasury and Chinese pride. The rebellion was a serious political and military problem, but it was one that a fit, powerful emperor such as Zhu Di in his prime would have solved with ruthless efficiency. Weighed down by his domestic troubles, he failed to suppress the revolt; Le L'oi then inflicted on the Chinese armies the first serious defeat the Ming dynasty had ever experienced. It was another shattering blow to the morale of the Chinese and their emperor, and though Le L'oi did not secure his country's formal independence until 1428, Zhu Di had effectively abandoned Vietnam by July 1421.

The demoralized old emperor had also lost control of his cabinet, and of China itself. There had always been an inherent contradiction at the heart of Zhu Di's government: it was effectively two separate administrations – a mandarin cabinet in charge of finance, economics, home affairs and law and order, and the eunuchs, who led the armed forces and executed Zhu Di's foreign policy. At the peak of his powers, Zhu Di had tolerated his mandarin critics, allowing them to influence his favourite son and successor, Zhu Gaozhi. Deep down the mandarins loathed Zhu Di's grandiose plans, his foreign policy, and the bleak northern location of the Forbidden City. They seized the opportunity offered by his illness and waning powers and looked to the crown prince, Zhu Gaozhi, to reverse his father's policies.

A diplomatic crisis accelerated the disintegration of Zhu Di's government. Sensing the emperor's weakness after the fire in the Forbidden City, the Mongol leader Arughtai refused to pay the tribute demanded by China. Zhu Di saw a heaven-sent opportunity to reassert his authority; the emperor himself would lead an army to bring Arughtai to heel. As a young man, Zhu Di had relied on the speed of his cavalry to outwit and outmanoeuvre the Mongol army. Now, he and his eunuch generals assembled an enormous, ponderous force of almost a million men and 340,000 horses and mules and plodded northwards into the steppe. Some 177,500 carts were needed just to transport the grain to feed this vast army. The mandarin Minister of Revenue, Xia Yuanji, the financial genius who had raised the funds for the Forbidden City, for widening the Grand Canal, for the fleet of grain barges and for Zheng He's armada, baldly stated he could not find the money for this latest imperial adventure. The Minister of Justice, Wu Zhong, also objected. Zhu Di had both ministers arrested. Fang Bin, Minister of War, then committed suicide. By the end of that terrible year, Zhu Di had lost his most able, loyal and long-serving ministers and his cabinet had disintegrated.

As his ministers had feared, Zhu Di's expedition was a fiasco. Arughtai simply disappeared into the vastness of the steppe. On 12 August 1424, while still pursuing Arughtai, Zhu Di, a broken man, died at the age of sixty-four. Some of the army's pots and pans were melted down to make a coffin to carry him back to the burnt remains of the Forbidden City in Beijing, where his body lay in state for one hundred days.

Zhu Di's funeral had the same epic quality as his life. The

procession was led by the old emperor's honour guard. Ten thousand soldiers and officials surrounded the cortège as it slowly zigzagged on its two-day march to the magnificent imperial mausoleum at Chang Ling in the foothills north-west of Beijing. There, in hazy autumn sunshine, they marched down an avenue lined with stone animals to lay the emperor's body in his magnificent tomb. Animals were sacrificed to his ancestral gods and then his cloak of imperial yellow and military decorations were laid beside him. Sixteen concubines were buried alive with Zhu Di. The complex was sealed as the cries of the doomed women marked the end of the mortal life of one of the greatest visionaries and gamblers in history.

On 7 September 1424, Zhu Di's son, Zhu Gaozhi, ascended the throne. That very day he issued an edict:

All voyages of the treasure ships are to be stopped. All ships moored at Taicang [a Yangtze port] are ordered back to Nanjing and all goods on the ships are to be turned over to the Department of Internal Affairs and stored. If there are any foreign envoys wishing to return home, they will be provided with a small escort. Those officials who are currently abroad on business are ordered back to the capital immediately ... and all those who have been called to go on future voyages are ordered back to their homes.

The building and repair of all treasure ships is to be stopped immediately. Harvesting *tieli mu* [hardwood for shipbuilding] is to be conducted in the same way as it was in the time of the Hongwu Emperor [Zhu Di's father]. [Additional harvesting] is to be stopped. All official procurement for expeditions abroad (with the exception of items already delivered at official depots), the making of copper coins, buying of musk, raw copper and raw silk must also be stopped ... All those employed in purchasing should return to the capital.[10]

Zhu Gaozhi also ordered the immediate release of those senior officials who had been imprisoned by his father, including the former finance minister, the mandarin Xia Yuanji. Xia took immediate steps to control inflation, forbidding the mining of gold and silver and stabilizing the amount of non-paper currency in circulation (paper money had been invented by the Chinese in AD 806, centuries before it came into use in Europe). Such was the value of pepper that it had been used as a means of payment by the Chinese. Now, all the pepper in the imperial warehouses was given away, the purchase of all luxury goods banned, the budget deficit slashed and all expenditure on the treasure fleets curtailed. China's territory produced all goods in abundance, so why buy useless trifles from abroad?[11]

The young emperor, fat, studious and religious, had shown no interest in military affairs and had hardly ever accompanied his father on his military expeditions, preferring to remain surrounded by his mandarin advisers. His priorities were in strict accordance with their Confucian values; 'Relieving people's poverty ought to be handled as though one were rescuing them from fire or saving them from drowning. One cannot hesitate.'[12] He saw no need to listen to the eunuchs who, in aiding and abetting his father's expansionary schemes, had brought China to the brink of disaster.

The last of the battered remnants of the great treasure fleets limped home in October 1423 after two and a half years at sea. Zheng He's men had no idea of the dramatic events unfolding at home and must have been expecting a heroes' welcome. Their voyages had been a remarkable success. They had reached countless unknown lands and immeasurably furthered their knowledge of navigation, but instead of plaudits, the returning admirals were spurned by those who now ruled China. Only Zheng He was spared from humiliation; perhaps his prestige was too great to strip him of his rank. The old admiral was pensioned off as an imperial harbour master in Nanjing, but was allowed to keep his sumptuous palace there and to continue building his mosque.

Zhu Gaozhi died in 1425 after only a year as emperor, and was succeeded by his son, Zhu Zhanji, who intensified his father's policies. Social harmony returned, but China had reverted to rule by traditional rural gentry. As long as the irrigation systems were maintained, the farmers were well fed and famine averted, there was little requirement for economic or political change, or the exercise of China's inventive genius. The country's institutions remained as if preserved in amber. Merchants wielded little political power, bankers and soldiers virtually none, and revenue from foreign trade dropped to less than 1 per cent of government income. Zhu Zhanji did allow Admiral Zheng He his swansong – one final voyage to Mecca – but with Zhu Zhanji's death in 1435, complete xenophobia set in. All voyages of the treasure fleets were halted and the first of a stream of imperial edicts banned overseas trade and travel. Any merchant attempting to engage in foreign trade was to be tried as a pirate and executed. For a time, even learning a foreign language or teaching Chinese to foreigners was prohibited.

The embargo on overseas trade was rigidly maintained throughout the next hundred years, and the Qing dynasty that succeeded the last of the Ming emperors in 1644 went even further. To prevent any foreign trade or contact, a strip of land along the southern coast 700 miles long and 30 miles wide was devastated and burnt, and the population moved inland. Not only were the shipyards put out of commission, the plans for building the great treasure ships and the accounts of Zheng He's voyages were deliberately destroyed. The mandarin Liu Daxia, a senior official at the Ministry of War, seized the records from the archives. He declared that 'the expeditions of San Bao (Zheng He) to the Western ocean wasted myriads of money and grain, and moreover the people who met their deaths may be counted in the myriads'. The goods the fleets had brought home – 'betel, bamboo staves, grape-wine, pomegranates and ostrich eggs and such like things' – were useless, and all the records of these expeditions – 'deceitful exaggerations of bizarre things far removed from the testimony of people's eyes and ears' – should therefore be burned. Liu then blandly reported to the Minister of War that the logs and records of Zheng He's expeditions had been 'lost'.[13] Not only was the priceless legacy of the greatest maritime expeditions of all time gone for ever, foreign lands were to be banished from the minds of the Chinese people. Only piracy and smuggling would be left to connect the fallen colossus with the outside world. The colonies established in Africa, Australia and North and South America were abandoned and left to their fate.

By late 1421, China's history was set for centuries to come. The legacy of Zhu Di, Zheng He and their great treasure fleets would be all but obliterated. What oceans they had sailed, what lands they had seen, what discoveries they had made, what colonies they had created were no longer of interest to the Chinese hierarchy. The ships that had made those voyages were left to rot and were never replaced. The logs and records were destroyed and the memory of them expunged so completely over the succeeding decades that they might never have existed. As China turned its back on its glorious maritime and scientific heritage and retreated into a long, self-imposed isolation from the outside world, other nations took up the torch. But all their explorers, colonizers and discoverers voyaged in the long shadows cast by Zhu Di's fleets.

THE
FLEETS
SET
SAIL

U NAWARE OF THE UPHEAVAL THAT WAS ABOUT TO OVERTAKE China, the great armada sailed majestically south across the Yellow Sea, beginning a journey that would take them to the ends of the earth. Early on the first morning of the voyage, 5 March 1421, the helmsmen kept the Pole Star, Polaris, dead astern while the navigators measured the star's altitude with their sextants. After taking their first readings, the navigators held their course due south for exactly twenty-four hours, then took another measurement of Polaris. By sailing due south, at the end of their first day at sea not only were they able to determine their change in latitude – their distance north or south of the equator – but could also adjust their compasses for magnetic variation, measure their speed and the distance covered, and calibrate their logs.

The methods of navigation employed by Zhu Di's admirals are revealed by one of the few documents of the era to have survived, the *Wu Pei Chi*. These Chinese sailing instructions, essentially a manual of the arts of seamanship and naval warfare, somehow escaped the purges of the mandarins.[1] There were instructions, inscribed on a long, thin strip of paper, for each regular voyage they made, giving detailed directions including star positions, latitudes, bearings and the physical description of islands, prominent headlands, bays and inlets that would be clearly visible along the route. By studying these sailing directions, it is possible to deduce not only the course the Chinese had steered but the accuracy of their navigation and their ability to set a course by the stars. It is an invaluable document.

The Pole Star was of great importance to the Chinese, both symbolically and for navigation. It was the fundamental basis of Chinese astronomy, for the celestial pole was regarded as the heavenly equivalent of the position of the emperor on earth. As mandarins, courtiers and servants circled around the emperor, so the other stars rotated around the Pole Star; as the clothes of the servants and their proximity to the emperor signified their importance, so did the brightness, colour and positioning of the stars that were 'tied' to the Pole Star. 'There is high Confucian authority. The master says,

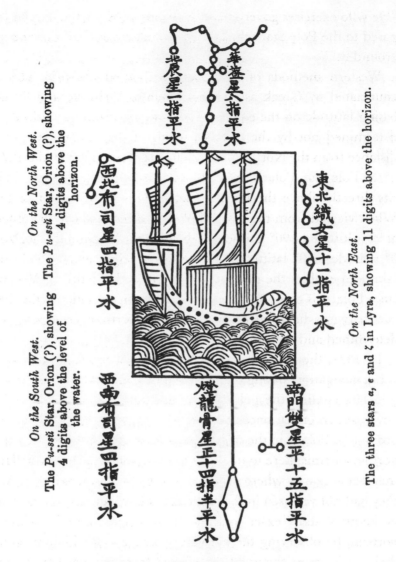

On the North West.

On the South West.
The *Pu-ssŭ* Star, Orion (?), showing 4 digits above the level of the water.

On the North West.
The *Pu-ssŭ* Star, Orion (?), showing 4 digits above the horizon.

On the North East.
The three stars α, ε and ζ in Lyra, showing 11 digits above the horizon.

西北布司星四指平水

東北織女星十一指平水

辰星一指平水

華蓋星六指平水

太

太

太

西南布司星四指平水

燈籠骨星正十四指半平水

南門雙星平十五指平水

On the South.

Navigational diagram used by Zheng He for the Sri Lanka–Sumatra run and reproduced in the *Wu Pei Chi*, 1628.

"He who exercises government by means of his virtue may be compared to the Pole Star which keeps its place while all the stars turn around it." [2]

Western methods of astronomy embodied the principles first enunciated by Greek astronomers such as Aristotle and Ptolemy, basing latitude on the equator. In Chinese astronomy, latitude was determined not by the distance north of the equator but by the distance from the North Pole, which was determined by the altitude of the Pole Star, Polaris. A bright and easily identifiable star, Polaris sits directly above the North Pole, billions of miles out in space. When viewed from the North Pole it is directly above the observer at 90° altitude or 90° latitude; at the equator it sits on the horizon at 0° altitude or 0° latitude. Measuring its height above the horizon (altitude) enables the navigator to calculate his latitude. Moreover, since Polaris is due north it enables magnetic variation – the difference between due north and the magnetic north of a compass – to be determined and adjustments made.

By 1421, the Chinese had well over six centuries' experience of ocean navigation, basing their calculations on both the Pole Star and the stars circling the pole at high altitudes which never rise and never set. In effect, once the Chinese had determined the absolute position of Polaris in the celestial sphere, they 'tied' other stars in the northern hemisphere to it. When viewing one star or constellation, they knew exactly where the others were in relation to it, even when they had not yet risen in the night sky. They were thus in a position to know a star's exact location, even when invisible below the horizon, by observing the meridian passage – the highest point of their track across the night sky viewed from any particular point – of the circumpolar stars to which it was 'tied'. However, the Chinese had not yet mastered using the sun to obtain latitude,[3] something the Portuguese first achieved in 1474 and which enabled them to measure latitude in the southern as well as the northern hemisphere. The Chinese could not determine their position south of the equator, where Polaris was invisible. It was a problem that had to be solved.

A star or stars in the southern hemisphere that could fulfil the function of Polaris in the northern had to be identified before Zhu Di's dream of charting the whole world could be realized.

By the seventh century, the Chinese could accurately determine the course to steer, for they had discovered the compass. They knew that the magnetic properties of lodestone could be transferred by induction to iron, and that this magnetized iron could be floated on oil, allowing it to swivel freely, one end pointing always to the earth's magnetic north. In 1421 the Chinese could steer to within two degrees of their chosen course using reliable magnetic compasses. They could also measure the distance travelled using hour-glasses of sand. One hour-glass equalled two and a half hours, the length of one watch for the seamen on duty.

The calculation of longitude, however, remained a problem they had not fully resolved at the start of this sixth voyage. Changes in longitude depend on four things: the course steered, the speed of the ship, the time that has elapsed and the distance north or south of the equator. By recording the number of watches, the speed through the water and the compass course, the navigator could estimate his change in longitude. But there was one great disadvantage to the Chinese method of navigation: if the body of water over which the ship was sailing was itself moving – for example, when a current was moving with or against the ship – the mariner had no way of measuring his change of longitude. This could only be achieved by measuring absolute time, something Europeans were not to achieve for another three and a half centuries, when John Harrison finally perfected a clock that could keep precise time at sea. At the start of the sixth voyage, this defect caused huge errors in Chinese calculations of longitude. Polaris navigation enabled them to calculate latitude and make landfalls north of the equator with astonishing accuracy, but a method of calculating longitude with anything approaching the same accuracy was not perfected until near the end of their voyages.

With centuries of experience in building ships to sail storm-tossed oceans, the Chinese marine engineers had evolved a robust frame built in sections. Each section was contained by watertight bulkheads at either end, resembling the internal partitions of a bamboo, and the watertight sections were bolted together with brass pins weighing several kilograms. Three layers of hardwood were nailed to a teak frame, then the planks were caulked (made waterproof) with coir (coconut fibre) and sealed with a mixture of boiled tung oil and lime. This hard, waterproof lacquer had been used to seal Chinese ocean-going ships since the seventh century, but so much tung oil was required to build Zheng He's treasure fleets that acres of land along the Yangtze banks were acquired to plant orchards of tung trees.

Marine engineers at the Longjiang shipyards designed their ships to survive the fiercest storms on the open ocean. Reinforced bows enabled the vessel to smash through the waves, and at either side of the bow were channels leading to internal compartments. As the square bow pitched in heavy seas, water was funnelled in; as the bow surfaced above the waves, the water drained out, modifying the pitching motion. A teak keel bound together by iron hoops ran the length of the ship, and specially cut, large rectangular stones were packed around it for ballast. Additional keels that could be raised and lowered were fitted at either side for more stability. In a storm, semi-submersible sea anchors could also be thrown overboard to reduce rolling. Even in the roughest weather and sea conditions, pitching and rolling were greatly reduced by these ingenious modifications.

The giant ships could survive typhoons and the sectional construction reduced the risk of sinking through a collision with a reef or an iceberg. They were designed to remain afloat even if two compartments were flooded after being punctured by coral or ice. To increase cargo capacity, the hulls of the junks were very wide compared with their length and they were flat-bottomed. Their sails were balanced lugs, four-sided sails hanging from a yardarm set at an oblique angle — the characteristic sail of China. They were stiffened by a series of bamboo battens, and the design was extremely efficient when sailing before the wind. It also allowed the sails to be reefed, or lowered, quickly in an emergency.

The most reliable ships in the world in the fourteenth and early fifteenth century, and by far the biggest, were these Chinese junks. Ibn Battuta, the Moroccan traveller and writer who journeyed through Asia in the fourteenth century, wrote that the trade of the whole world between the Malabar coast of India and China was carried in Chinese ships. Centuries later, in 1848, a junk built to the designs of that era was sailed from Shanghai via New York to London by a party of British naval officers. They sailed before the wind all the way and the junk handled beautifully. But magnificent though these ships were, they had been designed to operate primarily between China and Africa, sailing before the monsoon winds (which changed direction twice yearly), as they had for centuries. Although a lug-sail is also quite efficient when sailing into the wind, the combination of the hull shape and sail design meant that the Chinese monsters were crab-like and inefficient when attempting to do so. They had to wear rather than tack, and for all practical purposes were constrained to sail before the wind – a severe limitation when outside the monsoon belt of the Indian Ocean and South China Sea. It was to be one of the crucial factors when it came to tracking the course of the Chinese fleets during the great voyages of 1421 to 1423.

The eunuch captains and admirals of these great treasure ships were men of awesome ability but, like the European explorers who followed them, they often drew their crews from the lowest levels of society. Most were criminals, sent to sea in lieu of imprisonment or internal exile, and in some respects life as a crewman was far better than a prison sentence. They were provided with a uniform – a knee-length white robe – food and wine, and were well cared for when at sea. The admiral's staff included 180 medical officers, and every ship and company of soldiers had a medical officer for every 150 men. There was a varied and plentiful diet on the treasure ships, but the perils of voyaging through uncharted waters meant that life expectancy was short: only one in ten returned from the great voyages of exploration and discovery. But those who had survived the earlier voyages of the treasure fleets had been well rewarded. They were often freed and given endowments or pensions.

Like all sailors, the Chinese were superstitious. Each of Zheng He's ships had a small cabin dedicated to Shao Lin, the mariners' deity, and prayers were said to her every evening before supper. When the crew went ashore in foreign lands, they carried round bronze mirrors to ward off evil spirits; on the reverse was the eight-spoked Buddhist wheel.

The elite of the crew were the navigators and 'compass-men', operating from an enclosed small bridge and living and dining separately from the rest of the men. The junks also carried artisans and craftsmen of every description, capable of performing any task. Caulkers, sailmakers, anchor- and pump-repairers, scaffolders, carpenters and tung oil painters would keep the ships in good repair on their long voyage into the distant oceans. Their work in the Forbidden City complete, stone-carvers and stone masons were also embarked to leave permanent legacies of the fleets' voyages across the world. There was even a historian, Ma Huan, to document the voyage. His diaries, *The Overall Survey of the Ocean Shores*, were published in 1433, after Zheng He's final voyage.

The staple foods – soya beans, wheat, millet and rice – were carried in separate grain ships, enabling a fleet to stay at sea for several months without replenishing supplies, but if the grain ships sank, the whole fleet was in desperate trouble. Soya beans, grown in tubs all year round, were used in several ways. Soaked in water, they sprouted 'yellow curls' from the green bean. The sprouting process increased the content of ascorbic acid, riboflavin and nicotinic acid, the basis of vitamin C, and protected the crew from the deficiency disease scurvy. The Chinese knew well the dangers of scurvy and the remedies to prevent it. Enough citrus fruit – limes, lemons, oranges, pomelos and coconuts – was taken aboard to give every man protection against the disease for three months. Pomelos – a grapefruit-like fruit, also known as a shaddock – had been particularly valued ever since the Warring States period from the fifth to second centuries BC. 'The candid and ingenious prince should know . . . the State of Chu must necessarily gain wealth from its groves of orange and pomelo trees.'[4]

Rice was brown, not polished, and the husks contained vitamin B1. As a result, beri-beri – a disease causing degeneration of the nervous system – was rare among the crew. Fresh vegetables mainly comprised cabbages, turnips and bamboo shoots. When they ran out, the sprouting soya beans were particularly valuable. Soya beans also produced 'milk'. When boiled, it became curd, or tofu, rich in vitamin D, and fermentation of soya produced soy sauce. Tofu and vegetables were flavoured with a sauce made from fermented fish, soy, dried herbs and spices, or glutamate made by chewing wheat flour. The grains were chewed, spat out into a container and left to ferment. The method is still used in South America today. Noodles, pasta and dumplings were also made from wheat flour. Sugar cane was used to sweeten dried fruit and was also chewed raw by the crew.

Fruits and vegetables were preserved in ingenious ways. Fruit was dried or caramelized, pears, bamboo shoots and grapes were buried in sand, and vegetables were salted, pickled and marinated in vinegar and sugar.[5] Meat was limited, for the most part comprising dogs bred for the purpose and frogs kept in tubs. Chickens were kept for divination and were never eaten, but fresh, salted, dried and fermented fish were plentiful. They were caught by the trained otters, working in pairs to herd shoals into the nets, and by an array of hooks and nets. The crew drank green oolong and red tea, carried in both leaf and cake form, and rice wine (*jiu*) was hugely popular. 'In the sixth month [August] we gather wild plums and berries; in the seventh we boil marrows and beans; in the eighth we dry the dates; in the tenth we take the rice to make with it the spring wine so that we may be granted long life.'[6]

Wine was also distilled into liqueurs, brandy and vinegar. The junks carried huge quantities of fresh water and replenished their tanks whenever an opportunity arose, but they also knew how to distil it from sea-water, using paraffin wax or seal blubber for fuel. Their capacity to desalinate sea-water and the fresh vegetables they carried gave them the ability to cross the broadest oceans. The overall diet was infinitely more varied and nutritious than that provided for his crew by Magellan the best part of a century later – 'We ate only old biscuits turned to powder, all full of worms and stinking of the urine the rats had made on it.'[7] On the junks, rats were hunted by the sailors' little ship-dogs. Arsenic was used to kill bugs and insects and to promote the growth of plants.

The concubines for the treasure fleets were recruited from the floating brothels of Canton.[8] They belonged to an ethnic group called the 'Tanka', descendants of people who had emigrated from the remote interior of China to the coast to engage in pearl fishing. They spoke a peculiar dialect and differed from Chinese women by refusing to have their feet bound. They were prohibited from going ashore at any ports of call and from marrying Chinese men. They attended the sumptuous banquets aboard the treasure ships and were taught how to hold their drink; they consumed huge amounts. They were well educated and, as well as satisfying the sexual demands of the ambassadors and envoys, were expected to play cards and chess, to act in plays and to sing and dance. Most of them were Buddhists, a creed they adopted because of its teaching of universal love, compassion and equality of all beings, man and woman, emperor or prostitute.

Concubines were not viewed with contempt because of their profession; they were regarded as a long-established, legitimate and necessary part of society. Indeed, sex was viewed as a sanctified act. 'Of all the ten thousand things created by heaven, man is the most precious. Of all things that make man prosper, none can be compared to sexual intercourse. It is modelled after heaven.'[9] All men were free to have concubines, and 'class or fortune mean nothing in the selection as the only standard of preference is physical beauty'.[10] The Chinese invariably invited rulers back to Beijing, and foreign envoys could dwell in heaven from the time they left their home country until they returned, often a year or more later. Little wonder that they accepted invitations to Beijing with such alacrity.

Sex aids and aphrodisiacs were available to concubines and their guests. The most popular aphrodisiac was a pair of red lizards caught while copulating and drowned alive in a jar of wine. The wine was left for a year before being sold. There were also 'the genitals of a lewd animal, the beaver, with the drug so obtained to anoint the penis', and 'bald chicken potion'[11] was very popular. The name derived from a prefect of Shu who started drinking the elixir when he was seventy. His wife was so exhausted by his subsequent virility that 'she could neither sit nor lie down', and insisted that her husband throw the potion away. A cockerel then ate it, jumped on a hen and 'continued copulating several days without interruption, pecking the hen's head until it was completely bald'.[12]

The 'classic' concubine's bed was decorated with symbolic fruit. Bedspreads were embroidered with patterns of blossoming plum branches – the plum denoted sexual pleasure and fulfilment. The peach represented women's genitalia, and pomegranates represented the vulva. When envoys boarded treasure ships they frequently gave pomegranates as gifts. By day, concubines wore pantaloons, wide trousers; they usually made love wearing the *mo xiong*, a red brassière and silk stockings. Envoys and concubines were expected to wash their private parts before and after intercourse. A male contraceptive, a condom called *yin jia*, was available, and agar-agar jelly acted as a lubricant and mild disinfectant; venereal disease in the era of the treasure ships was rare, though it was to spread like wildfire in the late Ming period.

For the courtesan, the voyages offered an opportunity to attain the ultimate aim: to be freed to join a man who loved her. An envoy would request that a particular favoured concubine be disembarked with him at his home port, and she would remain with him as the fleet sailed on. Aboard she was respected and protected. If she failed to attain her dream and became too old to attract men, she was given the job of instructing the younger women in dancing and singing. By the time the foreign envoys left the treasure ships, some of the courtesans would undoubtedly have been pregnant. What happened to their children is not recorded. The concubines probably assumed other duties – cooking, weaving and sewing silk, making hemp ropes and looking after the tubs of beans and coops of chickens – until they were next required for the entertainment of foreign envoys. The eunuchs clearly had no use for the concubines and crewmen would have been executed for even approaching their quarters.

As the armada continued south on the first stage of the great voyage, the power to drive its huge ships was provided by the massive energy of the monsoon winds. Monsoons had always determined sailing patterns from China through the Indian Ocean to India and Africa. Ports such as Malacca (modern Melaka in Malaysia) developed where goods could be stored between the monsoons, the south-west in July and the north-east starting in January. Chinese ships took advantage of the north-east monsoon to sail before the wind to India, returning home on the next monsoon. The south-west monsoon reaches India in July, several weeks before it breaks over the coast of China. Ships from India sailing before the north-east monsoon winds arrived in Malacca before the junks from China had even set sail, and had unloaded and sailed for home by the time the junks arrived in Malacca.

According to Ma Huan, Zheng He's fleet arrived in Malacca six weeks after leaving Beijing. First established by the Chinese as a port where spices from the Moluccas – the Spice Islands (the modern Maluku Islands of Indonesia) – could be collected, Malacca soon expanded into a distribution centre for Chinese porcelain and Indian textiles, and grew to become one of the principal hubs of Indian Ocean trade. Halfway between India and China and 120 miles up the west coast of Malaysia from modern Singapore,

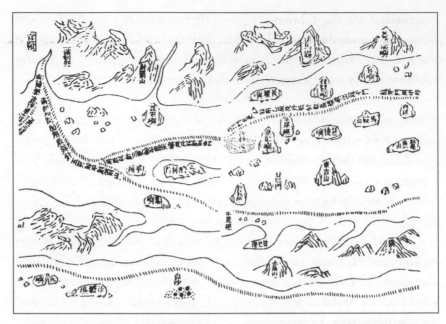

Chart of the Straits of Malacca from the Mao Kun map in the *Wu Pei Chi*. Malacca is in the top left-hand corner and Sumatra runs along the bottom.

Malacca lies on a strait through which sailing vessels must pass and has a sheltered location protected from storms by a ring of islands. There were rich tin mines in the surrounding area, a freshwater river bisected the town and the abundant water and teak from the surrounding forests made Malacca an ideal port. The trade in spices remained of paramount importance, offering merchants and traders the chance to amass vast fortunes. The attempt to exploit and control this vastly lucrative spice trade was later to be one of the principal engines driving the European voyages of discovery.

The Chinese set up a series of trading ports such as Malacca and Calicut on the south-west coast of India throughout south-east Asia and around the Indian Ocean. They were used as forward bases by Zheng He's fleets, providing fresh provisions, water and wood all the way from China to East Africa. They were an essential pre-requisite for Zhu Di's plan to bring the entire world into China's tribute system. In 1421, trade throughout the Indian Ocean was dominated by the Chinese and Arabs from Egypt and the Gulf States; relations between them were friendly. Like the rest of the known world, the Arabs craved Chinese porcelain and silk, and Chinese junks were almost always welcomed in Arab ports.

A report came from Mecca, the honoured, that a number of junks had come from China to the sea ports of India and two of them had anchored in the port of Aden, but their goods, chinaware, silk, musk and the like, were not disposed of there because of the disorders of the State of Yemen . . . The Sultan wrote to them to let them come to Jeddah and to show them honour.[13]

Chinese and Arabs met in equal numbers at the great Indian port of Calicut. Hormuz in the Persian Gulf and Malindi, Kilwa and Zanzibar in East Africa were Arab ports used extensively by the Chinese, but Malacca was virtually a Chinese colony and epitomized the Chinese forward base.

Formerly this place [Malacca] was not designated a 'country' . . . There was no king of the country; it was controlled only by a chief. This territory was subordinate to the jurisdiction of Hsien Lo [Thailand]; it paid an annual tribute of forty Liang of gold [approx. 48 troy ounces]; if it were not [to pay] then Hsien Lo would send men to attack it.

In the seventh year of the Yung Lo [1409] the Emperor ordered the principal envoy the grand eunuch Cheng Ho [Zheng He] and others to assume command and to take the imperial edicts and to bestow upon the chief two strong seals, a hat, a girdle and a robe . . . Thereafter Hsien Lo did not dare to invade it (Ma Huan, 1424).[14]

The diaries of Ma Huan also give a vivid picture of south-east Asia – the crocodiles that inhabit the mangrove swamps, rubber being tapped, the tin mines and coconut plantations.

The coconut has ten different uses. The young tree has a syrup, very sweet and good to drink; it can be made into wine by fermentation. The old coconut has flesh, from which they express oil, and make sugar, and make a food stuff for eating. From the fibre which envelops the outside they make ropes for shipbuilding. The shell of the coconut makes bowls and cups; it is also good for burning to ash for the delicate operation of inlaying gold or silver. The trees are good for building houses, and the leaves are good for roofing houses.[15]

Ma Huan also described the procedures followed by the Chinese fleets when in port:

When Malacca is visited by Chinese merchant vessels, [the inhabitants] erect a barrier [for the collection of duties]. There are four gates in the city wall, each furnished with watch and drum towers. At night men with hand bells patrol the precincts. Inside the walls, a second small enclosure of palisades has been built where godowns [warehouses] have been constructed for the storage of specie and provisions. When the government ships [Zheng He's fleet] were returning homewards, they visited this place in order both to repair their vessels and to load local products. Here they waited for a favourable wind from the south and in the middle of the fifth month [June] they put to sea on their return voyage.[16]

As well as trade, the Chinese were also greatly intrigued by the erotic Malaccan women. 'The mental capacity of the wives far exceeds that of their husbands. Should it happen that one of their wives is on terms of great intimacy with one of our countrymen, and allows him to feast and carouse with her, her husband looks calmly on and is not angry, but simply remarks: "My wife is beautiful and the Chinaman is delighted with her." '[17] Malaccan men went to considerable lengths to give pleasure to their women. Chinese-made glass beads assisted them, a custom still practised in some parts of south-east Asia today.

When a man has attained his twentieth year, they take the skin which surrounds the penis (*membrum virile*), and with a fine knife shaped like an onion they open it up and insert a dozen tin beads inside the skin . . . [The beads] look like a cluster of grapes. The King and the great chiefs or the rich people use hollow beads of gold in which is placed a grain of sand. After these have been inserted, when they walk there is a tinkling sound which is considered beautiful. Men who have no beads inserted [in the manner described] are people of the lower class.[18]

All manner of peoples visited Malacca – Bengalis, Gujaratis, Parsees, Arabs and many others conversed in eighty-four languages – and all returned home with Chinese goods. Boats that brought spices from the Spice Islands of Ternate and Tidore in the Moluccas returned with Chinese porcelain. Arab dhows sailed north-west for India, the Gulf, Egypt and Venice laden with silk, supplemented with batiks and tin from Malacca and Java. After the Chinese junks had unloaded their silk and porcelain, they refilled their holds with spice, Indian gems and Venetian glass.

[The Chinese] go about the country, scales in hand, buying up all the pepper they find, and after weighing a small amount so that they can judge approximately the quantity, they offer the payment for it in a lump sum, depending on the need for money of those who are selling it, and in this way they amass such a quantity they can fill the ships from China when they arrive, selling fifty thousand caixas' [a Portuguese trading currency] worth, which has cost them no more than twelve thousand.[19]

Throughout the archipelago and the whole of south-east Asia, trade was focused on Malacca and dominated by the Chinese. China consumed a hundred times more spice than distant Europe, and the Chinese merchants not only controlled commodity and currency markets but property prices too, even amusement and gambling. For ten months on end there was a Chinese fair where merchants gambled. 'As their merchandise is sold, they occupy less room and rent fewer houses. As sales fall, the gaming increases'.[20] Malacca was used as a forward base on each of Admiral Zheng He's voyages, and the importance he attached to the port is demonstrated by the temple he established there. It still stands in the road that bears his name, a few yards east of the Malacca River. According to legend, his flagship was once holed on a reef but its triple hull and watertight compartments enabled him to reach Malacca without sinking.

Zheng He's expeditions had become progressively more adventurous. His first, between 1405 and 1407, had sailed in sixty-two treasure ships manned by 27,800 men. En route for Malacca, they visited Cambodia and Java, then sailed on the next south-west monsoon for Sri Lanka and Calicut on the west coast of India. An incident on this voyage cemented a belief among the sailors that Zheng He's fleet was under divine protection. In the midst of a storm so ferocious that the sailors were praying to Shao Lin to save them from death, a 'divine light' – presumably St Elmo's Fire, a luminous electrical discharge sometimes seen during a storm at sea – appeared at the tips of the masts of Zheng He's flagship. 'As soon as this miraculous light appeared, the danger was appeased.'[21]

By the time of the third expedition, 1409 to 1411, Zheng He had established a settled programme. The fleet used Malacca as its forward base and there divided into squadrons that sailed on independently to separate destinations. The next great fleet set sail from China in 1413. One squadron departed from Malacca for Bengal, the Maldives and Africa; another sailed for the Arabian Sea and up the Persian Gulf to Hormuz. The fleets of the following expedition, 1417 to 1419, visited every major trading port in Africa, Arabia, India and Asia, then brought back the rulers and ambassadors travelling to Beijing for the inauguration of the Forbidden City. They were to spend almost two years enjoying the lavish hospitality of the emperor before the inauguration of his capital. Now, another fleet led by Admiral Yang Qing had been sent on ahead of the main armada. After returning rulers and ambassadors to the Gulf states, his daunting task was to solve the problem of determining longitude.

The rest of Zheng He's armada was embarked on the greatest

voyage of them all. After provisioning in Malacca, they sailed northwards for five days before anchoring off Semudera (modern Sumatra) at the entrance to the Indian Ocean. There, the admiral divided his armada into four fleets. Each carried an army equipped with gunpowder weapons. Three of these great fleets were placed under the command of Grand Eunuch Hong Bao, Eunuch Zhou Man and Eunuch Zhou Wen.[22] The fourth, by far the smallest fleet, remained under Zheng He's direct command. He was the emperor's right-hand man and could not be spared for the entire duration of the voyage. He would return envoys to south-east Asia and then sail for home, arriving in November 1421.

Assuming that Zheng He would have taken only a handful of ships with him for what amounted to no more than a brief and relatively easy passage home, it is safe to estimate that each of the remaining Chinese fleets numbered between twenty-five and thirty ships. Zheng He delegated powers of life and death to his admirals, and command was further delegated within each fleet: two brigadiers and ninety-three captains commanded regiments, and 104 lieutenants and 103 sub-lieutenants reported to them. The first task of the fleets was to return the rulers, ambassadors and envoys to their home ports in India, Arabia and East Africa. They were then to rendezvous off the southern coast of Africa and set sail into uncharted waters to fulfil Zhu Di's vision. They knew exactly what was expected of them. They would proceed all the way to the end of the earth to collect tribute from the barbarians beyond the seas or they would die in the attempt.

II

The Guiding Stars

4

ROUNDING

THE

CAPE

IN ORDER TO TRACE THE STORY TO THIS POINT, I HAD HAD TO learn the history of medieval China almost from scratch; my previous knowledge of Chinese history and culture had been modest at best. However, as I began to trace the voyages of the great treasure fleets in the 'missing years' from 1421 to 1423, I was entering familiar territory, making use of knowledge and skills I had acquired over many years' experience as a navigator and commanding officer on the high seas. During that sixth voyage, the fleets of Hong Bao, Zhou Man, Zhou Wen and Yang Qing sailed the oceans for two and a half years, but the mandarin official at the Ministry of War, Liu Daxia, had ordered the destruction of all written records and there was virtually no evidence to show where they had sailed or what discoveries they had made. But where before I had been plodding in the footsteps of academics and historians far more knowledgeable and gifted than myself, I could now use my skills to decipher the fragmentary evidence offered by ancient maps and charts, and those few documents and artefacts to have survived.

Two of these artefacts were carved stones. Old, virtually ignored by the new regime in China and perhaps fearing that he might never return, Admiral Zheng He erected two carved stones in palaces of the Celestial Spouse, a Taoist goddess, before he set sail on his final voyage in late 1431. The first was in Chiang-su, Fujian province, and the second at Liu-Chia-Chang. Only rediscovered in 1930, the stones commemorate the crowning achievements of his life, the great voyages of the treasure fleets. Their inscriptions are the key to unlocking the riddle of the sixth voyage.

Inscription at Chiang-su

From the time when we, Cheng Ho [Zheng He] and his companions at the beginning of the Yung Lo Period [or Yong Le – Zhu Di, 1403], received the imperial commission as envoys to the barbarians, up until now seven voyages have taken place and each time we have commanded several tens of thousands of government soldiers and more than a hundred oceangoing vessels. Starting from T'ai Ts'ang and taking the sea, we have by way of the countries of Chan-Ch'eng (Champa), Hsien-Lo (Siam), Kua-Wa (Java), K'o Chih (Cochin) and Ku-Li (Calicut) reached Hu-Lu-Mo-Ssu [Hormuz, in the Gulf] and other countries of the western regions, more than three thousand countries in all.[2]

Inscription at Liu-Chia-Chang

We have traversed more than 100,000 *li* of immense water spaces and have beheld in the ocean huge waves like mountains rising sky-high, and we have set eyes on barbarian regions far away, hidden in a blue transparency of light vapours, while our sails, loftily unfurled like clouds, day and night continued their course, rapid like that of a star, traversing those savage waves.[3]

The original English translation of Zheng He's Chiang-su inscription had been made by that great scholar of medieval China J.J.L. Duyvendak in the 1930s. In his article 'The True Dates of the Chinese Maritime Expeditions in the Early Fifteenth Century', the translation of a key phrase in the inscription was given as 'three thousand countries'. He and later scholars[4] thought that such a claim was so wildly implausible that the stone mason who carved the inscription must have made a mistake. On these grounds, the translation was amended to read 'thirty countries'. This was then repeated by subsequent writers and historians, and it was only when I consulted Duyvendak's text that I realized the original translation could have been correct; there was no logical reason why the mason who carved the inscription should have made such a gross error. But could such an extraordinary claim really be true? Had Zheng He's fleets reached three thousand countries? If so, the history of the exploration of the globe would have to be rewritten.

In attempting to reconstruct the voyages the fleets had made, I first had to put myself into the shoes of the Chinese admirals. There was no better way of doing that than by sailing in their wake, as I had done as a young officer in the British Royal Navy aboard HMS *Newfoundland*. Our captain was a very brave and distinguished sub-mariner, now Vice-Admiral Sir Arthur Hezlet KBE CB DSO and bar DSC. *Newfoundland* left Singapore in February 1959, passed through the Malacca Straits into the Indian Ocean and then turned westwards for Africa. We visited the Seychelles in the Indian Ocean before continuing west, making landfall on the East African coast at Mombasa. From there we went on to call at Zanzibar and Dar es Salaam before arriving at Lourenço Marques. We then sailed on down the east coast of Africa, visiting East London and Port Elizabeth before rounding the Cape, calling in at Cape Town, and sailing up the west coast round the 'bulge' of Africa to Sierra Leone, through the Cape Verde Islands and back home to England.

That journey gave me an invaluable insight into the winds, currents and navigational problems the Chinese admirals had encountered. Without that experience I could never have followed the elusive trail of evidence across the globe that revealed the incredible journeys made by the great Chinese treasure fleets. If I was able to state with confidence the course a Chinese fleet had taken, it was because the surviving maps and charts and my own knowledge of the winds, currents and sea conditions they faced told me the route as surely as if there had been a written record of it.

After parting company with Zheng He, the three remaining Chinese fleets sailed for Calicut, the capital of Kerala in southern India and by far the most important port in the Indian Ocean. The Chinese had been trading with Calicut since the Tang dynasty (AD 618–907). It was not only an important Chinese forward base but a great trading port, holding a huge stockpile of Indian cotton and textiles (calico), and the foremost centre for the trade in pepper. Its rulers, the Zamorins – Hindu kings – had built up an extensive network of trading relations throughout the Indian Ocean, East Africa and south-east Asia. Nearly all the celebrated travellers and explorers of the Middle Ages, such as Marco Polo (1254–1324), Ibn Battuta (1304–1368) and Abdul Razak (active 1349–1387), travelled to Calicut. In Zhu Di's reign, the Chinese explicitly recognized Calicut, which they called Ku-Li, as the leading emporium of the Indian Ocean, describing it as 'the most important harbour in the western ocean' and 'the meeting port of all foreign merchants'.[5] Chinese sailing directions for the Indian Ocean specified distances to and from Calicut and gave courses to steer between Calicut, Malacca, northern India, the Gulf and Africa. For their part, Calicut's rulers venerated China; between 1405 and 1419 they sent a series of diplomatic missions to Nanjing and Beijing, and a delegation attended the inauguration of the Forbidden City and presented Zhu Di with valuable horses.

The official historian Ma Huan described the Chinese voyage from China via Malacca to Calicut in great detail: no fewer than nine pages of his account were devoted to the city. He gave an enthralling account of life in a medieval Indian city through Chinese eyes, noting the religious practices of the Zamorin king in contrast to those of his Muslim subjects, and bringing to life the habits of the people, their festivals, music and dancing, clothing and food: 'The King of the country and the people of the country all refrain from eating the flesh of the ox. The great chiefs are Muslim people, they all refrain from eating the flesh of the pig.'[6] Ma Huan went on to describe local crime and punishment, in particular how the guilt or innocence of a person was determined in a 'trial by ordeal' in which the accused's fingers were held in boiling ghee, or clarified butter, before being wrapped in cotton. He also detailed the way in which goods from the treasure fleets were sold, and the form of contract used:

> If a treasure ship goes there, it is left entirely to the two men to superintend the buying and selling: the King sends a Chief and a Chei-Ti [a port customs official] to examine the account books in the official bureau; a broker comes and joins them [and] a high officer who commands the ships discusses the choice of a certain date for fixing prices. When the day arrives, they first of all take the silk embroideries and the open-work silks ... when the price has been fixed, they write out an agreement ...
>
> The Chief and the Chei-Ti with his excellency the Eunuch all join hands together and the broker then says: 'In such and such a moon on such and such

a day, we have all joined hands and sealed our agreement with a hand clasp. Whether [the price] be dear or cheap, we will never repudiate or change it.'[7]

By an extraordinary coincidence, at the very time the treasure fleets were in the city in 1421, a young Venetian, Niccolò da Conti (c. 1395–1469), also arrived. A well-connected trader, da Conti had left Venice in 1414 for Alexandria. The Islamic rulers in Egypt, the Mamluk sultans from the steppes of Asia, did not then permit Christians to travel south of Cairo for they were determined that the Indian Ocean should remain an Islamic lake. While in Egypt, da Conti had learned Arabic, married a Muslim woman and converted to Islam. Now travelling as a Muslim merchant, he journeyed to the Euphrates delta (in modern Iraq) and on to India, arriving by late 1420. He made for Calicut, because at the time it was a centre for Nestorian Christians – a cult of followers of St Thomas, also known as 'The Holy Apostolic Catholic Assyrian Church of the East', that had thrived in Syria in the sixth century and still exists in parts of western Asia – who were allowed to worship there by the tolerant Zamorins.

Years later, as penance for da Conti's renunciation of Christianity, Pope Eugenius IV made him relate the story of his journeys to the papal secretary Poggio Bracciolini, who had them published.[8] Da Conti described Calicut as 'eight miles in circumference, a noble emporium for all India, abounding in pepper, lac [a kind of insect gum used in making lacquer] and ginger'. There can be no doubt that da Conti was in Calicut when the Chinese fleets passed through, nor that he had at the very least boarded a junk, for he later described them in conversation with his friend, the Castilian Pedro Tafur: 'Ships [junks] like great houses and not fashioned at all like ours. They have ten or twelve sails and great cisterns of water within . . . the lower part is constructed with triple planks. But some ships are built in compartments, so that should one part be shattered, the other part remaining entire, they may accomplish the voyage.'[9] The description could only refer to warships of Zheng He's fleet; Chinese merchantmen did not have that type of construction, or that number of sails. I felt certain that da Conti also met Ma Huan in Calicut, for he described scenes almost identical to those Ma Huan recounted, as I discovered when comparing their two accounts. It was as if two different witnesses were describing the same things: the land surrounding Calicut, the trial by ordeal, capons and partridges kept in coops, the price and quality of ginger and pepper. Only in writing about sex did their emphases differ: da Conti described how women's orgasms were heightened by the beads inserted in boys' penises; the more fastidious Ma Huan mentioned only the tinkling noise the beads made.

Having travelled through India and the Far East on many occasions over several decades, I can vouchsafe for the accuracy of da Conti's descriptions – durians (a luscious but curious fruit) smelling of cheese in Malaysia, the musk of civet cats on the Malabar coast, the sweet smell of the scent used by Goanese women. He describes African ostriches and hippopotami, the rubies of Sri Lanka, Hindu women practising suttee (self-immolation on their husbands' funeral pyres), vegetarian Brahmins (the priestly caste of Hindu India), the

Chart of the Arabian Sea from the Mao Kun map in the *Wu Pei Chi*. At the top is the west coast of India and at the bottom the coast of Arabia.

dusty smell of cinnamon. Da Conti's descriptions of his subsequent travels in Chinese junks were to prove a vital link in solving the riddle of where the Chinese fleets had gone in the 'lost' years, for, as Ma Huan's account makes clear, with his role as official chronicler apparently over, he left the treasure fleets at Calicut. His departure meant that one useful source of information had dried up, and I had to look for other sources to replace him. The importance of da Conti to the story of the Chinese voyages became increasingly clear. Someone must have brought back copies of maps showing the discoveries made by the Chinese fleets, for how else could this information have reached Europe and become incorporated in the charts that were later to guide the Portuguese explorers? If it turned out that da Conti had also conversed with the Chinese on their return journey, he would be a prime candidate. Those charts were now proving equally vital to me as I endeavoured to trace the routes the Chinese fleets had followed.

The first task of the Chinese admirals after leaving Calicut was to return ambassadors to the coastal states of East Africa. Their passage

plan was marked on the Chinese Mao Kun chart compiled after the sixth voyage. The Mao Kun forms part of the much larger *Wu Pei Chi*. That part of the Mao Kun that has survived – no-one knows how large it originally was – is in strip form, 21 feet long and plastered with hundreds of names of ports and prominent coastal features, and the courses to steer and distances between them. It is 'believed to have been compiled in about 1422 from a mass of information brought back by Zheng He's fleet or collected for their use'.[10] Only a part of it has been translated to date, and as I write, scholars of medieval Chinese are working on the remainder. The translations of the Mao Kun and the *Wu Pei Chi*, and other documents of the period, will almost certainly produce further evidence of the great Chinese voyages. The quest to find further records will be formally inaugurated at a conference in Nanjing on 18 October 2002.[11]

The treasure fleets sailed from Calicut on the tail end of the north-east monsoon into the Indian Ocean, altering course to the south-west to make landings in Africa to return the ambassadors to their home ports – the route we followed over half a millennium later in HMS *Newfoundland*. It would have been uneconomical for all the fleets to have gone to each African state, so they would almost certainly have divided, with one returning ambassadors to Mogadishu (in modern Somalia) in the north, another to Zanzibar in the middle of the east coast, and a third to Kilwa (in modern Tanzania) further south. After all the ambassadors had been returned to their home countries, the Mao Kun indicates that the fleets rendezvoused off Sofala (near Maputo in modern Mozambique).

Finding the rendezvous must have posed a major problem, for during a voyage from India to southern Africa, Polaris, the Chinese guiding star, would have sunk closer and closer to the horizon and become invisible at 3°40′N, north of Mogadishu in Somalia. Until they found another guiding star in the southern hemisphere to fulfil the same purpose as Polaris in the north, they were sailing into the

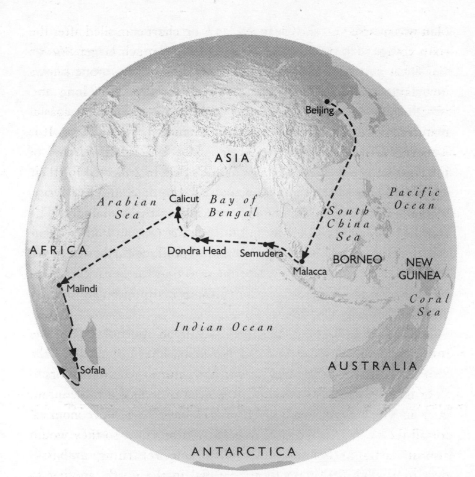

The voyage to Sofala.

unknown. They could use the Southern Cross for direction, for they knew that its leading stars, Crucis Alpha and Crucis Gamma, pointed to the South Pole, but as yet they had no star they could use to determine latitude. To locate one, they would have to sail far into the icy waters of the deep south. This was to be one of the most important aims of the expedition.

Allowing for sailing a hundred nautical miles (115 statute miles) in a day (the average speed recorded in the surviving records of

Chinese voyages in the Indian Ocean) and for remaining a maximum of one week in each port to re-provision (it usually took two to four days), all three fleets had probably completed the return of the envoys and ambassadors to their home ports by July 1421. By the time they had arrived at the rendezvous off Sofala, the admirals had already sailed some ten thousand miles since leaving China four months earlier. They would not return for over two years, but they did leave signposts of where they had sailed. The Chinese were rightly proud of their great voyages, and whenever they landed they usually carved stones in commemoration, like those erected by Zheng He in China. There are other similar stones near Cochin and Calicut in India, and near Galle in Sri Lanka. Some of the masons and stone-carvers who had worked on the Forbidden City had been brought with the fleets for precisely this purpose. The discovery of such stones was to prove one of the crucial links in the chain of evidence I was assembling. From the inscriptions on the carved stone erected by Zheng He in the Palace of the Celestial Spouse at Liu-Chia-Chang, I knew they had sailed forty thousand miles on their sixth voyage – almost twice around the globe.[12] The *Wu Pei Chi* and the Mao Kun covered only the Chinese routes across the Indian and Southern Oceans. Without Chinese records to help me, how could I find out how far they had sailed, what new oceans they had traversed and what new lands they had discovered?

My first recourse was to turn to the other great seafarers of the fifteenth century, the Arabs. My initial instinct has always been to look first for evidence in maps. The British Library holds copies of the great collection of early Arab maps assembled by Prince Youssuf Kamal, a wealthy Egyptian. These maps showed that the Arabs had certainly visited the east coast of Africa, and made regular voyages from the Gulf to collect slaves. However, dependent upon the prevailing winds, they had never ventured beyond the monsoon belt that spans the Indian Ocean but stops short of southern Africa. They set off from the Gulf on the north-east monsoon, sailed down to Zanzibar or sometimes further south to Kilwa and Sofala, then returned on the next south-west monsoon to the Gulf, laden with their tragic cargoes of slaves. I could not trace a single Arab chart that accurately depicted the east coast of Africa south of Sofala.

I knew of, but at that stage had never seen, a planisphere – a map of the world – showing the Indian Ocean and southern Africa. It was drawn in 1459 by Fra Mauro, a cartographer based on the island of San Michele in the Venetian Lagoon but working for Dom Pedro of Portugal, Henry the Navigator's brother and another leading light in the first wave of European journeys of exploration, who was then compiling a map of the world. I wondered if Fra Mauro's map, now held by the Biblioteca Nazionale Marciana, could throw some light on the Chinese voyages.

When I flew to Venice, the curator, Dr Piero Falchetta, took me into his office and proudly showed me Fra Mauro's map, a grandiose undertaking: the first map of the entire world to be drawn since the days of the Roman Empire. It was to be the first, vital clue to the course taken by the Chinese fleets. Dr Falchetta pointed out that Fra Mauro had correctly drawn the Cape of Good Hope (which he had called Cap de Diab) with its easily identifiable triangular shape, and had done so thirty years before Bartolomeu Dias rounded the Cape. That this was no mistake was emphasized by Fra Mauro himself, for he had appended notes stating that a ship or junk had rounded the Cape:

> Around the year 1420, a ship or junk [coming] from India on a non-stop crossing of the Indian Ocean past 'the Isles of Men and Women' was driven beyond Cap de Diab [Cape of Good Hope] and through the Isole Verde and obscured islands [or darkness] towards the west and south-west for 40 days, found nothing but sea and sky. In their estimation, they ran for 2,000 miles and fortune deserted them. They made their return to the said Cap de Diab in 70 days.[13]

Near the note, Fra Mauro had drawn a picture of a Chinese junk. It had the highly unusual broad, square bow, like a modern tank landing-craft, typical of Zheng He's junks, and was shown much bigger than his depiction of European caravels. Another inscription, placed in the middle of the Indian Ocean, read: 'The ships or junks that navigate these seas carry four masts or more, some of which can be raised or lowered, and have 40 to 60 cabins for the merchants.'[14] A further note described the huge eggs the crew found when replenishing at Cap de Diab and the giant size of the birds that laid them. That description could only have applied to ostriches.

Fra Mauro's planisphere of 1459 showed the Cape of Good Hope correctly drawn, had an accurate depiction of Zheng He's junks and described birds unique to southern Africa several decades before the first Europeans, Dias and da Gama, got to the Cape. The immediate and obvious question was, how did Fra Mauro get his information? How did he know the shape of a junk, and that the Cape was triangular? I found a partial answer in another fifteenth-century document describing the Portuguese conquest of Guinea: 'Fra Mauro has himself spoken with "a trustworthy person" who said that he had sailed from India past Sofala to Garbin, a place located in the middle of the west coast of Africa.'[15] There was no other clue to help identify the location of Garbin; the name does not correspond to that of any modern place. It is a bastardized version of the Arabic Al Gharb, meaning 'a place in the West'. The identity of the 'trustworthy person' would vitally affect the provenance and credibility of the notes on Fra Mauro's planisphere.

I was convinced that the person could only have been Niccolò da Conti. He was in Calicut when the Chinese junks berthed to offload passengers and cargo and take on supplies on their way across the Indian Ocean. The notes on Fra Mauro's map alluding to the voyage of the junk refer to 'the Isles of Men and Women', a peculiar name also used by da Conti in the account related to the papal secretary Poggio Bracciolini. Da Conti (c. 1395–1469) was a contemporary of Fra Mauro (c. 1385–1459), both came from Venice, and both were engaged in exploration or documenting exploration. Fra Mauro was working for the Portuguese government, and as well as publishing da Conti's stories, Poggio Bracciolini was also the intermediary between the Pope, Fra Mauro and the Portuguese government. There are no records of other Venetian merchants in India at the time, let alone in Calicut, when the Chinese passed through. It would be extraordinary if Fra Mauro's 'trustworthy person' were not da Conti.[16]

This was the crucial link in the chain connecting the maps drawn by the Chinese cartographers during the great voyages of exploration by the treasure fleets to the later Portuguese discoveries based on the mysterious maps they were soon to obtain. Chinese knowledge and Chinese maps passed from da Conti to Fra Mauro, and from him to Dom Pedro of Portugal and Prince Henry the Navigator. The Papal Secretary, Poggio Bracciolini, was, as we shall see, a key intermediary.

If Fra Mauro's description did come courtesy of da Conti's travels aboard a Chinese junk, it came from a reliable and accurate eyewitness, as I had already discovered. In those circumstances it seemed sensible to examine Fra Mauro/da Conti's claim that a ship or junk had indeed rounded the Cape of Good Hope and then sailed into the South Atlantic. If so, it was a towering achievement, for Pedro Álvares Cabral (1467–1520) and Bartolomeu Dias (c. 1450–1500), the first Europeans to round the Cape and venture into the Indian Ocean, did not do so until 1488. To have drawn the Cape so accurately Fra Mauro must have had a copy of a chart showing the exact shape and location of the southern tip of Africa. Only da Conti could have brought him such a map, obtained during his voyages aboard the Chinese fleet.

As I know from my own naval career, rounding the Cape remains an emotional experience for sailors today. As the clouds peel off the strange flat mountain tops of the fabled Cape, another ocean and another world – the exotic East – beckons. To the Chinese in 1421, coming from the opposite direction, it must have seemed that at last they had reached the brink of the unknown – not even the great admirals of the Tang dynasty had sailed this far. As they saw the lengthening waves and deepening troughs, they must have prayed that their ships would prove equal to the colossal challenges the vast and stormy Atlantic Ocean would surely bring.

I now had to discover where the mysterious ship described by Fra Mauro had sailed after rounding the Cape, and look for further independent evidence that it was a junk of one of the Chinese fleets. I started from the treasure fleets' last recorded position, shown on the Mao Kun chart of 1422 as off Sofala, sailing southwards at 6.25 knots, a good speed explained by the Aghulas current that sweeps southwards along the east coast of South Africa down to the tip. At that speed, the Chinese would have rounded the Cape of Good Hope in approximately three weeks, by August 1421.

As they have for millennia, winds and currents in the South Atlantic circle anti-clockwise in a huge oval loop from the Cape of Good Hope in the south to the 'bulge' of Africa in the north. At the Cape, the mariner meets the Benguela current that carries him due north up the west coast of Africa. After some three thousand miles, the current starts to hook first to the north-west, then westwards to South America. Off the coast of South America the current continues its anti-clockwise movement, running southwards off Brazil and Patagonia down the east coast as far as Cape Horn before sweeping to the east, back to South Africa. If a sailing ship, carrying sufficient supplies and robust enough to withstand the 'Roaring Forties' – powerful winds that circle the globe for hundreds of miles north and south of the latitude that gives them their name – were to hoist its sails off South Africa and sail before the wind and current, then several months later, having crossed thousands of miles of ocean in this great anti-clockwise loop, it would return more or less to where it started. An illustration of this is provided by the epic voyage of a very brave and distinguished submarine captain, now Vice-Admiral Sir Ian McIntosh KBE CB DSO DSC, once captain of the submarine squadron in which I served. He wrote to me:

In March 1941 I was a Sub Lieutenant in a merchant ship taking passage to Alexandria. She was sunk by gun-fire by an armed commerce raider some

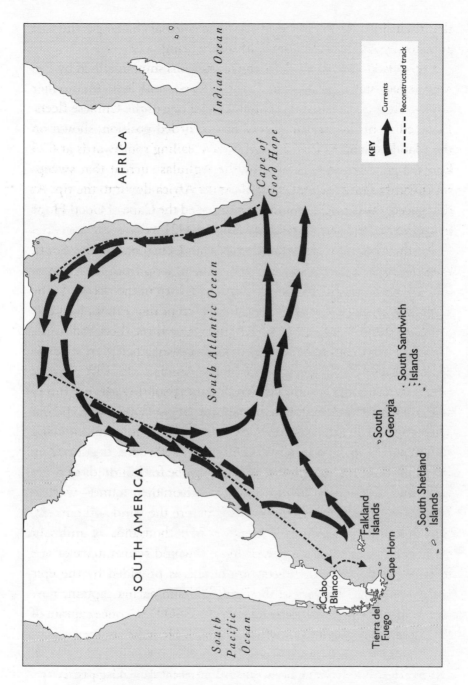

The circulatory winds and currents in the South Atlantic Ocean.

500 to 600 miles west of Freetown at about 08°N 30°W. The 28-foot standard wooden lifeboat, 'authorised' capacity 56, finally had 82 souls on board.

Even when I had repaired the shrapnel holes in the hull and the boat was reasonably dry I could not get her to sail closer than 5 or 6 points to the wind, a brisk NE Trade. This would never have allowed us to reach Africa, and to run before the wind to Brazil some 1,600 miles distant by the route chosen seemed preferable.

The plan was to steer due west until reaching 33° West then alter course to SW. This made full use of the NE Trades and gave us only a few days of shifting winds (and some most welcome rain) in the Doldrums before picking up light SE Trade winds. We made the [South American] coast on the 22nd day, ran NW along the coast looking for a suitable landing, which we found on the afternoon of the 23rd day.

I had estimated a maximum of 28 days for rationing purposes knowing that the equatorial currents were helping us but I had no idea at our latitude and time of the year whether they were a quarter knot or more than 1 knot, so I disregarded it in my noon DR [Dead Reckoning] positions.[17]

It is entirely feasible that the treasure fleets did reach the Cape of Good Hope where they would have been swept by the wind and current around the Cape and up the west coast of Africa to the 'Garbin' described by Fra Mauro. What I now urgently needed was independent evidence that this had happened. I pondered this question for months. Then I had a stroke of luck. John E. Wills Jr, Professor of History at the University of Southern California, and Dr Joseph McDermott, Professor of Chinese at Cambridge University, England, suggested to me that although the charts and records of the treasure fleets in China had been destroyed, there might be copies in Japan, for Japanese scholars were particularly interested in the early Ming era.

Subsequent research revealed that Ryukoku University in Kyoto held a copy of a Chinese/Korean chart known colloquially as the Kangnido. The Korean ambassador had presented Zhu Di with this extraordinary world map in 1403 after his inauguration as emperor.

The original map, however, has been lost, and the Ryukoku version of the Kangnido was extensively modified after 1420. It is nearly square and strikingly large, measuring 1.7 by 1.6 metres. Painted on silk, it remains in excellent condition, its colours little faded by the passing centuries. It is 'nicely organized and well worth admiration. One can indeed know the world without going out of the door.'[18]

The Kangnido gave a grandiose panoramic view of the world as seen in the early fifteenth century, and was compiled from many different sources. Names for Europe were in Persian Arabic, central Asia came from the Mongols, China and south-east Asia from old Chinese maps. Europe was covered in names as far north as Germany (named Alumangia). Spain was depicted, as were the straits of Gibraltar leading into the Mediterranean and the North African coast with the Atlas mountains. Europe, Africa, Asia, Korea and China were in their correct positions relative to one another, though Korea, perhaps for reasons connected with national pride and its traditional rivalry with Japan, was shown vastly larger than it should be and Japan much smaller. Nonetheless, it was an extra-ordinary piece of mapmaking.

For the moment, the part of the Kangnido that interested me most was Africa. So accurately does the Kangnido depict the coasts of East, South and West Africa that there cannot be a shred of doubt that it was charted by someone who had sailed round the Cape. Europeans did not reach South Africa for another sixty years; Arab navigators on the west coast never sailed south of Agadir in modern Morocco, eight thousand kilometres away, and the Mongols never reached Africa at all. The accuracy of the Kangnido told me that Mauro/da Conti's description made absolute sense. A Chinese navigator could indeed have reached 'Garbin' and then drawn the Kangnido. Still I had no precise location for Garbin save that, from the shape of the coastline shown on the Kangnido, it appeared to be near the Bay of Biafra, off western Nigeria. It was a problem I would have to address later. For now, I felt justified in assuming that the 'junk' referred to by Fra Mauro and drawn on his planisphere was

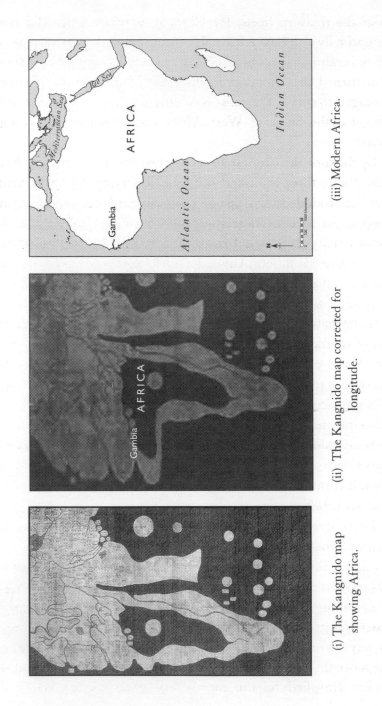

(i) The Kangnido map showing Africa.

(ii) The Kangnido map corrected for longitude.

(iii) Modern Africa.

from the treasure fleets, for Chinese merchant ships did not sail beyond Kilwa in East Africa. The Kangnido was much less accurate when it came to the 'bulge' of Africa north of the Bay of Biafra, so I next turned my attention to that part of the voyage. If they had managed to survey the coast of southern Africa with such accuracy, why was the bulge of West Africa not shown on the Kangnido chart?

By the time the Chinese fleets reached the Bay of Biafra, they had sailed some three thousand miles north from the Cape. I assumed that they rounded the Cape on their outward journey some time in August. At their average speed of 4.8 knots it would have taken about twenty days to sail from the Cape to 'Garbin'. They would have reached it in late August or early September 1421, the end of summer and towards the end of the rainy season. As I well know from my own time at sea in the South Atlantic, there is an extraordinary natural phenomenon in this part of Africa. Starting in the Bay of Biafra, the south equatorial current runs first to the north past São Tomé e Príncipe Island (where the bulge starts) then hooks westwards to flow due west along the south coast of the bulge, past Nigeria, Ghana and the Ivory and Gold Coasts until it peters out a thousand miles out into the Atlantic around 21°W. This massive body of cold water flows westwards with considerable speed the whole year round; a minor change occurs in summer when it extends further north to reach 5°N, a similar latitude to Monrovia in modern Liberia.

This current would have had two important implications for the Chinese: they would have been carried due west for some 1,800 miles, but they would not have known that this had happened. At this stage of their voyage the Chinese could only measure longitude by estimating their speed through the water, and if the great body of water was itself moving, either against them or with them, there was no way that they could determine their position with any accuracy, any more than a man walking up an escalator can judge the distance he has travelled by the number of paces he has taken. With mounting excitement, I realized that the charts drawn after they had entered the south equatorial current had to be adjusted to take account of this discrepancy, and the land they showed moved by up to 1,800 miles further to the west. I went back to my copy of the Kangnido and adjusted the land north of the Bay of Biafra to allow for this longitudinal error. The result was startling: the familiar outline of Africa became immediately recognizable. It appeared that the Chinese had been carried by the wind and current to the 'bulge' of Africa forty years before the first Europeans set eyes on it.

The south equatorial current gave them a 'free ride' westwards until the current petered out a thousand miles into the Atlantic. By then, they were in the south-east trade belt and being blown towards the coast of Senegal. In the wet season, running from April to October, the Sénégal current off this coast of West Africa reverses its normal direction and runs northwards along the coast at a rate of 0.6 to 1 knot. Yet again the junks would have had a free ride, this time to the north for around five hundred miles until the current itself petered out off Dakar, the modern capital of Senegal. By then they were in the belt of the north-east trade winds, blowing them south-west to the Cape Verde Islands. These lonely islands, then unknown to Europeans, were to play a vital part in unravelling the mystery of the Chinese voyages.

I checked and rechecked my calculations. By late September the junks that left the Cape of Good Hope in August would have found themselves approaching the Cape Verde Islands from the north-east. The design of the ships and the prevailing winds and currents would have prevented these flat-bottomed, broad-beamed monsters from sailing south at any point. It was now clear that Fra Mauro's account was entirely possible and that the Cape Verde Islands could have been the 'Isole Verde' reached by the ship or junk from India, forty days after leaving the Cape of Good Hope; they even had the same name. At 4.8 knots, the speed the treasure fleets averaged over all six great voyages, this would have taken forty days. Vasco da Gama took thirty-three days to make the same passage in the closing years of the century.

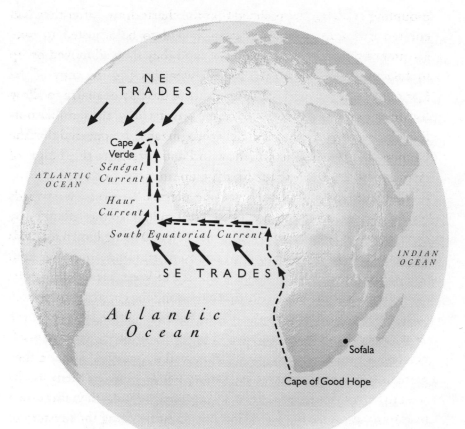

The journey to the Cape Verde Islands.

To have been called the 'Isole Verde', the islands Niccolò da Conti described to Fra Mauro must have been strikingly green. I knew the Cape Verde Islands well, having sailed through them in HMS *Newfoundland*. They are divided into two groups, and the windward (*balaventos*) are significantly wetter than the leeward (*sotaventos*). Of the windward islands, the biggest, highest, wettest and greenest is Santo Antão. It is an island of savage grandeur, awesome and eye-catching from the sea, particularly to a mariner seeking fresh water.

The Chinese admirals would have been approaching from the north-east on the trade winds, and from that direction they would have sighted Santo Antão first. On the north coast of Santo Antão, clearly visible from miles out as you approach from the north-east, there is a dramatic volcano. Streams pour down its sides and rush through lush valleys to the sea around what is now the small settlement of Janela. That strip of coast would have been an obvious and immediate place for the Chinese fleets to anchor and obtain water. If the Chinese had indeed landed there, I was confident that a legacy of their visit should exist.

The Cape Verde Islands were uninhabited when the first European, Cà da Mosto (1432–88), a Venetian explorer in the service of Henry the Navigator, arrived in 1456, so I could not expect to find goods that the Chinese had traded for food, such as the blue and white plates that were their currency on the south-east coast of Africa. On the Cape Verde Islands the Chinese could have obtained any amount of food and water for nothing. The seas teemed with swordfish, sole, shark, octopus, crayfish and tiny sweet mussels, the island was lush with fruit, and flocks of tame birds could be picked up by hand, for they had never learned to be wary of humans, as Cà da Mosto's crew found to their joy thirty-five years later. Nonetheless, there should have been other mementoes. A carved stone similar to the one erected by Zheng He on the estuary of the Yangtze stands at Galle, near Dondra Point in southern Sri Lanka. Inscribed in Chinese, Tamil and Persian, it extols the virtues of Hinduism (the local religion), Buddhism (Emperor Zhu Di's faith) and Islam (the religion of most Indian rulers in the early fifteenth century). There are other similar stones near Cochin and Calicut. I wondered if a carved stone might have been erected here.

The Chinese were always careful to respect local sensibilities; the language school in Nanjing, the Ssu-i-Quan, was, after all, set up by Zheng He specifically to train interpreters, and the fleets on this sixth voyage carried interpreters fluent in seventeen different Indian and African languages. It was highly probable that they had also left a stone on one of the Cape Verde Islands, carved with inscriptions in a language they thought people from the surrounding areas would understand. Such stones were always sited in prominent places where they would readily be discovered by others – what would be the point of erecting a monument to your achievements and then hiding it where it would never be found? If such a stone existed, the first Europeans should have found it when they reached Santo Antão thirty-five years later.

I referred to the journals describing Antonio da Noli, Cà da Mosto and Diego Alfonso's first voyages to the islands, and discovered that they had indeed found a large, free-standing stone near the coast at Janela. The stone still stands there today, in a dramatic setting framed by encircling mountains, beside the Ribeira de Penedo. Until a century ago, a clear, rushing stream tumbled down the side of the volcano, but now the stream has dried up and the stone is surrounded by agave plants. The stone, called locally Pedra do Letreiro (Stone of Letters), is of red sandstone, some three metres high and covered with inscriptions from top to bottom. The later carvings are in medieval Portuguese, commemorating the death of a mariner, Antonio of Fez, but underneath them I could see more calligraphy, unfortunately obscured by moss and lichen. The stone was so badly weather-worn and defaced by recent graffiti that it was very difficult to decipher the underlying calligraphy. A series of experts had tried – first a Frenchman, M. Chevalier, in 1934, then several learned Portuguese and Cape Verde historians over the past twenty years. They could tell me what the calligraphy was not – it was not Arabic, Judaic, Berber, Tifnaq, Aramaic, Phoenician, Latin, or any other European language – but they could not tell me what it was.

After receiving the necessary approval from the Cape Verde authorities, some of the lichen was removed. This revealed two pieces of calligraphy. I hoped that, helped by computer enhancement, I would at least be able to determine the language, but the calligraphy was quite extraordinary, unlike anything I had ever seen in my travels anywhere in the world. It appeared to have two characteristics: whorls like interlocking ram's horns, and a number of concentric circles.

My first thought was that it could be medieval Chinese, either the Zhu Qi Shan script or 'Flowinghand'. I sent photographs to experts at the Forest of Steles in Xian, China. Once the Temple of Confucius, it is now a museum and library holding a huge collection of steles, or engraved stone tablets, a timeless memorial to the Chinese written language. It is neither script, the experts replied. Could it be Tamil, similar to the writing on the stone the Chinese erected in southern Sri Lanka? It does resemble Tamil, but not closely enough. Nor is it Swahili, the lingua franca of the east coast of Africa. I then wondered if it could be another Indian language, perhaps one of the thirteen shown on today's high-denomination Indian banknotes. Could the Bank of India help? I faxed them a photo of a small section of one of the pieces of calligraphy.

'It looks like Malayalam,' they replied.

It was a language I had never even heard of. I faxed again.

'Where was this language spoken?'

'It was the language of Kerala.'

'Was it in use in the fifteenth century?'

'Yes, it had been in common use since the ninth century. It has largely ceased to be spoken today, though it is still used in a few out-lying coastal districts on the Malabar coast.'

Once I'd put down the phone, I punched the air in my excitement. In 1421, Kerala's capital was Calicut, the great port of India from which the Chinese had sailed. Once again, Fra Mauro and Niccolò da Conti seem to have been correct: a ship or junk from India appeared to have reached the Cape Verde Islands before the Portuguese arrived.

I next trawled through the learned experts' research[19] to see whether they had come across another, similar stone while they were attempting to decipher the writing at Janela. They had, but not in the Cape Verde Islands. The other stone was sited at the Matadi Falls

The third Ming emperor, Zhu Di, under whom exploration flourished.

From 1406 to 1420 Zhu Di presided over the building of the Forbidden City with the Imperial Palace (*below* and *bottom*) as its centre. The Temple of Heaven was its place of ritual; it encompasses the Hall of Prayer for Good Harvests (*opposite left*) where the emperor came to pray at the new year. When the capital moved north, the renovation of the Great Wall (*opposite right*) became a priority.

The Ming court in life and death: the emperor sits ensconced at the bottom level of a Taoist shrine (*above*) between a civil and a military adviser and flanked by two guardian figures.

The Spirit Way leading to the Ming tombs in Beijing is lined by stone warriors (*above left*) and high officials, here a Grand Secretary (*above right*), as well as powerful beasts – exotic elephants (*below*) and the mythical quilin (*opposite, below*).

The treasure ships took with them not only the much-prized blue and white porcelain (*above* and *top*), but also jade (*middle*), lacquer (*right*) and luxurious silk textiles (*opposite*).

A giraffe, with its attendant, sent from Africa to the Ming imperial court as tribute.

in the Congo. My first impression was that this was a wild goose chase. Why should a ship voyaging from India have visited a waterfall in Africa? But closer examination revealed the Matadi Falls to be at the upper navigable limit of the Congo River, where a mariner may anchor in beautiful surroundings and obtain clean, fresh water. A succession of ships had done just that down the centuries, from the Portuguese in 1485 to the Chinese today. The river pours over a series of cataracts before reaching the falls. The carved stone stands sentinel above a dark pool near the foot of the falls, where in days gone by fishermen would sit motionless while prostitutes patrolled the banks awaiting the arrival of the crews of foreign ships sailing upstream to water and gather provisions.

I had to retrace my route back to the coast of Africa to investigate this discovery. Like its Janela counterpart, the Matadi Falls stone has calligraphy beneath medieval Portuguese. The Portuguese writing once again commemorated a deceased comrade, here the navigator Álvares. There is less underlying material than at Janela, but the same experts confirmed that it was the same calligraphy. Its identity appeared to have been solved, although the concentric circles remained a mystery. It was likely that the Chinese had come here on their journey up the African coast. Not only is the Matadi Falls an ideal place for watering, it is 'in the middle of the west coast of Africa', and fits the description of 'Garbin' given by Fra Mauro. It is a busy port today.

Once again, Fra Mauro and da Conti appeared to have been vindicated: a ship sailing from India 'around the year 1420' seems to have reached Garbin. This does not, of course, guarantee that the ship was Chinese rather than Indian, but there is no other independent evidence that any Indian ship sailed beyond the monsoon winds of the Indian Ocean – they never sailed south of Madagascar – and I had the Chinese/Korean Kangnido showing the Cape of Good Hope and the west coast of Africa. The Chinese must have reached there. The simple and obvious explanation was that the calligraphy carved on the 'Garbin' and Janela stones was inscribed by interpreters travelling with the Chinese fleet, just as they had carved inscriptions in foreign languages at Dondra Head, Cochin and Calicut.

Despite the wholesale destruction of Chinese records carried out in the fifteenth century, I now had a trail of evidence of the treasure fleets' movements from departure from Tanggu to arrival in the Cape Verde Islands in September 1421. Ma Huan had described the voyage from China via Malacca to Calicut, and the Mao Kun chart of 1422 had then put the armada off Sofala in south-eastern Africa. My evidence for it having rounded the Cape of Good Hope and sailed north up the west coast of Africa was provided by the Kangnido map in Japan, and corroborated by Mauro/da Conti's descriptions. Their accounts, together with the inscribed stones, also showed that 'Garbin' in the middle of the west coast of Africa was the Matadi Falls, and that 'Isole Verde' was Santo Antão in the Cape Verde Islands. The Chinese were sailing before the wind and current all the way. It was precisely the route a ship sailing from India would have been obliged to follow, and at the Chinese average speed of 4.8 knots the latter part of the voyage would have lasted the forty days Fra Mauro had stated.

The great Chinese armada had already voyaged far into the distant and uncharted oceans, but I now had to discover where they had sailed next. The account by Mauro/da Conti described a seventy-day voyage after leaving the Cape Verde Islands, through *le oscuritade*, which can be translated as 'the obscured islands' or 'darkness'. My task was now to identify them. My first line of approach was to search for independent evidence of the next part of the Chinese voyage, for example in another chart that might throw some light on the location of these 'obscured islands'. In that era, Venice was the cartographic capital of Europe. If such a map existed, Venice was the most likely source.

During my researches in Venice I was told of a description by the Portuguese historian Antonio Galvão (died 1557) of a world map the Portuguese dauphin, Dom Pedro, Henry the Navigator's brother, had brought back with him from Venice in 1428 (my italics):

In the yeere 1428, it is written that Dom Peter, the King of Portugal's eldest sonne, was a great traveller. He went into England, France, Almaine [Germany] and from thence into the Holy Land, and to other places; and came home by Italie, taking Rome and Venice in his way: from whence he brought *a map of the world, which had all the parts of the world and earth described. The Streight of Magelan was called in it the dragon's taile: the Cape of Boa Esperança, the forefront of Afrike* and so foorth of other places: by which Map Dom Henry the King's third sonne was much helped and furthered in his Discouveries.[20]

Here was an unequivocal assertion that by 1428 both the Cape of Good Hope (Boa Esperança) and 'the Streight of Magelan' (separating Argentina from Tierra del Fuego) had been charted on a map. It was an extraordinary claim. How could the Strait of Magellan have appeared on a map – for simplicity, I shall call it the 1428 World Map – nearly a century before Ferdinand Magellan discovered it? To emphasize that this was no mistake, Galvão continued:

It was tolde me by Francis de Sousa Tavares that in the yeere 1528, Dom Fernando, the King's sonne and heire did show him a map which was found in the studie of the Alcobaza [a renowned Cistercian monastery traditionally used as a library by Portuguese kings] which had beene made 120 yeeres before which map did set forth all the navigation of the East Indies with the Cape of Boa Esperança according as our later maps have described it; whereby it appeareth that in ancient time there was as much or more dis-covered than now there is.[21]

This 1428 World Map was of huge importance to the Portuguese government, for in December 1421 the overland route to China and the Spice Islands – the great Silk Road running from China right across central Asia to the Middle East – had been blocked when the Ottomans surrounded Byzantium. In that same climactic month, on 6 December, the Mamluk Sultan Barsbey seized power in Egypt and nationalized the spice trade. The effect of the two events was to ruin the merchants who had controlled the spice trade, seal Egypt's borders to international trade and sever the sea route through the Bosphorus to the western end of the Silk Road. With the canal linking the Red Sea and the Nile (completed in the tenth century) collapsing and unusable, all land and sea routes to the East were now closed to Christians. A new ocean route to the East had to be found.

I knew from Antonio Galvão's description that the 1428 World Map showed the 'East Indies' (the Indian Ocean and what is now Indonesia) and revealed the ocean routes to the Spice Islands (Ternate and Tidore in eastern Indonesia), Asia and China round the Cape of Good Hope and through the Strait of Magellan. The information it contained was of incalculable commercial value and it was kept for decades under lock and key in the Portuguese treasury in Lisbon. However, the secret eventually leaked out and others became determined to get their hands on this vital map, even though the penalty for stealing it was death.[22] Certainly, Christopher Columbus was in possession of a copy in 1492 (see chapter 18).

The 1428 World Map has long been lost, but the information contained on some sections of it has survived, the most important of which is the section showing South America. A Spanish seaman who had sailed to the Americas with Columbus kept that portion of the map together with some notes Columbus had written about it. In 1501, the Ottomans captured the ship in which the seaman was serving; he still had the map in his possession. Neither the seaman nor any other who sailed with Columbus could have been the originator of this map because Columbus never sailed south of the equator. The information can only have come from the 1428 map.

Appreciating the extraordinary value of this captured document, the Ottoman Admiral Piri Reis incorporated it into a map known from that day to this as the Piri Reis map of 1513. This beautiful map can be seen today in the Topkapi Serai Museum high above the Bosphorus in Istanbul. It was based on several different maps, pieced together by the admiral from a number of different sources, and parts of it are unreliable, but the south-western portion based on the map taken from Columbus's seaman is very accurate. The trail I had begun to follow the day I visited the Torre do Tombo in Lisbon and read Antonio Galvão's description of a mysterious map that had come into Portuguese hands in 1428 had now led me to another chart that would prove one of the most valuable keys to unlocking the secrets of the Chinese voyages.

In recreating the Chinese route I remained certain of one thing: because of the hull shape of the Chinese junks, they would have had to sail before the wind. Their route after leaving the Cape Verde Islands was not hard to establish for there, as Admiral McIntosh described so many centuries later, the wind blows relentlessly westwards, towards South America. Moreover, at the Cape Verde Islands 'the north equatorial and south equatorial current converge, forming a broad belt of current setting west. Average rates reach two knots.'[23] The converged currents separate near the Caribbean: the northern part sweeps through the Caribbean to New England where it becomes the Gulf Stream; the southern part turns southwest towards South America.

My study of the old maps and charts, together with the evidence from wrecks and artefacts found around South America and in the Caribbean (to be examined more fully in a later chapter), led me to conclude that the Chinese fleets had separated with the current. Admiral Zhou Wen sailed north-west through the Caribbean towards North America, while Admirals Hong Bao and Zhou Man took the south-west branch of the equatorial current towards South America. It must have been an emotional parting as the great ships began to drift apart, gathering speed as the wind filled their sails. They were sailing into hazardous, uncharted waters and the admirals and their men would have been well aware that they might never set eyes on their companions again.

The evidence of the Piri Reis map and of the winds and currents seemed conclusive; the Chinese fleet must have sailed in this direction from the Cape Verde islands. Perhaps I would find the answer to the mystery of the 'obscured islands' somewhere off the coast of the Americas. I would return later to track the north-ward voyage of Zhou Wen's fleet, but for the moment I had to follow the course of Zhou Man and Hong Bao on their south-west track towards the 'New World'.

THE

NEW

WORLD

五

THE FLEETS OF HONG BAO AND ZHOU MAN WOULD HAVE
sighted the coast of what is now Brazil approximately three
weeks after leaving the Cape Verde Islands. What a moment
that must have been, a sprawling, unknown land filling the horizon
before them, the air full of unfamiliar scents and the calls of strange
birds. They may well have wondered if this was the land of Fusang,
described by their forebears almost a thousand years earlier.

During the Northern and Southern dynasties in the first year of
the 'Everlasting Origin' Emperor, AD 499, a Buddhist priest named
Hoei-Shin ('Universal Compassion') returned from a land twenty
thousand *li* (eight thousand nautical miles) east of China. He named
this continent Fusang after the trees that grew there. The Fusang
tree bore fruit like a red pear, and had edible shoots and bark the
inhabitants used for clothing and paper. Coupled with his statement
that the country had no iron, Hoei-Shin's description suggests that
the Fusang was the maguey tree that grows only in Central and
South America. It bears red fruit and is also used in the other ways
he described. Iron is found in almost every part of the world except
for Central America, just as Hoei-Shin indicated. Whether or not
Hoei-Shin reached the Americas, the Chinese certainly believed he
had, for his report was regularly entered in the yearbooks or annals
(official histories) of the Chinese Empire. From there it passed not
only to historians but also to poets and writers, and down the centuries innumerable tales were told of Hoei-Shin's exploits and
adventures in the land of Fusang.

> Fusang is about twenty thousand Chinese miles [eight thousand nautical
> miles] in an easterly direction from Tahan, and east of the Middle Kingdoms
> [China]. Many fusang trees grow there, whose leaves resemble the *Dryanda
> cordifolia*; the sprouts, on the contrary, resemble those of the bamboo tree, and
> are eaten by the inhabitants of the land. The fruit is like a pear in form but is
> red. From the bark they prepare a sort of linen which they use for clothing . . .
> The houses are built of wooden beams; fortified and walled places are there
> unknown . . . They have written characters in this land [which the Olmecs

did have] and prepare paper from the bark of the Fusang [which the Olmecs did from the maguey tree, which indeed has red fruit like pears].[1]

Zheng He and his admirals certainly knew these tales when they set sail, as did the Chinese seamen crowding at the rail for a sight of this new land. Was it a land of no iron? Did it have the famous Fusang trees? No doubt they were nervous, perhaps even frightened, but they must also have been immensely curious. Their landfall must have been around the Orinoco delta, for the Piri Reis map shows that they had surveyed that small part of the coast with great accuracy. My search for the obscured islands Fra Mauro/da Conti had described during the junk's seventy-day voyage after leaving the Cape Verde Islands could now begin in earnest.

Just before the book went to print I was informed that a considerable amount of research had been carried out into the DNA of American Indian peoples and the diseases that they carried which were otherwise unique to China and South East Asia. Briefly, it concerns a skin disease of the Indians of the Mato Grosso of Brazil; hookworms occurring in the Lengua Indians of Paraguay; roundworm in Peru and Mexico; and ancylostoma duodenale in Mexico. It is conclusive proof of Chinese sea voyages to the Americas before Columbus. This evidence, coupled with that of wild rice and horses in South America before Columbus, will be incorporated in the paperback edition. For the moment, however, I had to continue with the charts.

After making landfall near the Orinoco, where they would have replenished their water and taken on fresh food, they would then have set sail once more for the south. The currents would have carried them down the east coast of Brazil to Cabo Blanco in southern Argentina. I had found an inscription on the southern part of the Piri Reis map stating: 'It is related by the Portuguese Infidel [Columbus] that in this place, night and day are, at their shortest period, of two hours duration, and at their longest phase of 22 hours.'[2] For the winter daylight to have lasted only two hours, the

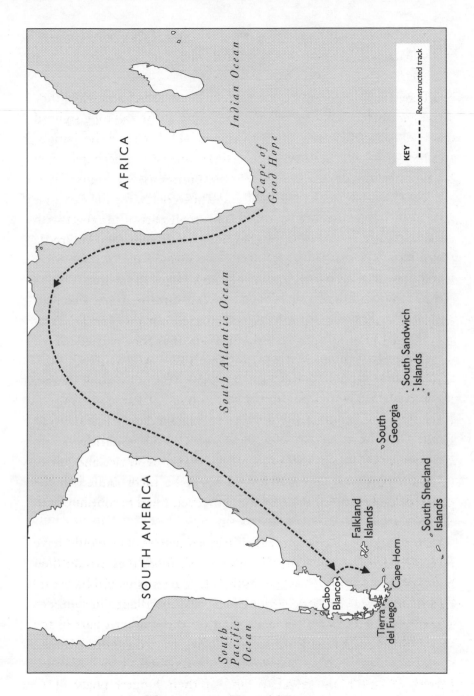

The journey to Tierra del Fuego.

man who originally drew the chart and made that note must have been in the deep south at a latitude of about 60°S, well to the south of the southern tip of Tierra del Fuego. The map also shows what appears to be ice connecting the tip of South America to Antarctica.

I was able to use the inscription on the Piri Reis map and the position of the ice shown on it to fix the southern tip of South America to approximately 55°S, the northern limit of drift ice. Establishing the latitude of Tierra del Fuego allowed me to make a closer examination of the southern part of the Piri Reis and compare it with a modern chart. This revealed at once that the original cartographer had drawn the east coast of Patagonia with great accuracy. The prominent features of the coastline – headlands, bays, rivers, estuaries and ports – tally from Cabo Blanco in the north to the entrance of the Strait of Magellan in the south. The cartographer of the Piri Reis also drew a number of animals on the land.

It is a bleak, desolate, windswept region, as Darwin recalled: 'Without habitations, without water, without trees, without moun-tains, they support merely a few dwarf plants ... The plains of Patagonia are boundless, for the area is scarcely passable, and hence unknown.'3 Columbus could not possibly have been the original car-tographer; he never got south of the equator. His knowledge of the region, including his description of the islands in the South Atlantic being in darkness – obscured – for twenty-two hours each day, can only have come from the inscriptions on the 1428 chart he had copied.

The first European, Magellan, did not set sail for Patagonia until years after the Piri Reis was drawn. So who originally provided the information to enable Patagonia to be drawn on the Piri Reis, and how did he obtain it? Knowing I was looking at Patagonia, a des-perate place but nonetheless one that supports animal life, I began to examine the five creatures depicted on the map.

The first, a deer with prominent horns, was superimposed on an area that has now been designated a national park, the Parque Nacional Perito Moreno. This animal is clearly a huemil, an Andean deer, with the head and antlers accurately depicted. There are still

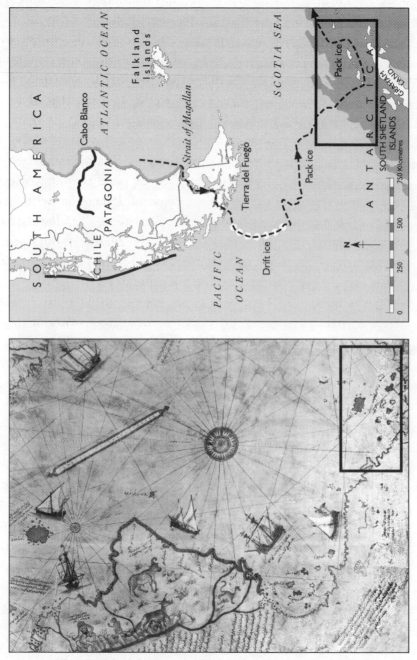

The Piri Reis map compared to modern Patagonia, showing
the Strait of Magellan.

huge herds of these deer where the animal is shown on the Piri Reis. The next creature was placed in what is now the Monumento Natural Bosques Petrificados, 150 kilometres south of modern Caleta Olivia. I have spent some time photographing animals in the Andes and instantly recognized the creature as a guanaco. Guanacos are members of the camel family. They have curious, floppy ears which are bent forwards when they are excited or anxious. Andean people decorate guanacos' ears with red tassels in the same way we would plait a horse's mane. From a side view, the bent ears resemble forward-pointing horns. Clearly, the cartographer who copied the original chart mistook the bent ears for horns. Large herds of guanaco are found in the Monumento Natural Bosques Petrificados, just where they are shown on the Piri Reis, and, like the huemils, guanacos are unique to South America. The third animal, a mountain lion, was placed in what is now the Parque Nacional Monte León where, as the name indicates, mountain lions are common. All three animals were shown exactly where they can still be found in Patagonia today and were drawn before Europeans arrived.

There is also a drawing of a naked bearded man. At first glance, he appears to have his head in the middle of his body, but on closer examination it seems perfectly possible that he had been drawn in a crouching position, allowing his thick beard to cover his genitals. I surmised that the Turkish cartographer who copied the captured Portuguese chart onto the Piri Reis was almost certainly a Muslim. Muslims are very conservative about exposing their bodies; if the cartographer had indeed been of that faith, he would not have been comfortable depicting naked men. When Magellan arrived in Patagonia long after the original map was drawn, he was surprised to find that despite the cold weather the people did indeed go about naked, keeping themselves warm with fires, even when they were travelling in boats. As a result, he named the land 'Tierra del Fuego' – the land of fire.[4]

That left one last creature to identify, a beast that appeared to have come from fable: a dog-headed man. There were two notes describing the creature: 'In this place there are ... wild beasts of this shape',[5] and 'These wild beasts attain a length of seven spans ... between their eyes there is a distance of only one span [the distance between the outspread tips of the thumb and the little finger]. Yet it is said they are harmless souls.'[6] The Piri Reis map had depicted the other Patagonian animals with remarkable accuracy and placed them precisely where they are found today. I could therefore expect the monster, if it ever really existed, to have lived in the south of the Santa Cruz province of Argentina or in the north part of the Chilean province of Magallanes. Did such monsters ever walk the earth there? London's Natural History Museum could offer no help in identifying the creature, so I contacted every natural history museum within a two-hundred-mile radius of where the monster was shown and described on the Piri Reis.

My first call, to the Museo de Fauna, Rio Verde in Magellanes province, Chile, was answered in the negative, with barely suppressed mirth. The fourth call, to the nearby Museo de Sitio in Puerto Natales, was much more fruitful.

'I'm looking for a monster twice the size of a human. Were there ever any creatures like that in your area?'

'Yes.'

'Does your museum exhibit one?'

'Yes.'

'What is its name?'

'The mylodon.'

The mylodon is a creature of which I had been wholly ignorant until then, but London's Natural History Museum now provided a wealth of information about it. The monster was a giant sloth weighing around two hundred kilograms, unique to South America. In 1834, Darwin found a skeleton on a beach at Bahía Blanca in Patagonia near to where the creature is shown on the Piri Reis map. He sent the bones to Dr Richard Owen at the Royal College of Surgeons in London, who reconstructed the skeleton. It resembled a giant man with a dog's head, rearing on its haunches

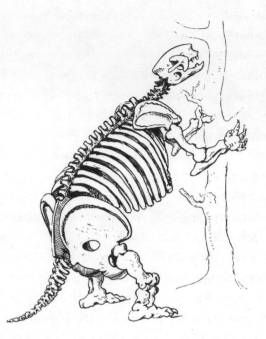

A nineteenth-century engraving of the skeleton of a mylodon.

and using its legs and tail as a tripod while it knocked down small trees. It would strip the branches bare of fruit before lumbering off to demolish the next tree. The animal was said to reach three metres, sometimes even more, in height and slept for most of the time. The native people of Patagonia harnessed them in caves during the winter, taking them out to graze in summer; their meat apparently tasted like bland mutton. The last of these 'harmless souls'[7] was thought to have died out some three centuries ago. However, in recent years, well-preserved pieces of this creature, apparently butchered by the local people, have been found in a cave, leading to speculation that it may still exist in the wilds of Patagonia.

Later I was to find a Chinese book published in 1430 entitled *The Illustrated Record of Strange Countries*. As its title implies, this book records the strange animals the Chinese found on their travels. A dog-headed creature very similar to that drawn on the Piri Reis map is shown, with a note – the only part of the document that has yet been translated – stating that it was found after travelling for two years west of China.

The Chinese must have looked upon such alien creatures with wonder, and at once would have begun efforts to capture some specimens. When encountering strange and exotic animals, it was their custom to take them back to China to present to the emperor for his zoo.[8] A stream of quilins (giraffes) had returned with Zheng He's captains to astound and delight Zhu Di, and I believe that a number of mylodons were also taken aboard the Chinese junks, two of which did reach China.[9] I could imagine the Chinese seamen luring these lumbering, dog-headed creatures out of their caves and onto the giant ships, accompanied by tons of leaves for them to eat.

The Piri Reis map was so accurate both in its depictions of physical features and its descriptions of animals unique to South America that it could only be charting Patagonia. For that reason, I was also certain that the mountains drawn on the western side were the Andes. These mountains, running northwards up the Pacific coast, are not visible from the Atlantic; they are hundreds of miles away from the east coast. The original cartographer must have sailed that Pacific coast long before the first Europeans reached South America or the Pacific, and the fleet that carried him can only have passed through the Strait of Magellan or braved the blizzards, incessant gales and mountainous seas of Cape Horn.

Knowing the size of Patagonia, I could accurately determine the scale of the Piri Reis map and fix the latitudes of the land and islands shown on it. Cabo Blanco is at 47°20′S, so the islands shown at the bottom of the Piri Reis must be at 68°43′S – exactly the latitude of the South Shetland Islands. I now knew that the original cartographer had been aboard a ship that had discovered the Antarctic continent and the South Shetland Islands four centuries before the first Europeans reached them. As I was later to discover, these obscure, almost uninhabited islands were of vital importance to the Chinese.

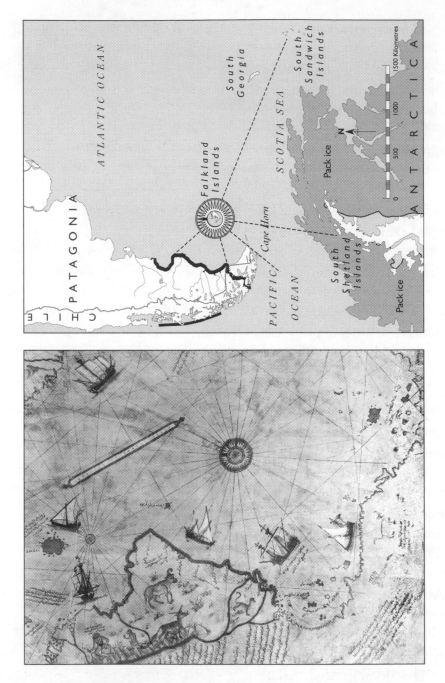

The Falkland Islands on the Piri Reis, compared to a modern map.

It must have taken thousands of man-hours for the skilled surveyors and navigators to chart such a large area of land and ocean, stretching thousands of miles from Antarctica in the south to the Peruvian Andes in the north. To cover such vast distances, the charting must have been co-ordinated, involving the use of different fleets. Before Europeans reached the South Atlantic, the only nation capable of putting such fleets to sea was China, and the only plausible opportunity was provided by the Chinese treasure fleets during the 'missing' two years of the great voyage of 1421–3. Although I was convinced I was right, I had not yet found any first-hand evidence of a Chinese visit to South America. The clearest evidence would come from the surviving wreck of a treasure ship full of early Ming porcelain. Such wrecks were to play a vital part in establishing the presence of the Chinese treasure fleets elsewhere in the world, but finding such a wreck on the coasts of South America is likely to be a lengthy task. The seas are buffeted by incessant storms and strong tides break up and sweep away wreckage and spilled cargoes. The search is in hand, but it is unlikely to yield short-term results.

Meanwhile, I needed an interim solution. For example, did the first Europeans to reach South America find plants or animals unique to China when they landed there, or were plants unique to the Americas seen in China when the first Europeans arrived there? If so, had the Chinese junks carried them home with them? Fortunately, a number of distinguished scholars have worked on this problem for many years.[10] I was led to their work as a result of waking at cockcrow on my first morning during a visit to Peru. I had lived in Malaysia and remembered well how the morning call of Asiatic hens – 'kik-kiri-kee' – was markedly different from the 'cock-a-doodle-do' of their European counterparts. As I lay in bed, I recognized the familiar 'kik-kiri-kee' and began to wonder how Asiatic rather than European hens had come to be in Peru.

The domesticated Asiatic cock and hen originated several thousand years ago in the jungles of south-east Asia, in South China,

Annam, Vietnam, Cambodia and Malaysia. The strain remains quite distinct from the European hen. When Magellan arrived off Rio (as it is now called), he 'picked up a great store of chickens . . . for one fish hook or a knife, they gave me six chickens, fearing even so that they were cheating me'.[11] But the chickens Magellan and the Spanish conquistadors found in South America had virtually nothing in common with European 'dunghill fowl'. They were of four principal, wholly different types. The Malay class were tall and thin – the cocks were able to peck food off a dinner table. They had thin heads, more like a turkey's than a chicken's, with a bare throat and a bare strip running down the breast. The Chinese class had stocky, heavy bodies, fluffy feathers, short wings and feathered legs. The cocks had modest tail feathers and very small, short, blunt spurs. They were poor flyers and notably tame. To this day, the silky-feathered melanotic chicken ('melanotic' denotes the black feathers, skin, flesh and bones of this strange bird) is found throughout Latin America. The fourth type of hen was the Asian frizzle fowl, with feathers that curve back towards the body instead of lying flat. Again, there was nothing remotely resembling this bird in the Mediterranean world of 1500, when frizzle fowl were found all over South America. Perhaps the most striking difference was that the Asiatic hens laid blue-shelled eggs whereas those of European hens were white or cream. Blue eggs are still found all the way from Chile to Mexico.

There were two other significant differences. If the Europeans had brought chickens, then the European name would have been adopted by the Indians of South America. This did not happen. The Arawak of northern South America called melanotic chickens *karaka*; the Indian name is *karaknath*. In north-west Mexico, chicken was *tori*; in Japanese it is *nihuatori*, meaning 'yard bird'. The Inca emperors, who were just embarking on a period of imperial expansion in 1421, frequently wore feathers and adopted the names of birds. In their Quechua language, chicken was *hualpa*, the name Topác Yupánqui (c. 1440–1493) adopted; Atahualpa was the formal

The frizzle fowl from Aldrovandi's *Ornithologia*, 1604.

name of the emperor overthrown by Francisco Pizarro. The Incas therefore had a word for chicken at least forty years before the arrival of the conquistadors.

Europeans of that era were almost unique in eating chickens and their eggs. In south-east Asia and China, chickens served a completely different purpose. The Chinese practices of divination using eggs or dripping chicken blood on bark paper before burning the paper, and the belief that a melanotic chicken protects the household from evil spirits, were also found in South America, and just as in China, neither chickens nor eggs were eaten by Amerindians. They used them for sacrifice, divination and healing the sick.

Asiatic chickens were found the length of both the Atlantic and Pacific coasts of the Americas as far north as Rhode Island. These birds cannot fly and must have been brought by ship. The only non-European ships that could travel such vast distances were Chinese.

The spread of Asiatic chickens prior to the European conquest closely correlates with the lands shown on the Piri Reis map – the Orinoco delta in Venezuela, Brazil, Patagonia, Chile and Peru. Even today, in areas of South America where there has been minimal Spanish (or other European) influence, one still finds chickens which lay pale blue eggs and possess other Asiatic characteristics unknown in European birds.[12] The conclusion is inescapable: Chinese fleets must have brought chickens to South America.

> Since the Asiatic chickens are very different from the Mediterranean chickens and most of the traits that reappear in the flocks of the Amerindians are found in Asia, the obvious conclusion would be that the Amerind chickens were first introduced [to South America] from Asia and not from the Mediterranean . . .[13]
>
> When one considers the total data available on the chicken in America, a conclusion for a Spanish or Portuguese first introduction of chickens into America is simply counter to all the evidence. The Mediterraneans, as late as 1600, did not have, and did not even know of, the galaxy of chickens present in Amerind hands . . . If a scholarly and scientific approach to the subject is taken, an approach that pays attention to the data instead of the clichés of the past, then the only possible conclusion is that chickens were introduced from across the Pacific, probably repeatedly, long before the Mediterranean discoveries of America.[14]

The second line of evidence came from maize, a very unusual plant that originated in the Americas and was unknown in China before Zheng He's voyages. Just as chickens cannot fly, maize is incapable of self-propagation. Wherever it is found, it has been propagated by man. There is considerable evidence that maize was carried to Asia before Columbus landed in America in 1492.[15] For example, within his description of the expedition landing at Limasava in the Philippines in 1520, Antonio Pigafetta, Magellan's diarist, noted this: 'The islanders invited the General [Magellan] into their boats in which were their merchandise, viz. cloves, cinnamon, ginger, pepper, nutmegs and maize.'[16] There is no possibility that Pigafetta had misidentified the plant. In his notes in the original Italian, maize is translated as *miglio* against which Pigafetta had written the Caribbean word, *maíz*. He knew what maize looked like – it had 'ears like Indian corn and is shelled off and called *lada*' – and not only had he spent months with Magellan in South America on his way to Limasava but several seamen aboard had also served with Columbus in the Caribbean.[17] Chinese records state that Zheng He's admirals brought back 'extraordinarily large ears of grain'.[18] The Chinese were used to rice with ears the size of barley. The only 'extraordinarily large' ears compared to rice were those of maize. There is a wealth of further evidence, for the Portuguese also found maize in Indonesia, the Philippines and China, and *metates* – utensils for grinding maize unique to South America – were found in the hold of a junk, built in 1414, that was recently discovered on the sea-bed at Pandanan in the south-west Philippines where it had sunk in about 1423.

There was now not a scintilla of doubt in my mind that the Chinese fleet had been in South America in 1421 and had surveyed the lands shown on the Piri Reis map a century before Magellan. But they were sailing on this epic voyage to bring the entire world into the Chinese tribute system. Why should they have taken such in-ordinate trouble to chart this part of inhospitable Patagonia, a land of driving snow and bitter cold occupied only by unsophisticated, naked people with nothing to trade and with little natural wealth save for burberries and fish?

Could the Piri Reis map provide a further clue? At first it seemed only to deepen the mystery, for it showed a series of 'spokes' extending from the Patagonian coast and intersecting in a hub – the centre of a compass-rose – in the wastes of the South Atlantic. These spokes are what navigators call 'portolan lines', used in portolan navigation, also known as triangulation. Comparing the Piri Reis with a modern map, I identified the prominent points on the Patagonian coast from where each portolan line was drawn. The cartographers must have been aboard seven ships that set sail from Puntas Guzmán and Mercedes on the northern coast, Cabos Curioso and San Francisco in the centre and Punta Norte, Cabos Buen Tempo and Espíritu Santo in the south.

Knowing the scale of the Piri Reis map, I could now readily identify the true location of the centre of the compass-rose. The portolan lines intersected in King George's Bay in the West Falkland Islands. At the absolute centre of the compass-rose is Mount Adams (2,917 feet), the most conspicuous mountain in the Falklands. Was either Zhou Man or Hong Bao a secret mountaineer at heart? Is that why the ships were ordered to steer towards a mountain peak? For weeks I was baffled by this conundrum, then suddenly the answer came to me. The Chinese needed a star in the southern hemisphere to replace Polaris in the northern, and in the event they selected two: Canopus for latitude and the Southern Cross for navigation.[19]

Canopus, a yellow-white, super giant star, sits in space three hundred light years from Earth towards the South Pole and pumps out more than a thousand times the power of the sun. The combination of its power and distance makes it the second brightest star in the sky, nearly as bright as Venus, and instantly identifiable because of the colour of its light. Like the Southern Cross, Canopus is in the far south but not directly above the South Pole. To use Canopus for latitude, the Chinese had to determine its precise position by sailing to a point directly underneath the star. The Southern Cross points to the South Pole but, unlike Polaris, it is not directly above the Pole. To be able to use the Southern Cross for accurate navigation, the Chinese also had to locate its position in the sky – its height and longitude. Once again, the only way to calculate the precise position of the Southern Cross was to sail to a position directly beneath it.

The Chinese had been attempting to locate the positions of both the Southern Cross and Canopus for centuries:

In the eighth month of the twelfth year of the Khai-Yuan period [in the eighth century AD] [an expedition was sent to the] south seas to observe Lao

Jen [Canopus] at high altitudes and all the stars still further south [Southern Cross] which, though large, brilliant and numerous, had never in former times been named and charted. They were all observed to about 20° from the south [Celestial] Pole [viz. 70°S]. This is the region that the astronomers of old considered was always hidden and invisible below the horizon.[20]

Only when Canopus and the Southern Cross had been located could new lands in the southern hemisphere be accurately placed on charts. When they reached Mount Adams in the West Falklands the Chinese cartographers were directly underneath Canopus. They were taking such pains to fix their position so that they could calculate their precise latitude: 52°40′ South. By cross-referencing Canopus to Polaris they could establish Canopus's height and then use that star to obtain their latitude anywhere in the southern oceans, just as they used Polaris in the northern hemisphere. Given the importance of this location to them, I would expect the Chinese to have erected a carved stone near Mount Adams, and I have asked the governor of the Falklands for his help in organizing a search for it.

Once the latitude of Canopus had been discovered, the fleets of Zhou Man and Hong Bao could have returned independently to China, sailing westwards across the Pacific and eastwards across the southern oceans, along the same line of latitude, directly under Canopus. By doing so, all ships would be conducting surveys from the same latitude. I also came to the conclusion that it would have been logical to survey the world at latitudes where the position of other stars could be precisely determined, for example at 3°40′N, where Polaris disappeared below the horizon. It also seemed logical to expect that other latitudes of particular significance to the Chinese, for example that of their capital city Beijing at 39°53′N, might also have served the same function. As will be seen, my hunches were to prove correct.

The first Chinese 'anchor point' was the Falkland Islands,

selected because they are not only directly underneath Canopus but also almost exactly half the world away (179°) from Beijing. At this stage, although the Chinese could not measure longitude they knew the earth was a sphere. Moreover, by using Polaris they could determine the semi-circumference of that sphere (180° × 60 nautical miles) and thus approximate when they were half the world away from Beijing (days sailed multiplied by average speed). If a fleet sailed westwards from this anchor position in the Falklands and found another island south of Australia at 52°40′ South, the cartographers could chart that continent by triangulation as precisely as they had charted Patagonia. Similarly, a fleet sailing eastwards and finding another island south of Africa at 52°40′ South could chart the Indian Ocean.

I pondered how I could track the onward movements of the Chinese fleets from this anchor position. I already knew the dates on which the fleets under Zhou Man and Hong Bao had eventually returned to China and the number of ambassadors each one had brought with them. I soon realized that by using the charts and maps, and noting the locations from which the ambassadors had been collected, I could make a rational deduction about the course each fleet had followed in the intervening period. It was another significant link in the chain of evidence leading me in the wake of the treasure fleets.

Whereas the fleet under the senior admiral, Yang Qing, had remained in the Indian Ocean throughout the duration of the voyage, and returned to China in September 1422 with seventeen envoys from states in East Africa and India, Zhou Man and Hong Bao did not reach China until the autumn of 1423. Zhou Man brought no ambassadors and Hong Bao only one, from Calicut. From that, I deduced that Admiral Zhou Man's fleet had sailed westwards to chart the Pacific and returned via the Spice Islands. Admiral Hong Bao's fleet had sailed southwards for Antarctica to measure the Southern Cross and then made its way home eastwards via the southern oceans, Malacca and Calicut. I began the search for traces of their voyages, first of all by tracking Hong Bao across the southern oceans.

III

The Voyage of
Hong Bao

6

VOYAGE TO ANTARCTICA AND AUSTRALIA

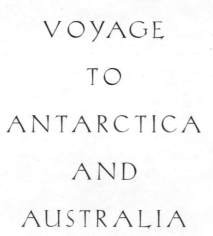

ADMIRAL HONG BAO'S DESIGNATED TASK WAS TO CHART the world eastwards from the fixed reference point established at the Falkland Islands, marked by the compass-rose on the Piri Reis – 52°40'S – but by now the brown rice in his container ships must have been running low and the bean shoots growing in tubs would all have been eaten. Before setting sail eastwards into the unknown waters of the southern oceans, he had to take on fresh supplies of food.

The Falklands offered cabbage, wild celery, penguins, geese and fish, but little other meat and no fruit at all. The only mammal ever discovered on the Falkland Islands was the warrah, an indigenous fox, described by Charles Darwin: 'There is no other instance in any part of the world of so small a mass of broken land, distant from a continent, possessing so large an aboriginal quadruped [the warrah] peculiar to itself . . . Within a very few years after these islands shall have become regularly settled, in all probability this fox will be classed with the dodo, as an animal which has perished from the face of the earth.'[1]

There is something curious about this creature which, as Darwin predicted, was wiped out in the Falklands by the 1870s. Darwin and other naturalists remarked on the warrah's extraordinary tameness. The British biologist Juliet Clutton-Brock has analysed the animal's physical characteristics from specimens in the Natural History Museum in London and concluded that, like the aboriginal dingo, the warrah had once been domesticated. It was a cross between the South American fox and a feral dog brought across the sea to the Falklands before the Europeans arrived. The most plausible explanation of its origins is that the Chinese left some of their dogs on the Falklands (they bred them on the junks for food) which then interbred with the local foxes. A request has been made to the Natural History Museum in London for DNA samples from the now-extinct warrah so that they can be compared to the DNA of Chinese food dogs. Results will be posted on the website.

If the Falklands offered a very limited food supply, Patagonia, three hundred nautical miles to the west, resembled an enormous larder, as later explorers were to find to their delight. Enough fish to feed the whole fleet could be netted in a morning; mussels the size of crabs littered the shallow pools. Guanaco, huemil and hares as large as dogs were almost tame; only snarling mountain lions stood between the sailors and limitless meat. Burberries and wild apples rich in vitamin C were also plentiful. Perhaps taking advantage of one of the periods of calm weather frequently found in an Antarctic summer, Admiral Hong Bao returned due west from the Falkland Islands to Patagonia to replenish his supplies. Still underneath Canopus at 52°40'S, he would have found what appeared to be a safe anchorage in a large bay just south of Cape Virgines. Unknown to him, the bay was the entrance to a strait leading to the Pacific. As he entered the bay, a ferocious current running at up to six knots would have dragged his fleet south-westwards through the strait like water down a plughole.

By the next morning the fleet had been sucked halfway through the strait. At last out of the current, they found themselves off the Brunswick Peninsula (the southernmost tip of the South American mainland), clearly identified on the Piri Reis map. By now the fleet was south of Canopus, and Hong Bao would have wished to sail north to get underneath his reference point once again, the latitude from which he was to chart the world to the east. The strait becomes narrower and narrower leading into the Canal Geronomino – less than a mile wide and far too narrow for his huge ships to manoeuvre, their turning circle being nearly a mile. As a result, the fleet was forced to reverse its course, and hence the cartographers drew the Canal Geronomino as a river, just as it must have appeared to them.

Back off the Brunswick Peninsula, the fleet took the Canal Magdalena south-westwards for the Pacific, entering the ocean near Isla Aguirre, a small, uninhabited island but one of the few out of the hundreds lining the coast to have been named, even today. The 'Strait of Magellan' had been discovered and charted by a complete accident: the latitude of the entrance to the strait is also the latitude of Canopus, the Chinese guiding star in the southern hemisphere. But although the Chinese had discovered the strait by chance, that does not diminish their astonishing achievement in piloting their enormous, square-sailed junks through such a narrow strait in the fierce gales and sudden violent snow squalls common in that region, which reduce visibility to a few yards. Magellan would not have known of this strait had the Chinese not charted it. Europeans thus owe a huge debt to the Chinese for pioneering the link between the Atlantic and Pacific Oceans, and opening up the sea route to the Spice Islands.

Not without reason was the remote, inhospitable land on either side of the dreaded strait named 'the uttermost part of the earth' by the earliest European explorers. Despite the near-endless snowstorms, often driven horizontally across the land by the force of the wind, Tierra del Fuego has an enthralling grandeur. Glaciers fall vertically to the ocean, and beyond them ice-bound mountain peaks glisten like diamonds against the pale skies. Today, as for centuries past, navigators dread the violent currents that seem to start and finish without warning or apparent cause, and the westerly gales that spring from nowhere and whip the seas into a boiling cauldron within minutes. Until the nineteenth century, its howling gales and bleak terrain discouraged settlement, leaving the Yahgan natives who inhabited this grim terrain to live in peace, huddling around the fires that led Magellan to name the region Tierra del Fuego. The Yahgan seemed to Darwin 'among the most abject and miserable creatures I ever saw, the difference between them and Europeans being greater than that between wild and domestic animals'.[2]

The discovery that the Chinese had made the first ever voyage through this daunting region was a tremendous moment for me. I wondered if Hong Bao had also realized its remarkable importance and significance. I returned to the British Library to see if the diaries of the Portuguese explorer Ferdinand Magellan and Antonio

Pigafetta, who sailed with Magellan's fleet, could offer any further verification of this ground-breaking voyage of a century before.

Magellan renounced his own country and set sail on his great voyage of circumnavigation on 20 September 1519 under the colours of Spain. He had a fleet of five ships and a crew of 265 men. Only one ship and eighteen men survived to complete the circumnavigation. Magellan himself was fatally wounded in the Philippines on 27 April 1521 after becoming involved in a dispute between two warring tribes. Pigafetta had this to say about the critical point in their journey:

> After going and setting course to the fifty-second degree towards the said Antarctic Pole on the festival of the Eleven Thousand Virgins (19th October), we found by a miracle a Strait [near what] we called the Cape of the Eleven Thousand Virgins [today Cape Virgines]. Which Strait is in length 110 leagues which are 440 miles and in width somewhat less than half a league.[3]

The fact that they were 'setting course to the fifty-second degree' indicates that Magellan knew that at 52°S he would find the strait that was later to bear his name, linking the Atlantic with the Pacific. His fleet reached the dark and forbidding region on 19 October 1520. By that stage, Magellan and his crew were in a wretched state. Howling gales battered the ships and blizzards obscured both the passage ahead and the rocky islands surrounding them. He had problems finding an anchorage, many of his sailors were dying from scurvy, and he had succeeded in quelling a mutiny only by the brutal expedient of hanging, drawing and quartering the leaders. Now mutiny was again in the air.

'This Strait was a circular place surrounded by mountains . . . and to most of those in the ships it seemed there was no way out from it to enter the said Pacific sea.'[4] Magellan could not persuade his men that it was safe to go onward through the strait, so he ordered his critics to put their reasons in writing for either continuing or returning to Spain. He read their opinions aloud, then, taking a sacred oath on St James whose insignia he wore upon his cloak, he solemnly swore to his men that 'there was another Strait which led out [to the Pacific] saying that he knew it well and had seen it in a marine chart of the King of Portugal, which a great pilot and sailor named Martin of Bohemia [Martin Behain] had made'.[5]

Magellan was telling the truth, though not the whole truth. The existence of the strait leading from the Atlantic to the Pacific was well known both to the King of Spain and Magellan before he set sail. He took with him on the voyage a marine chart that showed the strait and the Pacific Ocean beyond it. The contract he had signed with the king specified the aims of the voyage – to sail westwards for the Spice Islands – and the share of the profits each was to enjoy. Magellan wanted knowledge of the strait to be restricted to himself alone to prevent others from following in his wake and claiming their own share of the riches that awaited him, but the King of Spain was in no position to grant his request, for the Portuguese held the master chart.

Magellan's words, and his ruthless and inspired leadership, persuaded his men to continue, and they completed the passage of the strait that ever afterwards bore his name rather than that of the first man to do so, Hong Bao. In his description of the ships clearing the strait and entering the Pacific, Pigafetta made a vitally significant comment: 'When we had left that Strait, if we had sailed always westwards, we should have gone without finding any island other than the Cape of the Eleven Thousand Virgins ... in 52 degrees of latitude exactly towards the Antarctic Pole.'[6] Pigafetta's statement contained information that could only have been obtained by someone who had either sailed the world at that latitude or seen a chart showing the Pacific empty of land at 52°S. Magellan turned to the north towards the equator when leaving the strait and so could not have discovered for himself that there was no land at that latitude. He must therefore have seen a chart. Magellan knew that he was not the first to sail through the strait, nor the first to cross the Pacific.

Once again, Fra Mauro had been correct: a ship from India had rounded the Cape of Good Hope and sailed to the 'obscured islands'. The riddle of the Piri Reis map had also been solved. Patagonia and the 'Strait of Magellan' were indeed drawn long before Magellan set sail, but not by a civilization predating the Pharaohs, as one authority has suggested,[7] nor by aliens from outer space, as another, rather less academic writer argued,[8] but by a great Chinese treasure fleet during the 'missing years' of 1421–3.

After passing through the strait, Admiral Hong Bao took his fleet southwards, sailing to the west of the islands of Tierra del Fuego. The cartography of the Piri Reis map clearly shows the route the fleet took: while Patagonia is very accurately charted, the low eastern islands of Tierra del Fuego are not recorded at all, indicating that the Chinese had sailed down the mountainous west coast.

I compared the Piri Reis map with a modern satellite photograph and immediately identified the bays and small islands surrounding the Chinese passage to the south. Further down the coast, Cook Bay is accurately positioned, suggesting that Admiral Hong Bao had anchored there. From this anchorage, he would have seen the magnificent snow-capped mountains of the Cordillera Darwin towering in an arc to the east of him. They appear on the map as separate islands, for from that distance the cartographer could have seen only their snow-capped peaks. I magnified the Piri Reis map to the same scale as a modern chart[9] and found that all eleven 'islands' shown on the Piri Reis south of Patagonia coincide with mountain peaks on the islands that collectively form western Tierra del Fuego. My detailed workings appear on the website.

The Chinese had already established the position of Canopus in the sky, the nearest and brightest equivalent in the southern hemisphere to Polaris in the northern, but to fix its position relative to the South Pole they had to establish the precise position of the pole itself. Only then would they be able to navigate and chart lands as accurately as they did in the northern hemisphere. Since they already knew from their observations of the night sky that the two leading stars of the Southern Cross, Crucis Gamma and Crucis Alpha, were aligned with the pole, they believed that they only had to sail in the same direction to reach the pole.

The polar regions can be a terrible place for a mariner. In summer there are periods of flat calm, clear skies and limpid blue seas speckled with ice floes, but when the weather breaks massive waves crash over the bows and the wind screams through the sails, driving squalls and flurries of snow and ice that sting the skin like needles. For weeks in midwinter there is unbroken black darkness; even when the sun does begin to reappear it is no more than a brief, dim disc on the northern horizon. Often cloud and freezing mist cloak every outline, leaving the seamen on watch straining their eyes into the murk for the first warning sign of drifting ice floes or a towering iceberg in their track.

However, the prospect of sailing into these frozen regions would have held few terrors for the Chinese, who had eight centuries' experience of navigating in northern polar latitudes behind them and a thousand-year tradition of navigating in ice: the nearest port to Beijing, Tanggu, is ice-bound for three months each year. I found the first anecdotal evidence that the Chinese had indeed attempted to set sail for the South Pole after leaving Cook Bay in an account[10] of the travels of a young nobleman from Bologna, Ludovico de Varthema, in 1506. Ludovico de Varthema was sailing between Borneo and Java where he was told a strange tale. His companions, two Chinese Christians and an East Indian navigator, told him sailors from the other (Chinese) side of Java had sailed by the Southern Cross to regions where it was very cold and the days were only four hours long.[11] How could they have known without sailing there?

The Piri Reis map provided further evidence that they had sailed south. Ice is shown running due south of the Strait of Magellan, and to have drawn it the Chinese must have been sailing alongside it. They were heading due south, making straight for the South Pole. The two leading stars of the Southern Cross were overhead,[12] pointing in the direction they had to sail. Some two hundred miles south of Tierra del Fuego,[13] they met the first drift ice, which had begun to curve to the east, drawn as a C-shaped arc on the Piri Reis map. They attempted to continue southwards around the ice but were unable to do so and were obliged to alter course, first to the east and then to the south-east, all the time trying to find a way to continue towards the pole. After sailing another two hundred miles south,[14] they met pack ice that continued all the way down to the Antarctic peninsula. The ice depicted on the Piri Reis map corresponds with the normal maximum limits of drift and pack ice in midsummer.[15]

Admiral Hong Bao was now approaching the Antarctic Circle. At this latitude strange things happen. At the South Pole itself, longitude has no meaning. It becomes a dot; there are no directions other than north. In midsummer (December), the sun is always in the north and it is light all day; in winter, it is permanently dark. The navigational difficulties are exacerbated by magnetic anomalies caused by the South Magnetic Pole, far removed from the true South Pole. This would have played havoc with the Chinese magnetic compasses; the only navigational aids they could then rely on were bearings obtained from the constellation of the leading stars of the Southern Cross and the latitude of Canopus, both of which become circumpolar – never rising and setting and visible in the sky at all times – below 68°S. The intensity of its light and the clarity of the Antarctic air often make Canopus visible in daylight.

The Piri Reis map shows Graham Land, the northern extremity of the Antarctic peninsula, largely ice-free, confirming that the expedition reached the Antarctic in January 1422. The C-shape of the drift ice shown stretching from Cape Horn indicates that they had first met a current flowing from the east. Further south, where the current had more or less disappeared, the chart shows the pack ice stretching east–west before once again curving in a shallower curve to the south-east as it met another, weaker current. The uniform shape of these curves of ice showed that the Chinese were favoured with good weather and sailing into the circumpolar current before a light breeze, insufficient to break up the ice. I

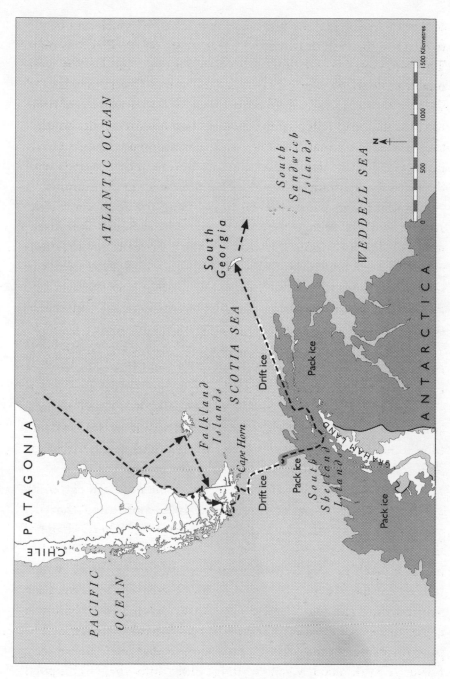

The journey to Antarctica.

estimated that they would have made an average speed of approximately three knots. At that rate the voyage from Cape Horn to the Antarctic peninsula would have taken approximately fourteen days.

A group of islands was shown on the Piri Reis map where none exists in reality. In shape they resembled the South Shetland Islands, and I wondered if they were indeed what the map was depicting. The Chinese could measure latitude precisely from Canopus, but they could not yet determine longitude with similar accuracy, and once again, I had to adjust the longitudinal positions of the islands recorded on the Piri Reis map to allow for the movement of the water in which the Chinese fleet was sailing, just as I had for the Kangnido map of Africa. Allowing for an average current of two-thirds of a knot against them during their passage south, the islands shown on the Piri Reis map would be in fact four hundred miles further west than they were charted – precisely the position of the South Shetlands.

I knew from the Piri Reis map that the Chinese must have approached Antarctica from the north-west, skirting the edge of the ice, and would have made landfall on the south-western edge of the South Shetland Islands. Three of the islands are charted very accurately: Snow Island in the west, horseshoe-shaped Deception Island in the south, and four mountains on Livingstone Island in the north. A note near Deception Island also states: 'Here it is hot'. At first sight this appears a curious comment to make about a snow-bound island in the Antarctic, but Deception Island is volcanic and active. Modern cruise ships anchor in the lagoon to allow tourists to bathe in the hot volcanic waters of Benjamin Cove.

Apart from Deception Island, the South Shetlands are an uninhabited wilderness of frost-shattered rock, glaciers and ice-fields, without so much as a blade of grass to be seen. As I knew from my own time in submarines sailing in polar regions, the cold can be so severe that metal objects stick to your fingers. To avoid tearing the flesh, you need to warm the fingers. The only way of doing so is usually to urinate on them, but if you attempt to do this while exposed to the Antarctic winds, you risk a very painful frostbite. The Chinese would have huddled below decks, trying to keep warm among their horses and dogs, returning to the upper deck for as short a time as possible. Their rice supplies would have had to be carefully covered and insulated to prevent the intense cold causing permanent damage to the grains, and the flooded sections of the holds where they kept their supplies of fish and their trained otters would have had to be emptied to prevent the water expanding as it froze, and forcing apart the seams of the hull. Furthermore, in these terrible conditions, surveying this part of the islands so precisely would have taken some considerable time. Why had the Chinese bothered to do so? I began to wonder if they really had gone there. Then the answer that I should have seen at once suddenly came to me. They had chosen this spot because they were right underneath Crucis Alpha, the leading star of the Southern Cross, at 62°49′S.

I could only shake my head in wonder at the skill and sophistication of these Chinese mariners of so many centuries ago. The Chinese astronomers' determination of the positions of Canopus and the Southern Cross in the sky was a pivotal moment in the history of man's knowledge of the globe. Because they knew the circumference of the earth, they could now calculate the true position of the South Pole. By observing the difference between the true bearing shown by the Southern Cross and that shown by their magnetic compasses, they could determine the position of the Magnetic South Pole and therefore make the necessary corrections to their compasses. In 1421–3, the stars of the Southern Cross and Canopus could be observed as far as 28°N – the latitude of the Canary Islands – where Polaris was also clearly visible.[16] A cross-reference to check latitudes could be obtained by comparing the latitudes derived from Canopus and Polaris. The *Wu Pei Chi* confirms that this was indeed a practice of Chinese navigators, whereas the Portuguese did not adopt this method of calculating latitude for another fifty years.

The Chinese could now steer a completely accurate course in the southern as well as the northern hemisphere and determine exact

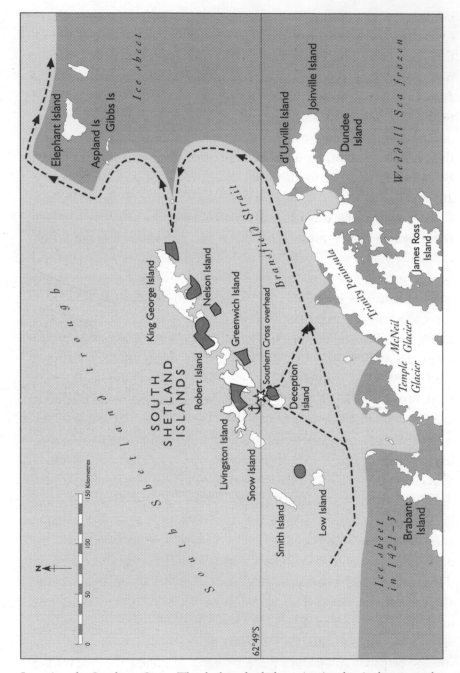

Locating the Southern Cross. The darker shaded portion is what is shown on the Piri Reis; the light areas are what is shown on modern Admiralty charts.

latitudes. Only the problem of longitude remained to be solved. Once true latitudes in the southern hemisphere could be calculated, Chinese charts could be drawn in a readily comprehensible form – not as a table or as a long strip of sailing directions such as the *Wu Pei Chi*, but as a recognizable geometric depiction. A note appended to the Piri Reis map confirms this change: '[This map was] drawn . . . from about twenty charts and mappae mundi . . . which shows the countries of Sint, Hint, and Cin [China] geometrically drawn . . . By reducing all these maps to one scale, this final form was arrived at.'[17]

To have found a way of accurately charting the whole world in a recognizable form must have been an incredibly exciting, triumphant moment for the Chinese astronomers, navigators and cartographers, just as it was for the Europeans when they made the same discoveries in 1473. The Chinese fleets could now go on to survey the world, using the latitude of Canopus as a baseline. They had accomplished one of the prime tasks their emperor had set them. They could now brave the biting cold of the air to enjoy a hot bath in the lagoon inside Deception Island, gather up penguins for food and cut off blocks of ice for fresh water. This would have been the moment to enjoy a cask of rice wine and feast on some of the dogs, before setting sail once again to explore the Antarctic mainland further south.

As the junks sailed through the strait separating the South Shetlands from the Antarctic peninsula, the islands would still have been visible thirty-five miles away to the north-west, with the mainland twenty miles to the south. At that range they would have seen only mountains, but they located them, with just a very small error. Their charting of mainland Antarctica was equally accurate. I was able to identify sixty-three prominent features of the Antarctic mainland on the Piri Reis map. My detailed working drawings appear on the website. Only one thing seemed out of place – a strange serpent shown resting on the ice of Elephant Island. But the leopard seal resembles a serpent as it slithers across the ice, and, like serpents, leopard seals have fangs. East of Elephant Island, the Weddell Sea was shown as solid ice, and it is indeed ice-bound throughout the year. It is remarkably accurate cartography.

There was no longer the slightest shred of doubt in my mind. There was no need to summon ancient Egyptians or space aliens to explain how the Piri Reis map could have depicted Antarctica with such accuracy four hundred years before the first Europeans arrived there. The information came from surveyors aboard Admiral Hong Bao's fleet in 1422, who had been charting the precise position of the Southern Cross.

The Piri Reis map also showed another, smaller compass-rose south-east of the Falklands and north-east of the South Shetlands. The centre of this secondary rose corresponds to Bird Island, the north-west island of South Georgia. As its name implies, Bird Island is populated by millions of sea-birds using it as a launching platform for feeding forays into the plankton- and fish-rich Antarctic Ocean. It is a tiny island, two miles long and nowhere more than half a mile wide, fringed by sheer one-thousand-foot cliffs on its north side but with sandy beaches to the south.

The compass-rose showed that Bird Island was used as a pivotal point by the Chinese cartographers. Having established the course and distances the fleet had sailed from the South Shetlands and the Falklands to Bird Island, they could reduce longitude errors by cross-referencing the three. I applied the same scale as I had worked out for measuring Patagonia and discovered that the distance shown on the Piri Reis map from Deception Island in the Antarctic to Bird Island was correct. The only mistake was that both the South Shetlands and South Georgia were shown further east than they should be. Once again, the circumpolar current accounted for the longitudinal error.

After he had reached and charted Bird Island, Admiral Hong Bao would have had no choice but to continue eastwards, sailing beneath Canopus, for around these latitudes, as the name implies, the Roaring Forties would have driven his ships before the wind to the east. These are winds to test the courage of the bravest sailor. They howl over towering seas, great walls of green water capped with foam, hurling spume through the air. Seamen would have worked frozen and soaked to the skin and shouted themselves hoarse in a vain attempt to be heard amid the shrieking of the wind through the rigging, the creaks and groans of timbers as the hull flexed and twisted in a swell like none other on earth, and the roar and hiss of waves breaking over the bows and foaming away through the scuppers. The prow would have dragged itself free of one giant wave only to bury itself immediately in the next. There would have been little respite for the men below decks, their clothes permanently sodden and the pitching and heaving of the ship so severe that sleep would have been all but impossible.

Driven eastwards by the relentless winds, Admiral Hong Bao would not have anchored until he next found land along 52°40'S, enabling him to conduct another detailed cartographic survey, just as he had in South America. But travelling eastwards at this latitude there is no substantial landmass, only a few scattered islands. At last, after a voyage of some five thousand miles across the southern oceans, all the time with the brilliant yellow-white Canopus directly above him, the increasing numbers of sea-birds – albatross, terns, skua and petrels – would have alerted him to the fact that land was nearby, and at last his look-outs would have spotted the volcanic Mawson's Peak on Heard Island silhouetted above a group of smaller islands just fifteen miles to the south. Now he could begin a survey to establish another 'anchor' position for his cartographers.

Heard Island would have seemed a far from inviting prospect to Hong Bao and his men. It is heavily glaciated and much of the coast-line is covered by ice cliffs. There are a few isolated patches of tussock grass, moss and lichen, but 80 per cent of the island is permanently ice-bound. However, a group of somewhat less forbidding islands, the Kerguelens – named after the Frenchman Le Comte Yves de Kerguelen-Tremarec, who is credited with discovering them on 12 February 1772 – lies three hundred miles to the north. The driving winds in that region mean that the Kerguelens can most readily be approached by square-rigged ships from the west – from South America, precisely the direction from which Hong Bao's fleet was sailing.

I found some independent evidence[18] that Hong Bao's fleet had reached the islands: the *Dictionary of Ming Biography* records, 'Some of the ships reached as far as a place called Ha-bu-er which may be identified as Kerguelen Island in the Antarctic Ocean.'[19] The island of Ha-bu-er is also shown on the Chinese Mao Kun chart, part of the *Wu Pei Chi*, compiled around 1422,[20] alongside a note stating that 'storms prevented the fleet sailing further south'. Hong Bao had found more new lands.

Dominated by the six-thousand-foot Mount Ross, the main island of Kerguelen is sufficiently barren to have been described as 'Desolation Island' by Captain Cook. Rain, sleet or snow falls on three hundred days a year and 30 per cent of the island is permanently ice-covered, but the coasts are rich in penguins and elephant seals, and Kerguelen cabbages, very valuable plants for seamen, grow among the tussock grass and moss. A relative of our own cabbage, Kerguelen cabbages are rich in vitamin C and were much harvested and eaten by whalers and sealers in the following centuries to prevent scurvy. Hong Bao's crew would almost certainly have been suffering from scurvy after their marathon voyage across the southern oceans and would have gathered as many cabbages as possible, but Kerguelen's sour and barren soil did not support anywhere near enough of the plants to feed the thousands of men carried by the fleet. The search for fresh supplies would now have been becoming urgent.

The revelation that the Chinese had discovered Ha-bu-er/ Kerguelen Island filled me with excitement, for after leaving the island Hong Bao's ships could have sailed in only one direction. As the Mao Kun says, the Roaring Forties would have prevented them from sailing further south, and they would also have stopped them from going north or retracing their route westwards. Instead,

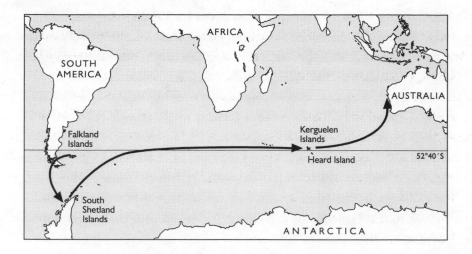

Hong Bao's journey to Australia.

the Chinese junks would have been propelled eastwards before mountainous waves along a sea-corridor that led straight to the south-west coast of Australia. I had no doubt that Hong Bao must have reached Australia, so I returned to the British Library to search for a chart of the continent that had been surveyed and drawn before the first Europeans discovered it.

Australia is not depicted on the Piri Reis map, but it is shown on another very early chart, held by the British Library. It was drawn by Jean Rotz, appointed 'Hydrographer to the King' by Henry VIII of England, and was included in the *Boke of Idrography* Rotz presented to the king in 1542, two centuries before Captain Cook 'discovered' Australia. Rotz came from the Dieppe School of Cartography, celebrated throughout Europe for the clarity and accuracy of the maps and charts they produced. He was the leading mapmaker of his day, renowned for the meticulousness with which he depicted new lands. He never invented or fudged; what is shown on his charts is exactly what he had seen on older charts.

It is commonly accepted[21] that Rotz, and indeed the other Dieppe cartographers of his day, copied much older Portuguese charts. The styles of the Piri Reis and Jean Rotz charts are very similar, and both use Portuguese names to describe the newly discovered lands. The Rotz chart shows Malaysia, Cambodia, Vietnam and China all the way up to modern Hong Kong, and the whole coast is extremely well charted. The Persian Gulf, India and south-east Asia are also instantly recognizable. The original chart can only have been drawn by someone with intimate knowledge of the coastlines of the Indian Ocean, China and Indochina. That at once ruled out the Portuguese, for although the Rotz chart was made after Magellan's circumnavigation of the world, neither Magellan nor the Portuguese explorers who followed him spent long enough on the Chinese coast to chart it with such compelling accuracy. Their target was the Spice Islands; they were making for the Moluccas far further south. If the original cartographer was not Portuguese, he in turn must have copied an earlier original.

Despite his accurate depiction of the coasts of China, Asia, India and Africa, many historians have failed to identify a vast new landmass Rotz showed south of the equator. It consists of two islands, 'Little Java' south of Sumatra and 'Greater Java', a huge continent stretching away from near the equator towards the South Pole. At its northern end, this continent has a protruding spit resembling Cape York, the northernmost tip of Australia. The north-east part of this southern continent also resembles the north-east Australian coast, but the land shown on the Rotz chart stretches far further to the south-east than Australia actually does.

The theories of Ptolemy – the astronomer, mathematician and geographer who lived in Alexandria in Egypt c. AD 87–150 – had been rediscovered in the late Middle Ages. Ptolemy's belief in the symmetry of the stars and the planets had led him to advance a theory in his book *Geographia* that a substantial southern landmass must exist to 'balance' the continents of Europe and Asia in the northern hemisphere. My first assumption was that when drawing the land in the far south the original cartographer of the Rotz chart had based it not on observation but on Ptolemy's forecast, but this did not square with Rotz's reputation for precision. For the moment I had to set that puzzle aside and concentrate my attention on the south-west coast of 'Greater Java', which was depicted with considerably more accuracy. The shape of the coast accords with Hong Bao's fleet having made a landfall near modern Bunbury, a hundred miles to the south of Perth in Western Australia. The prevailing wind and current would then have driven them up the coast to an anchor point in the estuary of the Swan River that separates modern Perth and Fremantle, shown as a deep indentation on the Rotz chart.

The Kerguelen cabbages they had collected would have been of only modest help in staving off scurvy among the crew of the fleet, but in south-west Australia they would have found plentiful supplies of vitamin C in the apples and plums that abound in the area. Blue fairy penguins and manna crabs were also there for the taking, the koala bears and quokkas (small wallabies) were slow, timid and easy prey, and the jarrah, marri and karri trees would have provided plenty of hardwood for repairing their junks. Although the Rotz chart also shows the eastern and northern coasts of the Australian continent with great fidelity, the west coast is drawn no further south than Bunbury, where it ends abruptly. The most plausible reason for this curtailment of the survey, I would argue, is that the junk despatched by Admiral Hong Bao to chart the south coast of Australia foundered off Warrnambool in modern Victoria, south-east Australia, where a wreck was indeed discovered 166 years ago that could well have been a ship from Hong Bao's fleet.

In 1836, when the state of Victoria was but two years old, three men hunting seals sailed into the muddy Hopkins River and continued westwards down the small estuaries and lagoons of that coast. Where the Merri River joins the sea, they came across the wreck of a very old ship known from that day to this as the 'Mahogany Ship' because of the timber used in its construction. Seven years later, Captain Mills, a local harbour master, inspected the wreck on behalf of the government. He was astonished at the hardness of the wood;

when he tried to cut a piece, his knife was useless, 'like glancing off iron'.[22] European ships were not then built of mahogany – the contemporary name used for any of a variety of reddish-brown hardwood trees – for there were no such trees in Europe, but Chinese ships were built of teak, a reddish-brown hardwood from the forests of Annam. Captain Mills was also baffled by the ship's origins: 'She struck me as a vessel of a model altogether unfamiliar and at variance in some respects with the rules of shipbuilding as far as we know them . . . As regards to the nationality of the wreck, I do not profess to be a judge . . . I should say the wreck in question is connected with neither [Spanish or Portuguese] build.'[23]

Twenty years later, an Australian woman, Mrs Manifold, examined the wreck, one of a further twenty-five people to record their impressions of it. She was impressed by the internal bulkheads, 'stout and strong'.[24] A bronze spike, an iron ladder and a piece of timber[25] were recovered; they have yet to be carbon-dated, but I am confident that this is probably a missing ship from Hong Bao's fleet. The Aboriginal Yangery tribe, who then lived on the mainland close to the wreck-site of the ship, have a legend that 'yellow men' long ago settled among them.[26] Since then many observers have commented on the distinctive colour and facial characteristics of Aborigines who come from this small area of southern Australia. Pending carbon-dating of the material to establish the date of the wreck, at the very least it is arguable that sailors aboard the ship detached by Admiral Hong Bao to chart the south Australian coast were shipwrecked, and that some of the men and their concubines managed to reach the shore and settled among the Aborigines. Professor Wei Chuh-Hsien (Wei Chu Xian) goes further, believing that the men wrecked at Warrnambool rode on horseback up the valleys of the Murray, Darling and Murrambidgee Rivers to what is now Cooktown, leaving traces of their journey along the route.[27] Professor Wei's theory seems to be corroborated by Toscanelli's map of 1474 which shows the rivers explored by the Chinese cavalry.

*

By March 1423, the Chinese fleets had been at sea for two years and had sailed the nethermost reaches of the oceans. Admirals Hong Bao and Zhou Man had accomplished the major part of their mission – locating Canopus and the Southern Cross and going on to chart the southern hemisphere – but one aspect of the voyage had not gone according to plan. After leaving the Indian Ocean, the admirals had expected to greet foreign potentates and present them with fine silks and porcelains, bringing their countries into China's tribute system. Yet the people they had met along the route were unused to trade and appeared to have no kings. The Bantu in South Africa, Aborigines in Australia and naked men in Patagonia had no use for silk or porcelain, and places such as the Antarctic and Cape Verde Islands were uninhabited. Life in the lands the Chinese had discovered was far more primitive than they had expected, and as a consequence the holds of their surviving ships must still have been full of their 'treasure' of porcelain and silks. But as he set sail from the west coast of Australia, Hong Bao would have known that he still had the opportunity to trade his goods before making for home, for the Spice Islands and the great trading port of Malacca were well within his reach.

The Rotz chart depicts western Australia, Sumatra, the Malay Peninsula, Indochina and the west coast of Borneo with considerable accuracy. This suggests that, having sailed north-westwards from Perth, the remainder of the fleet under Hong Bao circumnavigated Sumatra, berthed at Malacca, one of the prime trading ports in the Indian Ocean, and then returned home through the South China Sea, sailing along the west coast of Borneo – the east coast is not charted – and to the west of the Philippines before eventually arriving home on 22 October 1423.

Admiral Hong Bao's fleet had been the first voyagers ever to sail through the Strait of Magellan. They had discovered the Antarctic continent and reached southern Australia over two centuries before Abel Tasman (1603–c. 1659), who discovered the island of Tasmania that bears his name. Taken in isolation, Hong Bao's voyage would have been more than worthy of modern commemoration. He had made one of the epic journeys in the history of mankind's exploration of the planet and his name deserves to be remembered and celebrated. But that was not the end of the Chinese achievements. As Hong Bao prepared to return home in triumph, another Chinese fleet under Admiral Zhou Man was also sailing along southern latitudes making for Australia from the opposite direction, crossing the Pacific a century before Magellan.

IV

The Voyage of
Zhou Man

7
AUSTRALIA

七

THE DESIGNATED TASK OF ZHOU MAN WAS TO SURVEY THE world west of South America; like Admiral Hong Bao, who had sailed eastwards, Zhou Man would have needed 'anchor' reference points at 52°40'S as he crossed the oceans beneath Canopus. But as his fleet entered the Pacific, the square-rigged junks would have met the cold Humboldt current and been swept northwards up the coast of what is now Chile. Magellan, Carteret, Bougainville and countless other explorers following in the wake of the Chinese had the same experience. The depiction of the Andes on the Piri Reis map[1] gives clear evidence that this had also happened to Zhou Man's fleet, but I did not yet know how far north the Chinese had travelled and whether they had reached Peru or met the Incas, one of the great civilizations of pre-Columbian South America.

For once, there was a helpful Chinese document that had escaped destruction by the mandarins. Dr Wang Tao of the School of Oriental and African Studies in London told me of a novel about Zheng He's voyages written in 1597, the *Hsi-Yang-Chi* (*Xi Yang Ji*). It became hugely popular in China after its publication, but is now so rare that the copy held by the library of the School of Oriental and African Studies is the only one in the world. Although it was written the best part of two centuries after the voyages it describes, and most of the book is taken up with fanciful adventures, the author did the modern researcher a valuable service by giving a detailed list of the tributes offered to the Chinese fleet by the barbarians they encountered on their voyages. The descriptions differ from the lists of goods given by Ma Huan (who never sailed beyond the Indian Ocean), suggesting that the author must have drawn on a different, now vanished source, but the detail and oddity of the list makes a convincing impression:

One pair of whale's eyes, commonly called bright-eyed pearls.

Two bream whiskers. These are lustrous and may be used for hairpins or ear-ornaments. The price is very high.

One pair of camels that go to a thousand *li* [four hundred miles – possibly a reference to the distance the animals could travel without water].

Four boxes of dragon's saliva [ambergris].

Eight boxes of frankincense.

Four pairs of landscape porcelain bowls. In these is a landscape; by pouring water into the bowl, the mountains become blue and the water green.

Four pairs of porcelain bowls with representations of men and things: by pouring water into them there is gradually a picture of men saluting each other.

Four pairs of porcelain bowls with flowers and plants. In these are flowers and plants. By pouring water into them, they appear to move and wave.

Four pairs of porcelain bowls with feathers. In these are feathers, and by pouring water into them, they appear to fly.[2]

Clearly, these bowls greatly impressed the Chinese, who had prided themselves on making the world's finest and thinnest porcelain. These bowls must have been even finer. They became translucent when filled with water, allowing scenes painted on the undersides to be seen through the porcelain. It was beyond the capacity of any Indian, African or Islamic states of that or any earlier era to produce ceramics of such quality, and Europeans did not discover the technology to produce fine porcelain until the early eighteenth century. The only porcelain of that thinness at the time came from Cholula (in modern Mexico); the Aztec emperor Montezuma II (1480–1520) was eating off Cholula ware when the Spanish conquistadors encountered him. It was literally eggshell-thin, extremely expensive and much sought after, and was exported from Cholula to the Pacific coast and South America.

At the time of the Chinese voyages, Cholula was in its prime, producing huge quantities of this renowned porcelain and building pyramids more colossal than those of Egypt. Assuming that 'the pair of camels' were llamas (camelids), then everything in the tribute list, including the ambergris (from small whales called cachalots), could have been found in northern Peru. Asiatic hens were found there when the Spanish first landed, and at the very least it is arguable that they could have been left by Zhou Man's fleet after an exchange of gifts with the bird-loving Incas. I was later to find overwhelming evidence of pre-Columbian voyages between China and the Americas in Mexico, Guatemala, Colombia, Ecuador and Peru, as will be discussed in later chapters.

I returned to the task of tracing the course taken by Zhou Man. After leaving Peru, his fleet would first have been carried by the equatorial current as far north as Ecuador, where the current turns due west and carries mariners across the Pacific, the route along which explorer after explorer was swept in later centuries. Don Luis Arias, a Spanish envoy to South America in the sixteenth century, sent a memorandum to his king describing a South American legend of a Pacific crossing from Chile before the European voyages of discovery, carried out by 'light coloured or white skinned people . . . who wore white woven garments'.[3] When those legendary voyagers reached the mid-Pacific off Samoa, they found that the south equatorial current split there, just as it does today. The northern part carries on towards the Carolines, New Guinea and the Philippines; the southern part sweeps south-west towards Australia.

There is substantial evidence that Zhou Man's fleet separated at this point. The northern squadron built observation platforms at Kiribati in the Carolines, and another five in New Guinea. They were stepped pyramids with truncated tops like those in China. Rose-pink beads, made by rubbing a spiny oyster against cowrie shells, exactly similar in size and design to those found in the rivers of Mitla in Central America were found in the Caroline Islands last century, together with a fragment of obsidian and a piece of iron resembling a spearhead – all items foreign to the islands. Chinese hens were found in Peru by the first European explorers; maize, indigenous to the Americas, was found by the first Europeans to reach the Philippines; *metates* – tools used to grind maize – were in the holds of the junk found on the sea-bed in the Philippines in 1993, which was believed to have sunk about 1423. All of this is consistent with the Chinese sailing with the wind up the west coast of South

America (shown on the Piri Reis map) and then across the Pacific.

The course followed by the southern squadron along the south-west branch of the equatorial current would have taken it through the Tuamotu archipelago, four thousand miles west of South America. In 1606, Pedro Fernandez de Quirós (1565–1615), a Portuguese explorer working for the Spanish Crown, landed at Hao Atoll in the Tuamotu archipelago.[4] There he encountered an old lady wearing a gold ring set with an emerald. He offered trade goods for it but she greeted his offer with disdain – it was far too valuable. Neither gold nor emeralds are found within thousands of miles of the Tuamotu archipelago, but it is well documented that such rings were exported during the early Ming dynasty and given as presents by Zhu Di's ambassadors. Stepped pyramids were also found along this south-western route, in Tahiti and Australia, and the first Europeans to reach Fiji found that someone had been mining copper before them – something the locals did not do. Polynesians could have carried artefacts across the Pacific in their canoes, but that does not explain the Chinese hens and artefacts found in the Americas or the sheer volume of goods carried from the Americas to the Pacific. I would suggest that the only logical explanation is that they were carried by the junks of a Chinese treasure fleet and the ships of the traders that accompanied them.

The Chinese fleet swept on to chart Norfolk Island and, still carried westward by the current, made a landfall on the east coast of Australia just north of where Sydney is sited today. The great voyage across the Pacific had covered more than seven thousand miles and taken around three months. The current turns to the south when it meets the Australian coast, and Zhou Man's fleet would have been carried with it towards the latitude of Canopus, their reference point.

Admiral Hong Bao's voyage to Australia has been described in chapter 6. Admiral Zhou Man knew of Australia's existence before he landed there, for since Sui dynasty times (AD 589–618) the Chinese had known of a great landmass peopled by men who threw

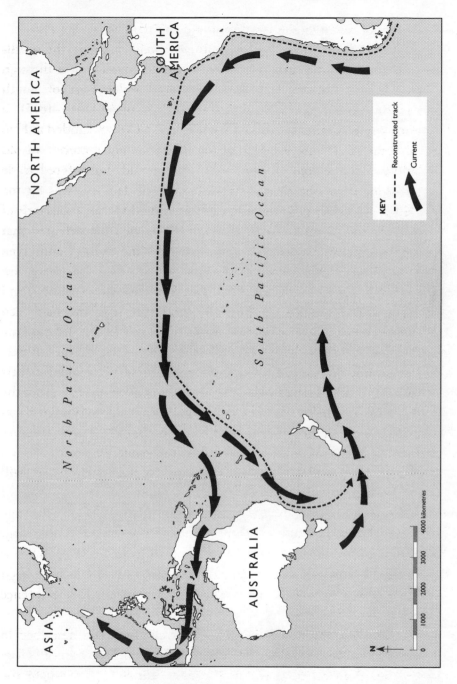

Zhou Man's journey to Australia.

boomerangs, one hundred days' sailing south of Asia.[5] Chinese historians of that era described an animal, *Shan Lai Jing*, with the head of a deer, that hopped on its hind legs and had a second head in the middle of its body – the baby in the pouch. By the time Marco Polo reached China in the thirteenth century, Chinese charts were showing two Javas – the island we know today as Java and 'Greater Java', the source of the trepangs, or sea slugs, the Chinese ate with such relish. They remained a lucrative catch for fishing vessels and are still a highly prized delicacy in China. After his visit to China, Marco Polo called Greater Java 'the largest island in the world', and even before his time there were kangaroos in the imperial zoo in Beijing. Kangaroos, of course, are unique to Australia. Further evidence of the Chinese voyages to Australia could be seen at Taiwan University: a map on porcelain dated to 1447 showed the coastline of New Guinea, the east coast of Australia as far south as Victoria, and the north-east coast of Tasmania. Unfortunately, at the time of writing it appears this map has been lost.

It seemed probable that cartographers aboard Zhou Man's fleet had surveyed these lands and provided the information for the charts, but since the records of his voyage were destroyed after he returned to China in 1423 I had to look abroad to find corroborative evidence of his landfall in Australia. My analysis started from the assumption that this great southern continent was already well known to the Chinese, but was surveyed in more detail during their 1421–3 voyage. If so, I expected the cartography to be of a very high standard, with the latitudes and the alignment of the land correct, but possibly with substantial errors in longitude.

The great landmass shown on the Jean Rotz chart (pp. 151-2) could be Australia, but with some longitudinal errors and some distortion of the land in the south-east of the continent. I began my investigation by examining the eastern coast of the continent from just south of Byron Bay in New South Wales down to Flinders Island off the south-eastern tip of Australia. A close examination of this part of the Rotz chart in comparison to a modern map showed that it depicted eastern Australia to a great degree of accuracy from Nelson Bay[6] down to the southern tip of Tasmania.[7] I could readily identify Port Stephens, Broken Bay and Botany Bay with their correct latitudes.

If Zhou Man's fleet had reached south-east Australia after crossing the Pacific, there should be evidence of that landfall in the area depicted with most precision on the Rotz chart. As soon as I started a search of the coastline south of Newcastle, I found a mine of information. In the 1840s, a ruined fortress was found by Benjamin Boyd, one of the earliest European settlers, at Bittangabee Bay near Eden in the far south of New South Wales. He noted a large, fully mature old tree with its roots growing under the stones of the complex. Bittangabee's substantial ruins comprise a square platform surrounded by large rocks that had once formed a sturdy, defensive perimeter wall. Foundations and parts of the walls of a blockhouse formed by large stones bound with mortar lie inside the perimeter wall. It must have taken a large labour force to bring the stones to the site and then dress and erect them. There is no evidence anywhere in Australia of Aborigines constructing such fortifications, and the age of the tree and the position of its roots show that construction can only have been carried out long before the British first arrived. More stone buildings erected before Europeans reached Australia can be found south of Sydney; a group of twenty, like a small village, are set beside the coast, and there are well-built paths leading from a reservoir to a fifteen-metre stone wharf beside the sea. Similar stone dwellings are found at Newcastle.

Further indications that visitors had landed in Australia were found in ancient Aboriginal rock carvings depicting a foreign ship similar to a junk on the Hawkesbury River north of Sydney. There are similar carvings further up the coast at Cape York, Gympie, and in Arnhem Land. This does not, of course, guarantee that the foreigners were Chinese – they might have arrived on an unknown Portuguese voyage – but rock carvings near the Hawkesbury River show people wearing long robes, which narrows the choice to Asian or Chinese people. Furthermore, an Aboriginal tradition from the Tweed River area tells of strange visitors attempting to mine metals in the Mount Warning area, south-west of Brisbane, many generations before the British did so.

The most compelling evidence for the date of these foreign visits came from shipwrecks, especially one found near Byron Bay in northern New South Wales. Two wooden pegs were unearthed, provisionally carbon-dated to the mid-fifteenth century but with a potential error of plus or minus fifty years. Before sand-mining destroyed the wreck, local people had described part of the hull and three masts protruding from the sand. In 1965, sand-miners unearthed a huge wooden rudder from this site; some said it was 40 feet (12.2 metres) high. If this description was even remotely accurate, it eliminates the possibility of an unknown Portuguese or Dutch voyage, for their caravels weren't much bigger than that rudder. It can only have come from an enormous ship several hundred feet long – the rudders of treasure ships were 36 feet high. The wreckage of another ancient ship was found at Wollongong on the coast south of Sydney, and two more were found in swampland near Perth. An ancient Chinese stone head depicting a goddess has

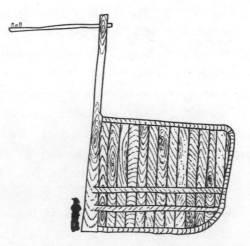

Reconstruction of the rudder of a treasure ship with a figure to the left for scale.

also been found at Ulladulla,[8] south of Wollongong, and a similar votive offering was unearthed on the Nepean River.

The 'mahogany ship' at Warrnambool, the similarities of the three wrecks at Perth and Wollongong, the age of the wooden pin and the size of the huge rudder in Byron Bay point to a Chinese origin. Only the Chinese built ships that could house a rudder the size of that found in Byron Bay, and only they could afford to lose so many ships in one area. The addition of the findings from the wrecks to the Aboriginal legends and carvings depicting foreigners in robes arriving by ship, the groups of stone buildings and the votive offerings produces powerful if not yet conclusive evidence that a large Chinese fleet visited south-east Australia in the fifteenth century.

South of Bittangabee Bay, the original cartographer of the Rotz chart drew the southern curved part of Tasmania, but the chart also

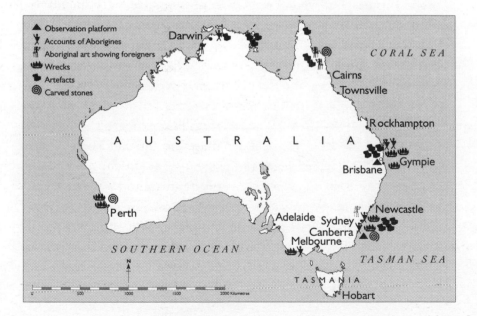

Evidence of the visit of the Chinese treasure fleet to Australia.

shows what appears to be a great landmass running first eastwards then southwards. This has always baffled professional carto-graphers, but when I compared the Jean Rotz and Piri Reis charts at the same latitude I saw at once that what appears to be land south of Tasmania is in fact ice. It is drawn in identical fashion to the ice shown on the Piri Reis map, and the line drawn on the Rotz chart corresponds to the northern limit of pack ice to the south of Tasmania in midwinter (June) in 1421–3. The precession of the earth's axis – its 'wobble' over the centuries – causes the limits of the ice to advance and retreat, and the limit then was approximately three hundred miles north of the normal maximum today.[9]

At a stroke this would have solved the mystery of the apparent landmass to the south and south-east of Australia were it not for two rivers shown on the Rotz chart flowing eastwards out of the ice. These two 'rivers' are shown well south of New Zealand; there are none there, of course. There appeared to be nothing but ocean at those latitudes, but when I examined a large-scale map I discovered two small islands of which I had previously been ignorant, Auckland Island and Campbell Island, at a similar latitude to Tierra del Fuego. Both have identical long thin bays lying east–west, precisely as drawn on the Rotz chart, and at the same latitude.

The two islands were shown at the edge of the normal limit of the pack ice that links them in midwinter. This explains the apparent anomaly on the Rotz chart. The Chinese could not possibly have known that they were islands rather than part of an ice-bound land-mass because continuous ice lay between them and stretched away north to Tasmania; once again, they had drawn precisely what they saw. They were sailing to Campbell Island to fix the position of Canopus – 52°40′S, precisely the latitude of the southernmost tip of the island. They had their reference position, and they could now start a detailed survey of this part of the world.

I found further indications that Zhou Man's fleet had reached Campbell Island in the accounts of the early Europeans who explored the island, discovered by Frederick Hasseburg, the captain

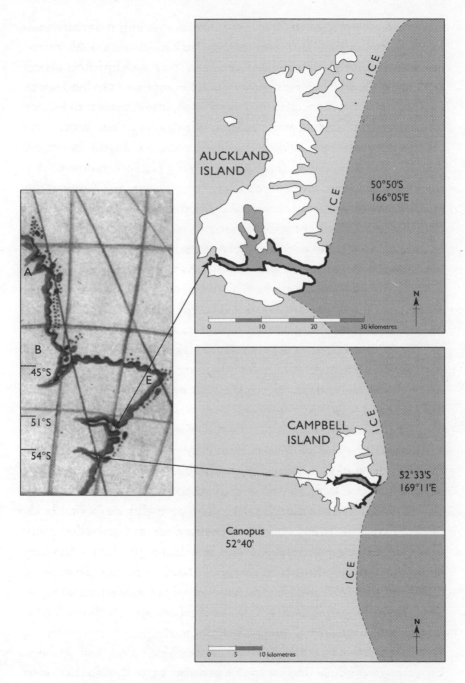

Auckland and Campbell Islands, as shown on the Jean Rotz map.

of a sealing ship, in 1810. In Camp Cove, they found the wreck of an old wooden ship and a tree stunted by the endless winds, but recognizable as a mature Norfolk Island pine, a tree unique to Norfolk Island. It was the Chinese custom to collect saplings, seeds and pine-cones on their voyages, planting them as shrines at places where they made landfall and burying votive offerings in the roots. The Norfolk Island pine on Campbell Island could well have been brought there by one of Zhou Man's junks.

The fleet had now surveyed and charted eastern Australia from Nelson Bay down to Campbell Island in the far south, but they were faced with real difficulties when it came to setting course back to Australia. Unknown to them, the Antarctic drift current was pushing them to the east, towards the South Island of New Zealand. I have many happy memories of that beautiful land after taking my submarine there at Christmas in 1969. The South Island is a place of rugged grandeur, spectacular mountains and crystalline lakes, a land where the Antarctic winds scour the skies clean. However, the Tasman Sea is a nightmare for navigators. The skies are frequently clouded and the currents are irregular. They can reverse their direction without warning.

The Chinese would have had to claw their way back against the current; as they did so, at least two of the great treasure ships were lost. The wreck of an old wooden ship was found two centuries ago at Dusky Sound in Fjordland at the south-west tip of New Zealand's South Island. It was said to be very old and of Chinese build and 'to have been there before Cook', according to the local people.[10] A Sydney packet visited Dusky Sound in 1831 and two sailors from the crew 'saw a strange animal perching at the edge of the bush and nibbling the foliage. It stood on its hind legs, the lower part of its body curving to a thick pointed tail, and when they took note of the height it reached against the trees allowing a metre and a half for the tail, they estimated it stood nearly nine metres in height. The men were to windward of the animal and were able to watch it feeding for some time before it spotted them. They watched it pull down a heavy branch with comparative ease, turn it over and tilt it up to reach the leaves it wanted.'[11] The animal described corresponds in size, posture and eating habits with the mylodons the Chinese could have taken aboard in Patagonia. Perhaps a pair escaped from the wreck, survived and bred in similar conditions to their home territory in Patagonia – the latitudes are the same. Sea-otters, which are not indigenous to New Zealand but, of course, were kept in the Chinese junks to herd fish, have been seen swimming in the fjords of South Island.

Further north, on the west coast of the North Island of New Zealand, the deck and sides of part of a large and very old ship were exposed in 1875 after a violent storm. The wreck was found near the mouth of the Torei Palma River at Whaingaroa; it is known as the Ruapuke Ship after the beach of that name. The wreck was said to have diagonal planking, and its internal bulkheads were bolted together by large brass pins, each weighing 6.3 kilograms. There has, though, been some dispute about the wood from which the wreck was built. Those who originally found it said that it was teak, but in May 2002 pieces of European oak were found in the area, leading certain experts to conclude that a European ship was wrecked there.

However, a huge stone carved in what local experts say is Tamil calligraphy stands at the point where the river empties into a little harbour. In shape, size and location this stone corresponds with those set up by the Chinese mariners in the Yangtze estuary, at Dondra Head, at Cochin on the Malabar coast of India, at Janela in the Cape Verde Islands and by the Matadi Falls in the Congo delta. In addition to the calligraphy, the Ruapuke stone has the same patterns of concentric circles as the stone at Janela. I had already found a number of carved stones at sites visited by the Chinese fleets, so my next step was an obvious one. Sure enough, a search on the internet soon revealed several more on the route from the Cape Verde Islands down to Patagonia, at Santa Catarina, Coral Island, Campeche and Arrorado Island on the east coast of South America. Each is also sited beside a watering place and overlooks the sea, and

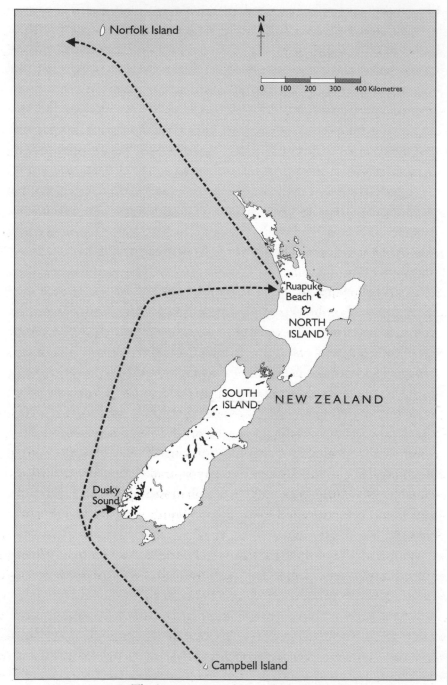

The journey around New Zealand.

the concentric circles inscribed on them match those at Ruapuke. But this could still have been a coincidence; after all, pyramids were built in Central and South America as well as in Egypt. The proof would be more conclusive if I could find similar carved stones in China. Another long search produced three more, at Wong Chuk Ha, Chang Zhou and Po Ti in Hong Kong. Again, these stones had similar markings to the ones I had already found. I now believed that the concentric circles were a 'signature' agreed upon before the armada set sail, denoting where each fleet had landed and watered.

Perhaps the most controversial piece of evidence unearthed in New Zealand is the celebrated bell found near the wreck on Ruapuke beach, named the 'Colenso Bell' after Bishop Colenso who discovered it being used as a kettle by the Maoris. It looks like a smaller version of Zheng He's bell cast after the sixth voyage, and the lip of the bell is inscribed in Tamil calligraphy similar to that carved on the stone near the wreck. It has been translated as 'Bell of the ship Mohaideen Baksh'. The inscription suggests that the owner was a Muslim Tamil, probably from one of the well-known ship-owning families based on the port of Naga Pattinam on the eastern coast of Tamil Nadu in south-east India.[12] At first sight, this appears to be evidence of an Indian not a Chinese ship, but, as the Pandanan wreck found in the Philippines (see chapter 10) demonstrates, it was common for local ship-owners to sail with Zheng He's fleets for they not only provided protection from pirates, they also afforded valuable opportunities to trade. It seems most unlikely that a Tamil ship would have travelled from India to South America and then to New Zealand on its own.

Within a mile of the Ruapuke wreck is a large fallen tree. When it was blown over in a gale, a duck, beautifully carved in dark green serpentine, was revealed nestling among its roots. The duck could well have been a Chinese votive offering. A similar offering, a lion, was found in East Africa, and others have been found in Queensland and the Northern Territory of Australia. This type of shrine is typical of, and unique to, the culture of southern China. Although they are clear evidence of Chinese visits to Australia, I accept that on their own the votive offerings are not proof of a landing by a treasure fleet; they could have been carried by Chinese merchants. However, the collective evidence – the ship, the votive offering, the bell, the stone and the carving – leads me to the conclusion that the ship at Ruapuke was almost certainly the wreck of a Tamil junk attached to the Chinese fleet.

The final piece of evidence is another votive offering found on the banks of a tributary of the Waikato River some thirty miles north of the Ruapuke wreck. The find was made in the late 1800s by Eldon Best, the distinguished historian and then curator of the Dominion Museum in Auckland. The small oriental figurine was

> found under singular and interesting circumstances at Mauku near Auckland. The lands around the place of discovery have been uninhabited since the arrival of Europeans until twenty years ago, and since then merely occupied by farm employees; nor have these lands ever been ploughed. In pre-European times, however, natives occupied the place, as shown by the remains of old settlements . . . The figurine is undoubtedly Oriental in design and workmanship . . . having the grotesque aspect so common in Oriental designs, some form of turban-like head dress is depicted, also a loose cloak or wide-sleeved garment . . . Altogether, this snub-nosed Tartar-looking figure represents an interesting discovery when the conditions of that discovery are noted.[13]

The Chinese fleets were losing ships with almost every landfall, a rate of attrition that continued throughout their voyages across the world, for of the 107 treasure ships that left China in 1421, a mere handful survived to return home in 1423. As the mandarins complained, 'Myriads were lost.' Those huge losses increase the likelihood that the wrecks at Ruapuke and elsewhere on the Chinese route were ships from the treasure fleets.

If the ship at Ruapuke is a wrecked treasure ship, then tales of the shipwrecked crew must exist in local legends, just as they do in

Central America and southern Australia near wreck-sites. When I investigated, I found that Maoris living near Ruapuke had just such a legend.[14] The strangers who settled among them were called 'Patupaiarehe', or pale-skinned, almost supernatural people. Another meaning of the word is 'fairies'. They wore white woven garments and also differed from the Maoris in having no tattoos and by carrying their children in their arms. Some married Maori women. I believe this local legend is true, and that the first non-Maori settlers in New Zealand were not Europeans, but Chinese.

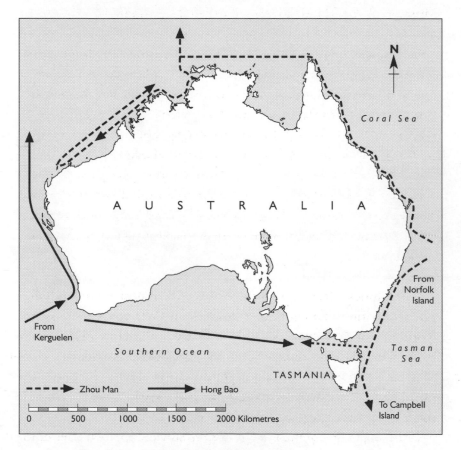

The routes of Hong Bao and Zhou Man around Australia.

8

THE
BARRIER
REEF
AND THE
SPICE
ISLANDS

ONCE BACK IN THE TASMAN SEA, ZHOU MAN'S SURVIVING ships entered a counter-clockwise, circular current that at last propelled them back to the Australian coast. The shape of the south-east Australian coast, coupled with the location of Campbell Island on the Jean Rotz chart and the wrecks in the south-west and north-west of New Zealand, are all consistent with the junks being swept before the winds and currents from the Australian coast down to Campbell Island and then in a loop with the wind back past New Zealand. Continuing before the wind would have caused them to make their second landfall on the Australian coast just north of Brisbane. Assuming an average speed of 4.8 knots, reduced to 3.8 by the current and storms, the journey down to Campbell Island and back again would have taken at least ten weeks.

The coast around Brisbane is shown on the Rotz chart with incredible precision, and that chart was not the only one of Australia to be drawn by cartographers of the Dieppe School, all of them drawn centuries before Europeans reached Australia. The Dauphin chart of 1536 and those of Desliens (1551) and Desceliers (1553) gave an almost identical depiction of the continent. Two decades ago, the La Trobe Library, Brisbane, exhibited one of these Dieppe maps. Visitors to the exhibition were stunned: 'Look at Brisbane. Look, there's Stradbroke Island, Moreton Island, the Pine River, the Heads and Fraser Island. There's the lagoon at Surfers' Paradise.'[1] The accuracy with which the eastern Australia coast had been drawn left me equally dumbstruck. To have surveyed it with such precision, the Chinese fleet must have spent some time on the east coast of Australia in what is now New South Wales and Queensland, and one obvious reason for that is the mineral wealth of the region.

Perhaps the most commercially valuable scientists carried by the great treasure fleets were mining engineers. At that time, China and India together accounted for almost half the world's entire wealth[2] and Indian engineers led the world in mining technology. They had opened up gold and iron fields in East Africa, stimulating a flow of raw materials eastwards across the Indian Ocean. Indian engineers and metallurgists sailed with the treasure fleets, but China also had centuries of experience in geology, mineral extraction and processing. As is claimed to have been described in Chinese records of a much earlier period,[3] the treasure fleets would have mined ores and carried gemstones and refined metals back to China in their holds, but the Chinese would also have set up longer-term settlements to exploit the mineral riches they discovered on their voyages.

Chinese scientists had classified minerals into groups by the first century AD.[4] Those early Chinese scientists could distinguish between different chlorides, sulphides and nitrates, and knew how to exploit them. They used mercuric sulphide (cinnabar) for red inks and paints; steatite was added to paper as a filler; and skins were first dried with saltpetre (potassium nitrate), then treated with ammonium chloride, and finally dyed with ferrous sulphate.

They were equally skilled in geological prospecting, capable of detecting minerals and metals by magnetic surveys or by measuring shock waves caused by explosive detonations, even by the lie of the land. They also knew that the ores and minerals they sought were often geologically linked with others. Greenstones always occurred in the neighbourhood of copper ores. They even had a rhyme for such associations: 'When there is cinnabar above, gold will be found below; when there is magnetite above, copper and gold will be found below.'[5] Similarly, iron was associated with haematite on the surface, and both sulphur and iron pyrites signified alum. Chinese chemists had also deduced that certain plants thrived on particular minerals, to the extent that they changed colour and taste when growing near them. Cybule onions signified silver; shallots, gold; ginger, copper and tin. Western scientists did not establish until the eighteenth century what the Chinese had known for centuries, that some plants can indeed signal the presence of gold and other metals.[6]

The Rotz chart of Australia and the wealth of wrecks and Chinese artefacts found in and around that country show that, by luck or design, the great Chinese fleets had discovered the location of some of the most varied and rich mineral seams in the world. They had done so accompanied by horse-ships. The Chinese took inordinate care in the selection of their horses. Their favourites were the famous 'blood ponies' of Tajikistan, so named because they supposedly sweated blood (the red markings on the skin were actually caused by a skin parasite). Blood ponies were bred in the high, rolling valleys of China's Tian Shan – 'Heavenly Mountains' – where they galloped through the walnut forests that cloak the slopes. They were incredibly swift, but also hardy and strong enough to make their way through dense snow and survive the worst weather. Zhu Di imported millions during his reign, placing such a strain on the imperial treasury that a special 'Tea for Horses' bureau was established to barter tea for the animals, thus avoiding further payments in silver.

Thousands of horses for the Chinese cavalry were carried on the horse-ships accompanying the treasure fleets. They were fed on mashed boiled rice, necessitating two gallons of water per horse per day. There is evidence that the Chinese took them ashore. Horses were then unknown in Australia, but they are beautifully depicted in drawings on the Vallard chart of the Dieppe School, although not, it must be said, on the Rotz chart. There was good pasturage for them around Sydney, from where an easy trail led up the Nepean and Hawkesbury valleys into the interior. A huge range of minerals including gold, silver, gemstones, coal and iron can be found within two hundred kilometres of Sydney. Further up the coast at Newcastle, also clearly identifiable on the Rotz chart, there was an equally spectacular array of riches. Within a week's ride from the coast were diamonds, sapphires and a wealth of other minerals.

Like their modern counterparts, the Chinese and Indian geologists with Zhou Man's fleet must have felt they had arrived in a mineral paradise. Many of Australia's minerals were of direct use to the fleet. Combining copper and zinc gave them brass; saltpetre mixed with sulphur and charcoal made gunpowder. Arsenic was a poison and insect repellent, yet also accelerated the growth of silkworms. White paint made of lead and copper prevented wood decay along the hull line. Kaolin was available for ceramics, while oxides of cobalt, copper and lead served for colours and glazes. Alum was particularly useful for making hides supple, for making drinking water potable and for its astringent properties. Asbestos had been used for fire protection for six centuries: 'When King Mu of the Zhou dynasty made an expedition to the western people . . . fireproof cloth was cleaned by being thrown into a fire . . . when taken out and shaken it became as white as snow.'[7] Local Aboriginal legends mention foreign people coming to these parts and mining materials while 'dressed in stone clothes'.[8]

There is further evidence in the accounts of Franciscan missionaries to China in the sixteenth century, who spoke of Chinese expeditions to Australia recorded on copper scrolls (dating from the sixth century onwards) together with maps of the continent.[9] These early Chinese records, which have since disappeared, described voyages carried out by gigantic fleets of massive junks (sixty to a hundred ships), each carrying several hundred men, with the aim of gathering minerals.

The wrecks on the coast and the stone buildings ashore, Aboriginal rock carvings and paintings depicting foreigners in their long robes, and the carved votive offerings are all signs of a Chinese presence in the mining areas of New South Wales. A beautiful carved stone head of the goddess Shao Lin, the protector of mariners at sea, was recovered from the beach front at Milton, New South Wales, in 1983. It is now in the Kedumba Nature Museum in Katoomba. Each of Zheng He's ships had a small cabin dedicated to her. However, the most direct and persuasive evidence of the Chinese visits to Australia comes from Gympie, a mining area further up the coast, four hours' drive north of Brisbane. In 1422, a creek connected Gympie to Tin Cat Bay and the Pacific; according to ancient Aboriginal tradition, a race of 'culture heroes' sailed up this creek and into Gympie's harbour in ships 'shaped like birds'. They later returned to their ships carrying rocks.[10]

While ashore, these mysterious people built truncated pyramids, one of which was discovered by a local researcher, Rex Gilroy, in 1975 and subsequently photographed. Now sadly vandalized, the pyramid was built of granite blocks and stood a hundred feet high, with the stepped construction typical of the other pyramids I had seen in South America and right across the Pacific. Mr Gilroy describes local people uncovering pre-European opencast copper, tin and gold mines, and he personally found an ancient pipe similar to those used to pour mercury to separate gold from ore. Half a mile from the Gympie pyramid, near an ancient opencast gold mine, were hearths that contained nodules of melted metal. Until 1920, Gympie remained Queensland's largest and richest goldfield. Many other artefacts have been found in the area. Two beautifully carved votive offerings are of particular interest: one is of the Hindu god Ganesh, the elephant god, carved in beige granite; the other is of Hanuman, the Hindu monkey god, this time made of conglomerate ironstone. Ganesh and Hanuman are two of the most important deities of Hindu worshippers in southern India, whence the fleet sailed and where they embarked Hindu priests, mining engineers and geologists.

Two equally fascinating carved animals can still be seen in the Gold Museum at Gympie today. The 'Gympie ape', dug up in 1966, is a monster with a head much larger than a human's. Its snout has been broken off, but a photograph of the second animal (it has now disappeared) shows the snout, nose and mouth[11] of a beast closely resembling a mylodon. Whether through intent or happenstance, animals were collected and carried from one continent to another – giraffes, ostriches and rhinoceros from Africa to China, Asiatic chickens to South America, Chinese ship dogs left in South America and on islands across the Pacific to New Zealand, kangaroos from Australia to China and otters from China to New Zealand. A number of mylodons might well have been captured and taken aboard the Chinese ships in Patagonia; one pair might have escaped in New Zealand and another pair landed in China. Perhaps Chinese sculptors wished to immortalize these strange creatures before the memory of them faded. A century later the arrival of exotic species brought back from the New World was to create a similar sensation in the courts of Europe.

The purpose of the Gympie pyramid has baffled Australian observers, but its size, height and shape are typical of Ming dynasty observation platforms, and it would have been wholly logical for the Chinese to build observatories to determine precisely the location of the phenomenal riches they had discovered, so that future fleets could return to the same place.

When Zhou Man's fleet resumed its voyage, it sailed north up the Great Barrier Reef, again shown with amazing accuracy on the Rotz chart. The reef itself and the islands inside and outside it have the correct latitudes and can be clearly identified for more than a thousand miles. However, when they returned to Australia after their voyage to Campbell Island to locate Canopus, their calculations of longitude (as shown on the Rotz map) are twenty degrees in error. Why should they have believed they were 1,800 miles further west than they really were? The answer, of course, was that they had been in the Antarctic drift current during their ten weeks in the southern oceans. The body of water in which they had sailed was itself moving eastwards, and Admiral Zhou Man as yet had no means of measuring longitude accurately.

I realized that the coastline of Australia on the Rotz chart north of where Zhou Man's fleet returned had to be adjusted to the east by 1,800 miles. As soon as I did this, the result was electrifying. Australia was laid out before me. The cartographer had done a remarkable job and had made only one mistake — longitude, which he had had no means of measuring. He had drawn the eastern Australian coast and the Great Barrier Reef with phenomenal accuracy 247 years before Captain Cook was to do so. When I further corrected the southern coast of New South Wales and Tasmania by removing the ice, I had an instantly identifiable map of Australia.

Cook was awestruck by the size and shape of the Great Barrier Reef, a type of structure 'scarcely known in Europe. It is a wall of coral rock rising all most perpendicular out of the unfathomable Ocean.'[12] For a mariner, any voyage near razor-sharp coral reefs is a nerve-racking prospect, particularly at night or in low visibility when the only warning is the noise of breaking surf. If your ship hits coral, it punctures the hull and it is difficult to get off the reef without tearing the vessel to bits. I knew the dangers only too well from my own experience of taking my submarine HMS *Rorqual* inside the Barrier Reef, and that was with accurate charts at my disposal. A voyage through uncharted reefs is a constant waking nightmare. At night one sees not a single light ashore, by day nothing but an unbroken belt of grey-green jungle, as if man had never penetrated this beautiful but forbidding region. The Barrier Reef stretches for more than 1,500 miles from Hickson Bay, south of Brisbane, up to Cape York in the north. Captain Cook narrowly escaped death after striking it, and like me, he had a chart to help him. It is inconceivable that Zhou Man's fleet could have made the passage through those uncharted waters without suffering severe damage or loss of ships. To have got through it at all was an incredible feat.

The Rotz chart shows the Great Barrier Reef, the islands between the reef and the coast, and yet more islands in the ocean beyond the reef. In many places, once inside the reef it is not possible to leave it. I remember very well how my submarine was hemmed in by the reef, and the relief I felt as I escaped from the straitjacket where the reef ends off Brisbane. The wealth of detail on the Rotz chart indicates that several Chinese ships must have been charting the coast, reef and islands. They would have been more or less in line abreast as they sailed north, some inside the reef and others in the ocean outside it. I estimate that there must have been at least six, probably ten or more ships to have gathered such a mass of information.

The Barrier Reef itself, the coastline and the islands both inside and outside are particularly accurately charted around what is now

Cooktown, indicating that the Chinese had spent some time surveying there. Captain Cook later used some of the maps of the Dieppe School to get to Cooktown, where he beached his ship, HMS *Endeavour*, after it hit a reef that was also shown on the earlier charts. The detail and precision of this part of the Rotz chart suggests that the Chinese might well have been forced to make a similar halt for repairs.

The Barrier Reef ends abruptly a few miles north of the tip of the Cape York Peninsula. The nightmare was over, and those Chinese junks that had survived the hazardous passage – and there must have been several casualties – could at last set course to the northwest for China. What an incredible sense of relief the eunuch captains and navigators of the surviving Chinese ships must have felt as they rounded the northern tip of Australia and sailed on past Cape York and the islands to the west. Here, the junks entered the Torres Strait, separating Australia from New Guinea, where the current flows from the east, sweeping the mariner westwards across the Gulf of Carpentaria. The Gulf is shown on the Rotz chart narrower than it should be; once again, the Chinese underestimated their change in longitude as the body of water in which they were sailing moved westwards across northern Australia.[13]

In the folio of charts he presented to Henry VIII of England, Jean Rotz included another map of this part of Australia drawn in greater detail and to a much larger scale. He drew the island of Lesser Java – the Chinese knew it as Little Java – separated from Greater Java by a narrow channel, though some of his contemporaries in the Dieppe School showed it as a river. It was a simple matter to determine who was right. I compared it with a modern map at the same latitude and saw at once that the channel Rotz had drawn was the Victoria River in the west and the Roper River in the east. Lesser Java on the Rotz chart is Arnhem Land, part of the mainland of Australia. The shape of north-east Australia was now instantly recognizable.

A number of descriptions in medieval Portuguese were written on Rotz's more detailed chart. The names are easy to translate and all of them correspond to what is found there today. *Canal de Sonda* – 'narrow sea ford' in medieval Portuguese – is marked where the long, narrow Apsley Strait bisects Melville and Bathurst Islands. *Aguada dillim* – 'waterway leading to inland sea' – corresponds to the Dundas Strait that does indeed lead into the Van Diemen Gulf. *Agarsim* – translated as 'yes indeed water is here' – is inscribed beside the Yellow Water Billabong in the Kakadu National Park, designated by the United Nations as 'wet lands of international importance'. *Nungrania* means 'no farmland' – there is none there – and *lingrania* means 'lime trees', which still grow there today. The Gova Peninsula, the eastern tip of Arnhem Land, is *finjava*, or 'the end of Java'. Only one inscription had me baffled – *chumbão*, or 'lead'.

The west coast of Arnhem Land is drawn with great fidelity. Rotz showed the main coastal features at their correct latitudes right up to 10°S, beyond the northern tip of Australia, and drew a mass of fishing stakes straddling Trepang Bay – as its name implies, the centre of sea-slug fishing. Chinese boats still fish this part of the coast today for the much-prized trepang. All this remarkably precise information predates the arrival of the first Europeans by over two centuries. The chart also shows details of the interior – the Finniss River wending westwards, and trees recognizable as eucalyptus and blackwood pines, both common in Arnhem Land. A tall rock is also depicted on the chart by what is now the Nourlangie Anbanbang Billabong in the Kakadu National Park. The original cartographer must have seen the rock to have drawn it so accurately.

As I studied the modern map of Arnhem Land, I realized I had found the answer to the mystery of the word *chumbão*. Lead is still mined in substantial quantities at the huge Jabiru Ranger Mines. It is the natural derivative of uranium 235 as it breaks down through the process of nuclear decay. Uranium is, of course, highly radioactive, and lethal to touch or ingest. The Jabiru Ranger Mines contain one of the world's largest deposits of uranium 235. Not realizing the danger they were placing themselves in, the Chinese must have been digging uranium out of the ground alongside the lead ore they sought. This may help to account for the appalling loss of life among Zhou Man's fleet, for only a tenth of the original nine thousand men remained alive when it finally reached home in October 1423.

To discover the lead, the Chinese had to penetrate well into the interior of the country. At that time, as now, Aborigines had made Arnhem Land their spiritual home. They were skilful artists, painting beautiful frescoes in caves, and I hoped to find evidence of the Chinese visit depicted in their cave art. George Grey, later the governor of South Australia, led an expedition to Arnhem Land in 1838. When they entered a group of caves twenty miles upstream from where the Glenelg River pours into Colliers Bay, they saw a group of paintings prominent among which was 'the figure of a man, 10ft 6in in height, clothed from the chin downwards in a red garment which reached to his wrists and ankles'.[14] Captain Grey's description fits precisely with the picture drawn by the native Mexican tribes at Jucutácato (see chapter 10) of the Chinese arriving in their red robes reaching to their ankles. Grey's find also accords with Aboriginal lore, which records that long before the Europeans a honey-coloured people settled north-east Arnhem Land. The men wore long robes and the women pantaloons. They went far inland for freshwater prawns, sandalwood and tortoiseshell, grew rice and lived in stone houses, unlike the Aborigines whose dwellings were of wood. The women wove silk dyed with local herbs.

Adze anchors with the curved fluke (the piece that holds the anchor in the mud) set at right angles to the stock of the anchor – a Chinese design – have been discovered on the coastline of north-east Arnhem Land, and substantial quantities of broken Chinese ceramics dating from the Han dynasty (202 BC–AD 220) to the early Ming (1368–1644) have been found at Port Bradshaw on the eastern shore of the Gulf of Carpentaria and on the nearby mainland, just where the currents and the reefs would make it likely that wrecks would be found.

Even with horses, the Chinese would have needed several months to carry out the detailed survey of the coast and interior lands depicted on the Rotz chart. For this they would have needed a base in a protected anchorage with fresh water. I expected to locate it on the most accurately charted part of the coast. The Beagle Gulf off the north-west part of Arnhem Land is very well drawn, and Darwin, at the south-western end of the gulf, has a splendidly protected anchorage. Today, a hotel, the Banyan View Lodge, stands on Doctor's Gully, shaded by a magnificent banyan tree. The stream running through Doctor's Gully is now paved over, but in those days fresh water would have been available from it. The lodge is a popular haunt of backpackers drinking lager, oblivious of the history that surrounds them.

Late in the nineteenth century, a figure of a Taoist immortal, Shu Lao, was found buried beneath that banyan tree. It is now in the Chinese collection of the Technological Museum in Sydney. Although very valuable, it had been deliberately wedged deep down in the roots. Dated by one expert as early Ming (late fourteenth century),[15] the figure sits upon a deer and in its right hand carries a peach, the symbol of longevity. It is made from very fine pinite and is beautifully carved and polished. Shu Lao is one of the Triad of Gods of long life in the Taoist pantheon; unlike Buddhism and Confucianism, Taoism is a religion peculiar to China and was never disseminated overseas.

Moreover, the banyan is foreign to Australia and must have been imported. This one was already several hundred years old when the statue was discovered over a century ago. In southern China, shrines were often built in cavities between the spreading roots of large trees such as banyans. The shrine at Darwin was almost certainly built by a Chinese centuries ago, and in structure and location it resembles the one at Ruapuke in New Zealand. It is theoretically possible that the shrines were created by the crews of Chinese boats fishing for trepang, but the possibility is very small indeed. No fishing boat would carry such a valuable statue – it would be worth a lifetime's wages to the crew; it is far more likely that it belonged to a wealthy Chinese captain or admiral from a great ship. By far the most plausible explanation is that Zhou Man's fleet used Darwin as its base and created a shrine in which the figure was placed in thanks for having survived a long voyage.

I am strongly inclined to believe that the Venetian Niccolò da Conti was telling the truth when he informed the Papal Secretary, Poggio Bracciolini, that he had landed in Greater Java on a Chinese junk and had spent nine months there with his wife. Perhaps she was one of the women in pantaloons.

When Europeans eventually arrived, they were not sailing blindly into a great unknown. The Dauphin chart, one of the other charts from the Dieppe School and almost identical to the Rotz chart, came into the possession of Edmund Harley, Earl of Oxford and First Lord of the Admiralty, in the mid-eighteenth century and became known as the Harleian. It was later acquired by Joseph Banks, the young scientist who sailed in the *Endeavour* with Captain Cook. At the time Captain Cook sailed, the British government therefore had access to both the Harleian and Rotz charts, since the latter was at that stage owned by the Admiralty. Cook's orders from the Admiralty were to search down to 40°S – the latitude of South Australia shown on both charts – where they 'had good reason'[16] to suppose the southern continent existed. They certainly did – they already had two charts showing such a continent at 40°S.

As they left Australia, like Hong Bao's fleet before them Zhou Man's ships were still laden with porcelain and silk, but the fabled Spice Islands lay between Australia and home, and spice was then an extremely valuable commodity in China. Even when the fleet had been reduced to a few ships, their holds could still carry thousands of tons of ceramics, and by sailing for the Spice Islands Zhou Man would at last have an opportunity to exchange them for goods of real value, such as nutmeg, pepper and cloves.

If the Rotz chart was based on an earlier map drawn by

cartographers aboard Zhou Man's fleet, it should show the Spice Islands. It does. The importance of Ambon, then the collecting centre for the two Spice Islands of Ternate and Tidore – so tiny one can walk around them in a couple of days – is emphasized by its being coloured red. In the Middle Ages, Ternate and Tidore were the hub of the spice trade, far and away the most productive islands. They were legendary, and had been fought over for centuries, for virtually all spices could be obtained there in huge quantities. To this day, the distinctive scent of cloves is detectable far out at sea, long before the islands themselves are sighted.

Further north, at a latitude of 10°N, the Rotz chart shows the channel between the Philippine islands of Mindanao in the south and Leyte in the north, but Rotz drew only the south coast of Leyte, leading to the obvious conclusion that the cartographer was in a ship passing down the middle of the channel. Using a similar common-sense approach, I could determine the angle from which the Spice Islands and the other islands between Australia and the Philippines were drawn, and hence deduce the route taken by Zhou Man's fleet through the islands. Along the way, now sailing in calm and sunny seas, Zhou Man would have had many opportunities not only to obtain spices but to barter his porcelain for batiks, artefacts, fresh water, fruit and meat, especially pigs. The Chinese were and are particularly fond of pork, and Zhou Man's men had probably lacked it for many months.

There would once have been plentiful examples of the silks and porcelain Zhou Man's fleet had exchanged for spices and supplies, but would any traces remain today? How could I find such evidence after an interval of nearly six hundred years? I wondered if Magellan had also sailed this way on his circumnavigation of the world. If so, his account might throw some light on the question. When I went to the British Library and consulted a copy of the detailed map of Magellan's route produced after his death, I was staggered to discover that his course from the Pacific through the Philippines and down to the Spice Islands, a distance of well over a thousand miles, was identical but in the opposite direction to the track of Zhou Man's fleet I had just reconstructed. It was as if the two were using the same passage drawn on the same chart. The chances of this being a coincidence are microscopic. I surmise that Magellan's chart showed Zhou Man's route.

As well as Pigafetta's description of Magellan's voyage, I found that the British Library also held an account by the Genoese pilot who sailed with Magellan. He described Magellan's landfall in the Philippines and how he found a strait leading from the Pacific to the Spice Islands – the same strait between Mindanao and Leyte shown

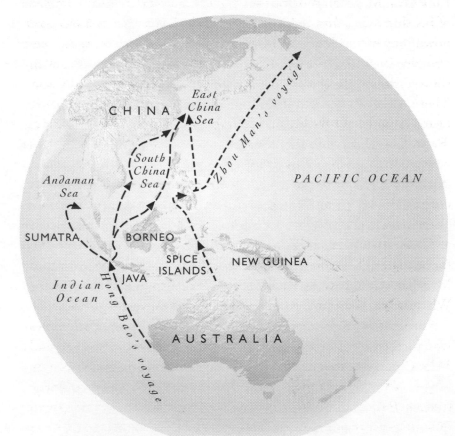

Hong Bao's journey home and Zhou Man's journey through the Spice Islands.

on the Rotz chart. Magellan passed through this strait and anchored at the first island, Limasava, where the king greeted him. Pigafetta described the king and queen wearing Chinese silk and eating off Chinese porcelain that had been buried for fifty years to increase its value. Their houses had silk curtains and porcelain ornaments, and their trading currency was Chinese coins with square centres. The same story was repeated on island after island visited by Magellan's ships en route to the Spice Islands. Zhou Man must have emptied his holds of porcelain as he went along, a century before Magellan.

Pigafetta also recounted Magellan's meeting with the King of Limasava. Magellan showed him '*the marine chart* and the compass of his ship *telling him how he had found the Strait to come hither* and how many moons [months] he had spent in coming; also, *he had not seen any land*, in which the King marvelled' (my italics). Magellan showed the king a chart depicting the strait and the empty Pacific. There was also a letter from Sebastian Alvarez, the King of Spain's factor (a merchant buying and selling on commission), to his king: 'From Cape Frío until the Islands of the Moloccas throughout this navigation there are no lands laid down in the maps they [Magellan's expedition] carry with them.'[17] Taken together, these accounts can mean only one thing. When Magellan sailed, he had with him a chart that not only showed the Strait of Magellan but also the Pacific at 52° South and an empty ocean from there to the Spice Islands on the equator. Someone must have sailed through the Strait of Magellan and across the Pacific before Magellan to make that chart. Who else but the Chinese, 'the yellow men wearing long robes'?[18]

Fortunately, the evidence from Magellan's visit to the Philippines was further confirmation of a Chinese voyage between 1421 and 1423. Chinese porcelain, silk and coinage of Zhu Di's reign, seen by Magellan in the Philippines, might have been the result of Chinese trade before Zhou Man's voyage, but Magellan noted substantial quantities on island after island. Clearly, huge amounts must have been exchanged, and that in turn must have resulted in Zhou Man taking aboard a vast quantity of traded goods, principally the greatly valued pepper. If so, that pepper would appear in the records of the Chinese stockpiles of the spice soon after he returned to China in October 1423.

I searched among copies of the few Chinese records that exist and found that my deductions were absolutely correct. By 1424 there were such massive stocks of pepper in the imperial warehouses that on his accession that year Emperor Zhu Gaozhi ordered much of it to be given away: 'To each banner bearer, housekeeper, soldier and guardsman one catty [half a kilo] of pepper . . . to each first degree literary graduate and licentiate, district police chief, prison warder, astronomer and physician, one catty . . . to each resident of the city and the environs of Beijing, each Buddhist or Taoist priest, artisan, musician, professional cook . . . one catty.'[19] The population of Beijing in 1423 certainly exceeded one million and the soldiers of the imperial army and their dependants accounted for another six hundred thousand people. The weight of pepper distributed is likely to have been more than 1,500 tons. When Magellan's ship returned home, he had less than twenty-six tons of usable pepper aboard. It was sold at ten thousand times the price he had paid for it in the Spice Islands, sufficient to generate a profit for the entire voyage. Contrary to the claims of the Chinese mandarins, the voyages of the treasure ships brought substantial tangible rewards, for the pepper added to Chinese stockpiles late in 1423 was of colossal value on the international market.

Pigafetta's account of Magellan's voyage yielded still more evidence that Zhou Man's fleet had sailed from the Americas to the Spice Islands and the Philippines. Pigafetta described maize growing in the Philippines and Magellan's crew loading it. Maize is not only unique to the Americas but a crop that can only be propagated by man. Furthermore, some of the surviving Chinese records state that Zheng He's fleets brought back maize from their voyages. Not only had junks brought porcelain, silk and currency from China and carried pepper back there, they had also brought maize from South America to the Philippines.[20]

THE
FIRST
COLONY
IN THE
AMERICAS

A LTHOUGH HE WAS NOW LITTLE MORE THAN A THOUSAND miles from the Chinese mainland, Zhou Man's remarkable voyage was still far from over. I next had to track his fleet as it sailed onwards from the Philippines to reach the coast of yet another new land. After leaving the Spice Islands with his rich cargo, the most direct route home for his fleet would have been to continue north, sailing west of Mindoro in the Philippines. From there, the prevailing summer wind would have blown him north towards China. Yet the manner in which the islands were drawn on the Rotz chart suggests that Zhou Man had chosen to alter course to the east, passing south of Leyte and re-entering the Pacific.[1] Assuming that he had left Darwin at the beginning of the southwest monsoon, in late April, he would have entered the Pacific by early June. I knew that Zhou Man had arrived in Nanjing on 8 October 1423, carrying no foreign envoys. What had he been doing and where had he sailed in the four months he had been in the Pacific?

The north Pacific is a vast circulatory system, with winds constantly blowing in a clockwise oval direction. In June, the prevailing wind off Leyte is to the north. As Admiral Zhou Man's fleet entered the Pacific, the Kuroshio or Japanese current would also have carried them northwards before starting a clockwise sweep towards the coast of North America. In fact, had Zhou Man simply unfurled his sails off Leyte, the winds and currents would have carried him to the Pacific coast of modern Canada. The California current would then have taken over, sweeping the fleet southwards down the western seaboard of the United States to Panama. From there, the north equatorial current would carry a square-rigged ship back across the Pacific towards the Philippines. The whole round trip, before the wind and current all the way, would have been about sixteen thousand nautical miles. At an average of 4.8 knots, the voyage would have taken some four months, matching the date of Zhou Man's return to Nanjing in October. My surmise, for reasons which will become apparent later, was that squadrons of ships from the main fleet were detached to establish colonies along the Pacific coast from California down to Ecuador.

I began the search for corroboration that Zhou Man's fleet had indeed reached the Pacific coast of North America. The first European to explore that coast was Hernando de Alarcón in 1540. Having sought fame and fortune in New Spain, he left Acapulco on 9 May of that year in command of a fleet supporting the conquistador Coronado's expedition to New Mexico. Alarcón first charted the peninsula of Bahía California, and then California itself. I knew that he was the first European to chart it, for neither Columbus nor any of the other early explorers reached any part of the west coast of North America, so any map of the Pacific coast predating Alarcón's voyage would be powerful evidence that he was not the first to reach it.

Such evidence does exist in the form of the Waldseemüller world map, a beautifully coloured large map published in 1507 and the first to chart latitude and longitude with precision. Originally owned by Johannes Schöner (1477–1547), a Nuremberg astronomer and geographer, it had long been thought lost and was only rediscovered in 1901 in the castle of Wolfegg in southern Germany. It remained there in relative obscurity until 2001, when in a blaze of publicity the US Library of Congress acquired it from Prince Johannes Waldburg-Wolfegg for ten million dollars. The man who drew the map, Martin Waldseemüller (c. 1470–1518), was German-born and one of the foremost cosmographers – combining the study of geography and astronomy – of his era. The globe and wall maps he made in 1507 and 1516 are the first ever to call the continent 'America'. The map, *Carta Marear – A Portuguese Navigational Seachart of the Known Earth and Oceans*, was 'the first and only printed version of the world charts previously known only to Spanish and Portuguese explorers and their patrons'.[2] The west coast of North America from modern Canada to the equator is drawn boldly and clearly on the map.

The Caribbean and Florida, shown on the Waldseemüller map,

Europe and Africa from Fra Mauro's planisphere of 1459: south is at the top. The surface is a glittering pattern of text and schematic walled medieval towns, but the map itself is informed by real geography, the result of up-to-date knowledge gleaned from contemporary explorers.

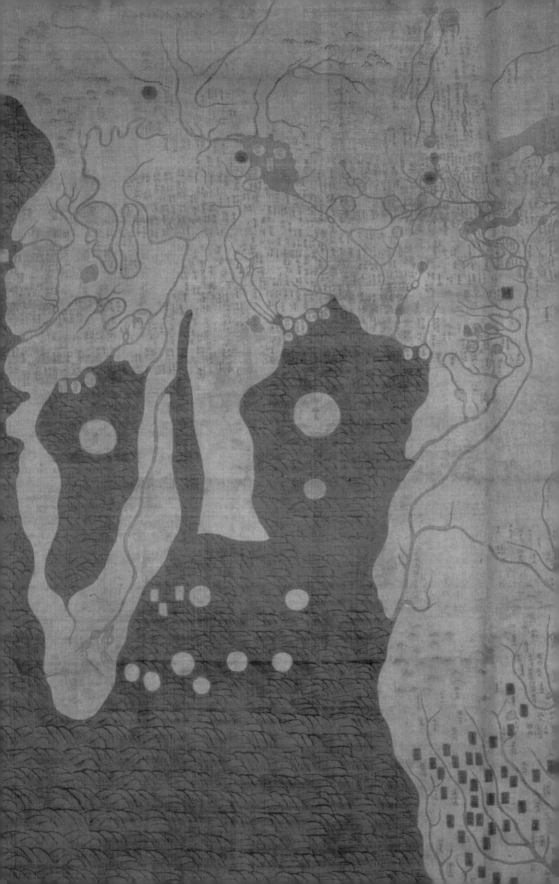

A detail of Africa and Asia from the Kangnido world map of 1402 (*opposite*) by Ch'uan Chin and Li Hui, the most advanced of its day. The Cape of Good Hope is delineated with extraordinary accuracy.

Chinese supremacy in the Indian Ocean: the Galle stele (*above left*), inscribed in four languages, testifies to Zheng He's attempts at diplomacy with the diverse inhabitants of Sri Lanka. By the time Zheng He set sail, the Chinese had well-established routes along the Malabar coast (*below*), where Chinese fishing nets are still used (*above*), and across the ocean to East African trading forts such as Kilwa (*opposite, below*), where Ming porcelain is incorporated into the mosque, just as in these pillar-tombs further up the coast at Kunduchi (*opposite, inset*).

The Piri Reis map of 1513, oriented with north to the left, so that South America is at the bottom of the page and Africa and Europe at the top.

The inhospitable shores of Antarctica (*above*): it is easy to see how giant icebergs (*below*) could be mistaken for islands.

were also depicted on two earlier charts, the Cantino (1502) in the Biblioteca Estense, Modena, Italy – a map which would play a significant role in my researches elsewhere in the world (see chapter 11) – and the Caverio map (1505) in the James Ford Bell Library at the University of Minnesota, Minneapolis. They too showed lands drawn before the first Europeans had reached them, but those maps cannot have been the original source of the Waldseemüller. The Great Bahama Bank is drawn identically on all three maps, but the Caverio map shows the Yucatán Peninsula in Mexico, which was not depicted on the earlier Cantino. Hence the Caverio cannot have been a copy of the Cantino, any more than the Waldseemüller is a copy of them, for the latest of the three, the Waldseemüller, shows the Pacific coast of North America and the Cantino and Caverio do not. All three maps have different original features, and all must have been copied from an even earlier map.

The Pacific coast of America is strikingly drawn on the Waldseemüller chart and the latitudes correspond to those of Vancouver Island in Canada right down to Ecuador in the south. This is completely consistent with a cartographer aboard a ship sailing down the Pacific coast, but not charting the coast in great detail. Oregon is clearly identifiable, and several very old wrecks have been discovered there on the beach at Neahkahnie. One was of teak with a pulley for hoisting sails made of caeophyllum, a wood unique to south-east Asia. The wood has yet to be carbon-dated, but if it proves to be from the early fifteenth century it will provide strong circumstantial evidence that one of Zhou Man's junks was wrecked in Neahkahnie Bay. Some examiners of the wreckage there claim to have found paraffin wax, which was used by Zheng He's fleet to desalinate sea-water for the horses.

Even without finds from wrecked junks, the Pacific coasts of Central and South America are full of evidence of Chinese voyages. The Asiatic chickens found from Chile to California were described in chapter 5, and many other flora and fauna were carried across the globe by the Chinese fleets. On my first visit to California many years ago, I remember coming across a bank of beautiful camellia roses (*Rosa laevigata*). It was a still summer's evening and their lovely fragrance filled the air around me. In 1803, European settlers found a beautiful fragrant rose growing wild; they named it the Cherokee Rose. Yet it was indigenous to south-east China and had been illustrated in a twelfth-century Chinese pharmacopoeia. 'When and by what means it reached America is one of the unsolved problems of plant introductions,'[3] but it was a common practice for sailors aboard Zheng He's junks to keep pots of roses, their scent an enduring reminder of home. The Chinese also took plants and seeds home with them. Amaranth, a native North American grain with a high protein content, was brought from America to Asia in the early fifteenth century, as of course was maize – brought to the Philippines and seen there by Magellan. Coconuts, native to the South Pacific, were found by the first Europeans on the Pacific coasts of Costa Rica, Panama and Ecuador and on Cocos Island west of Costa Rica. The carriers of grain from the Americas to Asia, of roses and chickens from China to the Americas, and coconuts from the South Pacific to Ecuador can only have been the Chinese.

San Francisco and Los Angeles are clearly depicted at the correct latitudes on the Waldseemüller chart, and I was certain that Zhou Man must have sailed down that coast. Crossing such an enormous expanse of ocean after two years at sea must have left some of his junks in bad condition and in urgent need of repair. Even the best-built ships could not remain at sea for such long periods without suffering at least some damage from storms and the pounding of the waves. At the very least they would have required running repairs and careening – scraping the barnacles from their hulls – and the most badly damaged might well have been cannibalized to repair the others. If so, the remains of these wrecked ships should have been found off the coast of California, just as other wrecks had been in Australia and other parts of the globe.

My enquiries into strange wrecks on the coast of California drew a blank, but I did discover that museums there held substantial quantities of Ming blue and white ceramics. The accepted wisdom is that these items were brought to California in the holds of Spanish galleons, but a number of medieval Chinese anchors have been found off the California coast, and these are unlikely to have been brought by Spanish ships. I began to question seriously the provenance of the Ming porcelain; had it really been brought by the Spanish? Medieval Chinese porcelain can be dated by its cobalt content: the greater the amount of iron in the cobalt, the deeper blue the glaze. The dark cobalt of the Mongol era came from Persia, also ruled by the Mongols, but Zhu Di's father sealed the Chinese borders after he drove out the Mongols in 1368 and Persian cobalt was no longer available. However, Zhu Di reopened the frontiers and restored trade along the Silk Road through Asia allowing Persian cobalt to be imported once more. The period when Chinese pale blue porcelain was produced and used in Ming China is thus limited, and the colour of the porcelain held by Californian museums would indicate whether or not it was made during this period in China's history.

I was certain that a great treasure fleet had discovered the Pacific coasts of North and South America, but my researches failed to uncover conclusive evidence such as the wreck of a Chinese junk. In the hope that others might have found traces I had missed, I decided to 'go public' on the issue in a lecture at the Royal Geographical Society in London in March 2002. It was broadcast around the world; within forty-eight hours reports began to come in from California, drawing my attention to the wreck of a medieval Chinese junk buried under a sandbank in the Sacramento River off the north-east corner of San Francisco Bay. My first reaction was to discount the reports – the site was more than a hundred miles from open sea and the discovery seemed too good to be true – but over the next few days more e-mails describing the same junk continued to arrive. As soon as I had carried out some preliminary research, I discovered that the prevailing north-easterly winds on this coast could have blown a junk straight across the bay and into the Sacramento River. Six centuries ago the river was broader and deeper than today, for deforestation has reduced rain- and snowfall in the area causing the water level to fall. It was indeed possible, if not probable, that a junk entering San Francisco Bay would have been driven by the winds into the Sacramento River.

Dr John Furry of the Natural History Museum of Northern California first became aware of the junk twenty years ago when he read an account of the strange armour that once had been found in its hold (the wreck was then evidently less deeply buried in sand and silt than it is now). The armour was of an unusual metal (native Americans did not know how to forge metal) and curiously silver-grey in colour. It was shown to a local expert who is said to have identified it as of medieval Chinese origin. Dr Furry's attempts to pursue the story met a brick wall – the expert had died in the intervening years, and the armour had been lent to a local school and was now lost – but he was sufficiently intrigued to begin investigating the wreck-site.

The site was covered with a 40-foot layer of the accumulated sand and silt of centuries, so Dr Furry began by taking magnetometer readings of the area. These showed a strong magnetic anomaly outlining a buried object 85 feet long and 30 feet wide, very similar in size and shape to the trading junks that accompanied Zheng He's fleets. Core samples were then extracted from the site. The fragments of wood brought up were carbon-dated to 1410, indicating that the junk was built in that year, 'a period that included a maritime highpoint for the ancient Chinese',[4] as local newspapers laconically reported.

The evidence from the carbon-dating encouraged Dr Furry to drill again with more sophisticated equipment. This yielded much larger samples including further pieces of wood and a compacted 80lb mass of millions of black seeds. He sent fragments of the wood and the seeds to China for analysis, and according to Dr Furry, the Chinese Academy of Forestry have provisionally identified the wood as Keteleria, a conifer native to south-east China but not to North America. In the Middle Ages, the Chinese cultivated

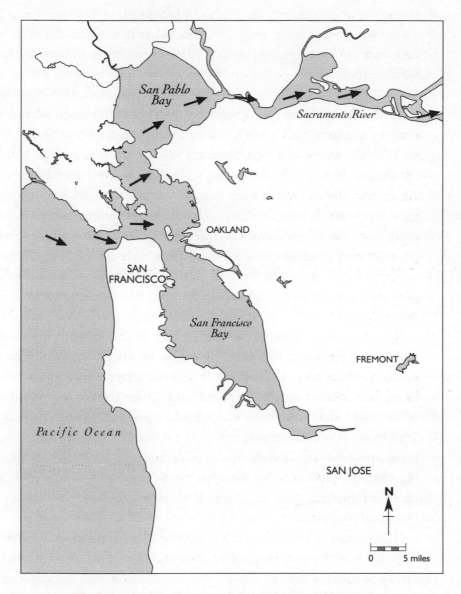

The San Francisco Bay area, showing the winds blowing into
the Sacramento River.

Keteleria for ship-building. Dr Furry also told me that Dr Zhang Wenxu, a former professor at the Chinese Agricultural University in Beijing and the leading Chinese expert on ancient seeds, had provisionally identified four different types of seeds in the black mass brought up from the wreck-site. Three were native to both China and North America, but the other was found only in China. Most interesting of all, however, was Dr Furry's further discovery of rice grains and the body of a beetle among the material raised. Rice, indigenous to Africa and China, was unknown in the Americas in the fifteenth century. Further analysis of the rice and the beetle is being carried out as I write, but to date no written reports on the analysis of the wood or the seeds have been received from China.

I now had little doubt that the site contained the wreck of a Chinese junk; it was exactly the evidence I had been looking for. It seemed highly improbable that the crew would have drowned when the junk grounded on the sandbank in the Sacramento River. It was far more likely that they had come ashore onto the lush, fertile lands of the valley. Their first task would have been to rescue as much rice as possible from the holds of the ship. Much would have been needed to meet their short-term food requirements, but they would also have set some aside as seed and planted it in a suitable location – the floodplain of the Sacramento River.

It has long been claimed that rice was introduced to West Africa by Europeans and then to the Americas by the Spanish, but Professor Judith A. Carney of the University of California has argued that this thesis is fundamentally flawed. It is widely accepted that the Chinese made a major contribution to developing agriculture in the rich soils of California, particularly the cultivation of rice in the swamplands of the lower Sacramento. By the 1870s, 75 per cent of the farmers in California were of Chinese origin. 'The Chinese actually taught the American farmer how to plant, cultivate and harvest.'[5] But were these Chinese working in the fields and plantations of the Sacramento Valley all part of the great nineteenth-century waves of immigration into the United States, or could some have been descendants of settlers left on the banks of the Sacramento by Zhou Man in 1423? I found a clue to this mystery in an unlikely source.

In 1874, Stephen Powers, an official inspector appointed by the government of California who had spent years collecting data on the languages of the tribes of California, published an article claiming that he had found linguistic evidence of a Chinese colony on the Russian River in California, some seventy miles north-west of the Sacramento junk.[6] Powers also claimed that diseases brought by European settlers had decimated this Chinese colony as well as the other Indian people of California, '[the] remittent fever which desolated the Sacramento valleys in 1833 and reduced these great plains from a condition of remarkable populousness to one of almost utter silence and solitude ... there was scarcely a human being left alive'.[7] Powers' report was badly received by his government employers, and although he courteously and bravely attempted to maintain his position, his official report, published in 1877, is a watered-down version of his claims. Nonetheless, it makes for fascinating reading.

Quite apart from his claim of a Chinese colony based on linguistic evidence, Powers described Chinese settlers as having intermarried with local Indians over centuries. Their descendants were paler than the people of the coast, and, unlike other Indian tribes, the older generation had magnificent beards while the women 'are as proud of their black hair as the Chinese'. Rather than skins, women wore 'a single garment in the shape of a wool sack, sleeveless and gathered at the neck, more or less white once'. They were 'simple, friendly, peaceable and inoffensive'. After death, 'they generally desire like the Chinese to be buried in the ancestral soil of their tribe'. Again like the Chinese, but unlike other hunter-gatherer tribes of North America, the peoples around the Sacramento and Russian Rivers were sedentary: 'at least four fifths of their diet was derived from the vegetable kingdom ... They knew the qualities of all herbs, shrubs, leaves, having a command of a much greater catalogue of [botanical] names than nine tenths of Americans.' Their ancestors' legacy could also be seen in pottery beautifully formed in classic Chinese shapes, whereas the '[modern] Indian merely picks up a boulder of trap [a dark, igneous rock] or greenstone and beats out a hollow leaving the outside rough'. The ancestors of the Sacramento and Russian River tribes also used 'long, heavy knives of obsidian or jasper' their descendants, Powers found, no longer knew how to make. And while the ancestors had fashioned elegant tobacco pipes from serpentine, their descendants made use of simple wooden ones. They had also 'developed a Chinese inventiveness'[8] in devising methods of snaring wildfowl using decoy ducks – a Chinese custom, but one not found among the Indians. Like the Chinese, they ate snails, slugs, lizards and snakes, and built large middens of clam shells.

On the eastern side of San Francisco Bay, some seventy miles south of the site of the Sacramento junk, there is a small, stone-built village with low walls. In 1904, Dr John Fryer, Professor of Oriental Languages at University College, Berkeley, California, stated, 'This is undoubtedly the work of Mongolians ... The Chinese would naturally wall themselves in, as they do in all their towns in China.'[9] This accords with Powers' succinct description of Chinese people who had created a colony and then intermarried with native Americans.

It certainly seems that Zhou Man's fleet left a settlement in California. Were they the first to cultivate rice in the Americas? And was the wealth of blue and white Ming porcelain found in California really brought by Spanish galleons, as conventional wisdom has it, or was it carried in the holds of the junks of Zhou Man's fleet? The investigation is ongoing, the definitive conclusion yet to be written; meanwhile, I had to press on with my own research, tracking the fleet as it set sail once more from San Francisco Bay.

After emerging from the bay, Zhou Man's fleet would have been carried southwards by the wind and current to New Mexico. The Waldseemüller map shows the coast with reasonable accuracy, charted just as one would expect from a ship passing by, but there is a gap at the latitude of the Gulf of Tehuantepec in Guatemala, as if the Pacific and Atlantic Oceans met there, which of course is not the case. This is consistent with the Chinese having sailed into the Gulf, but finding it too shallow to proceed, turning back and then drawing what they could see from the entrance: water stretching away for miles in front of them, marking an apparent opening between North and South America.

I made the assumption that they had sailed beyond the isthmus of Panama, clearly shown on the Waldseemüller, and then been driven back across the Pacific towards China by the winds and current, as one would expect with a square-rigged sailing ship. But on their way down that coast they would have been swept across the Gulf of California and could have made a landfall on the Mexican coast somewhere near Manzanillo in the modern province of Colima. Here a spectacular volcano, the Colima, some 12,700 feet high and clearly visible for miles out to sea, would have attracted them.

I decided to make a search for another wreck between Manzanillo and Acapulco, a stretch of coastline only around three hundred miles long and again clearly shown on the Waldseemüller map. I started my search with the accounts of the first Spaniards to reach that coast in the 1520s, Fra Bernardino de Sahagún[10] and Bernal Diaz del Castillo,[11] both of whom described the exotic Mayan civilization, still surviving in 1421 but in decline when they arrived. Many of the things de Sahagún and del Castillo described – chickens, lacquer boxes, dye-stuffs, metalwork and jewellery – seemed to have the imprint of China all over them.

As in California, when they arrived in Mexico the conquistadors found Asiatic chickens quite different from the European fowl they had left behind. The Mayan names for the birds, *Kek* or *Ki*, were identical to those used by the Chinese; like the Chinese but unlike the Europeans, Mexicans used chickens only for ceremonial purposes such as divination, not for eggs or meat. These were such remarkable similarities that for these reasons alone I felt a visit to that small strip of the Mexican coast was justified.

Before departing, I also investigated whether plants originating in China grew in New Mexico or western Mexico. The Chinese Rose did, but that could have been propagated southwards from California. Other than the rose, I found no plants growing in Mexico that had originated in China, but I did find the opposite; plants indigenous to Central America had found their way across the world before the European voyages of discovery.[12] Sweet potatoes, tomatoes and papayas were found in Easter Island, sweet potatoes in Hawaii, and maize in China and the Philippines. Maize could have come from South or North America, but the other plants had come from a much narrower area, from what we now call Mexico, Guatemala and Nicaragua.

The Mayan civilization the Chinese would have encountered was almost as old as their own. The Maya's predecessors were the Olmecs, the earliest civilization in Central America and possibly the whole of the Americas, whose capital was at La Venta on the Atlantic coast of Mexico. By 1200 BC, the Olmec people had constructed two large artificial plateaux at La Venta and San Lorenzo on which they built religious cities nearly as old as Babylon. These great mounds stretching for miles were the centre of a settlement system that integrated Olmec villages and hamlets into one social, political and economic unit straddling what we now know as southern Mexico.

They set up extensive trade networks with the peoples to the south, importing obsidian, basalt, greenstone and iron ore, and exporting pottery, jaguar pelts, coca and wonderfully expressive sculpture. Examples can be seen to this day in Parque La Venta: mischievous stone monkeys hang from trees; stone dolphins, so lively that one can almost see the water splashing off their bodies, leap between ponds; a man crawls out of the entrance of a tomb carved out of basalt; a distraught mother cradles her dead child in her arms. It is fabulous sculpture, the work of a truly amazing people. But around 300 BC, the Olmecs vanished for reasons that remain unclear. They were followed by the Maya, who created a trading empire spanning Central America. The Mayan epoch was already coming to an end by 1421 and civil war had broken out in Yucatan, but the Chinese would have found a very old and very distinguished civilization.

I saw traces of that great Mayan civilization everywhere as I took a bus from the Atlantic to the Pacific coast of Mexico. The Atlantic coast is littered with mooring posts, each of which seems to have its own sentinel pelican, watching over a sea teeming with fish. Then come mile upon mile of marshes, with flocks of ducks and skeins of geese crossing the sky. Ibises and storks stand motionless in pools and lagoons. This is Mayan country, with a system of agriculture unchanged for centuries. *Milpas* – cultivated fields – sprawl across the jungle, the result of the slash and burn system. In the dry season, around Christmas, farmers cut trees with their machetes. From March until May there is little rain and the heat becomes oppressive, an ideal time for burning dried wood, leaving a cleared area for cultivation covered with a nutrient-rich bed of ashes.

The first rains come at the end of May, preceded by silent lightning. Now farmers take long thick staffs and poke small holes into the wet earth into which they drop kernels of maize, beans and squash seeds. This marvellous trio has provided the healthy diet on which the peoples of the Americas – Olmec, Maya, Toltec, Inca and Aztec – have sustained themselves for millennia. As the corn grows, the beans wind around the stems and the squashes spread across the ground. By July, the sun is blistering but there is abundant rainfall, and in September it is time for harvest. The Chinese would have found such rich agriculture spread right across the land together with a sophisticated irrigation system and raised fields supporting a far higher density of population than is found in the Mexican countryside today. It rivalled their own.

Beehives are scattered along the fringes of the forest; honey was important to the Maya for sugar, as a basis for wheat-fermented alcohol and as a cash crop enabling the farmers to buy shoes and the cotton cloth their wives embroidered in traditional patterns. To this day, their children wear smocks exquisitely embroidered in vivid colours identifying family and village, very similar to those painted in the frescoes of long ago. The traditional *Na* houses peep out of the rainforest, unchanged for millennia. The foundations, an oval platform of rocks, are bound together by limestone cement. Horizontal beams are lashed to the uprights with rope made from fibres of the agave plant. Smaller bamboos complete the framework and the roofs are of dried fan palms. This traditional construction is still used in hotels and resorts throughout southern Mexico and Guatemala. The Maya still sleep in hammocks, and their everyday greeting remains 'Have a hammock.'

The jungle of Central America provides a rich and varied diet; man only needs to hunt, fish and gather fruit for two or three days each month, and in the sultry heat he needs few clothes. Building materials, vegetables, medicines, coca, coffee, edible birds and animals of all descriptions surround him. The jungle is never silent; night is punctuated by cries, whistles, screams, muffled roars and croaks. In this rich jungle environment, the Maya built glorious stone cities. Nothing I have seen on this fabulous planet, not even Machu Picchu or the Acropolis, has equalled the Mayan city of Palenque in Chiapas, Mexico, rising out of the white mist of a perfect summer's day. The city was built by the Maya in their glorious golden age (c. AD 325–925) and lay hidden under its cloak of jungle for a thousand years. Constructed on a series of adjacent hills overlooking the plains, it spreads over three and a half square miles. Each hill group comprises a cluster of buildings – pyramids, temples and palaces. Within each group, white stone palaces surround an enchanting central plaza with a backdrop of verdant, bottle-green jungle. The buildings have been superbly positioned to accentuate the natural features of hill and valley, while a placid river wends through the middle of the site. When the Chinese met the people of Mexico it is highly probable that they would have been shown Palenque, the finest Mayan city.

At the time, Palenque would have appeared to the Chinese as the work of a people whose talent equalled their own. It is the complete Mayan city, suddenly abandoned with its treasures intact. Here there is everything the archaeologist or historian could wish for: the fabulous tomb of a 'pharaoh of the jungle', filled with treasures; palaces of kings and priests covered in hieroglyphics telling the story of the site; observatories, temples, ball courts and, perhaps most important of all, the houses of ordinary people. Every aspect of art is here, from masks, statues, jewellery and ceramics to the humble pots and pans, fishing hooks and spears used by ordinary folk to hunt game.

The extraordinary white pyramid of King Pakal dominates the site. The Cuban scholar Alberto Ruz Lhuillier spent years digging down a secret stairway into the chamber at the very bottom. In 1952 his team wrenched aside a huge stone and entered a darkened vault.

> Out of the dim shadows emerged a vision from a fairytale, a fantastic ethereal sight from another world. It seemed a huge magic grotto, carved out of ice, the walls sparkling and glistening like snow crystals . . . the impression, in fact, was that of an abandoned chapel. Across the walls marched stucco figures in low relief. Then my eyes sought the floor. This was almost entirely filled with the great carved stone slab, in perfect condition . . . Ours were the first eyes that gazed upon it for more than a thousand years.

In feverish excitement, Alberto Ruz Lhuillier and his team jacked up the huge lid and peered inside.

> My first impression was that of a mosaic of green, red and white. Then it resolved itself into details – green jade ornaments, red painted teeth and bones, and a fragment of the mask. I was gazing at the death face of him for whom all this stupendous work – the crypt, the sculpture, the stairway, the great pyramid with its crowning temple – had been built . . . This, then, was a sarcophagus, the first ever found in a Mayan pyramid.[13]

The most spectacular of the exotic treasures that accompanied Pakal to the next life was his burial mask of jade, with shell eyes and obsidian irises. It must be one of the finest works of art ever made by man, of incalculable value. The dead king's wrist, neck, fingers and ears were adorned with exquisitely carved jade jewellery. Here were objects to rival or even eclipse the finest products of the Chinese or Japanese craftsmen. The beautifully proportioned pyramid with its simple, smoothly faced stone, the hidden stairway, the interior crypt and the superb mask and jewellery are the work of a people of immense architectural, engineering and artistic talent.

A walk downriver from Pakal's pyramid brought me to a museum filled with Mayan decorative art, mostly symbolic plants and animals – jaguars, serpents with fangs and claws, birds with their feathers and scales, so lifelike they appear to leap out of the display cases. It is an astounding cornucopia of artistic treasure. At last, after years of sailing the storm-tossed oceans, the Chinese had met a civilization nearly as old and as fine as their own. They had found jade jewellery as exquisite as theirs, and Cholula ware even thinner than the best Chinese porcelain, Jingdezhen from Jiangxi province. At long last, they could exchange their silks and blue and white ceramics for wonderful works of art.

COLONIES
IN
CENTRAL
AMERICA

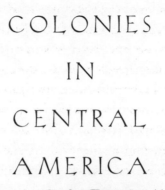

IFOUND SOME OF THE STRONGEST SIGNS OF CHINESE INFLUENCE
when I arrived in Uruapan in the mountains of western Mexico.
It lies approximately two hundred miles upriver from the Pacific,
with the river and the sea to the south and the mountains to the
north. The town owes its name to the Spanish monk Fra Juan de
San Miguel who was so impressed by the lush vegetation when he
arrived in 1533 that he christened the area Uruapan – 'eternal
spring'. To this day, it is renowned for its avocados and fruit, and for
the beautiful lacquer boxes and trays that delight tourists.

Lacquer, known in Mexico as *maque* and in China as *Ch'i-ch'i*, is
a highly unusual, complex and time-consuming method of decoration. The lacquer tree occurs in a wild state in China, regarded
as the original birthplace of lacquer, and is also cultivated in
plantations. The Chinese recognized the protective qualities of
seshime, the resin extracted from the branches of the lacquer tree, at
least three thousand years ago. They introduced it throughout
south-east Asia; the Chinese and Japanese lacquering processes are
essentially the same. The oldest known Chinese examples date from
the Shang dynasties (c. 1523–1028 BC) when the Middle Kingdoms
began using lacquer on household utensils, furniture and art objects,
and to preserve historical objects carved on bamboo. To their
astonishment, the first Europeans to reach southern California and
Mexico found that the process of lacquer decoration was flourishing
in the states of Chiapas, Guerrero, Michoacán and as far north as
Sinaloa on the Gulf of California.[1] Uruapan is considered to be the
centre of the *maque* art, but how could the people of Pacific Mexico
have come to know of it? Was it developed independently, or did the
Chinese introduce it?

Lacquer's unique characteristic is its need for a moist and
temperate atmosphere in order to dry. Warm dampness converts the
sap into a dense mass that hardens as enamel. Density and drying
vary with temperature, thickness and humidity. Perfect conditions
are found in the moist, warm Pacific winds of Uruapan. Before
applying lacquer in the traditional way, the surface of a box or other

object is prepared by filling all the cracks with a mixture of rice flour and seshime. The correct consistency is achieved by mixing it with rice paste, or, in the case of Mexico, with volcanic ash. The box is then sanded down and the first of between ten and a hundred coats of lacquer applied with a very fine brush made of human hair. Each layer has to be completely dry, sanded and polished before the next is applied. Polishing was an art in itself, using a whetstone and deer-horn powder applied with a soft cloth; sixty or seventy coats were common.

This process is virtually identical in China and Mexico, with Chinese technology being adapted to the climate and materials found in Mexico. Preparation of the surface is identical: cracks are filled with a mixture called *nimacarta*, the object is sanded until completely smooth, and as many coats of *nimacarta* as necessary are applied, each one dried, sanded and polished with a whetstone.

Although the process is the same, the ingredients in Mexico do vary. The *maque* is a semi-liquid paste formed using a mixture of animal and vegetable oils and natural refined clays. The principal animal ingredient is grease extracted from the *aje* insects (*Coccus lacca*) bred by the local people around Uruapan. The insects are gathered during the rainy season and dropped alive into boiling water until their bodies release a hard, waxy substance that floats to the surface. When the water cools, the substance is collected, washed and reheated to remove any water. It cools like slabs of butter. The second ingredient, *chia* vegetable oil, serves to thin the *aje* mixture. The oil is extracted from the seeds of the sage plant, a native of Mexico. *Chia* oil has a high glycerine content that quickly absorbs oxygen from the air, forming a hard elastic surface when dried. The third ingredient, finely ground dolomite called *teputzuta*, a mineral clay, gives body to the *maque* mixture.

The decorative techniques and colours used in Mexico and China are also remarkably similar, with spectacular reds incised into a deep black background. In both countries, the traditional colour is black obtained from the fine powder of burnt animal bones or burnt corncobs. Decorative *maque* techniques used in today's states of southern Mexico are the same as in China and Japan. The design is carved using the point of a sharp cactus needle inserted in a turkey quill. The soft plume of the feather is used to brush off the excess clay, or *maque*, as it is carved off. The fine incised lines are then filled with contrasting colours, one colour at a time, with plenty of drying, scouring and polishing after each application. The end result, the wonderful decorated plate or box, is so similar in Uruapan and China that it is almost impossible for those who are not experts to differentiate between them.

Theoretically, if very implausibly, this elaborate and time-consuming process could have evolved simultaneously in China and Mexico, countries thousands of miles apart, but lacquering is not the only congruity when it comes to the artwork of western Mexico and China. Both also have extraordinarily similar and highly unusual methods of obtaining the dyes used in their artwork. Madder red, indigo blue, scarlet and shellfish purple are obscure dye-stuffs producing brilliant colours but requiring complex procedures to extract and fix them. Again, I would argue, too large a coincidence to be probable.

Madder is a red dye derived in China from the roots of shrubs of the Rubiacea family. The dye is prepared by digging up, drying, cleaning and pulverizing the roots, then soaking the mash overnight and steeping it for a short time at about 150° Celsius. The fabric is first mordanted, or fixed, with an aluminium sulphate before being boiled in the dye bath. It is then rinsed in water mixed with wood ash. In Mexico, the roots come from relatives of the Rubiacea – *R. relbunium* and *R. nitidum*, small, sub-tropical shrubs found as far south as Argentina. The New World mordant includes aluminium, oxalic acid and tannin.

The brilliant blue indigo, used for millennia throughout south-east Asia, is the oldest of all the natural dye-stuffs and requires the most complicated technology. The plant must be very carefully cultivated. The fresh cut leaves, whole or ground, have to be steeped in hot water for nine to fourteen hours, during which time the leaves ferment and produce the most unpleasant smell. The resultant liquid is clear, but yarn or cloth soaked in it turns a vivid blue upon oxidization with the air. The process used for dyeing in pre-Columbian Central America was almost identical, save that ash and lime were employed as solubility enhancers.

Vermilion dyes, obtained from tiny insects scraped off oak leaves, were extensively used in south-east Asia. The insects were drowned in a vinegar bath, giving them a reddish brown colour, and when crushed they yielded a dye that was dissolved in alcohol and then fixed with alum or urine. The other red dye that occurred throughout south-east Asia was lac (laccaic acid), obtained from wild or domesticated curmese or lac insects parasitic on various trees. The twigs were broken off, dried in the sun and dropped into a hot soda solution from which the liquid was evaporated and the residue made into cakes. Both Ma Huan and Niccolò da Conti described them on sale in Calicut.[2]

The New World equivalent made use of another scaled insect, the cochineal, parasitic on cactus plants. The insect envelops itself in a cottony white film, and when crushed produces a spectacular scarlet colour ten times richer than the curmes and lac of Asia. After the Spanish invaded Mesoamerica, they exported cochineal to the Middle East and Asia. As in China, cochineal's colour was associated with royalty. True Mexican cochineal had reached southern Asia before Columbus set sail.[3]

The final dye was royal (tyrian) purple obtained from marine snails. This was the most celebrated of all colours used in the Old World. It was so expensive that only the wealthy could afford it, and purple robes became synonymous with high rank. The rulers of Byzantium were brought up in purple rooms and clothed in purple robes. In the New World, shellfish purple was produced from the region of Michoacán – the province surrounding Uruapan – and as far afield as Ecuador, and was very widely used on the Pacific coast. As early as 1898, this method of extracting shellfish purple was considered a possible indicator of pre-Columbian transoceanic trade.

... in many areas where the step of applying these substances as colorants might have occurred, it didn't, and sophisticated application of them to fiber is so involved that it seems remarkable that it developed at all, not to say multiple times ... thus when we find several of these dye stuffs, together with use of mordants, shared by distant regions, we must consider the possibility of historical contact, and rather intimate, repeated contact at that – especially in light of a host of other shared, and often arbitrary, traits.[4]

It is inconceivable that these dyeing processes could have been accidental, independent discoveries; 'a common source of the two civilisations must therefore be assumed'.[5]

But the links between Mexico and China do not end with natural dyes, lacquerwork, hens and plants. Lake Pátzcuaro, upriver from Uruapan, is surrounded by mountains rich in copper ore. To this day, lakeside towns such as San Christobal sell beautiful copper artefacts to swarms of tourists, and the museums are filled with treasures from the past. In Michoacán, as in China, metals were separated after they had been mined, stored in different warehouses and catalogued according to the quality and type of the metal and whether it was to be used for religious offerings or as tributes.

The *Florentine Codex* – Fra Bernardino de Sahagún's great book,[6] completed in 1569, describing pre-Hispanic civilizations in Mexico – illustrates the processing of the metals by blowing oxygen through them to separate impurities, an advanced process not used in pre-Columbian North America. The metals used by the Michoacáns were copper, gold, silver and metal alloys. They were particularly adept at casting bells, which took up nearly 60 per cent of the metals fabricated. The resonance of a bell is determined by the type of metal alloy used; just as in Asia, the proportions were carefully measured to give the correct resonance. Metal bells using these same alloys were important symbols in the Buddhist religion, and visitors to Thailand, Burma, China and India are still charmed by the sweet notes of such bells through the day, as I know from dreamy afternoons spent in monasteries in central China and Tibet.

Metal *hachuelas* – burial offerings in the shape of a crescent moon – are also found in abundance in Mexican tombs. *Hachuelas* were often placed in the mouth of the deceased, just as jade marbles were placed in the mouth of the dead in China. The curved, moon-shaped form was an important universal symbol of Lamaist Buddhism. Emperor Zhu Di made significant efforts to encourage Lamaism in China by inviting the Tibetan Karmapa to visit him and bestowing honours upon him. Moon-shaped ceremonial knives were used symbolically to sever the attachment with life, and can be found in Buddhist temples and tombs throughout Tibet and China to this day. While the eunuch captains were Muslims, the crews of Zheng He's fleet were almost all Buddhist, attracted by Buddha's teaching of universal compassion to all sentient creatures.

Mirrors also had an important place in the cultures of both Central America and China. In China, a mirror was believed to assist the transition of the soul to other planes, to the abodes of the spirits of gods and the souls of the ancestors. Most Chinese bronze mirrors were round, embodying the Taoist concept of the circle as a universal space. In China and Japan, the reverse side of a mirror was inscribed with symbols of animals and flowers, and with religious reliefs. It became a tradition to carry a symbolically decorated, round, bronze mirror as protection from evil spirits. In Michoacán, round metal discs called *rodelas* were used in ceremonies and rituals. Like bells, they were produced in large numbers from gold, silver, copper and alloys, and were decorated on the reverse side with symbols of nature and the universe.

As a result of this research, I was certain that the Chinese had been to Uruapan, had traded hens there, and that they must have stayed for months or possibly years to impart their knowledge of lacquer-work and dye technology to the Mexicans. My tentative conclusion – that squadrons or individual ships had been detached as the fleet passed down the coast in order to set up colonies – seemed more and more plausible. There was corroboration of that in the oral history of the Nayarit, to the north-west of Guadalajara – tales of a pre-Columbian ship from Asia that arrived on the Mexican coast and was cordially received by the chief of the Coras, a prominent Nayarit people. I began to search through the museum collections. It was a long haul with little to show for it at first. Then I came across the *lienzo de Jucutácato* (the linen of Jucutácato), a painting discovered in the nineteenth century in the village of that name.

The *lienzo* comprises around thirty-five squares, thirty of which are about the same size, and each square tells a little story. The first scene shows men disembarking from a ship. Running ahead of them is a dog with a distinctive tail curved in a bow over its back. In shape, size and gait, especially its peculiar tail, it resembles the Chinese shar-pei, a hunting dog originally from Guangzhou, and much prized by poor Cantonese for its extreme devotion to its keeper and his family.[7] At least one of the men is on horseback, a creature the local people would have found very strange and worthy of note; there were none in the Americas prior to the Spanish conquest. The leader emerging from the bows is dressed in a red tunic (the same garment Governor Grey described in the Aboriginal paintings in Australia) and he holds a round mirror. The mirror clearly had symbolic importance for it is repeated no fewer than fourteen times in the other pictures. In some of them the reverse side of the mirror is shown 'marked with eight divisions'; this 'wheel of doctrine' relates to a major event in the life of the Buddha, particularly his preaching and enlightenment. The mirror being carried by the red-robed leader is entirely consistent with a Buddhist religious leader coming ashore to meet local people.

In the centre of the picture, a leader sits while local people lay trays of minerals on the ground at his feet – to my mind an obvious reference to their selling copper to the Chinese. At the bottom is a tree with rays of light emanating from it. It may symbolize the tree of enlightenment under which the Buddha sat. Finally, there are several drawings of a large bird with a drooping tail trailing on the ground. In size and posture, the bird resembles the Asiatic Malay chicken. Taken as a whole, the picture is wholly consistent with Chinese disembarking on horseback and on foot from a great ship, striding ashore with their mirrors to ward off evil spirits, assisted by the tree of enlightenment and the wheel of doctrine. The local people brought them minerals and perhaps in return the Chinese bequeathed their chickens, lacquerwork, dye-stuff and mineral technology.

According to the historian Nicolás León,[8] the first person to have the *lienzo* analysed and copied, it was painted with black vegetable ink on a coarsely woven cloth and dates to long before the Spaniards arrived in Mexico. He states that it was altered in the sixteenth century by the Spaniards who added buildings and words in an attempt to explain it. These alterations were made with a different type of ink and at a later date.

Was it plausible that the Chinese had reached Jucutácato, even though it lies inland from the coast? The village stands some ten kilometres south of Uruapan where the Cupatitzio River ceases to be navigable. The Cupatitzio empties into a large lake some forty kilometres further south, which in turn is connected to the sea by the Balsas River. Just as at Sacramento, it is entirely possible that a junk could have reached Jucutácato from the sea, to obtain minerals and plants in return for trade goods and technology.

If the Chinese had made such a visit to trade and teach the Maya the secrets of lacquer technology, evidence of their stay should still exist. Professor Needham, one of the great experts on Ming China, visited Mexico in 1947 and described his experiences. 'I was deeply impressed during my stay with the palpable similarities between many features of high Central American civilisations and those of East and Southwest Asia,'[9] he wrote, then listed more than thirty cultural parallels. In addition to the metallurgy described earlier, he cited Mayan drums resembling those found in China, tripod pottery, games, computing devices, jade used to demonstrate a panoply of complex beliefs, music (more than half the types of Mayan musical instruments are also found in Burma and Laos), Chinese carrying poles and Chinese neck-rest pillows. With respect to the great professor, I would go even further. From the Pacific coast of Mexico down to central Peru one can be forgiven for thinking one is in China, so similar is the atmosphere, so familiar the bustle, so reminiscent the 'kik-kiri-kee' of the hens in the morning, so alike the people.

To my mind, direct evidence of an early Chinese presence is littered right across the Mayan landscape. Pre-Columbian Chinese bronze figures were found in Peru, and Nazca figurines of the sun god have on their base a Chinese figure for heaven. The museum at Teotihuacan, then an important city, has Chinese medallions, and Chinese jade necklace decorations were found at Chiapa de Corzo in the modern state of Chiapas. Don Ramón Mena, then director of the National Museum of Mexico, described one medallion as 'centuries old ... carried to America when the Chinese came to this continent'.[10] In the celebrated Cueva Pintada caves on the Mexican peninsula of Bahía California, there are paintings of men pierced with arrows and a depiction of the Crab Nebula supernova of 1054 recorded by the Chinese (see chapter 1). In the debris at the foot of the paintings, charred wood has been found and carbon-dated to between 1352 and 1512.

Further evidence of a Chinese stay in Mayan lands comes from Guatemala. The distinguished biologists Carl Johannessen and M. Fogg describe the divination and witchcraft practised by the local people using black-fleshed melanotic chickens.[11] They make a compelling case that not only were the chickens brought from China, but the Chinese must have spent a long time indoctrinating the different groups of people.

Seemingly incontrovertible proof of Chinese colonies in Central America also comes from the foothills of the mountains west of the Gulf of Venezuela, an area clearly shown on the Waldseemüller chart. I have seen these mountains from far out to sea, their snow-capped peaks silhouetted against the setting sun – an unforgettable sight. Some of the native tribes living in this remote area have traces of Chinese genes in their blood.

In 1962, Dr Tulio Arends and Dr M.L. Gallengo of the Instituto Venezolano de Investigaciones Científicas, Caracas, reported the findings of their electrophoretic study of the distribution of transferrin phenotypes (the study of the migration of suspended particles in particular protein macro-molecules under the influence of an electric field) in linguistic and ethnological groups of the mature population of the American continent. They identified transferrins (proteins transporting iron in blood) in the Irapa, Paraujano and Macoita people who inhabited the foothills of the Sierra de Perija (9° to 11°N; 72°40′ to 73°30′W). These tribes were primitive populations on the verge of extinction. In 58 per cent of these people, the scientists found a slow-moving transferrin indistinguishable from one which to date has been found only in Chinese natives of the province of Kwantung in south-east China.[12] As the report says, 'this finding is additional evidence for the existence of a racial link between South American Indians and Chinese'. A goodly proportion of the crews of Zhou Man's and Hong Bao's fleets would have been born in Kwantung, for then, as now, its ports – Kowloon, Hong Kong and Macao – were among the busiest in China, thronged with boats and the seamen who sailed them. It appears that some of the Kwantung sailors aboard Zhou Man's ships interbred with Venezuelan women.

There is also linguistic evidence of Chinese visits to South America. A sailing ship is *chamban* in Colombia, *sampan* in China; a raft, *balsa* in South America and *palso* in China; a log raft, *jangada* in Brazil, *ziangada* in Tamil. Until the late nineteenth century, villagers in a mountain village of Peru spoke Chinese.[13] A mountain of evidence – wrecks, blood groups, architecture, painting, customs, linguistics, clothes, technology, artefacts, dye-stuffs, plants and animals transferred between China and South America – points to a pervasive Chinese influence the length of the Pacific coast of Central and South America, and inland. So broad and deep is the influence that one may almost call the continent of that era 'Chinese America'.

There is one further incontrovertible proof that the Chinese reached Mexico. When I commanded HMS *Rorqual*, I took her through the South China Sea and Philippine Islands to Subic Bay. There were many legends about Chinese junks lying on the sea-bed with their treasures intact. I searched for them with my sonar, but alas without success. Then I discovered that on 9 June 1993 a pearl-fisher diving off Coral Bay in south-west Pandanan, a small island to the south-west of the Philippines (and marked on the Rotz chart), had found the wreck of a Chinese junk. The wreck was encrusted with barnacles, but much of the hull – of teak – remained intact. Under the supervision of Dr Eusebio Dizon, the head of the under-water archaeology section of the National Museum of the Philippines, the wreck was excavated in the spring of 1995 and 4,722 artefacts brought to the surface. They provide a vivid illustration of trade between China, south-east Asia and the Americas.

The wood of the hull has been carbon-dated to 1410, the same date as that of the Sacramento junk. Both are of the same length and beam, approximately 97 feet by 26 feet, and both apparently carried iron woks in their holds – those at Pandanan have been photo-graphed on the sea-bed and those at Sacramento were located by 3D magnetometer readings. Both junks carried exotic as well as ordinary commercial goods. The Pandanan junk had millions of tiny glass beads the size of those used by the Chinese as a sex aid, a practice noticed by both Ma Huan and Niccolò da Conti in south-east Asia (see chapter 3), and extant in the Philippines today. The Sacramento junk carried millions of tiny black seeds, some of which have been provisionally analysed as those of a poppy unique to south-east China. If this analysis is confirmed, it is possible the Chinese were trading in drugs. The Pandanan junk also carried *metates* – pestles for grinding maize – which were then unique to South America, and what appears to be Cholula ware, the eggshell-thin ceramics made in Mexico. The junk had been trading throughout south-east Asia before she sank, for the hold contained porcelain from eight separate countries, including superb ceramics from Vietnam and blue and white Chinese porcelain from the celebrated kilns at Jingdezhen. Complementing these beautiful pieces were ordinary household goods such as clay cooking pots and stoneware storage jars for rice, beans and seeds. There were also three bronze gongs from Dongson (Vietnam) and a peculiar bronze scale balance that may have been the compensating mechanism for a Chinese water clock.

Of the 4,722 items brought up, about a thousand currently remain to be identified. When they have been, it should be possible to reconstruct the junk's route. On the evidence already available, it appears to have returned from Central America with the north equatorial current (the route sailed by Zhou Man's fleet) and been wrecked off Pandanan, perhaps in a sudden squall. This would put the date of its demise at about early September 1423, towards the end of the southwest monsoon, a time when there are unpredictable squalls.

Uncovering the evidence of these early-fifteenth-century Chinese voyages of discovery had been immensely stimulating and exciting, but the implications of what I was learning were now beginning to dawn on me. There seemed to be a mass of powerful evidence that the Chinese had not only traded with the Americas but set up colonies from California to Peru. They had also explored the world long before the Europeans and appeared to have been well on the way to setting up colonies in East Africa and Australia and across the Pacific as well as in America. If all this was true, history would need to be radically revised, but it seemed extremely presumptuous for a retired Royal Navy submarine captain to be the one initiating this process. Although I was confident in the veracity of the evidence I had assembled, the thought of the potential responses in academic circles was causing me nightmares. I decided it was imperative to find corroborative evidence from the academic world, for, generous though they had been in helping me so far, I could well imagine the reaction of some distinguished professors of history to a radical reinterpretation of the subject they had devoted their lives to studying and teaching.

Although all the Chinese records had allegedly been destroyed, I felt sure that somewhere something like the *Wu Pei Chi* and Ma Huan's diaries must have been missed; the mandarins could not have been so thorough that they had obliterated every description, every letter, every mention of what had been found during the voyages. Surely another private memoir or account must have survived somewhere.

My first approach was to the Zheng He Museum in Nanjing. The museum is situated in the centre of the city in what used to be the private park encircling Zheng He's palace and has been built in early Ming style, surrounded by bamboo groves and carpets of green grass dotted with flowers. The principal exhibit is entitled 'Historical Relics and Material Exhibitions of Zheng He's Expeditions'. The most interesting and important relic is the 36-foot-high rudder post. By the standards of conventional ship engineering, a vessel carrying such a gigantic rudder must have been around four hundred feet long. The only other artefacts of interest I found in the museum were Zheng He's bell, resembling a larger version of that found at Ruapuke Beach, and the highly unusual claw-shaped anchors like those found in Australia.

These findings, though interesting, were inconclusive. I then wrote to professors in the Chinese or Asian Studies departments of the universities of California, world-renowned for their research into medieval China, to the relevant professors at Oxford and Cambridge and to the librarians of the great libraries of England, America and Australia to enquire if their collections included books of the early Ming era unknown to the outside world.

After a wealth of friendly but negative replies, I at last struck lucky. Professor Charles Aylmer, the librarian of the East Asian Collection at Cambridge University in England, informed me of a unique book, *I Yü Thu Chih* – 'The Illustrated Record of Strange Countries' – a compilation of the people and places known to the Chinese in 1430. The book's cover page is missing so the author is not known for certain, but it is believed to have been written by the

Ming prince Ning Xian Wang (Zhu Quan) and printed within a year or so of 1430. It formed part of the magnificent collection donated to the University of Cambridge in the late nineteenth century by Professor Wade, who had spent most of his life in China and was the first professor of Chinese at Cambridge. The Cambridge copy is the only one in existence, anywhere in the world. It has never been translated and only one photocopy has ever been taken, by the Chinese Embassy in London. Professor Aylmer and other learned sinologists are absolutely convinced of the provenance and authenticity of the book.

I hurried to Cambridge. Although the book itself is in very poor shape, Professor Aylmer had arranged for it to be photographed onto a microfiche which showed all ninety-eight pages with remarkable clarity. There are some eight thousand characters in medieval Chinese and 132 illustrations drawn by different artists. Some are quite brilliant, catching the atmosphere with a few strokes of the brush. There are plants, animals and people from practically every continent in the world. It is a most concise and powerful illustration of Chinese knowledge of the world and its creatures in 1430 – hence the title of the book. The Chinese incorporated only what they found strange, and there are therefore very few scenes of China itself. Instead, the illustrations showcase all the principal religions on earth: Muslims in long robes praying to Mecca; the Hindu trinity of Lord Brahma, the creator and supreme being with his four arms, Lord Vishnu, the maintainer and preserver of the universe, and Lord Shiva, its destroyer; there is Ganesh, the elephant god, and a wonderfully lively picture of monkeys dancing around Hanuman, the Indian monkey god; Buddha is depicted in contemplation under the holy tree and praying towards the holy mountain. The artist has drawn Sikhs in their turbans and Venetians in their distinctive hats, long boots and flowing cloaks, but most vivid of all are the animals: a well-fed zebra with its fat, rounded belly; African elephants and lions; Indian peacocks and tigers, all drawn with masterful economy of line. There are pictures of the deer of south-east Asia and the steppe, and the hunters who pursued them with their different weapons – the double-ended bow of the Mongols and the western Asian longbow. There are also drawings of creatures unique to the Americas: llamas, an armadillo plodding across the ground in search of ants, a jaguar with its slack belly, men chewing coca, the naked men of Patagonia, and the dog-headed mylodon, 'which is found two years and nine months' journey west of China'.[14]

Two things particularly surprised me. The first was the emphasis placed on people from the far north. There were Eskimos in their fur-lined hoods carrying harpoons, and a wonderful Cossack dancer. At that time, Moscow was the leading principality of Russia but had not yet started to expand eastwards across Asia. The Chinese could conceivably have seen Eskimos in the Aleutian Islands, but not Cossacks. There are no records in that era of any Chinese expeditions overland into Muscovy, yet somehow the Chinese must have reached a Muscovite port. It was yet another mystery that had to be set to one side for the moment.

The second curious aspect was how little space was devoted to Australia; I could only assume that was because by 1430 it was no longer considered a 'strange country'. By the fifteenth century there had been many descriptions of fleets of junks, each carrying hundreds of people on voyages from China to Australia. In one, the north coast of 'the great south land of Chui Hiao' was described as lying thirty thousand *li* – approximately twelve thousand miles – from China and being in the south temperate zone, where seasons are opposed to those in the northern hemisphere.[15] It was inhabited by a race of small (just one metre tall) black people identified by the Australian anthropologist Norman B. Tyndale as Aborigines from the mountains above Cairns in north Queensland.[16]

In March 2002, the talk I gave at the Royal Geographical Society in London was broadcast live to Australia. The television station Channel 9 then invited me to take part in a live interview in which a number of distinguished Australian professors participated. The fact that Zheng He's fleet had reached Australia came as no surprise to them, and I was subsequently referred to several books that made the same claim. If my theory seemed to be broadly accepted in Australia, did this hold true in China? Dr Wang Tao of the School of Oriental and African Studies, University of London, kindly offered to introduce me to the widow of Professor Wei of Nanjing. Professor Wei's life work was a study of Zheng He's voyages, in particular his fleet's discovery of the Americas. He was about to publish a book entitled *The Chinese Discovery of America* when, sadly, he died. Professor Wei's work is widely known in the academic community in China, though it is yet to be translated into English (or published in China). The revelations in my book caused no particular surprise there either.

I began to wonder why American and European historians had managed to persuade the world for so long that Columbus had discovered America and Cook Australia. Were they ignorant of the Chinese voyages to the Americas before Columbus? I decided to find out. To my amazement, I discovered that there were more than a thousand books providing overwhelming evidence of pre-Columbian Chinese journeys to the Americas. This literature has even been summarized in a two-volume bibliography.[17] As Professor George F. Carter, an expert on hens in the Americas and author of several fascinating books on the subject of early Chinese voyages, remarked, 'Sinologists and Asiatic art historians are normally struck by the overwhelming, all-pervasive evidence of Chinese influence in Amerindian civilization. Seemingly the Americanists are not aware of the Chinese literature suggesting not only discovery but colonization of America.'[18] Professor Carter's phrasing is a masterpiece of tact. Perhaps, as he suggests, those academics are not aware of the evidence; perhaps they have chosen to ignore it, presumably because it contradicts the accepted wisdom on which not a few careers have been based. Academics with rather more open minds will look again.

The thesis that the Chinese explored virtually the whole world between 1421 and 1423 might be a radical departure from con-

1 Neahkahnie Bay – wooden pulley
2 Sacramento junk – plus Chinese speaking
  peoples and location of a Chinese village
3 Los Angeles – Chinese anchor
4 Cave art – depicting foreigners arriving
5 Michoacán artefacts – lacquers, dye-stuffs, both
  with Chinese influence

6 Asiatic chickens
7 Gulf of Fonseca
8 Venezuelan Indians with Chinese DNA
9 Peruvian village with Chinese-speaking
  people
10 Peruvian bronzes with Chinese inscriptions
11 Ecuador – Chinese anchor and fish hooks

Evidence of the visit of the Chinese treasure fleet to the Americas.

vention when it comes to the dates of the discovery of these 'new worlds' and the identity of those who first explored and charted them, but I was confident that there was solid evidence to support it. My training in astro-navigation had also enabled me to find further proofs that no academic, unless he were an astronomer, could have reached. No matter what heavy artillery was brought to bear, I was confident the thesis could withstand it. Reassured, I turned the spotlight onto Admiral Zhou Wen and his fleet.

V

The Voyage of Zhou Wen

11

SATAN'S
ISLAND

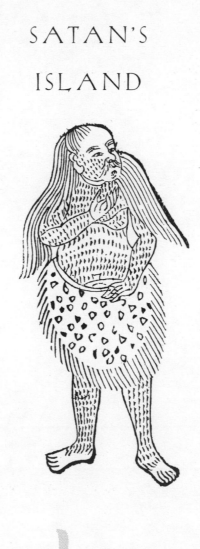

十一

I N OCTOBER 1421, WHEN THE FLEETS OF HONG BAO AND ZHOU Man had sailed south-west from the entrance to the Caribbean towards the coast of South America, they had left the fleet of Admiral Zhou Wen taking a course to the north-west following the northern branch of the equatorial current. I already knew that this fleet must have later reached the Azores, at the latitude of Beijing, for the islands appear on the Kangnido map, drawn before the first Europeans discovered those islands. My task was now to find where Zhou Wen had sailed between those two landfalls.

When Admiral Zhou Wen reached the Cape Verde Islands he had already sailed across a substantial part of the globe and must have known that the mysterious land of Fusang lay to the west of him. By the time of the great cartographer Chu Ssu Pen (1273–1337), the Chinese had made an accurate estimate of the distance from the Pacific to the Atlantic, but how far to the west Zhou Wen thought Fusang lay would depend on how far he considered he had already sailed. The Kangnido shows that, because of the effects of the ocean currents, the Chinese fleets had underestimated their voyage across the 'bulge' of Africa by a couple of thousand miles. As he lay at anchor at Santo Antão in the Cape Verde Islands, Zhou Wen might well have assumed that Fusang lay four thousand rather than two thousand miles to the west of him, but that was still well within his range, without the need for fresh provisions or water en route.

North of the equator, the Atlantic is a vast oval-shaped wind and current system rotating clockwise day in, day out, throughout the year. British Admiralty sailing directions advise mariners on how to make use of these winds and currents: 'From Madeira the best track is to pass just west of, but in sight of, the Cape Verde Archipelago . . . from Cape Verde steer a direct course [for the Caribbean] . . . thereafter . . . the north equatorial current and south equatorial current converge, forming a broad band of current setting west. Average rates reach 2 knots.'[1] From the Cape Verde Islands they carry the mariner due west to the Caribbean, then north-west towards Florida and north up the American seaboard before taking him clockwise to the east, where the current becomes the Gulf Stream carrying the mariner across the Atlantic to the Azores, a thousand miles west of Portugal. It then hooks southwards, back once again to the Cape Verde Islands. The commander of a ship with sufficient provisions can hoist sail off the Cape Verde Islands and sit back and do nothing. Provided he is not capsized by a storm, a common occurrence in the North Atlantic, he will eventually end up more or less where he started.

The westerly current from the Cape Verde Islands reaches its strongest flow when approaching the Caribbean at the latitude of the island of Dominica. As a result, explorer after explorer down the centuries – Columbus on his second voyage, the Spanish explorers Rodrigo de Bastida and Juan de la Cosa in the early years of the sixteenth century, the French and English fleets during the Napoleonic Wars – has entered the Caribbean through the passage between Dominica and Guadeloupe. I would put the likelihood as high as 80 per cent that if, having replenished with fruit and fresh water, the Chinese had sailed from the Cape Verde Islands in October they would have been entering the Caribbean by early November.

The track of the junks of Admiral Zhou Wen's fleet through the Caribbean should logically have been the same as that of Columbus, for the winds and tides have remained unaltered from that day to this. Whatever the Chinese discovered should have been re-discovered by Columbus seventy years later. By examining Columbus's diaries of his second voyage, I should be able to reconstruct the most likely track. If the Chinese had found any islands or land on their voyage across the North Atlantic, I could expect those discoveries to be recorded on charts drawn after they returned to China in 1423. Just as I had done for South America and Australia, I now began to search for a chart that, like the Piri Reis and Jean Rotz maps, appeared to depict lands Europeans had yet to discover.

In that era, Venice, the base of Fra Mauro, the Venetian cartographer working for the Portuguese government, led the West in mapmaking. As I expected, Venetian and Catalan charts

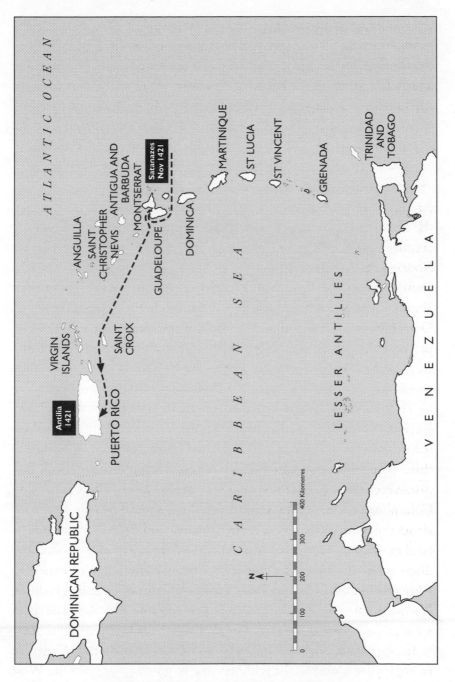

Zhou Wen's journey through the Caribbean.

(Catalonia was then part of the Kingdom of Aragon; the Catalans were redoubtable seafarers) drawn before 1423 disclosed nothing new in the western Atlantic, but a chart dated 1424 and signed by the Venetian cartographer Zuane Pizzigano was an entirely different matter. The Pizzigano chart was rediscovered some seventy years ago and in the early 1950s it was sold to the James Ford Bell Library at the University of Minnesota. Its authenticity and provenance have never been questioned and several books have been written about it by distinguished historians.

> [The 1424 chart] is a document of capital importance to the history of geography. From the historical point of view, it is undoubtedly one of the most, if not the most, precious jewel yielded by the disclosure of the almost unknown treasures contained in the unique collection of early manuscripts assembled by Sir Thomas Phillips during the first three-quarters of the nineteenth century. The great importance of this chart lies in the fact that it is the first to represent a group of four islands in the western Atlantic, called Saya, Satanazes, Antilia and Ymana ... there are many and good reasons for concluding that the Antilia group of four islands shown for the first time in the 1424 chart should be regarded as the earliest cartographic representation of any American lands.[2]

This was high praise indeed. I made a close study of the chart (see Introduction). It is markedly different from its contemporaries. It is not centred on the Mediterranean, as earlier charts were, but looks westwards across the Atlantic, where two large islands, Antilia and Satanazes, hitherto unknown to Europeans, are depicted. Two smaller islands are also shown: Saya, a parabolic island to the south of Satanazes, and the box-shaped island of Ymana to the north of Antilia.

Other accounts of the era put the islands '700 large leagues'[3] west of the Canaries, which would put them near the Bahamas, but no large islands are located there. Were the islands imaginary? Other chartmakers clearly believed they were genuine, for the group was subsequently represented on at least nineteen fifteenth-century maps and two globes, all of them drawn before Columbus set sail (see chapter 17). But as time went by, successive cartographers relocated the islands further and further to the south-west, until they ended up in the Netherlands Antilles.

The Portuguese names on the chart had made me presume that they were the original cartographers, but the names on the Piri Reis and the Jean Rotz charts were also in Portuguese and they could not possibly have been the discoverers of the Antarctic, Patagonia or Australia. Portuguese records in the Torre do Tombo, the National Archives of Portugal in Lisbon, state unequivocally that Henry the Navigator sent caravels to discover Antilia after he had received a similar but slightly later chart (the 1428 World Map discussed in chapter 4).[4] Moreover, in 1424 the Portuguese simply did not have the capacity to survey the islands with such accuracy – for the cartography of Antilia was amazingly good. I concluded that it could only have been the Chinese. However, I needed further proof that this was the case, and I found once again that the best way of tackling this puzzle was to put myself in the cartographers' shoes. When in submarines, we used to spend time in the Barents Sea photographing military installations. Part of our training was in periscope photography and the obscure art of constructing charts from near sea level. At the time I was working from about the same height as the cartographers of the Pizzigano chart, standing on the deck of a medieval ship.

As Zhou Wen's ships approached the Caribbean, they would have had warning some two days out that they would shortly sight land. Clouds, winds, weather and sea-bird types would all change, and finally, a few hours before the islands became visible, the crew would have begun to detect the soft, subtle smell of wet foliage. Because Columbus sailed through the Dominica Passage on a Sunday, he named the island to the south Dominica, the Spanish name for that day of the week; that to the north was named Marie-Galante after his flagship. He first landed at Marie-Galante but found little and pushed on northwards with the current, landing the next day at an island he named Guadeloupe in memory of his visit to a monastery of that name in Extremadura in Spain. Had they known, the monks might have raised objections to his choice of name, for the inhabitants of the island were Carib cannibals. Dr Chanca, a chronicler of Columbus's second voyage, recorded his men striding through the soft sand into the coconut groves where they found 'houses, about 30, built with logs or poles interwoven with branches and huge reeds and thatched ... with palm ... square and cottage like ... For dishes [they use] calabashes [a gourd] ... and, oh horrors!, human skulls for drinking vessels.'[5] Only women were left in the villages; the native men had fled to the hills in terror at the sight of the sails of Columbus's fleet.

The stench of bodies horrified Columbus's men. 'Limbs of human bodies hung up in houses as if curing for provisions; the head of a youth so recently severed from the body that the blood was yet dripping from it, and parts of his body were roasting before the fire, along with savoury flesh of geese and parrots.'[6] The natives used arrow-heads made from human bones, and

in their attacks upon the neighbouring islands, these people capture as many of the women as they can, especially those who are young and beautiful, and keep them as concubines ... they eat the children which they bear to them ... Such of their male enemies as they can take alive they bring to their houses to make a feast of them, and those who are killed they devour at once. They say that man's flesh is so good, that there is nothing like it in the world ... in one of the houses we found the neck of a man undergoing the process of cooking in a pot. When they take any boys prisoners, they dismember [castrate] them and make use of them until they grow up to manhood, and then when they wish to make a feast they kill and eat them, for they say that the flesh of boys and women is good to eat. Three of these boys came fleeing to us, thus mutilated.[7]

Another contemporary writer noted that it was 'their custom to

Cannibalism in the Caribbean: a fanciful seventeenth-century reconstruction of
Columbus's encounter with the Caribs

dismember the male children and young slaves, whom they capture
and fatten like capons'.[8]

To fifteenth-century eyes, the cannibalism Columbus encountered could easily have been seen as the work of the devil.
Could that be the explanation of the name Satanazes – Satan's
Island? Was this what the Chinese had found, and was Guadeloupe
the Satanazes shown on the Pizzigano chart? If so, like Columbus
seventy years later, the Chinese would have approached the island
from the south-east on the prevailing wind and current.

I turned my attention to the island of Saya lying to the south-east
of Satanazes on the Pizzigano chart. I could vividly picture the scene
as the Chinese approached because I spent some time in the
Caribbean in command of the submarine HMS *Rorqual* and had
visited and photographed many of the islands. In many cases the
mountains appear black, surrounded by green jungle. Heavy

rainstorms occur without warning, blotting out the islands. Frequently, birds take flight just before the rains arrive, circling in flocks, shrieking with foreboding.

As soon as I consulted a modern map, I saw that Saya on the Pizzigano map corresponded to Les Saintes. It is approximately the same shape and lies in the same position relative to Guadeloupe as Saya to Satanazes. I assumed that Saya was indeed Les Saintes, Satanazes was Guadeloupe and, based on my calculations of their course and speed, that the Chinese had arrived off the islands in November 1421. Given the maximum height of Les Saintes (about a thousand feet) and the height of eye of a seaman on the deck of a Chinese junk, I estimated that they would have seen the island from twenty-five miles away, while still in the Dominica Passage. From that position they should also have seen the plateau island of Marie-Galante ten miles north of them and the mountainous Dominica ten miles to the south, yet neither was recorded on the chart. I made the obvious deduction that they had passed through the passage in darkness with no moon. When I checked the records, I discovered that the new moon occurred on 25 November 1421, so I took it that they had probably approached Les Saintes from the south-east around dawn, possibly on 26 November 1421.

Les Saintes is composed of two large islands, Terre de Basse and Terre de Haut, and three smaller ones, La Coche and Grand Ilet in the south, and Ilet a Cabrit in the north. The big islands are much higher than the smaller ones and, approached from the south-east, the lower Grand Ilet and La Coche would merge with the taller islands in the background and appear to form a single block of land. The south coast would appear as a single parabolic island, just as it is drawn on the Pizzigano chart. Knowing the height from which they had surveyed it – the deck level of a treasure ship – I could now make an estimate to within two miles of the location from where Saya was charted.

What else would the Chinese have seen from this position? Just what Columbus saw from the same spot seven decades later: 'Dawn reveals a most romantic landscape. A volcanic peak rises to an immense height, and cataracts pouring down its sides appear like water falling out of heaven ... Flights of brightly coloured noisy parrots and other brilliant tropical birds are winging their way from one island to another and the wind of the land is laden with sweet odours.'[9] The 'volcanic peak' is La Souffrière on Guadeloupe, eighteen miles to the north-west. La Souffrière is well inland, its peak frequently shrouded by clouds and heavy rain, and seven rivers pour down its eastern side, the most spectacular among them the 120-metre Karukera Falls. The Chinese junks would have been at sea for at least three weeks, and I am sure the chance to take on water would not have been spurned. They would have altered course for the cataracts.

I turned to the words *con* and *ymana* marked on Satanazes on the Pizzigano chart. My first attempt to solve the riddle of these names was to recruit an expert at crosswords, who came up with *con* as a shell, conical mountain or volcano – interesting, but not much help. Then Professor João Camilo dos Santos, an expert in medieval Portuguese attached to the Portuguese Embassy in London, translated these words for me as 'a volcano' (*con*) 'erupts there' (*ymana*). The description was highly significant. Transposing the location of these words on the Pizzigano chart onto the corresponding modern map placed them directly above the volcanoes of La Souffrière, La Citerne and L'Echelle. Had these volcanoes erupted in 1421? The Smithsonian Institution confirmed there were two eruptions of the three volcanoes between 1400 and 1440; the dates, calculated by radio carbon-dating, cannot be determined more precisely.[10] There were no further eruptions from these volcanoes for another 250 years, and no eruptions of other volcanoes in the Caribbean during the whole of the fifteenth century.[11] Since the Pizzigano chart can only have recorded an eruption of the volcanoes on southern Guadeloupe, I had first-hand evidence that a cartographer had been in the Caribbean no later than 1424, sixty-eight years before Columbus.

There are some anomalies in the map, but they are easily explicable when one retraces the route the ships must have taken. As the Chinese junks headed for the waterfalls on Guadeloupe, they would have had to sail closer and closer to Les Saintes, for all the time the current was pushing them westwards. As they passed the north-east tip of Les Saintes, the cartographer drew Baie du Marigot from half a mile away with the morning sun behind him. Because this bay was so close and so well lit, its size was somewhat exaggerated on the Pizzigano chart. As the junks neared land, the cartographer drew two further bays on the north coast of Saya. The third, Passe du Pain du Sucre, was drawn from a distance of seven miles, much further away than the first drawing, and it was now nearly noon (assuming their speed through the water was 4.8 knots) so the sun was in the cartographer's eyes. The combination of the position of the sun and the greater distance resulted in the third bay being drawn smaller than it should have been. To check that my conclusions were accurate, I showed the chart and my navigational workings to a fellow of the Royal Geographical Society, like myself a professional navigator. He was also convinced that Saya is Les Saintes; it is drawn precisely as it would have been seen from sea level when approaching from the south-east.

Having calculated the time of day at which the cartographer drew Les Saintes, I was able to estimate with some certainty that by noon the junks had landed in the Baie de Grande Anse on southern Guadeloupe. I could imagine them replenishing their fresh water supplies against a backdrop of white, purple and blue hibiscus and orchids ('the wind of the land is laden with sweet odours'). Cassava, peppers and yuccas were there for the taking. The sea is a kaleidoscope of fish, crabs bask on exposed coral and crayfish are abundant. I could visualize the mariners gambolling in the surf before they feasted, washed their clothes and stocked their ships with fruit. How delightful it must have been to swim in the warm water after being at sea for nearly a month. It used to be my practice when in command of HMS *Rorqual* to anchor off an inhabited bay and send the

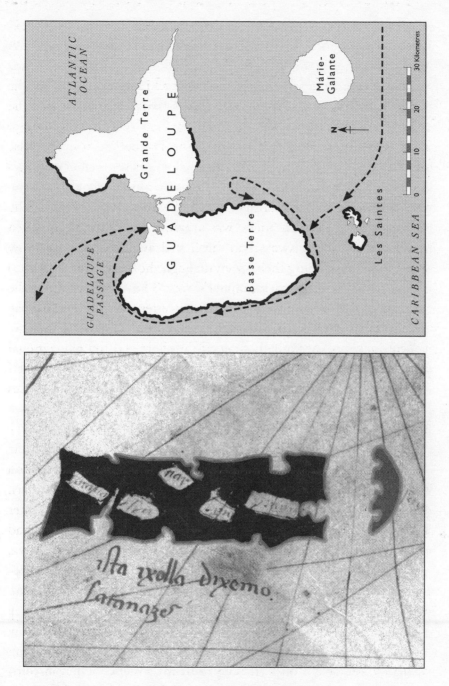

Guadeloupe shown on the Pizzigano map, compared with a modern map.

sailors ashore in the inflatable dinghies we carried. It always proved a popular excursion – a swim in the sea, followed by rum toddies and roast lobster.

In the eastern Caribbean, an offshore breeze usually springs up as the land cools in the early evening. The Chinese had landed on an exposed Atlantic shore and would have had to find a sheltered anchorage for the night. Two hours' sailing up the east coast would have brought them to a secluded anchorage between two coral islands in the southern part of Baie de Sainte Marie. My assumption was that the Chinese had landed, watered and anchored at precisely the same spot Columbus found seventy years later, and the French and English fleets centuries after that. At first sight that may seem an incredible proposition: why should ships of so many different nations over several centuries all end up at the same spot on a remote Caribbean island thousands of miles from home? They did so because they were all subject to the same natural forces.

The clockwise movement of current and winds drew Zhou Wen's fleet from the Cape Verde Islands to a latitude of 18°N, where the equatorial currents converged to sweep them towards the Dominica Passage. As they entered the Caribbean, they were greeted by the magnificent volcano of La Souffrière in Guadeloupe with its cataracts of 'water falling out of heaven'. After watering on the Atlantic shore they needed to find shelter for the night; their anchorage was the nearest sheltered bay to the waterfalls. What they did not know was that this seeming paradise was 'Satan's Island' – Satanazes – populated by cannibalistic Carib tribesmen. Guadeloupe was the Caribs' principal lair in the Caribbean, and they were skilful hunters of men, even when swimming. I spent a day in the British Library poring over Columbus's journal of his second voyage, which includes a description of a Carib attack on his fleet: 'These Caribs can fight about as well in water as in their canoe ... the Spaniard dies in consequence.' After a Spanish sailor was killed, Columbus retaliated, and one of the Caribs had his belly slit open. His intestines were floating on the sea but, according to the Spanish accounts, the wounded Carib pushed them back inside his stomach with one hand while still firing arrows with the other.[12]

On that gruesome note, I decided to end my researches for the day, but as I was making my way home that evening, it occurred to me that if the Chinese had landed on the island, they must have been attacked by the Caribs, just as Columbus was. Might there be some record or legacy of that landing? When I went back to the British Library to look again at the account of Columbus's second voyage, I made another extraordinary discovery as I read the following passage:

> In one house they find what seems to be an iron pot . . . but here is a curiosity amongst savages – the stern post of a vessel. This must have drifted across the ocean from some civilized country. Perhaps, it is a part of the wreck of the *Santa María*. Now all stand aghast at the sight of a pile of human bones – probably the remains of many an unnatural repast.[13]

Iron is not found on the Caribbean islands, nor indeed in Central America. The islanders used hollowed-out tree trunks for their boats, and they did not build them with stern posts, a sophisticated design. Stern posts had been in use in China since the first century AD; they did not reach Europe until the fourteenth century. Columbus's *Santa María* was wrecked off the north coast of Haiti, far away to the north-west of Guadeloupe, and the Gulf Stream would have carried flotsam from that wreck in precisely the opposite direction, north-west towards New England. I strongly suspected that the stern post came from a junk and the iron pot was one brought by the Chinese.

The Chinese would have put to sea to escape the Caribs, just as Columbus's fleet did. When safe in open water, three miles offshore, they would have rounded the southern tip of Guadeloupe and sailed before the wind up the west coast where they charted the headland of Vieux Habitants, the Bay of Anse de la Barque and the Bay of Deshaies. By the next evening they would have been sailing into the bay now known as Le Grand cul de sac Marin, and from there the cartographer drew what he could see of Grande Terre, the eastern island of Guadeloupe. It is a low-lying island, rising from fifty metres near the shore to no more than a hundred metres further inland. By this stage it would have been after dusk and Grande Terre would have appeared as no more than a hazy blur. The cartographer probably saw little of it, and never properly charted it. The Chinese then set sail once more before the wind and current, heading north-westwards across the Caribbean, probably making for 39°53'N, the latitude of modern Atlantic City, New Jersey, but also of Beijing, and another obvious reference point for the Chinese fleets to have chosen.

The cartographer had charted Les Saintes as he saw it from sea level, and placed it in the correct position relative to the western island of Guadeloupe, Basse Terre. He had accurately charted the east, south and west coasts of Basse Terre and Le Grand cul de sac Marin, placing the bays and rivers in their correct position, and had described the volcano La Souffrière and its sisters erupting. The chances of finding another island with erupting volcanoes, coupled with the same-shaped islands in the south and the bay in the north, are nil; there cannot be the slightest doubt that Satanazes is Guadeloupe (Basse Terre) and Saya is Les Saintes. Knowing Basse Terre's true size, I could adjust Satanazes' size to true, and as the Pizzigano chart gave Antilia's size and orientation in relation to Satanazes, I could also calculate the true size and orientation of Antilia. The Pizzigano chart also showed the relative positions of and distance between Satanazes and Antilia. To find Antilia, all I had to do was look for an island 135 kilometres long by 50 kilometres wide, aligned east–west, and lying some six hundred kilometres west-north-west of Guadeloupe, once again in the track of the prevailing current and wind.

I turned to a modern map to see if I could find a match for Antilia. The map revealed that Puerto Rico was in the correct position, had the true alignment and size, and lay directly on the route along which the wind and current would have swept the junks

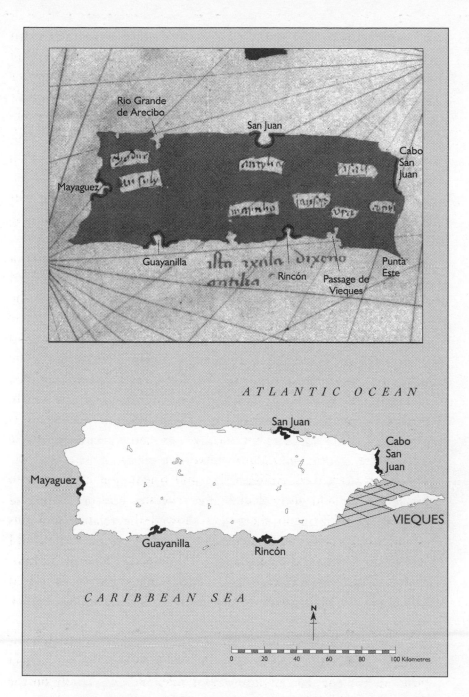

Puerto Rico shown on the Pizzigano map, compared with a modern map.

after they left Basse Terre. I compared the shape of Antilia on the Pizzigano chart with Puerto Rico. It was a very good match. I remember this still as a tremendous breakthrough. Overwhelmed by the importance of what I had discovered, I wandered off into the night in search of a celebratory drink.

I returned to the British Library early the next morning worried that tiredness and elation might have caused me to misread the evidence, but a comparison of a large-scale modern-day map of Puerto Rico with Antilia on the Pizzigano chart at once removed any residual uncertainties. There are striking similarities, particularly the overall shape and the bays of Guayanilla, San Juan and Mayaguez. Save for the south-east tip, Antilia and its harbours fitted Puerto Rico like a glove. The standard of the cartography was astounding, way beyond what the Portuguese could have achieved in 1424.

But the exaggerated south-east tip is easily explained. After leaving Guadeloupe, the winds and currents would have driven the Chinese to the north-west – the same track Columbus later followed – to a point sixty miles east of Puerto Rico. There, they would have sighted the menacing, anvil-shaped volcano El Yunque near the east coast and turned towards it for water. As they had done many times when surveying other islands during their voyages, the Chinese squadron would have been split in two, one sailing north and one south of Puerto Rico to chart both coasts simultaneously. Had they sighted the volcano in the evening, and if they were travelling at their average rate of 4.8 knots, they would have passed south of Vieques Island during the night. In the darkness they could not have seen that Vieques is a separate island, and accordingly drew it as part of the mainland of Antilia.[14] The Pizzigano chart is also inscribed with the word *ura* – hurricane – near the east coast of Puerto Rico, a clear indication that Zhou Wen's fleet had been battered by a hurricane as it sailed away from the island. It would have been prudent of him to run before the storm on as few sails as possible so as to find anchor in a sheltered bay. This is consistent with the

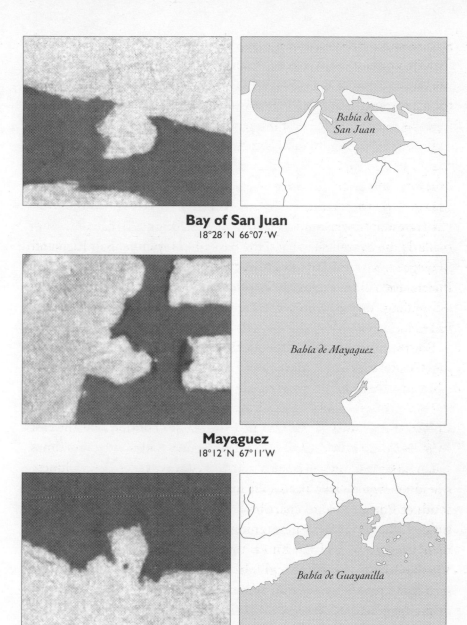

Bay of San Juan
18°28′N 66°07′W

Mayaguez
18°12′N 67°11′W

Guayanilla
18°00′N 66°46′W

The bays and inlets of Puerto Rico, depicted with extraordinary precision on the Pizzigano map.

astonishingly precise cartography of the harbours on Puerto Rico's south, west and north coasts, drawn before Columbus had even been born.

The storm-damaged Chinese fleet had completed its survey of Puerto Rico, and I could imagine the junks unfurling their great sails at the tail end of the hurricane and setting sail for the north from Puerto Rico towards the latitude of Beijing. If that theory was correct, there should have been evidence of their voyage at that latitude. I was confident that the Chinese had sailed to the North Atlantic, for the stone erected by Zheng He at Liu-Chia-Chang in south China after this epic sixth voyage states 'the countries beyond the horizon and at the ends of the earth have all become subjects and the most western of the western or the most northern of the northern countries, however far away they may be'.[15] From a Chinese perspective, the most northern of the northern countries and the most western of the western could only be referring to the Atlantic coasts of North America, but as ever, my problem was that the mandarins had destroyed all records of the treasure fleets. Once again, I had to look for clues in maps and charts of the northern hemisphere drawn before the first Europeans reached the Americas. I had to find a counterpart to the Pizzigano chart.

A world map popularly known as the Cantino came to my rescue. I had unearthed this extraordinary chart in the Biblioteca Estense in Modena, Italy, during my investigation into Zhou Man's visit to the Americas. It was drawn by an anonymous Portuguese cartographer and surreptitiously obtained by Alberto Cantino, the agent of the Duke Ercoli d'Este of Ferrara. The Cantino's provenance and credibility have never been questioned, and there is firm evidence for dating its acquisition to October 1502. The Chinese fleet had to sail before the wind and current; after leaving Puerto Rico, it would have been blown north-west towards Hispaniola and Cuba, and then through the Caribbean to the coast of Florida. The Cantino indeed reflects this, for it shows Hispaniola, Cuba and many other islands in the Caribbean and off Florida, but though it portrays the coast of Africa and the Indian Ocean and its archipelagos of islands with extraordinary accuracy, at first glance its depiction of the Caribbean appears woefully inadequate. Many of the islands seem to bear little relation to their present sizes and shapes, and I was baffled as to why it was so much in error.

I struggled to make sense of this for some considerable time; then, all at once, the answer came to me. Sea levels in 1421 were lower than they are today. Global warming has caused the polar ice to melt, causing sea levels to rise slowly but inexorably. The best estimate of the Proudman Oceanic Laboratory of Birkenhead in England is that they have risen over the past centuries by about one to two millimetres a year. Other reputable oceanographers put the rise a little higher, at an average of four millimetres a year. In the almost six centuries since 1421 it is safe to say that sea levels have risen between just under four and just under eight feet. For simplicity, I assumed that the overall rise had been one fathom, or six feet, roughly the midpoint of the range of estimates.

The British Admiralty charts of the Caribbean[16] enabled me to visualize a completely new picture of the region. In 1421, vast areas that today are submerged would have been either above water or with rocks and reefs showing as breaking water and shoals. The banks and reefs of the Great Bahama Bank, stretching south of Andros Island towards Cuba, would in 1421 have been above water down to the latitude of the Tropic of Cancer, and the numerous sand ridges today marked as 'almost uncovered' on the modern chart[17] would also have been above water. To the Chinese cartographers, everything from Cayo Guajava in the middle of Cuba's north coast as far as the latitude of Miami would have appeared as one large low-lying island, an extension of Cuba.

The prevailing wind and current would have driven the fleet along the north-east coast of Cuba, then due north to the east of Andros, up towards Grand Bahama. (Andros Island is a favourite submarine haunt, for there is a deep-water trench well to the east of the coast along which thousands of tons of nuclear submarine can hurtle at forty miles an hour in order to test its silence at depth and speed. Afterwards we would surface and relax under the palms on Andros beach, drinking Bacardi and Coke.) If the Chinese fleet had made the passage at night, they would never have seen any openings to the west and could only have drawn what appears on the Cantino. When I adjusted the modern chart to show everything to a depth of one fathom, many of the shallow lagoons between the Caribbean islands became dry land, and when I superimposed these adjustments onto the Cantino it was clear the Caribbean had been drawn with incredible accuracy, just as it would have appeared to mariners sailing through it on a following wind six centuries ago. Once again, it was extraordinarily good cartography.

The question I now had to face head on was whether this mapping could have been carried out by Columbus, who had reached the Caribbean in 1492, ten years before the Cantino was acquired. A number of learned professors have slightly different interpretations on the location of his first landfall in the Caribbean, varying between Samana Cay and Cat Island, and on where he first landed on the coast of Cuba. Columbus was a poor cartographer. On his first voyage his calculations of latitude were twenty degrees out – he believed he was somewhere in Nova Scotia – and his longitude was a thousand miles in error. Even if Columbus had a secret, and rather better, cartographer aboard who could have accurately drawn the Caribbean islands shown on the Cantino during all four of Columbus's voyages, that still left hundreds of thousands of square miles of ocean and islands shown on the Cantino that neither Columbus nor any other European explorer reached until twenty years after the chart was drawn. I concluded that the chart could not have been the product of any voyage by Columbus.

Could it have been drawn by an unknown Portuguese or Spanish expedition? One has to look at the overall picture of the lands covered by the Piri Reis and the Cantino together. By 1501, when the source chart was obtained from Columbus's sailor, the maker of the Piri Reis map could accurately depict South America and

Antarctica. By the next year, 1502, the Cantino was showing Africa, the Indian Ocean and the Caribbean. To achieve the remarkable precision and wealth of detail of the Cantino and Piri Reis charts would have required at least thirty ships just to survey the Indian Ocean, let alone South America, Antarctica and Africa. Neither Portugal nor Spain could have sent so many huge fleets simultaneously to different quarters of the world. Only China had the ships, the resources and the expertise to have done so. Cartographers aboard the Chinese treasure fleets had to be the originators of these remarkable charts.

By looking at the Caribbean islands charted on the Cantino, I could reconstruct the passage of the cartographers who had drawn them. To chart the islands, they had to see both coasts, and sailing always before the wind and current, square-rigged sailing ships had no opportunity of turning back for a second pass. To survey both coasts of an island required at least two ships, one either side of it. The way the charts are drawn, coupled with the prevailing winds and currents, leads me to believe that at least five squadrons of ships would have been needed to chart the Caribbean. By my best estimate, at least ten to twenty ships would have had to sail through the Caribbean to collect this mass of information in one pass. Assuming they were within sight of one another, working for ten hours a day, and travelling at an average speed of 4.8 knots, they would have charted fifteen thousand square miles per day and could have obtained the information in four to six weeks.

Many of the islands are very low-lying, and to survey them with the accuracy shown the junks must have been within ten miles of each one, exposing themselves to horrific risks. To cross the Great Bahama Bank from Cuba to the east of Andros Island and inside the Berry Islands (all shown on the Cantino), the ships must have passed, frequently and at night, what the British Admiralty charts call 'numerous sand ridges almost uncovered', and 'numerous rocky heads'. In one small stretch of forty nautical miles,[18] there are literally hundreds of rocks and reefs capable of ripping wooden hulls

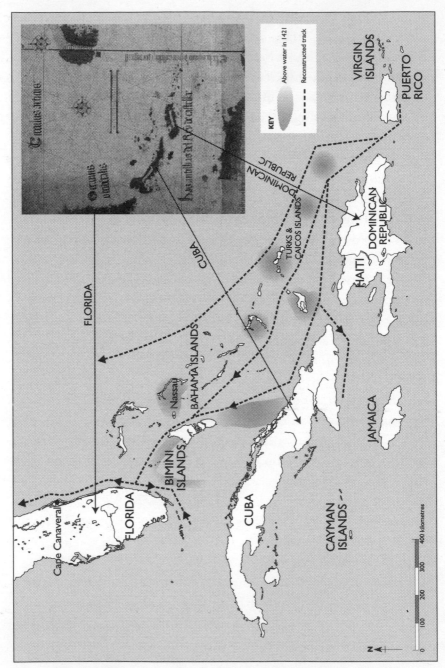

The Cantino map showing the Caribbean and Florida, compared with a modern map.

apart. That short distance must have been achieved at a terrible cost. I cannot conceive how they could have made that passage without losing ships. By the time the junks had crossed the Great Bahama Bank and reached the Berry Islands they would surely have been in desperate trouble, the internal compartments of many ships flooded. The calm, moonlit seas might well have been echoing with the cries of dying seamen.

It was a sombre thought, but it also highlighted the fact that I was closing on my quarry. The charts told me exactly where to look. I had to search for traces of the wrecks of treasure ships within a few miles of the Berry Islands in the Florida Strait.

12

THE
TREASURE
FLEET
RUNS
AGROUND

十二

AS YOU PASS FROM SHALLOW WATER INTO THE DEEPER waters of the open ocean, the pattern and length of the waves change and they have a different colour and smell. It is a phenomenon familiar to all blue-water sailors, and as his fleet passed the Berry Islands, Admiral Zhou Wen would have known at once that his fleet had entered deep water – the Northwest Providence Channel leading into the Florida Strait. I made the assumption that several of his junks had been damaged in crossing the reefs, and he would have had to find somewhere to beach his fleet before it sank in deep water. The search for a suitable island would have been a matter of desperate urgency, for many of the junks must have been in a critical condition, unable to survive in the open ocean.

My detailed research of the area surrounding the Berry Islands now began in earnest. Large-scale British Admiralty charts[1] and Coffman's treasure atlas[2] show wrecks strewn along the Chinese track. These wrecks have been classified by Coffman as Spanish galleons, later ships and earlier, unidentified ones. I focused my attention on the latter class of wrecks, and compared them with the Admiralty chart. It was a dramatic moment, for eight unidentified wrecks were disclosed within six hours' or forty miles' sailing from the point where the Chinese would have entered the Florida Strait. Four wrecks[3] are shown on the Little Bahama reef and the Florida coast; another four[4] are due south. When I examined a large-scale chart, it revealed that the track of these four southern wrecks was pointing towards a group of small islands, North and South Bimini, Gun and Ocean Cay, fifteen miles away. The position of the wrecks was consistent with four junks making a desperate but doomed bid to reach the islands; the last wreck is within a mile of North Bimini. All are in shallow water; if the sharks did not get them first, the crew could have swum ashore. I felt sure that there should be evidence of other wrecks – ships that had managed to struggle to land – on Bimini itself.

Before I flew there to begin a detailed search of the island, it

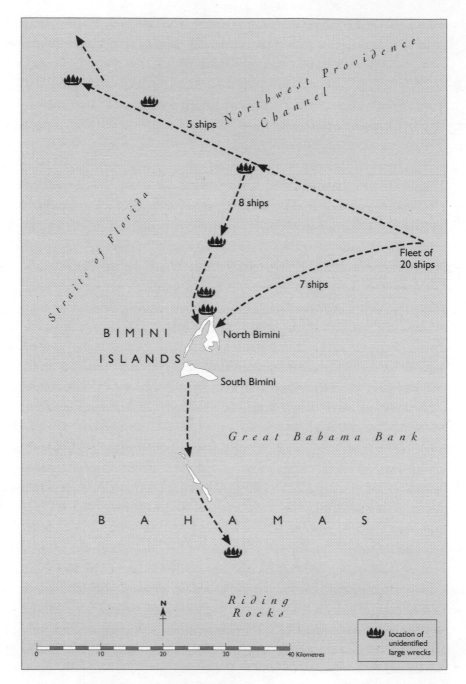

Locations of unidentified wrecks on the route to Bimini.

seemed sensible to see if the first European to reach Bimini had found anything, such as wrecks or porcelain, left behind by the Chinese. The first European on Bimini was Juan Ponce de León (c. 1460–1521), a Spanish conquistador and governor of Puerto Rico from 1510 to 1511. On 23 February 1512, he was given a commission by the King of Spain:

<u>The King</u>

To the officials of the island of Española upon the agreement which they have made with Juan Ponce de León upon that and the said island of Biminy which he has to go to discover.[5]

The king's eagerness to locate the mystical island of Bimini was based on the legend that its waters conferred perpetual youth on those who drank them: 'There is an island about three hundred and twenty-five leagues from Española in which there is a continual spring of running water of such marvellous virtue that, the water thereof being drunk, perhaps with some diet, maketh old men young again ... bathing in it, or in the fountain, old men were turned into youths.'[6] This legend was widespread before Columbus set sail. The waters have subsequently been identified as a foul-smelling sulphurous spring on the east side of North Bimini island. It can be reached via a shallow creek infested with caymans – members of the alligator family. Few kings could have resisted the allure of immortality, however remote the possibility, and such a discovery would have been of incalculable commercial value. There was not a rich man living who would not have exchanged the greater part of his wealth for the promise of eternal youth, as is the case to this day.

The bays to the north and south of Bimini are clearly marked on the Cantino chart, drawn twelve years before Ponce de León set sail. Someone must have been there before him, not only to draw the island that appears on the Cantino but to convey descriptions of its magical spring. Bimini is only a few feet high and can be circumnavigated in a day. It was uninhabited for centuries save for wreckers, who based themselves there for salvage during the hurricane seasons. In the twentieth century, Ernest Hemingway took a liking to the island and drank the night away in local bars while writing *The Old Man and the Sea*. Today, thousands of trippers come by seaplane and yacht from Florida to see Hemingway's haunts, oblivious of the history that surrounds them.

In September 1968, Dr Mason Balantyne, a zoologist and under-water archaeologist, was swimming off North Bimini. He was in ten feet of water about a thousand yards from the shore when he spotted hundreds of flat rocks, eight to ten feet square, arranged in regular patterns. His discovery, named the 'Bimini Road', comprises two parallel lines of stones on the sand dunes of Bimini Bay running south-west towards the deep ocean. The western section starts at an angle of 160° to the beach and curves round to run directly to the shore. The curved part, some 330 feet long, is composed of large, well-laid stones. The straight, shoreward section is 1,200 feet long by 200 feet wide and has a trench in the middle where there are no slabs. (The website has further details.)

In 1974, an American scientist, Dr David Zink, led an expedition (the first of nine) to survey these mysterious stones. He produced overwhelming evidence that the road was man-made. Small stones are placed underneath large ones, apparently to make the sea-bed level, and the larger of the two structures contains arrow-shaped 'pointers' that can only have been man-made. Parts of the road contain stones cut to the same size and laid in rows, and some small square stones have tongued and grooved joints. The mineral micrite, foreign to America and almost always found in association with lead and zinc ores, was also lying on the sea-bed around the stones. They have been submerged over a long span of time, for the edges of some have become rounded by wave action, giving them something of the appearance of huge loaves of bread. Some of them were not of Caribbean origin. The road is clearly visible from the air through the azure water. It runs straight as a die down into the depths, a broad band of beige stone. After Dr Zink's expeditions, Jacques Cousteau surveyed the 'road' in detail for a television programme,[7] and *National Geographic* has published several features. The 'road' has been surveyed by a number of different experts, and there is almost universal agreement that the structure is man-made.

Dr Zink later reached the bizarre conclusion that the stones of the Bimini road were part of the fallen pillars of a sacred temple built about 28,000 BC by a long-lost civilization, the Atlanteans, who employed aliens from the star cluster Pleiades to build a megalithic temple complex similar to Stonehenge.[8] Although I disagree with the strange conclusions Dr Zink reached, they do not detract from the value of his basic observations, measurements and surveys, which were meticulous.

As Admiral Zhou Wen's fleet made for Bimini, many of his ships must have been holed below the waterline, with one or more flooded compartments. The captains of the crippled junks desperately needed to beach them before they sank so that they could carry out repairs to the hulls and pump out the sea-water before it reached the rice that was their principal food supply. The standard practice with crippled ships, established over centuries and used extensively during the Second World War, is for damaged ones to be lashed alongside seaworthy ones to keep them afloat and offer all possible assistance. It is likely that some flooded horse and grain ships were tied to capital ships limping towards the shore. One can imagine the relief of the seamen and concubines as they saw the sandy spit of land fringed by palm trees.

As soon as they saw North Bimini, the ships' captains would have made straight for it. Since the water levels in 1421 were approximately one fathom lower than today, and the junks drew an average of two fathoms (twelve feet), depending on the cargo or ballast they were carrying, I calculated that the junks would have grounded where today there is eighteen feet of water – the depth of the seaward end of the Bimini Road. The inverted 'J' section at that end is in the exact position a junk rounding the Great Bahama Bank and then turning directly towards North Bimini would have beached.

This supposition enabled me to look at the Bimini Road with fresh eyes. As I studied it, I hit upon a possible solution to the mystery of the road's purpose. Could the road have been a slipway made of smooth stone to prevent further damage to the hulls of ships being beached and refloated? The curved section of the road could have acted as a turntable. When one of the treasure ships beached, its keel and rudder would have prevented it from being dragged sideways to the shore. The great ship's stern would have had to be swivelled to face the beach before it could be hauled ashore backwards. When I drew a treasure ship and a grain ship on the same scale as the road, and then rotated their sterns, the treasure ship ended up on the larger stretch of road and the grain ship on the smaller. Both roads had grooves for the ships' keels and rudders, enabling them to be dragged stern first to the beach.

Obtaining stones and rocks of the required size for the Bimini slipway would have been a simple exercise. The junks would have contained thousands of tons of stone ballast. Zhou Wen's fleet carried gunpowder that could be used to blow up rocks, and Chinese stone masons were aboard the ships. They had built thousands of miles of Great Wall between 1403 and 1421 using a wide variety of percussion hammers, drills, awls, saws and sledgehammers. Assuming, for reasons I shall explain later, that fifteen treasure ships had reached Bimini, about six thousand sailors and concubines would have been available as labourers. At first sight, laying the stones on the sea-bed appears problematic, but the Chinese also had more than six centuries' experience of building coffer-dams, water-tight enclosures pumped dry using 'Archimedes' screw-pumps (centuries before Leonardo da Vinci 'invented' them) to permit work below the waterline. By the early Ming period they even had diving equipment with breathing tubes and face masks.[9] Laying stonework under water was a problem they were well equipped to overcome.

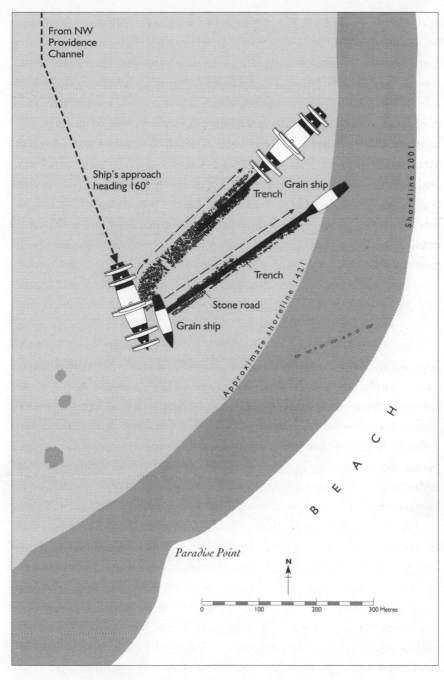

From NW
Providence
Channel

Ship's approach
heading 160°

Trench

Grain ship

Trench

Stone road

Grain ship

Shoreline 2001

Approximate shoreline 1421

BEACH

Paradise Point

N

0   100   200   300 Metres

The junks' approach to Bimini and the Bimini Road.

When the slipway had been completed, each huge ship would have had to be hauled ashore in turn, keeping the rudder and keel in the groove. Again, this appears to be a tremendous engineering challenge, but although the treasure ships displaced thousands of tons, Chinese engineers had developed a wide variety of capstans using wire or hemp ropes in order to haul ships. The capstans had geared ratchet-wheels and differential drives, and were designed to be powered by men or horses. The Chinese would have expected their square-rigged junks with shallow draughts and flat bottoms to run aground occasionally, and it is probable that the crew's training included practising hauling flooded ships ashore for repairs. It was reasonable to suppose that the necessary equipment would have been aboard each ship to enable them to do so.

There remained several unsolved puzzles that did not yet fit my scenario. Many of the big rectangular stones were not made from rock found at Bimini. The bedrock there was softer, and laid in a far more disordered pattern than the 'imported' slabs.[10] The 'cement' which appeared to bond the sections also differed. Dr Zink found one sample to be dominated by aragonite crystals, another by spalling calcite, implying that adjacent stones had different physical properties and hence had been formed in different locations. But why would it be necessary to transport huge stones and those square 'building blocks' to Bimini when there was plenty of usable rock there – unless they were part of the ballast carried by the Chinese junks?

Dr Zink sent a sample to the Brookhaven National Laboratory on Long Island. As it had never been fired in a kiln, they were unable to carbon-date the blocks but the head chemist, Dr Edward V. Sayre, confirmed that some of the smaller square blocks were made with a sandstone-limestone mixture and suggested that they 'might have been created by an ancient technique of mass production'. Moreover, each 'building block' was tongued and grooved to slot into its neighbour, and although they had square sides, they tapered in thickness. There appeared to be no need for the tongue and groove on the sea-bed, for the stones were not joined together with them. The solution could be that the building blocks were tongued and grooved so that they could be joined together around ballast in the bottom of a junk, preventing the large stones from moving in a heavy sea and damaging the hull.

A junk's beam was very wide in comparison to its length, and because it was flat-bottomed, substantial ballast was required. The displacement of the capital ships was around 3,400 tons; according to standard nautical engineering I would expect each of them to have carried between five and six hundred tons of ballast – around thirty tons in each of the eighteen watertight compartments. The slipway is composed of a mixture of local rock, building blocks and large 'imported' stones. Some 450 of the latter are still in place on the slipway, but in recent years dredgers have removed part of it to build a seawall in Miami. I calculated that originally there were about six hundred stones on the slipway, each weighing about ten tons, the equivalent of the ballast carried by a dozen junks.

I could now reconstruct a plausible scenario for what had happened. A junk hit the shore, its hull fractured, and some stones or building blocks spilled out onto the sea-bed – the first part of the 'road'. To increase buoyancy, other large stones might have been lowered through the ruptured hulls using long stones as 'straps' beneath them, held by ropes at either end. The 'support' stones on the sea-bed might have been the straps left when the stone reached the sea-bed.

Although the 'imported' large stones[11] are commonplace (save in the Caribbean) throughout the world, they are found in the Yangtze area and could have been mined and cut to size in the Ming quarries in the eastern suburbs of Nanjing, where the treasure ships were built. The building blocks on the sea-bed are one *chi* (thirty-two centimetres) square, and the sandstone-limestone mixture used to make them was widely available in the Yangtze area. Yangtze limestone's porosity is less than 2 per cent and its permeability almost zero, making it very suitable for building blocks; it is still used for that purpose in China.

That left one remaining mystery, the mineral micrite found on the sea-bed. Micrite is not found in the Caribbean; it was not traded in 1421 and had no commercial value, other than its association with metal ores. Why would the junks be carrying it? China's Qinlin Devonian belt, covering the upper Yangtze basin, contains one of the world's largest micrite deposits, with about twenty million tons of lead and zinc reserves. The most valuable deposit is at Changba, a short distance to the west of Wuhan in the middle Yangtze, some four hundred miles upriver from Nanjing. Ferries still ply between Nanjing and Wuhan. Emperor Zhu Di invested heavily in construction projects at Wuhan, the most spectacular among them the Golden Hall on Heavenly Pillar Peak, which can still be seen today. Built in 1416 entirely from gilded copper, it was the world's largest copper building and symbolized the importance of an area that had been a copper mining centre for two thousand years and a source of the copper used to mint the imperial currency. The scale and value of copper production at Wuhan can be illustrated by the canal Zhu Di commissioned, linking the Changba mine to the Yangtze. With copper and zinc deposits, Nanjing's marine engineers had the metals they needed to make brass, required in large volumes for the bolts – each of them six *chi* long and weighing around seven kilograms – that held together the watertight compartments of the treasure ships. Once the zinc and copper ores had been sifted from the micrite deposits, the residual micrite soil could well have been used for packing the stone ballast of ships in the Nanjing yards. That may explain the mineral's presence on the floor of the Caribbean around the stones of the Bimini Road.

Once the junks had been hauled onto the beach, the sea-water could be pumped out and the urgent task of drying the rice stores could begin. The Chinese crewmen would have been able to supplement their basic diet with the abundant conches, turtles and gamefish around Bimini. Water could be obtained from the celebrated spring, the bubbling pool of sulphurous water later described to Ponce de León as a fountain of life. But however skilful the

Chinese carpenters, some junks would have been damaged beyond repair. They would have been cannibalized, their holds emptied of stores, their hull planking used for the repair of potentially seaworthy junks and for firewood. The remainder of the hulls would have been left as giant wooden skeletons on the beach beyond the slipway. If this had happened, some evidence might remain.

In 1989, Raymond E. Leigh, a land surveyor attached to Dr Zink's expedition, flew across North Bimini and took measurements with infra-red equipment of the north-eastern end of the island, opposite the place where the slipway comes ashore. He discovered four rectangular sand mounds, the largest 500 feet long and 300 feet wide. Their size and shape suggest that they may be the sand-covered hulls of treasure ships, and they are just where I would expect to find the skeletons of junks swept ashore by a hurricane. Another mound was found by Dr Zink on the beach near the slipway. As Chinese warships, the remains of the junks may technically still be the property of the Chinese government. Negotiations are in hand between the Bahamian authorities and myself to resolve the issue of ownership of any artefacts that may be found. When these protracted negotiations are complete, archaeologists may be allowed to excavate the mounds. Their contents may yield detailed knowledge of Zhou Wen's fleet, and perhaps some of the treasure it carried. It could be a priceless discovery in every sense: each junk could carry two thousand tons of cargo, and a single early Ming plate was recently auctioned for £89,500.[12]

I concluded that four junks had sunk just short of North Bimini, another five had been abandoned on East Bimini and the remainder had been repaired and refloated. The lost ships would have carried several thousand sailors and concubines, and Bimini could probably not have supported more than a hundred. A large number would have been taken aboard the surviving junks, but it is inconceivable that room could have been found to carry all of them back to China. Some must have been left on Bimini, others put ashore wherever conditions seemed to offer better hope of survival. As Admiral Zhou

Wen's shrunken fleet continued its voyage, its upper decks crowded with crew and passengers from the abandoned junks, many others must have been left to their fate, as happened to sailors from Columbus's ships seventy years later: one of his ships and crew were left behind on Hispaniola. Once the available food on Bimini was exhausted, the abandoned Chinese would have had to attempt the crossing to Cuba, the nearest large island, some 180 miles to the south, or to Florida. Had they managed to do so, some of their descendants should have been alive when Columbus arrived.

In the summer of 1494, on Columbus' second voyage, he anchored his ships off Cuba near a beautiful palm grove to get fresh water and wood.

As the landing party cut wood and filled their water casks, an archer strayed into the forest in search of game, only to return a few minutes later to relate a baffling and frightening experience . . . He had come across a band of about thirty well-armed Indians . . . three white men were in the company of the natives.

The white men, who wore white tunics which reached to their knees, immediately spotted the intruder . . . one of them stepped towards the hunter and started to speak.[13]

The hunter then fled. Upon hearing his story, Columbus despatched another party who failed to find the men. White men with 'white tunics which reached to their knees' is the description local people in Mexico (Jucutácato) and Australia (Arnhem Land) gave to the strangers landing on their shores. Not without reason did Columbus conclude that the men were people of Mangon (China) and that he had reached the shores of Asia.[14]

In isolation, the description of the men in white tunics who greeted Columbus's men could be taken with a pinch of salt, but explorer after explorer in continent after continent reported the same story, all along the Chinese track I had reconstructed from the charts published before the first Europeans reached those continents. In South America, the Spanish envoy, Don Luis Arias, recounted tales in the sixteenth century of light-coloured people who wore white woven garments and crossed the Pacific after leaving what is now Chile. Father Monclaro, a Jesuit priest who accompanied a Portuguese expedition to East Africa in 1569, described the inhabitants of Pate whose claim to be descendants of shipwrecked Chinese sailors was reinforced by their story of the giraffe, the 'quilin' presented to Emperor Zhu Di. Indian sailors reported a Chinese expedition to Antarctica following the Southern Cross constellation. In southern Australia, the Yangery tribe, living beside the wreck of a 'mahogany' ship, claimed that 'yellow men' had settled among them; and in northern Australia the Aborigines said that a honey-coloured people, the men wearing long robes and the women pantaloons, had settled in north-east Arnhem Land. The Maoris made a similar claim, and the French explorer Bougainville reported meeting Chinese people in the Pacific in 1769. It is scarcely credible that all these accounts are imaginary or fabricated.

The Bimini Road has, of course, excited great controversy and interest. All sorts of exotic ideas and theories have been put forward; mine is but the latest. I fully accept that it requires some leaps of the imagination that are not, as yet, backed up by hard evidence. Only when the Bahamian authorities grant permission for the archaeological excavation of the sand mounds on the beach will we be able to determine whether or not my theory is correct. For the time being, frustrating though it was, I had to leave the mounds undisturbed and depart from Bimini, following in the wake of Admiral Zhou Wen as he assembled the remnants of his fleet and sailed northwards.

13

SETTLEMENT IN NORTH AMERICA

十三

IN SOLVING THE IMMEDIATE PROBLEM OF HIS DAMAGED AND destroyed ships, Admiral Zhou Wen had fallen foul of another. Some of his ships were again seaworthy and some of the rice had been salvaged, but he now had to make provision for the crews and concubines from the wrecks that had been left on the beach at Bimini. There would have been several thousand additional sailors and several hundred concubines to be accommodated and fed from a much-reduced food supply. The rulers of many Arabian, African and Indian states had been served by the concubines. Many must have been pregnant when the fleet left India, and some would already have given birth. The only way to cope with the chronic overcrowding in the surviving junks would have been to create settlements ashore where some of the crewmen, concubines and their children at least had a chance of survival. A later voyage would have to return for them.

If such Chinese settlements had been made in North America, evidence should exist, but my problem, as ever, was to locate it. Along the Florida coast marked on the Cantino map, the cartographer drew the Florida Keys, Port Sewall, Cape Canaveral and the Savannah estuary. I know Cape Canaveral well. I was operations officer on HMS *Resolution* when we fired Britain's first Polaris missile there in February 1968. It splashed down 2,800 miles away off South America, just fifteen feet shy of the target buoy – the splash as the warhead hit the water temporarily blinded the reading apparatus. As we surfaced back in Florida, we found sea snakes nestling in the conning tower, attracted by the submarine's warmth. The cape itself is a bleak place, renowned for its manatees, the strange sea mammals that gave birth to the legend of the mermaids. Both Cape Canaveral and St Augustine are littered with wrecks, some of them ancient and unidentified, but the fierce current has carried away the timbers to such an extent that identification is very difficult. Nonetheless, the attempt is in hand.

The Cantino ends abruptly at the estuary of the Savannah River, at Point Tybee. This suggested that, having reached this point, the

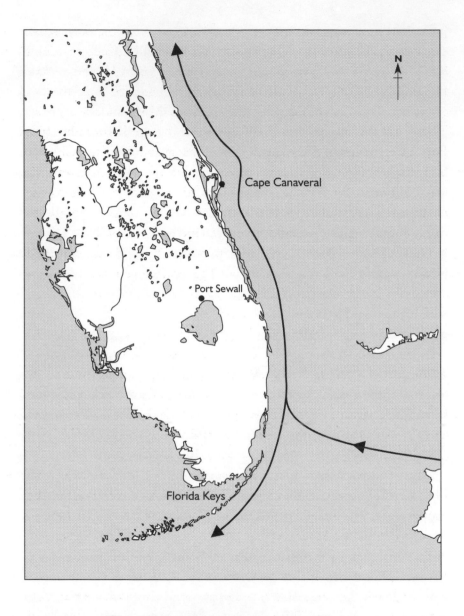

Zhou Wen's journey up the east coast of Florida.

junks had then been carried away from land towards the north-east, exactly the direction in which the prevailing winds and the Gulf Stream run there. These would have carried the junks up to Cape Hatteras in North Carolina. Off Cape Hatteras, the Gulf Stream divides in two, one branch flowing north-east towards the Azores. Those islands appear on the Kangnido, drawn before the first Portuguese reached the islands, and I was certain that the Chinese had reached them. The other, westerly branch of the current off Cape Hatteras flows at first due north, then slowly rotates to the north-east past Philadelphia. At latitude 40°N, the current flows inshore towards Long Island, Rhode Island and Cape Cod.

Once again, this part of the coast is littered with unidentified wrecks, many of them ancient, and a sensible point to begin a detailed search for traces of the Chinese was at the latitude of Beijing – 39°53′N. On the course the junks were taking, they would have reached this point off the coast of modern New Jersey. I have taken my submarine up that coast and can confirm that a huge volume of water flows north-east and the wind and current push ships directly towards Cape Cod. I began the search around Narragansett Bay and Buzzards Bay, and on the Cape Cod peninsula, making sure first of all to consult the accounts of the first Europeans to reach this part of the coast.

The renowned Venetian explorer Giovanni de Verrazzano (c. 1480–c. 1527) arrived there in 1524, twenty-two years after the Cantino was produced. Francis I of France had retained him to explore the North American coast with the aim of finding a seaway to the Pacific and the Spice Islands – 'the happy shores of Cathay'.[1] Verrazzano's voyage was carried out at the same time as the Spanish sent Magellan around South America and the Portuguese despatched a series of expeditions around the Cape of Good Hope. All three countries were in a race to find the most cost-effective and secure means of reaching the Spice Islands of Ternate and Tidore now that the overland route to the East, the Silk Road, had been severed.

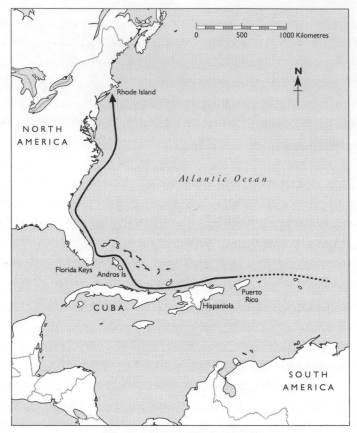

The journey to Rhode Island.

In 1524, Verrazzano with his small squadron sailed northwards up the coast from Virginia to the eastern tip of Nova Scotia, describing the pleasant land and its savage people as he went. When at the parallel of Rome, '41 degrees and 2 terstices north', he entered a large bay, corresponding with Narragansett Bay off Rhode Island, where he spent fifteen days. The local people were

the colour of brass, some of them incline more to whiteness: others are of yellow colour, of comely visage, with long and black hair, which they are very careful to trim and deck up; they are black and quick eyed, and of sweet and pleasant countenance . . .

The women are of the like conformity and beauty; very handsome and well favoured, of pleasant countenance and comely to behold; they are as well-mannered and continent as any woman, and of good education ... [women] use other kinds of dressing themselves like unto the women of Egypt and Syria; these are of the elder sort: and when they are married, they wear divers toys [jewellery] according to the usage of the people of the East, as well men as women.[2]

This is a very significant passage. Verrazzano was comparing elegant people with brass-coloured skin to the much darker and more uncouth people he had met further south. He referred twice to the women's connection with the East and their clothes – dresses rather than the furs and animal skins worn by the people he had encountered previously. Most important of all, Verrazzano was not describing local women married to foreigners, but women resembling those from the East who had somehow ended up in North America. Clearly they were from a different civilization and were not natives of North America, nor of Europe.

Verrazzano's description suggests that the younger girls were not following their grandmothers' traditions; the original customs they had brought were dying out, indicating that they had been there a few generations. The description would indeed have fitted Syrian or Egyptian women just as much as it would Chinese. All of these women would have worn long dresses and jewellery and had their black hair decked up, but Egyptian and Syrian seafarers never reached the Atlantic; in any case, their women were not taken on long voyages. The description would fit the descendants of the Chinese concubines pregnant by Middle Eastern rulers and ambassadors. It could have been they who greeted Verrazzano.

There is another clue in Verrazzano's account of leaving Narragansett Bay: 'In the midst of this entrance [to the harbour] there is a rock of stone produced by nature apt to build any castle or fortress there, for the keeping of the haven ... which we call La Petra Viva [the living rock].'[3] Verrazzano's description fits the rock

The Rhode Island Tower.

on which the Round Tower still stands, in a park in Newport, Rhode Island, on a promontory overlooking the harbour. The tower is a mystery; visitors muse over whether or not it was built by strange people who arrived before Columbus. To me it is a curiosity, quite unlike any other colonial building in America, placed in isolation, in a commanding position but not a fortress, and out of the wind, so unlikely to be a mill. Historians have furiously debated its origins. One school claims it was a sixteenth-century flour mill, another that it served as a lighthouse and was built around the end of the fourteenth century. Both theories could be correct; an earlier building could have been modified to serve as a flour repository, if not a mill. Historians in the flour-mill camp rely for their evidence on the first

Rhode Island governor, Benedict Arnold, a prosperous merchant whose will referred to 'my stone builte tower'.

A detailed survey of the tower by the respected Danish Committee for Research on Norse Activities in North America AD 1000–1500 took place in the early 1990s. The publication in 1992 of the results of investigations and analyses seemed to confirm the flour-mill thesis. The report, prepared by Johannes Hertz of the National Museum in Copenhagen, concluded that Arnold was the builder in 1667, but an American architect, Suzanne O. Carlson, who has made a meticulous examination of the tower, recently challenged these findings.[4] She argued that closer study of the report revealed the tower could not have been built by Arnold at that date, and she cited four specific pieces of scientific evidence in support of her argument.

Firstly, she contended that every seventeenth-century colonial structure in New England was built using English measurements – yards, feet and inches – yet not a single dimension of the Newport Round Tower conforms. Secondly, she claimed that the seventeenth-century trench surrounding the tower, which the flour-mill camp says supports their argument, could only have been built to stabilize an earlier building. Thirdly, she argued that the Danish committee's carbon-dating was based on a new and experimental technique that measured the carbon 14 in carbon dioxide bubbles in the mortar. The actual range of dates measured was between 1410 and 1970, and while the Danish committee attributed it to the late 1600s, the analysis could equally well apply to any date after 1409. Lastly, the tower was built using an unusual type of mortar made from crushed shells, rather than the standard lime mortar habitually used by colonial builders.

However, the details of the tower's construction do not reveal its purpose, which has been described as follows:

> The first storey of the tower served as a lighthouse. The larger windows of
> the first storey were so placed in relation to the fireplace that the light from

the fire at night seen through the south window would be a guide to a ship approaching the entrance to Narragansett Bay . . . fireplace light through the two-foot opening of the west window would guide a ship to the harbour landing at the bottom of Tower Hill . . . The ingenious builder of the tower had obviously had considerable experience . . . in designing lighthouses.[5]

The Norse were present in Greenland from the end of the tenth to the early fifteenth century. Greenland had no wood, so each summer they set sail to Vinland – North America – to gather wood, returning each autumn. At first sight the narrow windows and rounded arches of the Rhode Island tower appeared Romanesque, and my initial reaction was that it was a lighthouse built by the Norsemen. It could have been; they had penetrated nearly as far south as Newport. However, the Norse had little experience of lighthouse design and are not known to have built one overseas; and in my view the design and position of the windows closely resembled those on the Song dynasty (960–1279) lighthouse that guided Chinese and Arab trading fleets into the port of Zaiton (Quanzhou) in Fujian province in southern China. A number of the crewmen aboard the Chinese fleet would certainly have known Zaiton and its lighthouse, for at the time of the Chinese treasure fleets Zaiton was probably the largest commercial port in the world. Marco Polo described it as 'a great resort of ships and merchandise . . . for one spice ship that goes to Alexandria or elsewhere to pick up pepper for export to Christendom, Zaiton is visited by a hundred. For you must know that it is one of the two ports in the world with the biggest flow of merchandise.'[6]

The Zaiton lighthouse is twice the size of the Newport Round Tower and is five storeys high rather than three, but the windows are notably similar, as is the design of the central fireplace. Like Zaiton, too, the tower at Newport was once covered in smooth plaster. There are several other striking resemblances. The Rhode Island tower is a grey shell of stones rising above arches that span eight columns set on an octagonal base, just as at Zaiton. The masonry consists of stones of various shapes held together by a powerful and long-lasting mortar; neither the stones at Newport nor those at Zaiton have moved since the wall was built. Furthermore, the dimensions of the tower show that it conforms to the standard Chinese units of measurement used in the fifteenth century: the external diameter is 2 *chang* 40 *chi* and the internal 1 *chang* 80 *chi* (1 *chang* = 10.167 feet; 1 *chi* = 32 centimetres).

Professor William Penhallow, Professor of Physics and Astronomy at the University of Rhode Island, offered an alternative explanation for the purpose of the Round Tower. He made a study of astronomical alignments and discovered that the seemingly random openings and asymmetrical, splayed window-jambs framed specific astronomical events, notably lunar eclipses and the rising and setting of the sun at its solstices and equinox.[7] This accords precisely with the design of Ming observatories and observation platforms. The length of the sun's shadow at solstice and equinox at any particular latitude gives the precise time, and viewing a lunar eclipse gave the Chinese the opportunity to observe the leading star on the zenith and so determine the longitude of the Newport Round Tower when they returned to Beijing,[8] just as they did with observation platforms around the world.

The tower could thus have served two vital purposes. It could have been used to determine the exact location of the settlement set up by the Chinese crewmen and concubines left behind, so that they could be found and rescued on a subsequent voyage of the treasure fleets. It could also have been a lighthouse to guide the rescuers safely into Narragansett Bay. Although now obscured by encroaching woods, the tower was sited in a prominent position and was once a distinctive landmark clearly visible from the sea. Like the Zaiton lighthouse, it was angled so that the light burning from its fire could warn of danger through one set of windows, but also act as a guide through another set to bring mariners to a safe anchorage.

An analysis of the mortar used in the Newport Round Tower would settle the matter once and for all, for Chinese mortar had a very distinctive property – it contained gypsum as a hardening and rice as a bonding agent. It can also be dated; from analysis of the mortar on the Great Wall, it has been possible to determine the different rice and gypsum contents used in the Tang and Ming eras, and therefore when each section of the wall was built. I have asked the authorities at Newport for permission to arrange an analysis, but this has been denied. The first duty of the authorities is of course to preserve the fabric of the monuments in their care, not to make them available for experiments, but I hope they can be persuaded to change their minds. It would then be possible not only to determine the nature of the mortar but also to date it, and early Ming is particularly easy to date.

There is a substantial body of evidence that the Chinese landed at Newport. They had reached Bimini and later the Azores, and a detailed cartographic survey of the coast of Florida had been carried out before the first European reached North America. The route from Bimini to New England and then the Azores is precisely the one a square-rigged sailing ship would have followed, before the wind and current all the way. And the first Europeans to reach New England described civilized white- or bronze-skinned women living around Newport who wore clothes of the East and dressed their hair in buns, as Chinese women did.

In view of all this evidence, it is more likely that the tower was erected by the Chinese, who had centuries of experience of lighthouse and observatory building, than by Norsemen, who had virtually no experience of either. The Newport Round Tower faces south, the direction from which the Chinese would have arrived, sailing with wind and current. It would have been useless to Norsemen approaching from Greenland to the north, sailing against the prevailing winds and currents.

I contend that the people Verrazzano met at what is now Newport, Rhode Island, can only have been Chinese men and women, the descendants of sailors and concubines from Zhou Wen's great fleet. Knowing the longitude of the tower, the junks of the next treasure fleet would have been able to sail directly to Newport, and it would have been natural for those stranded there to have built a lighthouse to guide their rescuers safely into harbour, protecting them from the tragedy that had overtaken Zhou Wen's fleet in the Caribbean. If my surmise was correct that Zhou Wen had several thousand men and concubines to land around Narragansett Bay, a substantial amount of evidence should remain in the countryside surrounding the Newport tower. I would expect at least to find stones similar to those the Chinese erected elsewhere on their journey.

I began my search on the internet to see if there were any carved stones in eastern Massachusetts. My search produced immediate and dramatic results. Thirty miles upriver from the tower is the celebrated Dighton Rock. It is a free-standing, easily identifiable rock of a distinctive reddish-brown colour with an exposed face measuring approximately five feet high by eleven feet wide. It stands on the banks of the Taunton River and is covered with ancient carvings, on top of which is a Portuguese cross and graffiti. In that respect, Dighton Rock strongly resembles examples in the Cape Verde Islands and at the Matadi Falls. I felt that another link in the ever-lengthening chain of evidence had fallen into place.

Dighton Rock would have been the logical place for any explorer of the Taunton River to stop to leave a mark. It is the largest rock in the bay on the south side of what is now Perry Point, the northern-most point any large vessel can reach along the Taunton River. Above Perry Point, the river narrows to under two hundred feet and the depth falls to a few feet. It is the reason why the Taunton Yacht Club is located there rather than further north.

The rock was first drawn in 1680 by a local clergyman, Mr Danforth, who also related the legend associated with the rock that had passed into the folklore of the local Indians: 'Then there came a wooden house (and men of another country in it) swimming up the River Asooner [as the River Taunton was then called] who fought the Indians with some mighty success.'[9] The Chinese themselves described their junks as 'wooden houses', as did other observers such as Niccolò da Conti and Pedro Tafur, a Spanish traveller to whom da Conti related his story (see chapter 4). In 1421, the sea level was some six feet lower than today, and the rock, now covered at high water, would have been above the waterline in all but the highest spring tide. It was certainly respected and deemed old by local native Americans:

> This monument was esteemed by the oldest Indians not only very antique but a work of a different nature from any of theirs ... some reckon the figures here to be hieroglyphicall [sic] the first figure representing a ship without masts, and a mere wrack [wreck] cast upon the shoals. The second representing an head of land, possibly a cape with a peninsula. Hence a gulf.[10]

This description accords with the dreadful experiences a few weeks earlier of Zhou Wen's fleet.

After Mr Danforth's drawing of 1680, at least six more were made before 1830. However, it was the practice of local boatmen to take tourists to the rock and scrub off the algae to reveal the hieroglyphics underneath, and as time went by fewer and fewer of the hieroglyphics remained legible and the drawings grew more and more extravagant and fanciful, and bearing little relation to Mr Danforth's sketch. Whatever message the stone carried can no longer be read, and sadly all I or anyone else can conclude is that the rock was carved in a non-European language by foreign mariners sailing upriver in a ship like a house, that the inscription described a shipwreck and that the Portuguese later found the rock and inscribed a cross upon it.

I next searched the work of local historians for further evidence. Narragansett Bay is open to the North Atlantic and experiences brutal winter weather. Snowstorms lash the coast, and the native Americans who inhabited this bleak region, even the wild animals, sought refuge inland, away from the worst of the weather. It would have been natural for the Chinese also to seek shelter up one of the arms of the bay, and the Taunton River was the most obvious route.

It was the native Americans' highway to the interior, and it would have been logical for the Chinese to sail upriver to the highest navigable point, beside Dighton Rock, to escape the sudden squalls that might have caused the ships to drag their anchors and run aground.

In the 1950s, just before a housing development started at Perry Point, a cluster of very old stone buildings was found. They were all the same size, arranged in a cruciform pattern and held together by mortar. Hops and wild rice, not indigenous to the area, grew nearby. No-one at the time thought the matter sufficiently important to attempt to stop the housing development or to arrange an extensive excavation.[11] Could this have been a settlement established by the Chinese? Sadly we will never know as all traces of these buildings have been destroyed.

Professor Delabarre, a distinguished North American historian,[12] contended that there were noticeable differences in physiology and colouration between the 'pure blood Wampanoag Indians' living near Dighton Rock and adjacent tribes in Massachusetts. Based upon this, he postulated that while exploring what is now Narragansett Bay, the ship of the Portuguese explorer Miguel Cortreal was wrecked in 1510.[13] He and his crew were accepted by the Wampanoag and intermarried within the tribe. Professor Delabarre's theory could, of course, also apply to the bronze-skinned people Verrazzano met. The Wampanoag later proved hospitable to the first pilgrims, contrary to experiences elsewhere: male pilgrims were frequently killed by other tribes and women and possessions taken. One can speculate that the Wampanoag might earlier have been fairly treated by shipwrecked Chinese.

I began to search for more corroborative evidence such as other carved stones, without any great hope of finding any. After discovering the Cape Verde stone, I had spent considerable time searching for inscribed rocks around each Chinese landfall and had very rarely found more than one, at most two, in any one area. To my amazement, I discovered no fewer than twelve curious stones in one small area of eastern Massachusetts.[14] The size, position and aspect of these rocks was strikingly similar to those I located on the Cape Verde Islands, at the Matadi Falls on the Congo River and at Ruapuke beach in New Zealand. Many were propped up with round stones at one corner in precisely the same way as the Cape Verde stone. Someone must have pushed the rocks into this odd position, recalling the description given by the Aborigines of foreign visitors to Australia 'pushing the rocks in long lines'.

I decided to plot these stones on a map of eastern Massachusetts and immediately saw that they were either beside the Taunton River in the south, the Merrimack River in the north or around Massachusetts Bay. What appears highly likely is that the people who hauled the huge stones into position had sailed upriver, one 'great house' sailing up the Taunton River, another up the Merrimack.

One of these stones, the 'Shutesbury', appears to have carved upon it a figure of a seated Buddha in the classic position. If the carving could be dated to the pre-Columbus period this would be highly significant but unfortunately the museums I have approached so far have been unable to give a final opinion of the date. Curiously, at North Salem, a hundred miles south of Shutesbury, there is an instantly recognizable carving of a horse – pre-Columbus. If the people who raised the stones had used horses the likelihood would be that they came with horse-ships, for the rocks were found in place by the first European settlers and horses died out in North America round 10,000 BC. At this stage all one can say is that it is possible the huge stones were hauled into position by people using horses. The investigations continue and the results will be posted on the 1421 website.

It could be argued that the similarities of site, size, shape and method of support among the twelve large stones found in eastern Massachusetts and those in the Cape Verde Islands, at the Matadi Falls and at Ruapuke beach are coincidental, and that the in-scriptions on the Dighton Rock represented shipwrecked mariners other than the Chinese, but I was sure the Chinese fleet had reached

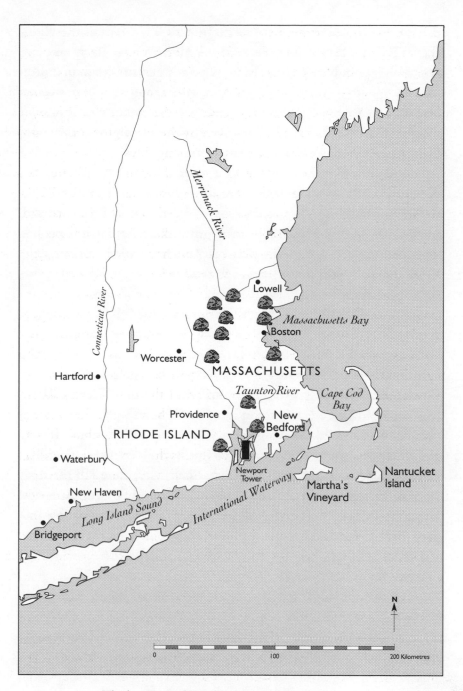

The locations of standing stones in Massachusetts.

the Caribbean, and later the Azores. In between these two landfalls, the winds and currents would have taken them to exactly the place where the rocks have been found. The most plausible explanation is that the rocks were erected by the Chinese and that the women Verrazzano met were the descendants of Chinese concubines. I suggest that the first settlers of North America came not with Columbus nor any other European pioneer, but in the junks of Admiral Zhou Wen's fleet, landing around Christmas 1421. Perhaps New England should now be renamed New China.

After establishing the settlements, the junks would have set sail. How desolate the crew and concubines left ashore must have felt, watching the great red sails unfurl and fill with wind, carrying the junks away. Those lining the beach would have strained their eyes until the ships were no larger than specks on the horizon, and as they turned away at last, their hearts must have been full of foreboding. No doubt promises were made that the next great treasure fleet would return for them, bringing fresh supplies and more people and carrying those who so wished back to their homeland. As the years passed, amid the daily struggle to survive – building shelters, catching fish, tilling the soil and foraging inland for food – they must have paused often to cast their eyes out to sea, raking the horizon for the first smudge of red that might signal the arrival of a rescue fleet. But as the years went by, hope must have faded, as must talk of their homeland, constant in the conversation of the old but dimming to a half-remembered tale and then forgotten altogether by succeeding generations. Not one single Chinese ship ever returned to collect them.

A magnificent Ming porcelain bowl, decorated with a phoenix and a quilin, recovered from the Pandanan wreck.

The Jean Rotz world map, 1542.

Chinese influence abroad: a contemporary lacquer chest produced in Mexico (*opposite, main image*); the Cherokee rose (*opposite, inset*) originating in China and found in North America.

Artefacts recovered from the Pandanan wreck, including a bronze ceremonial saluting cannon (*top*), a bronze mirror (*above left*), a coin of Zhu Di's reign (*centre right*) and grinding stones from Central America (*above and right*).

The Waldseemüller map of 1507.

The Pizzigano chart of 1424 and an enlarged detail of Antilia/Puerto Rico. The rectangular, blue island above is Satanazes/Guadeloupe.

EXPEDITION
TO THE
NORTH
POLE

ADMIRAL ZHOU WEN'S ALREADY DEPLETED FLEET WAS TO be further reduced in strength on the next stage of its epic voyage, for the surviving medieval maps suggest that as the Chinese fleet crossed the icy waters of the North Atlantic, it was divided into two squadrons. One set sail even further to the north; the other carried on eastwards and, swept before the winds and currents, it would have been approaching the Azores from the north-west within a month of leaving New England. The Azores chain stretches four hundred miles from north-west to south-east, and the first island the Chinese would have sighted approaching from the Americas is the most north-westerly of the Azores, the small but dramatic island of Corvo on the same latitude as Beijing.

Like Santo Antão in the Cape Verde Islands and Guadeloupe, Corvo is dominated by a huge volcano, the long-extinct Caldeirão, usually capped by a large white cloud. Streams tumble down the sides of the volcano, visible from miles out into the Atlantic. Only five miles long, the island looks verdant green, rising above a sea of the deepest blue, but the living is hard, for there is only a narrow strip of fertile land on the south shore around what is now the capital, Vila Nova, between the foothills of the volcano and the sea. All the houses huddle together as if begrudging even a single lost yard of the precious soil.

Here I began to look for a lighthouse, or a carved stone like the ones I had already located along the routes the Chinese had sailed. If it existed, it would have been placed in a prominent site and would have been noted by the Portuguese when they first discovered the island. The earliest account of the Portuguese arrival in the 1430s has this to say:

On the summit of a mountain on an island they call The Raven [Corvo] . . . a statue of a man seated upon a horse; his head is uncovered and he is bald; his left hand rests upon his horse, his right hand points towards the west. The statue is set firmly upon a stone base carved out of rock. At the bottom are inscriptions in a writing which we could not understand.

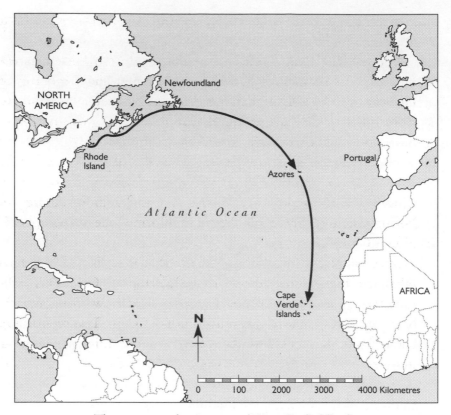

The voyage to the Azores and Cape Verde Islands.

This statement is significant on several counts. The people who carved the horse and the writing were clearly not European, and the horseman is not only hatless but bald. Some of the terracotta army guarding the Emperor Quin's tomb were depicted with shaven heads covered by a close-fitting stocking, like a tight hairnet. They do, indeed, look bare-headed and bald. The Corvo horseman is pointing to the west, to New England, the direction from which the Chinese would have arrived. The Azores are easy for a junk to reach from the Americas, but very difficult to reach from Portugal because from there ships would be sailing into the wind. That is why the Portuguese discovered them long after the Canaries and the Cape Verde Islands, despite the Azores being nearer to Portugal.

For me, the final confirmation that the Corvo horseman was indeed a Chinese statue, perhaps even of 'The Emperor on Horseback' Zhu Di, is that the Azores appear on the Chinese/Korean Kangnido chart, produced before the Portuguese discovered the islands. They had never appeared on any Arab maps, not even those of the famous historians Al Idrisi (1099–1166) and Ibn Khaldun (1332–1406). If the Azores were not discovered by the Chinese, who could have discovered the islands before the Portuguese, and why should they have informed the cartographer in distant China?

Surprisingly, corroborative evidence that the Chinese may have inhabited the Azores comes from Christopher Columbus, who reported a local story of non-European bodies washed onto the beach at Flores, some twenty miles south of Corvo. This report came before Columbus set sail for the Americas and Ferdinand Columbus indicates that his father believed these bodies, together with 'artistically carved pieces of wood', were evidence of contact between Cathay and the West.[2]

While one squadron of Admiral Zhou Wen's fleet set sail for home from the Azores via the Indian Ocean, the early maps show that the other squadron had taken a different route. South of the Grand Banks off Newfoundland,[3] the Gulf Stream separates. While the main body flows clockwise, carrying ships to the Azores and then via the Canaries to the Cape Verde Islands, a second, smaller part of the stream, the Irminger current, carries on to the east. Due south of Iceland, it veers counter-clockwise, first to the north, then the north-west and then north again, carrying a ship into the Davies Strait separating Greenland from northern Canada. There it becomes the West Greenland current, which flows up the west coast of Greenland, circles around the north coast and then comes back down the east coast as the East Greenland current, leading back into the Atlantic. Any ship circumnavigating Greenland in this way

The journey around Greenland.

would never have to sail into an opposing wind or current at any stage.

I was faced with two questions: why would the Chinese have wanted to circumnavigate such a barren, frozen land, and even if they had good reason to do so, was it actually possible? The answer to the first was easier to find than the second. The symbolic and practical significance of Polaris to the Chinese made fixing the absolute position of the North Pole of great importance. Not without reason had the emperor ordered them to reach 'the most northern of the northern ... countries', and to explore the nethermost parts of the earth – as their compatriots were doing in the far south, locating the South Pole.

I found the first circumstantial evidence that their thrilling gamble might have succeeded in two charts. The first was the Cantino, the remarkable medieval map that had already led me to so many discoveries about the Chinese voyages. The second chart was far more controversial: the Vinland map, dated to between 1420 and 1440. The Vinland map shows Newfoundland, Labrador and the whole of Greenland with great accuracy and in considerable detail. If it is genuine, it is proof that someone – perhaps the Chinese – had penetrated to within 250 miles of the North Pole four centuries before the first recorded European exploration of the High Arctic.

By using information from the Vinland map, I knew I would be opening a Pandora's box of controversy. The map's credibility has been attacked on many grounds. Its extraordinary provenance – it first appeared in 1965 from the back of a small Fiat car owned by a map-dealer – has made it suspect in many expert eyes. There is no shortage of historians who believe its cartography just too good to be true; Greenland is so accurately drawn that it simply must be a modern fake. Walter McCrone of McCrone Associates, a respected Chicago firm expert in chemical analysis, claimed in 1972 that the ink's composition, in particular its anatase content (a form of titanium that first appeared in inks in the 1920s) made impossible the purported date of the map's creation. However, in 1992, Dr Thomas Cahill of UC Davis found anatase in a variety of medieval manuscripts, reopening the question of the Vinland map's authenticity.

The other grounds for attacking the map's credibility are that the Norsemen who first settled Greenland had no cartographic know-

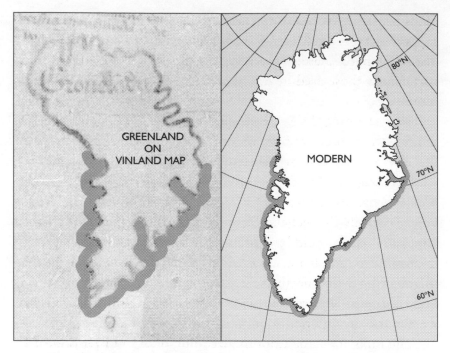

Greenland shown on the Vinland map, compared to a modern map.

ledge, only an oral tradition that substituted for map making, and the map could not conceivably have been drawn from an oral description. Furthermore, it was believed that Greenland could not have been circumnavigated, and that the names on the Vinland map supposedly placed there by Claudius Clavius, an eminent Danish cartographer who is believed to have drawn the map in about 1424, are fairytale names; surely the Norsemen would have told him what they had called places in the north. However, if the original cartographers had been Chinese, Clavius would probably not have been able to translate the names marked on the chart, which might explain why he felt the need to invent them. The ink remains the one controversial issue that has not yet been resolved. Several books have been written about it, and in addition to the research of Dr Cahill, McCrone Associates' assertion that it was faked has recently been challenged by no less an authority than the then Keeper of

Maps of the British Library, Mr R.A. Skelton. In this he has been supported by several learned professors corroborating Dr Cahill's discovery that anatase was in fact contained in some medieval inks, particularly those used in Alpine monasteries early in the fifteenth century.

Those claiming the Vinland map is a forgery have not remotely satisfied the burden of proof, and it is my belief that it is genuine and that the original cartographers who produced the information on which it was based were aboard several Chinese junks, at least one of which circumnavigated Greenland on a quest to reach the North Pole. To justify that belief, I had to answer the question of whether Greenland really could have been circumnavigated. It is completely impossible today, even in a nuclear-powered icebreaker, for the seas surrounding the far north are frozen solid all year round. However, there is direct evidence that conditions in the early fifteenth century were markedly different from those ruling today.

Contemporary accounts of the wedding of Sigrid Bjornsdottir in 1408, preserved in the state archives in Oslo, paint a very different picture of the land we know as Greenland. Sigrid was a widow; her father and sisters had died and she had inherited the family land, becoming the wealthiest landowner in Greenland. Her second marriage spawned a number of property transactions, allowing accurate deductions to be made about the livestock on her farms until she left Greenland in 1419. She possessed substantial flocks of sheep and cattle that fed on lush Greenland pastures, a scene quite unrecognizable from today's barren, ice-bound land. The church in which Sigrid was married still stands in bleak and splendid isolation above the dark fjord. We can imagine her that September Sunday as the service ended, hurrying from the church into the dark warmth of her house to begin her wedding celebrations.

Excavations of the floors of the houses in which she, her family and her retainers and servants lived show that the climate in Greenland was far warmer before the onset of a miniature Ice Age around the year 1450. The evidence is supplied by a change in the type of flies found during the excavations. Those that inhabit warm houses disappeared and were replaced by flies that can live in cold, empty houses off the rotting flesh of the dead. Evidence of an abrupt change in climate came from the skeleton of an elkhound whose throat had been slit – perhaps a last meal for the dying inhabitants. A valuable hunting dog would only have been slaughtered like this in the most dire circumstances, for without it a family's chances of killing enough game to survive the winter would be drastically reduced.

I found further corroboration of the change in climate in the accounts of Captain George Nares's voyage to the Arctic in 1875–6.[4] One of his ships reached 83°20' North, just nineteen miles from the northern tip of Greenland. An officer, Lieutenant Lockwood, marched the nineteen miles to the northernmost tip, Lockwood Island, later named after him.

The miniature Ice Age that started in 1450 (it is now ending) was partly caused by a shift in the earth's axis. By analysing the sailing directions and the star guide given in the *Wu Pei Chi* of 1422, I was able to calculate that the equator at that date was at 03°40' North. As a result, a corresponding shift of 3°40' northwards in the maximum and minimum limits of pack and drift ice would have occurred in both the northern and southern hemispheres. Corroboration that this shift did happen came from the ice shown on the Piri Reis map along the southern coasts of Tierra del Fuego, and from the Jean Rotz chart showing ice just south of Tasmania – approximately three hundred miles north of the normal limits today.

It is safe to conclude, therefore, that Greenland was circum-navigable in 1421–2, for not only was the maximum limit of the polar ice well to the north of its present position, the climate of Greenland was far warmer than it is today. In 1421 it would have been a country of green pastures where cattle grazed in the open from Pentecost (fifty days after Easter) to Cross Sunday (the second Sunday in September). The rivers were full of salmon, the coasts rich in walrus.

Additional corroboration that the Chinese did reach Greenland comes from a most curious letter written in 1448 by Pope Nicholas V to the bishops of Skalholt and Holar in Iceland, setting out the background to his desire to appoint a new bishop to Greenland: '[Thirty years ago,] the barbarians came from the nearby coast of the heathens, and attacked the inhabitants of Greenland most cruelly and so devastated the mother country and the holy buildings with fire and sword that there remained no more than nine parish churches . . . The pitiable inhabitants of both sexes they carried away . . . the greater number have since returned from captivity to their own houses.'[5] The Pope referred to 'barbarians' who came from 'the nearby coast of the heathens'. In other letters, he referred to the Inuit tribes of the Canadian Arctic as 'the heathen', so 'the nearby coast' can reasonably be assumed to refer to the Canadian Arctic. Addressing a Christian audience, the Pope distinguished between heathens and barbarians – they were not interchangeable terms. He cannot be referring to Norsemen – Greenland was a Norse colony – nor to any other Christian invader; they might have been heretics in the Pope's eyes, but they would not have been barbarians. In those days, as is commonly accepted, barbarians were people who invaded Europe from the East; the Pope was almost certainly referring to a Mongolian or Chinese invader of Greenland. The Pope would not have been referring to North American Indians as the barbarians, for these people had no 'swords' or 'fire' with which to fight. They used bows and arrows. I believe the only rational view to take is that this letter is describing a Chinese fleet arriving from North America and attacking the local people, perhaps with cannon (Hvalsey, Sigrid Bjornsdottir's home town and the main settlement of Greenland, was within cannon range from the sea). They took them away in their great ships then returned them. But why the Chinese should have acted in this uncharacteristic way is inexplicable. Perhaps they were attacked first.

Assuming that the Chinese did indeed reach the settlement at Hvalsey, the Vinland map should show where they had most accurately surveyed the coast, and therefore the sites where further direct evidence of settlements, wrecks and artefacts might be found. Peter Schlederman and Farley Mowat, two well-known authors and explorers, have carried out years of painstaking research in the High Arctic at the extraordinary villages of stone houses centred on the Bache Peninsula of Ellesmere Island, to the west of Greenland on the west shore of the Kane Basin, and made some remarkable discoveries.[6]

The colony on the Bache Peninsula is of particular interest. There are about twenty-five houses and a similar number of beacons on the peninsula, and some of the houses are immense – nearly 150 feet (45 metres) long and over 5 metres wide. The houses are so large and the stonework so well constructed that it is inconceivable they were built by Inuit peoples, who had no tradition of building in stone. They have other notable characteristics that make them quite unlike anything else found in the High Arctic. Stone beacons resembling small lighthouses were built alongside the houses, and there is one very curious omission: none of the houses has a roof. The Norse settlers of Greenland almost invariably roofed their houses with sod, but there is not a trace of such roofing on any of the houses on the Bache Peninsula. That there are no roofs at all is astounding. The buildings are large enough to have accommodated as many as three thousand people, but without a roof over their heads they would have been lucky to survive a single Arctic night. The ruined walls of the buildings can be seen today. Outside the houses, row upon row of hearths had been constructed, 142 in all, each separated from its neighbour by a stone wall. This multiple arrangement of outdoor hearths is again quite unique; nothing like it has ever been identified among prehistoric sites in the Canadian Arctic.

In trying to solve the mystery of these curious buildings, my first clue came from the local geography. The settlement at Ellesmere Island was built on a spit near a large polynya – a stretch of open water, a curious phenomenon found all the way to the North Pole. As I can vouch from navigating submarines under the ice in this part of the world, polynyas remain ice-free in both summer and winter. The reason for this is still not fully understood, but because they are permanently free of ice, they are extraordinarily attractive not only to submariners in search of fresh air but as breathing-holes for mammals. There, mammals can also seek their prey. The polynya off the Bache Peninsula is particularly rich in fish and attracts large numbers of walrus. Walrus were very greatly valued in the Middle Ages for their meat, their magnificent ivory tusks and their hides, which could be boiled to make blubber oil for heating and lighting and distilled to make pitch to seal the hulls of ships. That the villagers on the Bache Peninsula in the High Arctic were there for the walrus is confirmed by the superb artefacts of exquisite work-manship that have been found nearby, such as fish hooks made from walrus ivory.

Ellesmere Island also has another very valuable commodity: copper. Evidence of ancient mining and processing of copper has recently come to light on nearby Devon Island;[7] of course, the Chinese were adept at surveying for, mining and refining metals. Coal originating from Newport, Rhode Island, has also been found in Greenland. Someone must have carried it there.

All of this was reasonably logical, but it begged the question of why the Chinese, with their magnificent ships, should have bothered to build stone houses at all. Why not simply anchor off the polynya to hunt the walrus and prospect for copper? But if one or more of the great ships had been holed by ice and forced to beach, they would then have found themselves on land with thousands of tons of teak near a rich fishing ground that would keep them alive if only they could withstand the cold. In such circumstances they would probably have done what Shackleton was to do centuries later: they built houses of the local material – stone – and roofed them using the timbers of their ships. By my calculations, one three-thousand-ton junk could have roofed all twenty-five houses of the settlement on the Bache peninsula.

I next turned to the stone hearths. If they had been designed for cooking, they would have been inside the houses: sited outside, they must have been built for industrial purposes. The sheer number of them – 142 in total – supports this thesis. One explanation would be that the hearths were used to boil blubber, both to make pitch for sealing the wooden roofs of the houses and to provide heating and lighting oil for winter. They could also have been used for desalinating sea-water or melting snow for drinking water, but so many hearths would scarcely have been required for these purposes. I believe that the Chinese were also smelting copper.

Part of the Chinese fleet must have remained at the settlement for some time, but at least one ship must have gone on to circumnavigate Greenland because the northern and eastern coasts of Greenland appear on the Vinland map. The south-western and south-eastern coasts are very accurately drawn with correct latitudes, but the north-west coast has a substantial 'bulge' in the area from Cape York through the Kane Basin to Petermann Fjord and Peary Land. To work out how this might have happened, I studied modern ice maps of the region[8] and concluded that the bulge shown on the Vinland map is in fact ice protruding into the sea from the huge glaciers of Mylius Erichsen's Land and Kronprins Christian's Land. Superimposing the shape of the glaciers onto a modern map of Greenland reconciles the disparity on the Vinland map.

Excepting this one error, the coastline is well drawn. Once again, it is a staggering cartographic achievement. The cumulative evidence – the Chinese reaching the Caribbean, the currents and winds that could have carried them from there around Greenland, the Pope's letter and the stone village – is suggestive of a Chinese attempt to reach the North Pole. By reaching Greenland they failed only by four hundred nautical miles . . . or did they? The most exquisite artefacts – snow geese, polar bears, seals and walruses of sumptuous workmanship carved from walrus ivory – have been found in the High Arctic even further north than Greenland, within 250 miles of the North Pole. They were designed by artists of genius. Could the Inuit have made them, or were they the art of a civilization almost as old as time?

*

After setting sail from Greenland, the currents and prevailing winds would have driven the Chinese fleet on towards Iceland. Confirmation that this was feasible came from Christopher Columbus: 'In the month of February 1477, I sailed 100 leagues [approximately 470 nautical miles] beyond the island of Tile [Iceland], whose southern part is in latitude 73 degrees north . . . and at the time when I was there, the sea was not frozen, but there were vast tides, so great that they rose and fell as much as 26 braccia [about 50 feet] twice a day.'[9] Professor Mike Baillie of Queen's University, Belfast, a world expert on dendrochronology – the analysis of tree rings to establish dates – has shown that 1477 was indeed an un-usually warm year, hence Columbus's claim is perfectly acceptable. Such a voyage would have taken him to the coast of Greenland. Then came the bombshell. Columbus summarized his voyage in his own handwriting in the margins of his copy of Pope Pius II's book *History of Remarkable Things that Happened in my Time*. He wrote: 'Men have come hither [to Iceland] from Cathay in the Orient.'[10]

I now had separate testimony from a pope and from Columbus that the Chinese had reached Greenland and Iceland, documentary evidence corroborated by the Vinland map of c. 1424 that shows the south coast of Greenland with stunning precision. In addition, the great expert on Ming China, Professor Needham, says that there exist more than twenty separate Chinese claims that they actually reached the North Pole.[11]

When they rounded Greenland's North Cape, the Chinese would have been just 180 miles south of the North Pole, for its position in 1422, as determined by Polaris at 90° altitude (*Wu Pei Chi*), was well to the south of where it is today. To reach the pole, the Chinese had only to travel a further 180 miles to the north – less than two days' sailing. Could the Arctic waters have been ice-free over those last 180 miles? A current (2000) temperature chart for the Arctic in July shows a tongue of relatively warm water off the North Cape of Greenland – perhaps the last feeble remnant of a branch of the Gulf

Stream – extending northwards beyond the North Cape towards the North Pole. It is entirely possible that the Chinese claims are true, that they had indeed reached the North Pole five centuries before Europeans did. Having been in a submarine on patrol near the North Pole using a series of polynyas, I can only marvel at the Chinese achievement. They could now eat the last of the dogs and drain the remaining bottles of rice wine in celebration before at last setting sail for their homeland.

Their route home from these far northern latitudes may solve yet another mystery, for the Waldseemüller map, published in 1507, shows the north coast of Siberia from the White Sea in the west to the Chukchi Peninsula and the Bering Strait in the east. The whole coast, with its rivers and islands, is clearly identifiable. If not the Chinese, who could have surveyed that enormous coastline? How was this chart drawn, showing lands that were not 'officially' discovered by Europeans for another three centuries, unless the Chinese had also travelled there? The first Russian surveys of Siberia did not take place for another two centuries, and the first Russian map did not appear until the nineteenth century.

The only logical explanation is that it was surveyed by Zhou Wen's fleet as it made its way back to China through the Bering Strait. As discussed previously, *The Illustrated Record of Strange Countries* features drawings of Cossack dancers and Eskimos hunting. The Eskimos could have been those of the Aleutian Islands, known to the Chinese, but the drawings of Cossacks cannot be explained in this way. There are no records of any Chinese visits to Muscovy in the first half of the fifteenth century. How could the drawings have been made without a visit to the Arctic?

Another Chinese admiral, Zhou Wen, had now completed an epic voyage of discovery, equalling if not surpassing the extraordinary voyages of Hong Bao and Zhou Man. Yang Qing had also been at sea with a great fleet in the missing years of 1421 to 1423, and I now turned my attention to him. He may not have travelled as far as the others, remaining for the most part in waters already familiar to the Chinese, but his achievements during the voyage he made lose nothing in comparison to the successes of the other great admirals.

VI

The Voyage of
Yang Qing

15

SOLVING

THE

RIDDLE

WHILE HIS PEERS HAD BEEN LOCATING CANOPUS AND the Southern Cross, penetrating the polar regions and discovering new lands and continents across the globe, Grand Eunuch Yang Qing's fleet, having left Beijing a month before the rest, spent the entire voyage in the waters of the Indian Ocean. Nowhere was more familiar to Chinese seamen, for trade with the states of the Indian Ocean, particularly the vastly lucrative spice trade, was the source of much of the Chinese national wealth. Trade was carried on not just with the Spice Islands, the countries of southeast Asia, India and the Arab states of the Gulf, but with ports and states the length of the East African seaboard.

By the early fifteenth century, Arab ports along that coast traded directly with China, exporting gold, ivory and rhino horn. Rulers of East African states habitually travelled aboard the junks of Zheng He's fleets to the Forbidden City. Many were returned to their home states as the fleets made their outward voyages in 1421, and more were collected and taken to China by two of the fleets limping homeward at the end of their remarkable voyages: Yang Qing himself returned from the Indian Ocean in September 1422 bearing the envoys of seventeen states from the East African and Indian coasts, and Hong Bao sailed home in October 1423 with the ambassador of Calicut. Once again, the emperor's foreign policy had succeeded brilliantly. The Indian Ocean had become a Chinese lake.

As most of the Chinese records had been destroyed, I had as usual to look elsewhere for evidence of the route Yang Qing's fleet had taken around the Indian Ocean. I found it in a familiar source: the Cantino map of 1502. My belief that it was based on information obtained from the Chinese voyages of 1421–3 arose from Portuguese historian Antonio Galvão's comment about a map (the 1428 World Map) that 'set forth all the navigation of the East Indies, with the Cape of Boa Esperança' (see chapter 4).[1] In those days, the 'East Indies' meant India, the Indian Ocean, Malaysia and Indonesia. It was an unequivocal declaration that the Cape of Good Hope, the Indian Ocean and the East had been set out on a map drawn early in the fifteenth century. Further corroboration that the Portuguese had a map showing the Cape of Good Hope before Dias or da Gama set sail came from the instructions of King João II of Portugal to the explorer Pêro da Covilha (c. 1450–c. 1520) in May 1487, when he sent him on a voyage to search for a sea route to India:

> He recommended him very much to enquire whether beyond the Cape of Good Hope it was possible to navigate to India . . . Then the King sent two of his trustworthy men who could speak Arabic well and were experienced travellers, Pero de Covilha, a knight of his household, and Alfonso de Paiva . . . [the future] King Dom Manuel gave them a chart (*Carta de Marear*) taken from the Map of the World [1428 chart] . . . all these showed as well as they could how they would have set about going and finding the countries the spices came from [the Moluccas].[2]

Significantly, Dias had not 'discovered' the Cape of Good Hope in May 1487, when these instructions were issued.

By the fifteenth century, the Chinese had hundreds of years' experience of navigating the Indian Ocean and the east coast of Africa; they had been visiting Africa since the time of the Tang dynasty (AD 618–907). The chronicles of Ma Huan and Fei Xin, who sailed on five voyages prior to 1421, the detailed sailing directions in the *Wu Pei Chi*, listing the courses to reach East Africa, and the accounts of medieval travellers recording the wealth of early Ming blue and white porcelain in merchants' palaces along the East African coast as far south as Sofala, all show the extent of Chinese trade and influence.

When serving in HMS *Newfoundland*, I travelled thousands of miles along the East African coast from Kenya to South Africa. In 1958 it was largely unspoilt, lined by the remains of old Arab and Portuguese slave towns and the occasional musty British club, the last remnants of empire. One incident remains vivid in my memory. People on safari in Africa in those days carried guns, not cameras, as their essential equipment. We decided to go on a crocodile shoot in the estuary of the Limpopo, and duly borrowed the ship's motor boat, several rifles and a crate of rum. We arrived in the glassy, greasy estuary under a leaden sky, a scene Kipling would have recognized. There were no crocodiles but plenty of hippos with their ugly snouts and big ears showing above the muddy water. This was sport! We soon discovered two things: hippos' hides are tough (the bullets bounced off) and hippos do not enjoy being peppered with shot. One charged us; I can see the boat now, flying through the air upside down, its propellers whirring away as it passed overhead. Both we and the hippo retired bruised but otherwise undamaged. From then on I found my entertainment in more environmentally sensitive ways, by exploring some of the old Arab and Portuguese trading and slaving towns along the coast.

When the Portuguese first arrived in East Africa, they found that the kings and queens of Zanzibar and Pemba (in modern Mozambique)[3] were dressed in fine Chinese silk and lived in stone houses decorated with Chinese porcelain. Further evidence of the Chinese presence in the Indian Ocean comes from the Lamu archipelago or Bajun Islands, five hundred miles north-east of Zanzibar, off the northern coast of modern Kenya. The Bajun capital, Pate, was habitually used by Zheng He's fleets, and when the Portuguese arrived they found 'Bajuni', honey-skinned people with fine features. A Jesuit priest, Father Monclaro, wrote in 1549: '[They produced] very rich silk cloths, from which the Portuguese derive great profit in other Moorish cities where they are not to be had, because they are only manufactured on Pate, and are sent to the others from that place.'[4] Craftsmen from Pate also specialized in lacquerwork, another craft unknown to medieval Africa, and wove baskets using the same technique as in southern China.

An Italian anthropologist, Signor N. Puccioni, made an expedition to the Juba River in Africa in 1935 and concluded that the Bajuni at Pate were of 'a physical type absolutely different from other people in the region. The skin is rather light, in some lightly olive, and in the men you can spot flowing beards, and the women part their hair in the middle and then braid it into two side braids.'[5] One of the clans on the island, the Washanga, claimed that their forebears were Chinese sailors wrecked off the island, and their folklore relates that the King of Malindi, the most powerful local potentate, presented two giraffes to the Emperor of China.[6] This indeed happened in 1416.

Pate has changed little since the fifteenth century, save that for a while after the 1960s the island became a haunt of hippies. The people are Islamic, the men still wear the full-length white robes known as *Khanzus* with *Kofia* caps, and the women are shrouded in black capes known as *Bui Bui*. Dhows still ply the coast, their design unaltered for centuries – a triangular lateen sail and a broad, roughly planed hull sturdy enough to beach on the rocky shores. Most have coconut matting tied to their sides and a wooden 'eye' painted on their bow. Those of the Lamu archipelago are distinctive through having perpendicular bows. Dhows are remarkably fast and particularly good at tacking into the wind. Because of the stinking fish bait they carry, dhows can frequently be smelt before they are seen. I used to surface my submarine alongside to load up with flying fish, which made a very welcome variation from the standard Navy diet.

The remains of the former Arab trading town of Shanga, supposedly named after Shanghai, lie at the eastern edge of Pate Island. Today, the town is almost deserted save for mangrove pole cutters. Two centuries ago, large quantities of Chinese ceramics of the Song (960–1280) to early Ming (1368–1430) era were found there, together with the statuette of a Song lion, buried as a votive offering. Even the name for these settlers, Bajuni, may be of Chinese origin: *bjun* is Chinese patois for 'long-robed'. Native people on the East African coast wore loin cloths. Long, silken robes would have been striking and unusual enough for the name to be bestowed upon the settlers.

The Chinese were already sailing those waters and they certainly had the capacity in terms of both ships and scientific knowledge to make an accurate survey of the Indian Ocean. They could measure

A bronze Song lion statuette found off the Kenya coast.

time accurately, plot the course of the stars in the heavens, and determine accurate latitudes in both hemispheres. But could they also determine longitude? East Africa on the Cantino bears an astonishing likeness to a modern chart; the latitudes of inlets, bays and rivers are correct from the Cape of Good Hope in the south to Djibouti at the mouth of the Red Sea in the north, a distance of seven thousand nautical miles. Even more startling, the longitudes on the Cantino are correct to within thirty nautical miles – a mere thirty seconds of time. How had the cartographers achieved this incredible feat?

To date there is no connection between the Chinese and the calculation of longitude. All we can say is that an accurate calculation of longitude had been achieved before 1502 when the Cantino arrived in Italy.

Finding longitude without clocks has a long history. The key is to mark the precise moment when a heavenly event occurs, one which may be seen simultaneously across the globe. One of the oldest and best-tried methods was by observing lunar eclipses and elapsed time. Ptolemy in his *Geographia* in the first century AD records Hipparchos (c. 190–120 BC) advocating this method and giving an example of its use in 330 BC. However, Hipparchos does not explain how local time was to be found, a problem because the sun must be below the horizon during a lunar eclipse.[7] It is quite possible that a few Europeans knew of Hipparchos' method by 1415, when Ptolemy's *Geographia* was brought to Venice by two Byzantines escaping the Ottomans, who were by then threatening Byzantium. The Arabs certainly knew of Hipparchos' theory.

The observatories the Chinese built and the written records they kept show that they measured the passage of time by the length of the sun's shadow. The most famous observatory, the Zhou Gong Tower fifty miles south-east of Luoyang, still stands. Built seven centuries ago, it is a truncated pyramid with stairways leading from ground level to a 25-foot-square platform. A small building in the centre of the platform houses a thin vertical rod for observation of the stars on the local meridian, and a clepsydra, a large water clock. A gnomon – a 40-foot metal measuring pole – was set in a bed of stones extending for 120 feet to the north of the tower, between two parallel troughs of water. The stones were laid perfectly flat, parallel with the water surface. The Chinese measured the sun's noon shadow cast by the gnomon on to the stones. At the equinox on the equator, the sun rises due east and sets due west. At midday it is directly above the observer and casts no shadow at all. The longest shadows are cast at sunrise and sunset, and the length of the shadows between those points determines the precise time at that particular location.

As far back as AD 721, the Chinese had realized that the length of the sun's shadow varies not only with the time of day but with the day of the year and the latitude of the observation points. Using a smaller, standard 8-foot gnomon, they made simultaneous measurements of the lengths of shadows during the summer and winter solstices at several different locations from the latitude of modern Hue in Vietnam due north to Beijing. They calculated that the shadow lengths varied by just over 3.56 inches for every 400 miles of latitude, allowing them to make corrections for their position anywhere on earth on one particular day.

However, the shadow length also varied day by day throughout the year. In one remarkable measurement they calculated that the length of the shadow was 12.3695 feet at the summer solstice and 76.7400 feet at the winter solstice. By extrapolating from the two experiments described above, the Chinese were able to make corrections for each day of the year as well as for different latitudes on the earth's surface. Furthermore, by the length of the noon shadow they could establish which day of the year it was. At this time, neither Arabs nor Europeans had a means of measuring time other than hour-glasses, which could not give them either the date or any more than a rough estimate of time on any particular day.

A third adjustment was necessary to correct for the irregular motion of the earth around the sun, occasioned by the eccentricity of the earth's orbit and the difference between the equator and the ecliptic (the great circle of the celestial sphere representing the sun's apparent path through the sky during a year). This causes differences between absolute time and the apparent time obtained from the sun which reach a maximum positive difference of 14 minutes 30 seconds in February and a maximum negative difference of 16 minutes 30 seconds in November. The Chinese determined this with such accuracy that 'observations made from 1277 to 1280 are valuable for their great precision and prove incontestably the diminution of the obliquity of the ecliptic and the eccentricity of the earth's orbit between then and now'.[8] In layman's language, the earth's orbit around the sun has changed in the past seven centuries.

The Chinese replicated the Zhou Gong Tower first in Nanjing and then in Beijing after the capital was moved there. Zheng He's treasure fleets went on to build similar observatories around the world. Each was equipped with instruments for amplifying the sun's shadow and measuring its length, recognizing stars in the sky, determining the exact positions of the sun and moon at eclipses, and observing Polaris.[9] The stone tower at Rhode Island (see chapter 13) may prove to be one such example. Each observation platform thus had everything needed to measure latitude and longitude.

The Chinese had long known that the taller the gnomon and the longer the shadow it cast, the more accurate the measurement of time. However, as it grew longer, the shadow also became fainter and more attenuated. In the early Ming era, the Chinese devised a 'camera obscura' by cutting a tiny hole in the roof of the observation chamber. This resulted in a sharper shadow that was intensified through a type of magnifying glass. The long shadow could then be measured to an accuracy of one hundredth of an inch.

The outstanding precision of this Chinese measurement of time is illustrated by their calculation of the length of lunation – the interval between new moons – which they estimated at 29.530591 days.[10] This figure would produce an error of less than one second in a month. Using these methods, measurements of time could only be taken when the sun was above the horizon. Measurements after dark were made using clepsydras (water clocks) that were calibrated in daylight against a gnomon.[11] With their gnomons and clepsydras, the Chinese were able to determine the passage of time, day by day, minute by minute and second by second, both day and night. They could also forecast and make use of the full lunar eclipses that take place somewhere across the globe roughly every six months.

Solar and lunar eclipses occur when the sun, moon and earth are in line with one another and when the moon's orbit around the earth is in the same plane as the earth's orbit around the sun. In a solar eclipse, the moon's shadow blots out the sun over a small portion of the earth and it becomes night for a very short period. The spot of darkness, the umbra, travels across the earth as the moon rotates around the earth, and the earth itself rotates. Observers in different locations see the solar eclipse at different times. In a lunar eclipse, the earth is between sun and moon, and because the earth is so much bigger than the moon, its shadow obscures the moon. The great difference for astronomical observations is that the event may be seen simultaneously by observers across half the earth, whereas in a solar eclipse the event occurs only above a very small part of the earth at any one time. The ability to time a lunar eclipse with absolute precision and the fact that the same event could be seen simultaneously from different parts of the globe were to prove the vital steps in Chinese attempts to find a method of calculating longitude.

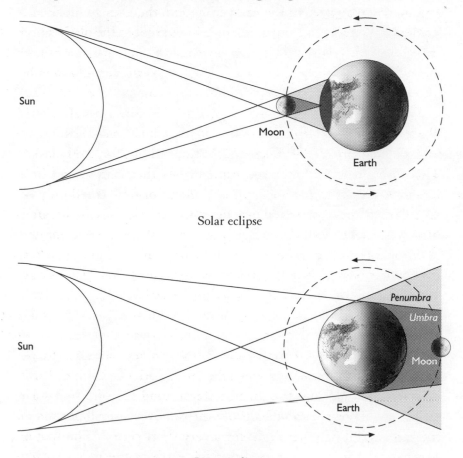

Solar eclipse

Lunar eclipse

The keys to using a lunar eclipse to determine longitude are, first, that the event is seen across half the world simultaneously, and secondly, while the eclipse is taking place, the earth's rotation makes the stars appear to move across the sky. There are four distinguishable events during an eclipse: U1 – first contact, when the moon enters the dark umbral shadow; U2 – second contact, when the moon has just fully entered the umbra and is totally covered; U3 – third contact, when

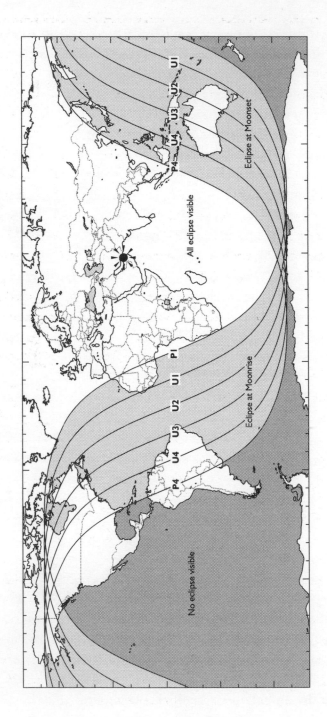

The progression of a lunar eclipse across the Earth's surface.

the moon first starts to emerge; and U4 – fourth contact, when the moon has just fully emerged. The Chinese concentrated on U3 and used it as the basis of their calculations.

After landing in an unknown territory, Chinese navigators and astronomers would have been instructed to observe the lunar eclipse, wait until the moment when the third event (U3) occurred, then determine what star was just crossing the local meridian in the night sky. The local meridian was the imaginary longitudinal line, starting on the horizon directly north of the observer, passing over his head and ending at the horizon due south of him. The known star crossing that line at the time of the third event of the eclipse was the key sighting for the observers in the new territory, and for those back in Beijing.

When the astronomer returned from his voyage, he and his colleagues in Beijing compared their data. Using their time-keeping device, calibrated from the gnomon, they timed the interval between the transits of the star observed in the new territory at the time of the eclipse and the star seen by the astronomers in Beijing at the same moment. The earth rotates 360° in twenty-four hours. If the elapsed time between the two transits was six hours, a quarter of the time it takes the earth to rotate, the difference in longitude between Beijing and the new territory would be a quarter of the total longitude around the world – 90°, one quarter of 360°. Errors could be reduced by timing each of the four events of the eclipse, U1, U2, U3 and U4, then averaging the results. By observing the same event at different locations around the globe and fixing the exact time at which this event took place, the Chinese could then compare their results. By determining the differences in the time when the event took place, as observed from the separate locations, they could then calculate the difference in longitude.

Professor John Oliver, Professor of Astronomy at the University of Florida, put the theory to the test by observing the lunar eclipse of 16 and 17 July 2000. He set up teams of observers across the Pacific from Tahiti to Malacca, near Singapore, choosing the same sites as the Chinese observation platforms (Appendix 4). The average longitudinal errors produced by this method were minuscule: 1.1 degrees in Tahiti, 0.1 degree in New Zealand, 0.1 degree in Melbourne and zero degrees in Singapore. This has startling implications. In Professor Oliver's experiments, there was a six-mile longitudinal error between Singapore and New Zealand, and none between New Zealand and Australia. In all, longitude was calculated across one-third of the world's surface, a distance of some eight thousand miles, with a maximum error anywhere of just sixty-six miles. And Professor Oliver's observers were amateurs; with more training and experience, the errors could have been reduced even further. Using their observation platforms at the same sites, the Chinese would have determined longitude just as accurately as Professor Oliver's team, maybe more so. The brilliance of the method is that, unlike calculations for latitude, neither a sextant nor a clock is required.

Having accurately determined the longitude of Malacca near Singapore, for example, the Chinese fleets could then use Malacca as a base to repeat the process using the observation platforms and gnomons on their other bases around the Indian Ocean: Semudera (Sumatra), the Andamans, Dondra Head (Sri Lanka), Cochin and Calicut on the Malabar coast of India, Malindi and Zanzibar in East Africa, and the Seychelle and Maldive archipelagos, all of which appear on the *Wu Pei Chi*. If a sufficiently large fleet was deployed, there is no reason why longitudes across the whole of the Indian Ocean should not have been established in a single lunar eclipse. Men would have been despatched to different locations in readiness to take readings of the lunar eclipse, all on the same night. They could then return to base to compare measurements.

One can imagine the ships of the great fleet dispersing across the Indian Ocean to take their measurements, the eunuch captains anxious to arrive in good time, the sailors doubtless far more interested in meeting the local women, renowned for their beauty and sexual appetite. They welcomed sailors with open arms, as Marco Polo noted: 'They are all black-skinned and go stark naked, both males and females, except for gay loin cloths: they regard no form of lechery or sensual indulgence as sin. Their marriage customs are such that a man may wed his cousin german or his father's widow or his brother's. And these customs prevail throughout the Indies.'[12] However, the crews would have had to postpone their pleasures until the business of the fleet had been completed and the lunar eclipse timed. The results of this Chinese expertise can be seen in the Cantino map of 1502, where the coast of East Africa is depicted with such accuracy that it appears to have been drawn with the aid of satellite navigation. Who else but the Chinese could have drawn this astounding chart two centuries before Europeans had clocks, and four centuries before they knew how to separate the South Pole from the magnetic pole? Was there even the remotest possibility that it could have been an earlier, unknown Portuguese voyage?

The Portuguese had no accurate method of calculating longitude; in 1541, thirty-nine years after the Cantino was drawn, a Portuguese attempt to determine the longitude of Mexico City by the measurement of a solar eclipse put it nearly 1,500 miles too far to the west. Yet the Cantino had longitudes correct to within thirty miles along thousands of miles of coastline. The reason was that the Portuguese were using solar eclipses, the Chinese lunar eclipses. The Portuguese did not have enough ships to determine longitude by trigonometry.

Three expeditions to the Indian Ocean had returned to Portugal before the Cantino was made. Vasco da Gama visited Sofala, Kilwa and Mombasa in 1498–9. At Malindi, he took an Arab pilot who guided him directly to Calicut, therefore he could not have charted the coast north of Malindi. Pedro Álvares Cabral's second expedition set off in 1499 and returned in June 1501. Early in the voyage, his fleet was hit by a terrible storm and four ships were lost. One, commanded by Diego Dias, sailed along the east coast of Madagascar, and from there to Mogadishu. His ship was severely damaged and he lost many men. On his voyage home, Dias stood well out to sea, and the only part of the East African coast he could have charted was between Mogadishu and Berbera. Cabral's broken fleet limped from Sofala to Kilwa, then to Malindi.

Thus none of the three fleets that arrived back in Lisbon before the Cantino was drawn had spent long enough on the East African coast to make such an accurate cartographic survey, and none could have charted the entire coast. Moreover, the Cantino covers about nine million square miles of ocean. It would have taken forty ships at least two years to carry out such a vast survey, an undertaking far beyond Portugal's resources at the time. Indeed, it took sixty years for the Portuguese to survey Africa's west coast. To expect a few battered caravels to have done the same on the east coast while simultaneously charting nine million square miles of ocean and six island archipelagos in the few months they were in the Indian Ocean before 1502 is as realistic as expecting a lone surveyor to map a continent with nothing more than a measuring stick and a horse and cart.

Having ruled out the Portuguese, I wondered if Arab navigators could have been the original cartographers. I made an exhaustive examination of the wonderful collection assembled by the wealthy and dedicated map collector Prince Youssuf Kamal, copies of which are in the Map Library of the British Library, but found not one detailed Arabic chart of the east coast of Africa in that whole monumental collection. The best Arabic medieval maps, such as those of Al Idrisi, bear no comparison in detail or accuracy to the Cantino of 1502. Although the Arabs understood how to calculate longitude by lunar eclipse, they never mastered how to measure time with the necessary accuracy, something that the Chinese achieved, and hence the Arabs could not have produced the Cantino, or the Waldseemüller chart.

Admiral Yang Qing journeyed much less far than the other Chinese admirals, yet the task he had been set was as vital and as demanding as those of Hong Bao, Zhou Man and Zhou Wen, and his success matches their towering achievements, for by the end of that voyage his men had perfected a method of determining longitude over three centuries before John Harrison's invention of the chronometer.

Though the Western world is largely silent on the origin of these extraordinary world maps, now correct both for latitude and longitude, the inscription on the stone erected by Zheng He in commemoration of his voyages shows where the credit is due: 'And now as a result of the voyages the distances and courses between the distant lands may be calculated.' It was another towering achievement by the Chinese fleets, one that should have burned like a beacon in the annals of global history. Instead, it was to be snuffed out and forgotten, along with the discovery of the Americas, Australia, Antarctica and the Arctic; Europeans would claim the glory that should have belonged to the great Chinese admirals and their fleets. The Portuguese were to lead this European wave of exploration and colonization. They more than any other nation benefited from the hard-won Chinese knowledge of the oceans and new lands that lay beyond them.

VII

Portugal Inherits the Crown

16

WHERE
THE
EARTH
ENDS

十六

IN JUNE 1421, AT THE SAME TIME AS THE CHINESE FLEET WAS rounding the Cape of Good Hope to head north for the Cape Verde Islands, far out in the Atlantic a little caravel – a small Portuguese sailing ship – lay at anchor in a wooded bay of the uninhabited island of Madeira. The great wave of European expansion and colonization that was to spread across the globe and, for better or worse, change the lives and destinies of billions of people had begun, in the most unobtrusive manner. This first small, hesitant step was taken by the Portuguese on their own initiative, but within three years news of the great Chinese discoveries and charts showing those far-flung lands and seas would be filtering into Portugal. No longer would they be sailing into the unknown.

On that June day in 1421, the Portuguese explorer João Gonçalves Zarco and his family must have felt they had arrived in paradise. A kaleidoscope of fish circled the caravel – black espadas, blue tunny, silver-striped mackerel, red bream and grey mullet – and sea lions were Zarco's only competitors for this bounty of nature. Streams of crystal water tumbled into a small lagoon, rich in langoustines and snails. The air was heavy with the sweet smell of jasmine and alive with the songs of birds that had never learned to fear man. Beyond the vivid banks of orchids, azaleas, begonias and jacarandas lining the Madeiran shore stretched mile upon mile of fennel interspersed with clumps of passion fruit.[1]

The same streams, the Ribeira de Santa Luzia and the Ribeira de São João, still tumble into the Atlantic, but in place of the lush fields of green fennel are now the quiet streets of Madeira's capital, Funchal. The statue of its founder dominates the Avenida Zarco. The Santa Catarina chapel, erected by Zarco's wife, stands on another street named after him, and next to it is the statue of Prince Henry the Navigator, the man who had made the expedition possible.

The colonization of Madeira, begun on that June day in 1421, was a pivotal moment in the history of European exploration. Zarco, a knight in the service of Prince Henry, discovered the island by accident. In December 1418, Zarco and Tristão Vaz Teixeira ('Vaz'), another Portuguese knight who had loyally served Prince Henry, had been ordered to explore the African coast down to Guinea, two thousand miles south of Portugal, but their ship was blown off course and driven before the wind to Porto Santo, an island sixty kilometres north-east of Madeira[2] then populated by crying seabirds and *câmara de lobos* (sea lions). One sunset, while on the island, Zarco spied a smudge on the horizon in the direction of the setting sun. They set off a week later and took formal possession of the new land in the name of the King of Portugal, of Prince Henry and the Order of Christ, naming the mountainous, densely forested island 'Ilha da Madeira', the Island of Wood. They returned almost immediately to Portugal where Zarco, Vaz and their companions were received with acclaim. Zarco was knighted and given the title Count of Câmara de Lobos.

Prince Henry warmly endorsed Zarco's plan to colonize the islands and financed two further expeditions, providing Zarco with ships and stores. The island was to be divided in two, with Vaz governor of the northern half and Zarco of the southern. Another of Zarco's shipmates, Bartolomeu Perestrello, was sent to establish a colony on the neighbouring island of Porto Santo. It was an ill-starred choice. Perestrello's children had a pet rabbit, a doe. It gave birth to a litter during the voyage to Porto Santo, and when the colonizers settled on the island the rabbits multiplied so fast without natural predators to control their numbers that the island was soon reduced to a desert.

In contrast, the colonization of Madeira was an enormous success and vividly demonstrated the benefits of overseas exploration. Prince Henry pioneered the introduction of grape vines and sugar cane from Crete, which flourished in the warm, damp climate. The famous Madeira wines made from the grapes were exported throughout Europe, and sugar cane production showed equally spectacular profits. Entrepreneurs flocked to Prince Henry's court to participate in future bonanzas, and Portuguese explorers set sail on ever more adventurous voyages, in the vanguard of an expansion that was to see European nations dominate the world for another five hundred years.

Henry was the third son of King John I of Portugal and his wife, Queen Philippa, daughter of England's John of Gaunt. With English help, John had led an uprising in 1383 and replaced the old Portuguese nobility with a new landed aristocracy, the House of Avis, loyal only to himself. John proved a cautious and pragmatic king, negotiating a defensive treaty with England and exploiting that arrangement to make an uneasy truce with Castile. The existing treaty between the separate Spanish kingdoms of Castile and Aragon left the whole peninsula at peace. John's foreign policy was equally cautious, and he was particularly careful not to antagonize Castile by interfering in its sphere of influence abroad.

It was an era of massive Christian confidence throughout the peninsula. After six centuries, the Moors had finally been driven out of the Algarve, their last stronghold in Portugal. King Sancho I of Portugal had invaded the Algarve in 1189, and by 1249 the whole region, once the westernmost province of the majestic Arab caliphate of Cordoba, was in royal hands, allowing the capital to be moved south from Coimbra to Lisbon. With the *Reconquista* complete, Portugal's soldiers, like their counterparts in Aragon, had nowhere to go but overseas.

John and Philippa were devout Christians, but their court was one of the most enlightened in Europe, a centre for men of scholarship and ability regardless of religion. China remained years ahead of Europe in terms of science, technology and, arguably, culture, but fifteenth-century Portugal was beginning to flower and would quickly grow into the principal European centre for voyages of discovery and exploration. It was an age of rapid change, and his parents ensured that young Prince Henry received an appropriate education. In 1415, just out of his teens, he was entrusted with the command of the Portuguese attack on Ceuta, an important Arab port on the north coast of Africa overlooking the Strait of Gibraltar.

Plans were well advanced when Queen Philippa fell gravely ill. As she lay dying, she gave a sword to Henry with the words, 'I give you, Henry, this . . . sword. It is as strong as you are. To you I commend all the lords, knights, squires and those of noble blood.'[3] She also insisted that Henry proceed with the attack on Ceuta rather than remain at her bedside.

In past centuries, the Moors had launched three invasions of Spain using troops drawn from Senegal to Arabia, and Islamic rulers still controlled a vast empire. Even for someone as daring and resolute as Henry, an attack on Islam's heartland was a colossal gamble, the first European invasion of Africa since that of the Emperor Justinian eight hundred years earlier. Henry's army was drawn from all over Europe, the Christian forces uniting under the banner of a new crusader prince. The attack on Ceuta was preceded by all manner of ruses to disguise the real plan; Portugal even declared war on Holland as a distraction to mislead the Moors. When the assault on Ceuta began, Henry handled his forces so skilfully that the battle was quickly over.

The capture of Ceuta was the first European victory over the Moors in their own territories, an event of great moral and psychological significance. A despatch rider was sent post haste with news of the victory to the Holy Roman Emperor Sigismund and the royal houses of Europe. Henry's success brought him invitations to take up all manner of commands – from the Pope to head the papal armies, and from Henry V of England to lead a crusade against the infidels – but he declined all offers, preferring to act as his father's representative in Ceuta, from where he set about building a Portuguese empire based on the wealth of the gold trade that stemmed from the capture of the city.

The Mediterranean world cried out for gold; Arab camel caravans plodded across the Sahara from Mali through Marrakesh, Fez and Meknes – glorious, immensely prosperous cities – to Ceuta. Capturing Ceuta had given Henry's army a secure harbour on African soil, and the opportunity to intercept bullion shipments and strike at the wealth of the fabled Moroccan cities, in the process depriving the Arabs of the money to lubricate their trading routes. Henry had a stranglehold on one of Islam's prime sources of wealth.

Arabs had enriched Portugal and Spain in many ways, and were skilled at exploiting the trading opportunities presented by their far-flung empire. They brought Syrian engineers to irrigate Portugal's Algarve and improve rice cultivation, and developed the corn lands of the Alentejo, where they also introduced cotton and sugar cane. 'Persian' carpets were woven in Bera and Caleena, Chinese methods of paper manufacture were copied in Játiva, and 'Moroccan' leather and textiles were made in Cordoba where there were thirteen thousand leather workers and weavers. Islamic ships carried the finished products from the Tagus estuary in Portugal to Cairo and North Africa.

At the time of the attack on Ceuta, Portugal was still a medieval land, riddled with superstition. Books described the incredible wealth of lands beyond the seas, the extraordinary challenges that awaited explorers and the strange people and monsters lying in wait to attack them. On the way to India there was 'a sea so hot that it boils like water over a fire, and it is all green; and in that sea serpents breed bigger than crocodiles, having wings wherewith they fly, and so venomous that all people run from them in fear ... because [the serpent] grew in the boiling sea, no fire can burn it ... in that sea is a whirlpool, so terrible that men fear to venture'.[4] India was a land 'of wild beasts that are in the wilderness, blue dragons, serpents and other ravening beasts that eat all they can get. There are many elephants, all white; some are blue and of other colours, quite numberless; there are also many unicorns and lions and other hideous beasts.'[5] In those far-off lands, men had heads in the middle of their chests, their eyes were in their shoulders; 'They have two small holes, all round, instead of eyes, and their mouth is flat also without lips.' Women hid snakes in their vaginas 'which stung the husbands on their penises'.[6] By taking Ceuta, Prince Henry and his countrymen had the opportunity to learn the true facts. In his four

Sea monsters from Sebastian Münster's *Cosmographia*, 1546.

years in the city, Henry became familiar with the blinding African sun, the bite of sand in the air when the wind comes off the desert, the hot dusty streets, the soft smell of cloves and the extraordinary clarity of desert nights.

Ceuta was also an important port, attracting a cosmopolitan population, and a home to fine Islamic universities. The Arabs revered scholarship and had carefully stored the masterpieces of Greece and Rome, including the geographical works of Ptolemy. They did not subscribe to myths and superstitions about the world around them. They had been trading from the Atlantic to the Pacific for centuries. The Arab geographer Al Barouwi had charted North and East Africa from the Atlantic to Zanzibar by 1315, and in 1327 another famous Arab traveller, Al Dimisqui, had described the real world of the East peopled by ordinary beings and reached by sea voyages across natural oceans. Although the Arabs had not drawn accurate maps of Africa or the Indian Ocean, they did know the relative positions of Africa, India, China and the Far East as early as 1340, when Hama Allah Moustawfi Qazami drew his mappa mundi based on the work of Ptolemy. The Arabs described the sea route to India in 1342 and produced an encyclopedia of Asia in 1391, giving detailed descriptions of the major towns, cities and mosques.

It must have been a life-changing moment for Prince Henry to learn that Arabs had traded over the whole known world for centuries. He had only to follow in the wake of Arab dhows to discover those same exotic lands. The whole world lay at his feet if he could build an ocean-going fleet, and to do that he had to return to Portugal. By Christmas 1419 he had chosen Sagres in south-west Portugal as his permanent base. There Henry the Navigator built a *forteleza* (fortress) and founded a chapel, a hospital, and the school of navigation that earned him his name and changed the course of world history. A painting in Lisbon's Maritime Museum depicts Henry's court at Sagres, peopled by Catalan sea captains, Jewish cartographers, Arab astronomers, Portuguese knights, men-at-arms, sailmakers, priests, shipwrights, physicians, sailors and court retainers, all of whom lived, prayed, ate and worked together.

There are some parts of the ocean where a mariner knows his position by the smell of the sea. The Grand Banks off Newfoundland is one, the Straits of Malacca another, but most potent of all is the scent of pines off Sagres on a warm summer's night, a smell that for me always brings back memories of voyages to the East, for after Sagres one alters course to the south-east for the Mediterranean and the lands beyond. Even today, Sagres is daunting. It stands some two hundred feet above the Atlantic, jutting out into the ocean, looking out over Cape St Vincent, passing ships no more than a distant blur on the horizon. Below, long rolling breakers smash into the cliffs, their dull boom a constant background to the haunting cries of sea-birds. In winter and spring the promontory is lashed by rain; at many other times it is veiled in spray and sea-mist. The lush vegetation of the mainland gives way to stony scrub; neither flowers nor trees grow. A great grey wall, its stones hewn from the cliffs, guards the entrance, and through a dark oak door one can glimpse a row of austere houses and the simple chapel of St Catherine.

To the Portuguese, Sagres was the end of the world, 'where the earth ends and sea begins'.[7] Closer inspection reveals that the promontory was an inspired choice as a base. Each winter and spring, the prevailing north-west wind sucks vast quantities of water out of the Atlantic and dumps it onto the mountains of the Sierra Monchique; despite the torrid summer heat – it is further south than most of Spain – the area is sub-tropical in character. A day on horseback takes the rider into foothills where lush, verdant forests are interspersed with cork and oak trees, and white almonds, oleanders, hibiscus, lilies and geraniums thrive on the heat and moisture. Groves of orange and lemon trees, laden with fruit, grow among dark pine forests. Cabbages are planted beneath date palms, and vines are cultivated on trellises among the heather. The edge of the continental shelf is only a few miles offshore from Sagres where the ocean falls steeply to two thousand fathoms, over two miles deep. The seas teem with fish; over a hundred species have been found around Cape St Vincent. Fleets of small boats bring in heavy catches of cod, anchovies and sardines for drying and salting. The cliffs afford shelter, the small harbours safe mooring against the prevailing northerly storms.

Here, in the south-west Algarve, Henry the Navigator had access to everything necessary to build, fit out and provision a fleet – limitless supplies of soft pine for ribs, resinous pine for planking, oak for rudders and keels, gum for caulking, wool and hides to clothe the crews, bamboo and reeds for their beds and baskets. Provisions for a two-month voyage – salt fish, rice, wheat, olives, dates, oranges, lemons and almonds – were in abundant supply. Sailors also need alcohol; as in Henry's day, the full, fruity and strong Alentejo wine, made from Periquita grapes, is still fermented in large earthenware jars cast from the heavy red soil.

When Henry arrived at Sagres, Catalan cogs – small cargo vessels – were evolving into good ocean-going ships, but they were still square-rigged. From his experiences at Ceuta, Henry knew that Arab dhows bound for the eastern Mediterranean spent much of their voyage in light, variable winds, and had to be able to sail into the wind. Square-rigged ships, sailing always before the wind, often had no rudder. Dhows had rudders, and the Arabs had refined the lateen (triangular) sail so that two men, hoisting it on a simple block

A Portuguese caravel in full lateen rigging.

and tackle, could control a large area of canvas. Henry incorporated a stern rudder into the design of his new sailing ship, the caravel, a cross between a Catalan cog and an Arab dhow – the design lives on in the modern ketch – but of all the improvements Henry introduced, none surpasses his brilliant adaptation of the Arabic lateen sail. The later caravels had lateen sails on mizzen and main masts and a square sail on the foremast, and could be converted at sea to be either square- or lateen-rigged. A mariner could sail southwards from Portugal square-rigged before the prevailing wind, then convert to lateen sails to return north into the wind. Although tiny in comparison to Chinese junks, caravels were much more nimble and manoeuvrable.

Henry's next problem was to enable his captains to measure their position on the earth's surface. Determining the correct position of new discoveries and then finding the way home depended upon knowing latitude and steering the correct course, and that in turn depended upon the compass. Arabs had used compasses for centuries, after obtaining the device from the Chinese with whom they regularly swapped nautical knowledge. However, the Chinese knowledge of navigation, astronomy and the means by which latitude and longitude could be calculated, perfected on the last great voyage of the treasure fleets from 1421 to 1423, remained theirs alone. Others, even the Arabs but particularly the Europeans, were still floundering in their wake decades, and in the case of longitude centuries, later.

Henry was a dedicated mathematician, and by the late 1460s, just after Henry's death, his astronomers, assisted by Arabs, had solved the problem of latitude. Arabs had an old civilization and they, too, were dedicated mathematicians. In Henry's era they were far better educated than Europeans and were used to sailing the Mediterranean and Indian Oceans out of sight of land. To this day, many stars in the sky – Betelgeuse, Aldebaran, Mikah – have Arab names,

A European determining latitude, from Pedro de Medina's *Regimiento de Navigación*, 1563.

and British Admiralty charts credit Arab navigators in the use of names such as Ras Nungwi and Ras Al Khaimah. Arab navigators knew that the altitude of the meridian passage of the sun – its maximum height in the sky at noon each day – could be measured by lining up the sun with the horizon. Either wooden or brass instruments would do; one of the simplest and best was designed by Gil Eannes, one of Henry's captains, in the 1460s.

The sun's maximum height varies day by day throughout the year, and the difference between this daily height and the height at its lowest point in midwinter was named the declination of the sun. The Arabs had discovered that the sun's declination, when subtracted from its height at midday, gave the latitude of a place in the northern hemisphere.[8] In 1473, Regiomontanus, the Viennese astronomer who had attended Henry's court, produced a set of 'ephemerides tables' giving day-by-day declinations of the sun. A captain in the distant oceans now merely had to measure with a quadrant – a rudimentary type of sextant – the altitude of the sun at its meridian passage, then consult the tables to find the sun's declination for that day. By subtracting declination from altitude the mariner knew how many degrees south (and hence how many miles) he was from home. With a caravel and a quadrant, sailing back to Sagres was relatively simple. The mariner sailed due north, following the Pole Star by night and setting a course opposite to the sun's noon position by day, until he reached the latitude of Sagres, whereupon he altered course to the east, keeping to that same latitude until he could see Cape St Vincent or smell the scent of pines in the air.

By 1420 Henry had designed and built an ocean-going caravel that could remain at sea for weeks at a time and could return home. He knew from the Arabs that the medieval fables of monsters and boiling seas were nonsense, and that the oceans of the world could be crossed to discover new worlds. The last piece of the jigsaw was the production of accurate charts to enable his captains to reach the East. In 1416, Prince (Dom) Pedro, Henry's elder brother, 'seized with the desire to gain enlightenment by travel through the principal countries of Europe and Western Asia',[9] had set off on an odyssey to garner every possible piece of information about the world beyond the Mediterranean. King John had invested a substantial sum in Florentine bonds to cover his son's travelling expenses, and the King of Spain had provided him with a retinue of servants, translators and scholars. He travelled through Spain, Palestine, the Holy Land, the Ottoman Empire – 'the Grand Sultan of Babylon' – Rome, the Holy Roman Empire, Hungary, Denmark, England and Venice, and 'at the end of twelve years' travel Dom Pedro returned in 1428 to Portugal'.[10]

He had departed the year after Ceuta was taken, a time when the Portuguese were lionized throughout Christian Europe. All had shared in the excitement of Prince Henry's daring gamble to form a bridgehead in Africa, the heartland of Islam, and now Dom Pedro was treated as a conquering hero at whose feet Europe lay. He could go where he wanted, ask what questions he wished and receive all the knowledge his hosts possessed. In England, he had been created a Knight of the Garter; the Doge had personally entertained him in Venice; the King of Spain had showered him with gold; and Emperor Sigismund had given him valuable land in the March of Treviso, a fertile province a few miles north of Venice that had served as his base from 1421 to 1425.[11]

In many ways, Dom Pedro was the ideal complement to his younger brother. Henry was a practical man of action, Pedro a dreamer and a visionary of immense charm who was appalled by European conflicts and fired his hosts with his ideal of uniting Christians in Africa, India and Cathay (China) by voyages of discovery. His twelve-year odyssey was a brilliant success, and he returned to Portugal in 1428 with 'a map of the world, which had all the parts of the world and earth described'.[12] This seemingly incredible map showed the 'Streight of Magelan' and the Cape of Good Hope sixty years before Dias and nearly a hundred years before Magellan set sail (see p. 107). Until it appeared, most European maps of the world had Jerusalem at their centre, their edges patrolled by wild beasts. This new knowledge of the world, hard-won by the Chinese during their great voyages of exploration, was to become the driving force behind the European voyages of discovery.

Dom Pedro, like Henry, had been well educated in an enlightened court, and tutored by Venetian scholars. When the princes were young, the Council of Pisa (1409) had been convened, primarily in an attempt to end the thirty-year 'Great Schism' between the rival popes established in Rome and Avignon. It failed in its aim – the attempt to depose the rivals and install a new pope merely led to there being three popes instead of two – but Portugal sent a major mission to that council, and Dom Pedro and Prince Henry took great interest in its other deliberations. They could not have failed as a result to become acquainted with a revolutionary work, Ptolemy's *Geographia*, long forgotten in Europe but now translated into Latin. It was brought to that council and delivered to the newest pope, Alexander V.

The rediscovery of the *Geographia* created a sensation in Europe, for it maintained that the earth was not flat, but a sphere – something the Chinese already knew – and set out the principles of latitude and longitude by which man could determine his own position and that of new discoveries on that sphere. More than anything else, the reintroduction of Ptolemy into the mainstream of European political life revolutionized cartography and exploration. But brilliant as the *Geographia* was, it contained no maps, only explanations of how to use information to make them. This deficiency was rectified when the Byzantine cartographers Lappacino and Bonnisegni fled the Turks encircling Byzantium, to settle in Venice in 1415. They brought with them a number of maps based upon Ptolemy's *Geographia* showing Africa and India in their correct positions. At the latest, Dom Pedro would have known of these maps by 1428, when he paid his state visit to Venice, though almost certainly he knew of them by 1424, when Niccolò da Conti returned from his travels.

There are two versions of how da Conti returned to what we now call Italy. One school contends that he had returned from the East by 1424, but he had come in fear of his life, in disguise and under the *nom de guerre* 'Bartholomew of Florence' because he was a renegade who had converted to Islam at a time of intense religious persecution and wished to avoid being burned like John Huss, the Czech protestant reformer who had been executed for heresy only nine years earlier.[13] The other school claims that Dom Pedro instructed a famed Franciscan friar, Alberto de Sarteano, to bring da Conti back from Cairo, where he was in hiding, on the promise of absolution.[14] Fra Sarteano succeeded, escorting da Conti to Florence, and Dom Pedro then immediately summoned his envoy to Portugal for a complete debrief of his voyage with the Chinese fleet.

Dom Pedro's principal aim in this was to link Portugal with isolated Christian communities in the East supposedly founded by the apostle Saint Thomas, to encircle Islam and to find a new way to Cathay – a route urgently needed, for while Dom Pedro was travelling, the borders of Egypt were sealed by the Mamluk sultans who ruled the country. By the end of 1421, the Ottomans, who were already in possession of Asia Minor, had surrounded Byzantium and taken control of the terminus of the Silk Road across Asia. An impenetrable barrier had been erected across the eastern Mediterranean and the Near East.

Dom Pedro achieved a magnificent intelligence coup by retaining Fra Mauro and Poggio Bracciolini, the Papal Secretary, and by debriefing the 'renegade', Niccolò da Conti. By doing so he obtained the knowledge that da Conti ('Bartholomew of Florence') had acquired in twenty years' sailing the world – from India to the Cape Verde and Falkland Islands, to Australia and China. Dom Pedro now knew that Cathay and the Spice Islands could be reached by sailing westwards.[15]

The cartographer Paolo Toscanelli (1397–1482) made the same claim after meeting da Conti and extracting every scrap of usable information from him. He later relayed the material in a letter to Christopher Columbus:

I notice your splendid and lofty desire to sail to the regions of the East [China] by those of the West as is shown by the chart which I send you, which would be better shown in the shape of a round sphere . . . not only is the said voyage possible, but it is sure and certain, and of honour and countless gain . . .

I have had most fully the good and true information . . . of other merchants who have long trafficked in those parts, men of great authority.[16]

Toscanelli sent a map to Columbus showing the westwards route across the Atlantic via Antilia. He also passed on da Conti's information to Behain of Bohemia[17] (1459–1507), who was working for the Portuguese government. Behain then showed the strait leading from the Atlantic to the Pacific on both the globe he produced in 1492 and on his maps, and Magellan acknowledged that he had seen them in Portugal before he set sail.[18] A number of other accounts describe Magellan examining Toscanelli's charts in the Portuguese treasury. One can only imagine the extraordinary impact these charts, based on the Chinese voyages of 1421 to 1423, must have had on the Europeans, for they traced the boundaries of vast, unknown oceans and of lands such as South America and the Antarctic whose very existence had previously been clouded and uncertain.

Toscanelli's letter to Columbus and the statements of Magellan and his diarist Pigafetta are further evidence that, long before Magellan set sail, the Portuguese knew that the quickest way to China lay westwards through the strait later named after Magellan but first navigated and charted by the Chinese. The information came from Niccolò da Conti, 'the merchant who travelled in those parts'.[19]

With the reappearance of Niccolò da Conti, I felt I had almost come full circle. It had been in every sense a long and extraordinary journey since I had first seen a mention of his name and his presence in Calicut at the time Zheng He's treasure fleet passed through the port. It had led me to every corner of the globe, and everywhere I had found traces of the Chinese voyages da Conti had described. Now it was clear that the Portuguese and Spanish had read and heard the same accounts and been inspired to make their own voyages of discovery.

Having learned of the existence of new lands beyond the seas from da Conti in 1424, Dom Pedro carried back to Portugal in 1428 a map of the world showing 'all the parts of the world and earth'[20] – Africa, the Caribbean (Antilia), North and South America, the Arctic and Antarctic, India, Australia and China. The information it contained was hugely valuable, and for over a century afterwards the Portuguese went to considerable trouble to prevent any knowledge of it from reaching competing European powers.

Coupled with Henry's improvements to navigation and ship design, the world map revolutionized European exploration for all time. Henry knew that if he could fund his expeditions, Portugal could dominate the world. He needed substantial capital, for there was a large retinue to feed and house, a hospital to maintain, a chapel to be endowed and caravels to be built and fitted out for voyages that might last for months.

The Pope had appointed Prince Henry Grand Master of the Order of Christ in 1420, and its Red Cross motif adorned the sails of his caravels. Funded by tax revenues, the order's principal duties were to defend Portugal and to lead crusades against the infidel. Both Niccolò da Conti and Marco Polo had described a series of Christian states extending all across India.[21] Dom Pedro and Prince Henry now had the knowledge that would enable Portuguese seafarers to reach those Christian communities, and the Order of Christ could fulfil its destiny by linking them.

The order, then, was Henry's prime source of funds, but even its substantial wealth would have been swiftly exhausted without a return on the capital invested in those voyages of discovery. The return was to come first through the colonization of Madeira, an uninhabited island with fertile soil, abundant rainfall and plentiful sunshine. As we have already seen, by June 1421 João Gonçalves

Zarco had claimed the island for Portugal and begun the work of planting crops that were to yield huge profits for Portuguese investors and drive the search for new territories to explore, exploit and colonize.

Colonization was carried out methodically, and the governors of Madeira were required to produce monthly reports of progress. Although vast areas of virgin forest were devastated by fires soon after settlers began to arrive, it proved to be a blessing in disguise. By clearing the forest and enriching the soil with potash, the fires merely speeded the growth of an island economy based on the planting of grape vines and sugar cane, and ever larger quantities of sugar and Madeira wine were produced and exported.

The island provided a vivid illustration of the commercial gains to be won from successful exploration, and as increasing numbers of Portuguese entrepreneurs beat a path to Henry's court, financing voyages of exploration became easier. In the earlier years the strain of fund-raising had taken a heavy toll on the resources of the Order of Christ and on Henry's stamina, but after colonizing Madeira he was financially secure. Portugal could now begin to look further across the oceans to the west. If one small island could yield such wealth, what untold riches might be made from new colonies beyond the seas? Those lands were not unknown to Prince Henry and his sea-captains, for they had the Chinese charts to lead and guide them.

17

COLONIZING
THE
NEW
WORLD

THE PORTUGUESE LOST LITTLE TIME IN EXTENDING THEIR search for new territories in which colonies could be established westwards across the Atlantic: 'As early as 1431 we see Prince Henry the Navigator send Gonzalo Velho Cabral in search of the islands marked on the map which Dom Pedro, the son of King João I, had brought from Italy in 1428.'[1]

As they voyaged further and further, Prince Henry's caravels must have quickly discovered Antilia – Puerto Rico – and established a colony there. Andrea Bianco's 1436 chart describes the Sargasso Sea with the Portuguese name for seaweed, *mar de baga* – powerful evidence that they had reached the Caribbean, for the Sargasso Sea, a mass of floating seaweed, is unique in the world. It could only have been described by someone who had sailed there; and because of the circular wind and current systems, it can only be easily reached from Europe after passing through the Caribbean. The Portuguese could not have been the creators of the first map showing these lands, for of course it predates their voyages. I could only wonder if those first Portuguese settlers had found traces of the Chinese voyages – a carved stone, fragments of porcelain, utensils or artefacts, or a once neat but long overgrown plantation of rice. Would they have paused to wonder at them, or merely shrugged their shoulders, dismissed them as native curiosities and turned their minds from high-flown thoughts to the gritty reality of winning a living from the soil?

Unlike Guadeloupe, Puerto Rico was populated by peaceable people. If the Portuguese did settle here in 1431, some ten years after the Chinese visit, their descendants should have survived to greet Columbus or later explorers. Columbus's first visit to Puerto Rico in 1493, during his second voyage to the New World, was a fleeting one. He was in a hurry to reach the Spanish garrison of La Navidad and the gold mines in Hispaniola, the next island to the west, and visited a single port in Puerto Rico, remaining only a few days. Nonetheless, Columbus found the port to be a civilized one:

King Ferdinand sending Columbus to the New World. From Giuliano Dati's
verse rendition of Columbus's first letter to the King of Spain published in 1493.

The fleet moved on past Saint Ursula and her eleven thousand virgins [the
Virgin Islands] till it reached Porto Rico which was the home of most of
the captives taking refuge with the Spaniards [refugees taken aboard at
Guadeloupe]. On the west end they found a fine harbour abounding in fish.
Here was a native village with a public square, a main road, a terrace – all in
all quite an artistic home-like place.[2]

As I dug deeper into Columbus's records, I found another story:
'A storm driven ship landed at the Isle of the Seven Cities [Antilia]
in the time of the Infante D Henriques [Henry the Navigator].' The
crew were welcomed by the inhabitants, invited in good Portuguese
to attend divine service and urged to remain until their ruler showed
up.[3] Prince Henry, of course, had died long before Columbus set sail.
The story was corroborated by the sixteenth-century Portuguese
historian Antonio Galvão:

Guadeloupe. Les Saintes, approached from the south-east (*below*),
would look like one island curving to the north-west. La Souffrière
(*above*) on Basse Terre is not far to the north.

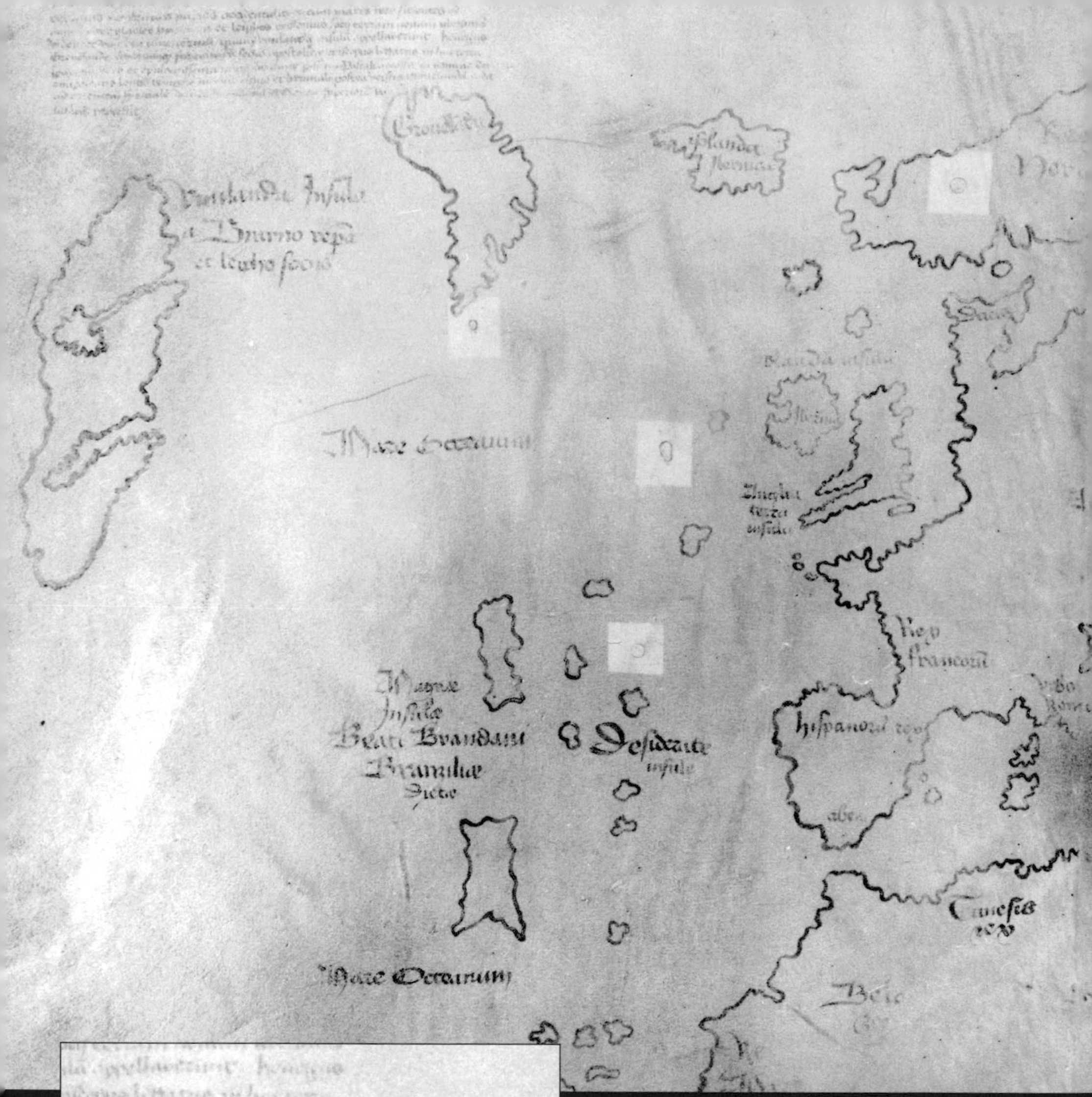

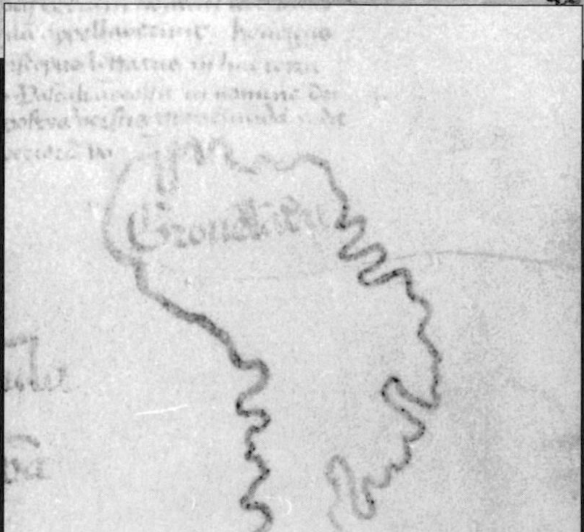

Gronelāda

Vinlāda Insula

Mare Oceanum

Magnæ Insulæ Beati Brandani Branliæ dicte

Desiderate insule

Mare Oceanum

hispanorū reg

Rego francorū

Gronelāda

The Chinese and the New World. The controversial Vinland map (*above*) and a detail of Greenland (*left*): further proof of the extent of Chinese exploration. The Bimini stones (*opposite, main image and opposite, right*) in the Caribbean: surely these are man-made? One of the pyramids (*opposite, left*) at Güimar in the Canary Islands. It shows a remarkable resemblance to a Chinese gnomon.

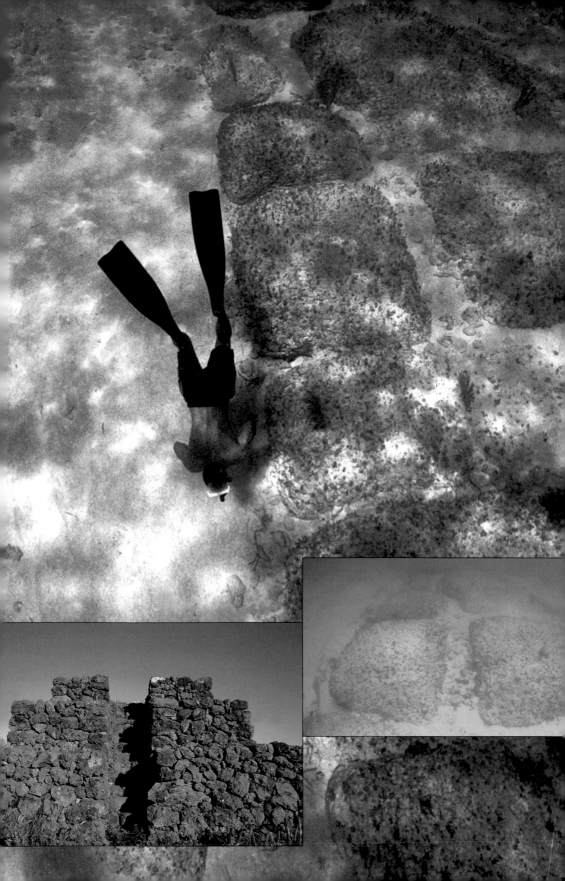

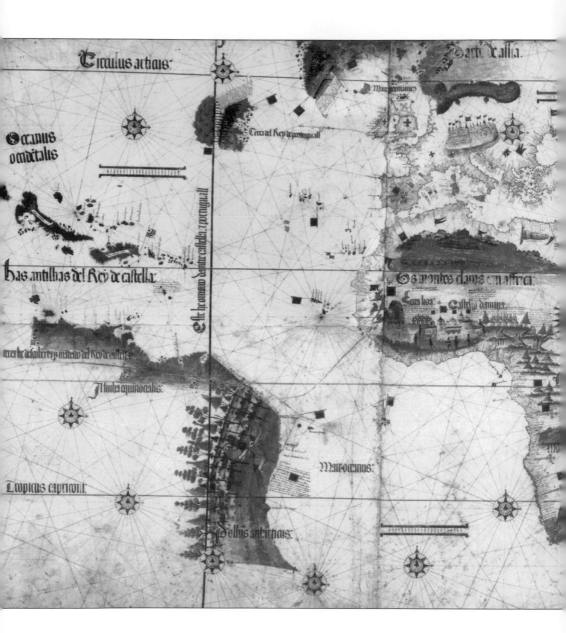

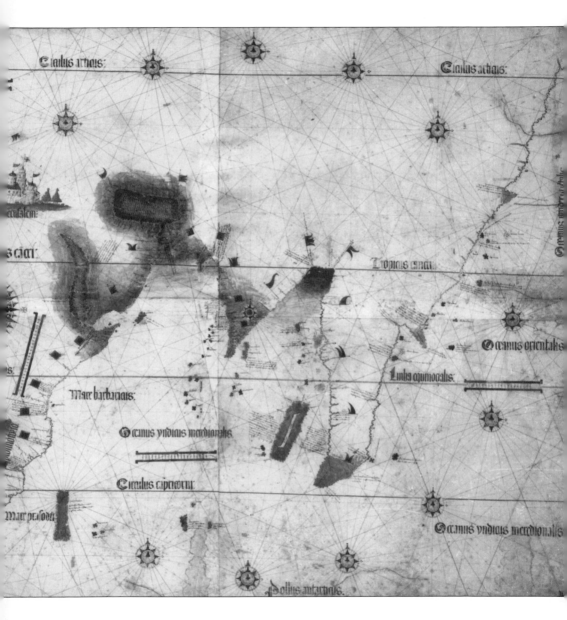

The influential Cantino world chart of 1502.

European exploration: in the fourteenth century Marco Polo with his father and uncle (*below*); in the fifteenth (*opposite, centre, left to right*) Christopher Columbus; Vasco da Gama and Ferdinand Magellan. By the sixteenth century trade with ports such as Calicut was thriving (*above*), but the level of scientific inquiry did not reach Chinese proportions until the advent of Captain James Cook and Joseph Banks (*opposite, bottom left*), who stopped off for water in Tierra del Fuego en route for Tahiti in 1769 (*opposite, bottom right*).

Prince Henry the Navigator
looking westwards from the
prow of the monument at
Belèm to four hundred years
of Portuguese exploration.

So in this year, also 1447, it happened that there came to Portugal a ship through the streight of Gibraltar, and being taken with a great tempest, was forced to run westward more willingly than the men would [wish], and at last they fell upon an island which had seven cities, and the people spake the Portuguese tongue, and they demanded if the Moors did yet trouble Spain . . . The boatswain of the ship brought home a little of the sand, and sold it unto a goldsmith of Lisbon, out of which they had a good quantity of gold.

Dom Pedro understanding this, being then governor of the realm, caused all the things thus brought home, and made known, to be recorded in the House of Justice.

There be some that think that those islands whereupon the Portugals were thus driven were the Antiles or New Spain, alleging good reasons for their opinion.[4]

It was compelling evidence that the Portuguese did settle Antilia in 1431, and were still there in 1447. The Portuguese regent, Dom Pedro, certainly knew of the island; it had appeared on the 1428 map he had personally brought back to Portugal. I was sure that records of what those visiting caravels found must have existed. It would be absurd to imagine that they had travelled for weeks across the oceans, come across an island of Portuguese-speaking people, then sailed on without making a record of the island and their com-patriots' way of life. It was also likely that some of the people who had landed in Puerto Rico in 1431 would have wished to return home by 1447. Some of them were doubtless yearning for their homeland, longing to hear once more the sad, lilting *fado*, and hoping to pass their twilight years in their native land. Those people who did return after the 1447 voyage would also have given the necessary information to the cartographers to correct the earlier chart.

Zuane Pizzigano, author of the 1424 map showing Antilia, never produced another chart and history does not record his fate – I assumed that he had died by the 1440s – but I returned yet again to the Map Room of the British Library and examined the first charts drawn after 1447. These proved a remarkable source of information. A series of charts followed one another in quick succession between 1448 and 1489.[5] In all, I looked at seven pre-Columbian charts, containing seventy-three names and describing features on Antilia and Satanazes. I would have expected these later charts to be updated with further information, but in fact the map drawn in 1463 by Grazioso Benincasa had the same number of cities as the Pizzigano chart. The only change was that all seven cities shown on the earlier chart had been renamed on the later one. The drawing of the island was identical, save for the addition of one more bay on the north coast of Antilia and a more accurate depiction of the south-west and east coasts. I could not understand why the cartographer had renamed all the cities. The mystery deepened with another chart, from 1476, which yielded yet another set of names. Why had they kept changing the names of the cities?

I was convinced that the names must be in medieval Portuguese because the caravels despatched by Prince Henry would hardly have been manned by mercenaries, so I turned to a dictionary for a translation. With the exception of Antilia, not a single name on the later charts appeared to be in medieval Portuguese. They were incomprehensible.[6] If the islands were indeed populated, why did the seven cities not have Portuguese rather than fairytale names?

I asked the owners of the Pizzigano chart for help. The Royal Geographical Society in London had a copy of a pamphlet[7] by Professor Carol Urness, the custodian of the chart, describing the efforts of historians over the last fifty years to solve the question of the identity of the islands. It appeared from the pamphlet that the experts were baffled, and it seemed presumptuous of me to expect to succeed where they had failed. I decided to abandon my quest and leave the mystery for others. I headed home from the Royal Geographical Society thoroughly despondent after being frustrated at this last hurdle, unable to get corroborative evidence that the Portuguese had settled in Puerto Rico after the Chinese had discovered the island but before Columbus set sail.

In times of trouble, my habit is to pray to the Virgin and eat bacon sandwiches. Having done so, a thought occurred to me. Sagres, the home base of the caravels, is only a day's sailing from Sanlúcar de Barrameda on the estuary of the Guadalquivir. In 1431, it was a major Castilian port. Had there been any Castilians aboard those caravels, and if so, could the writing be in medieval Castilian? I hurried back to the British Library. I found a Castilian dictionary in six volumes, but only A–D was available. That scarcely mattered, because six of the seven names on Grazioso Benincasa's 1463 chart began with the letter 'A'. Not one appeared in this massive medieval dictionary; the names were not Castilian. Were they from Aragon, then? The people of Aragon spoke Catalan, but once again, not one name appeared in the dictionary of medieval Catalan. I made a final, desperate search in the Basque and Latin dictionaries, to no avail. I was beaten.

I left the reading room and paced around the courtyard outside the library, cudgelling my brains without success. I then went back to the reading room to put away the dictionaries. There were seven of them strewn across my desk. As I closed the medieval *Dizionario Etimologico* my eye was caught by a section on the code employed in medieval times. Y meant 'there is' or 'and'; *a* meant 'towards'; *j* emphasized the letter before or after it; and *an* before a word meant *particular negativa*, 'the opposite of'. To describe black, they would write *anblanco* (the opposite of white). Was this the key I was looking for?

I went back to the charts. Six of the names began with *an*, 'the opposite of'. Instead of looking for *ansollj* in the dictionary, I should have been looking for its opposite, *sollj* – and *sollj* meant 'sun'. Feverishly, I worked through the medieval Catalan, Castilian and Portuguese dictionaries, cross-referencing with modern dictionaries. There were now ten of them scattered across the desk. One of the names was indeed Catalan, a few were Castilian, but the great majority were medieval Portuguese. I began to compile an alphabetical list. Sixty-three of the seventy-three names were in medieval

Portuguese, four of the remaining ten were Castilian, one was Catalan and five were unaccounted for. I expected the last five to be medieval Venetian – Pizzigano came from Venice – but surprisingly, only one was. Three were in the Veneto language of Treviso. One name, *anthib*, had me beaten.

I checked the names against a modern map of Puerto Rico and within half an hour I had found the solution: the names were not of the seven cities but descriptions of natural and man-made features, and the descriptions on the 1448–89 charts put it beyond argument that Antilia was Puerto Rico. Mountains, rainforests, harbours, rivers and salt-pans were described on Antilia exactly where they are found on Puerto Rico. There were no discrepancies between the charts: the later ones merely amplified the former. Some Castilian names were used on later charts, but they still described the same place. Only two islands in the whole world fit these descriptions: Puerto Rico and Guadeloupe.

Con is marked on the south-east part of the island of Antilia/Puerto Rico – the conical mountain of Pico del Este. To the north, the cartographer has placed *ansollj*, 'no sun', corresponding precisely to the El Yunque rainforest, deluged with 240 inches of rain a year. Similar tropical downpours – *choue, choue-due, cyodue* – are shown at the western end of the island at the end of the Cordillera Central. This area has an annual rainfall of a hundred inches, still prodigious by European standards. The draughtsman described marshes (*ensa*) around present-day Mayaguez, the water-logged estuary of the Grande Rio de Añasco, but one of the most interesting descriptions was *antuub* or *an tuub*, literally 'without drainage tubes', placed on the north coast to the east of Arecibo. Today, the area remains a vast mosquito-ridden swamp called Cienaga Tiburones. The name Tiburones is Castilian, *tiberon*, or 'drainage', in turn deriving from the Portuguese *tubaro*. Brilliant red and green Puerto Rican parrots, *ansaros*, are denoted in the south-west – presumably the Portuguese wore the feathers of these exotic birds in the same way Columbus's sailors later did. The forest of

Boquerón where the cartographer drew these parrots remains a bird watcher's paradise today. The lack of arable and fertile land is vividly caught in the descriptions of the cartographers (Puerto Rico to this day has less than 5 per cent arable land): *ansessel*, 'no grass', appears four times, supplemented by *an suolo*, 'no arable land'. Redeeming features are found on the narrow coastal plains.

The translation that caused me most difficulty was *asal*. My dictionary[8] said that the word is derived from the Latin *acinus*, meaning 'berry, especially grape, also any berry or the seeds in a berry', but *asal* is placed on the chart on a mountain slope behind Ponce. Winters in Puerto Rico are too hot for grapes – they need very cold winters to thrive – but *asal* was written above modern-day Yauco, the 'coffee capital' of Puerto Rico, so I wondered if the Portuguese were describing coffee beans. This theory provoked a vigorous debate among the historians advising me. Some pointed out that coffee was indigenous to East Africa and was introduced to the Caribbean by the Spanish, so it could not have been marked on charts made before the Spanish landed. But further research[9] revealed that at least nineteen strains of coffee were found in the Caribbean before the Spanish arrived. It grew on mountain slopes, usually between three and four and a half thousand feet, in temperate climates within the tropics where there is no wind but plenty of morning sun. These conditions are found on the southern slopes of the Cordillera Central behind Ponce, just where *asal* is marked on the charts of Antilia. Could the Chinese have introduced coffee when they arrived in late 1421?

The second translation that provoked a heated debate was *cua cusa* – pumpkin – shown on the coastal plain in the east near Naguabo. Had pumpkins and squashes really grown there? It transpired that they still do. On a visit to Puerto Rico while researching this book, I took photographs of twenty varieties piled in heaps beside the road: long yellow, champion market, hackensack, manu, rocky ford and white Japan musk squashes; yellow, crookneck, orange, white, delicate and golden scalloped melons; and an assortment of cucumbers, gherkins and eggplants.[10] They grow in such variety and profusion and to such a size because of the sunshine, volcanic soil and moderate rainfall particular to the eastern coastal strip of Puerto Rico.

The really fascinating aspect of the translations of these names is that they were shown on charts published before Columbus set sail and they describe plants foreign to Puerto Rico. Coffee was then native to Africa, cucumbers to India, mangoes to south-east Asia. Columbus also found coconuts, native to the Pacific. Not only had someone reached the Caribbean before Columbus and drawn Puerto Rico with incredible accuracy, they had also brought plants there from all over the world. It seems to me that only the great Chinese fleet commanded by Admiral Zhou Wen can have achieved these things.

Marolio was another interesting name, on a chart drawn by Albino Canepa in the 1480s. It was placed in the same position as *marnlio* on the Pizzigano chart; I assumed that the lower edge of the *o* had become erased. *Marolio* is medieval Portuguese for 'plants of the Annonaceae family' – star fruit, sweet and sour sops, pawpaws and custard apples. On both charts the cartographer had placed the description just north of modern Ponce in the middle of the south coast. This area remains the centre of the tropical fruit industry of Puerto Rico, rejoicing in plantations of star fruit, sour sops and papaya. Their juice is exported all over the Americas and forms the basis for the rum punches tourists continue to enjoy. These fruits were indigenous to south-east Asia and South America. Once again, I concluded that the Chinese had introduced them to Puerto Rico in 1421.

The cartographers depicted Satanazes (Guadeloupe) in an entirely different light to Puerto Rico. They changed the name from Satan's or Devil's Island to Saluagio (Island of Savages) in later charts.[11] Those later charts of Guadeloupe merely amplified what could be seen from the sea – a second volcano (*con*), Mont Carmichael at 1,414 metres, with a plateau (*silla*) between it and

La Souffrière. The waterfalls flowing down the east side of La Souffrière (Karukeka and Trois Rivières) had the soubriquets *duchal* and *tubo de agua* – 'showers from heaven'. Villages and cultivated fields (*aralia y sya*) are shown on the low land on the west coast of Grande Terre, just where Columbus described them as he sailed past years later. Satanazes is clearly a horrible place, summarized by Albino Canepa as *nar i sua*, 'nothing but sweltering heat', but the description of the island of Saya (Les Saintes), 'any number of tropical birds', was apt, for the island is still renowned for its kingfishers, hummingbirds and bananaquits – little flying jewels flitting across the turquoise sea that separates the islands.

The most unusual name Zuane Pizzigano had written on Antilia (in the south-east, covering Vieques Island) was *ura*, placed next to *con* on later charts. *Uracano* is Venetian for 'violent explosion', 'eruption' or 'tempest'. By 1421, the volcanoes on the south-east coast of Puerto Rico had long been extinct, and earthquakes were and are more prevalent on the west of the island, near Mayaguez, but hurricanes invariably approach from the east and roar northwestwards from Vieques Island to San Juan. I was sure that this was what the Chinese cartographer had seen when the junks arrived in November, during the hurricane season that runs from June to the end of November.

All these names, coupled with the extraordinary physical similarity between the islands on the Pizzigano chart (and others) and what is actually there, put it beyond argument that Antilia is Puerto Rico, Satanazes is Guadeloupe and Saya is Les Saintes. Although it is possible to quibble over the nuances of a few of the medieval Catalan or Castilian translations, continued debate about the identity of the Antilia group of islands is pointless. These names and maps are unequivocal proof that the islands were continuously settled by the Portuguese from before 1447 until 1492, the time of Columbus's first voyage. The plants foreign to Puerto Rico were brought there before Columbus set sail. To my mind, this is proof that the Chinese discovered Puerto Rico.

Although the depiction of the islands was accurate, their location and orientation was not. They were shown in the Atlantic rather than in the Caribbean, more than two thousand miles away from their correct position. The error was gradually corrected by succeeding cartographers. By 1448, the islands were 1,500 miles west of the Canaries (750 miles in error), and by 1474 they had again shifted westwards, just 500 miles in error. The mistake is easily explicable. In 1431, Henry's captains did not have good astrolabes (sextants), nor did they understand declination. Portuguese navigators did not know how to use Polaris until 1451; only after 1473, using declination tables, could they finally determine latitude with accuracy (Toscanelli's 1474 chart places Antilia at the correct latitude). Longitude remained a problem. Columbus put the Americas a thousand miles out for longitude, as well as twenty degrees for latitude. When he returned from his first voyage, he did not know where he had gone, what he had found or where it was. He thought he had reached China.

In the fifteenth century, the Portuguese navigated by compass and measured their speed through the water by throwing logs off the bow. They positioned the islands by dead reckoning, calculating their position by speed through the water multiplied by the number of days travelled. But they did not realize that the great mass of water over which they were sailing was itself moving, taking them away from their dead-reckoning position. Like Columbus, the Portuguese did not know where they had gone. When I made adjustments to allow for the movement of water during their ten-week voyage from Madeira to Guadeloupe,[12] I found that the Portuguese had placed the islands in their correct dead-reckoning position and orientation.

I felt that there were two further questions about the Pizzigano chart still to be answered. The first concerned the size of the islands. In the earlier charts, Antilia was depicted as bigger than Puerto Rico, and Satanazes was also shown larger than Guadeloupe; a mistake caused, I believe, by transposing not only the wrong position of the islands but their scale from the earlier (Chinese) map onto a

European one. The other outstanding question was when and where the Pizzigano chart had been made. It seems likely that he was working under the direction of Dom Pedro, whose cartographers were searching for information about new lands in order to create a world map for Prince Henry. I knew that the Holy Roman Emperor had given Dom Pedro substantial estates in the Veneto at Treviso, fifteen miles north of Venice, and this became the Portuguese delegation's base. It struck me that the Portuguese cartographers probably met Niccolò da Conti there in 1424. He, of course, had spent years aboard a junk of the Chinese treasure fleet, the original discoverers of Antilia. The chart was almost certainly made in Treviso, since the majority of the 'non-Portuguese' names on the chart were in the dialect of Veneto rather than Venice. Pizzigano may have been a monk at the great Dominican sanctuary of San Niccolò at Treviso.

The Pizzigano chart depicted Puerto Rico so accurately that whoever collated the information must have been a master of his craft; in that era, that meant the original cartographer can only have been Chinese. The importance of the chart and those that followed is twofold: not only do they provide evidence that the Chinese discovered the Americas seventy years before Columbus, they also show that Puerto Rico had become a permanent Portuguese settlement before 1447. The names on the subsequent charts continually hone the descriptions of the islands long before Columbus reached them. The positions of the islands were also continually corrected, and the charts from 1463 and 1470 contain a wealth of additional information about Antilia, including further bays on the north-west and east coasts, and the slightly exaggerated south-west tip was redrawn with greater accuracy. The island of Ymana, to the north of Puerto Rico, was also better drawn on later charts, its name changed to Rosellia. As European navigators discovered declination and the measurement of latitude, and improved their sextants and their measurement of time, the positions of the islands on the charts were moved to the south-west.[13]

Identifying Antilia and Satanazes enabled me to pinpoint the other 'islands' surrounding them on the medieval charts. Andrea Bianco's chart of 1448, for example, includes the north-east coast of Brazil, and Cristobal Soligo's 1489 chart[14] shows a further seven 'islands' – the tip of Hispaniola in the west, Trinidad, the Virgin Islands, St Vincent, St Lucia, Barbados and the north coast of Venezuela in the south – all before Columbus had even set sail.

I returned to the chart of Puerto Rico and began to search for the probable site of the first settlement. Both the Portuguese and the Chinese must have approached from the south-east on the prevailing winds. The southern and western coasts of Antilia were more accurately drawn on the Pizzigano chart than the northern or eastern coasts, so I concentrated the search there.

The Pizzigano chart has *cyodue*, 'incessant rain', to the west, *ansuly*, 'lack of fertile land', in the south-west and *ura*, 'hurricane', to the east; none of these sounded a particularly inviting place to settle. On the other hand, *marolio*, 'luscious tropical fruit', is shown just north of Ponce, and Ponce Bay was drawn with striking accuracy on all the charts, showing a prominent headland, La Guancha, to the east of the bay. For centuries, this headland has provided sheltered anchorage from the easterly winds. The sea abounds in fish and, located as it is in the rain shadow of the mountains, Ponce has by far the best climate in Puerto Rico. When I flew there to take a look on the ground, I could see the purple clouds of an afternoon thunderstorm breaking on the central Cordillera to the north, leaving the town dry. Not without reason was Ponce named 'the pearl of the south'. It is likely the Portuguese made their first settlement here; this is where they would have greeted newcomers on the 1447 voyage and invited them to attend divine service.

The river leading from the harbour into the old town still retains the name Rio Portugués. The brilliant-white cathedral of Our Lady of Guadeloupe stands on its banks, and as I sat in the main square of Ponce one evening, sipping bitter black Puerto Rican coffee at the end of another day spent combing the island for evidence of the Chinese voyages and the early Portuguese colonists, I watched people pouring into the cathedral to attend evening mass. Some men had red hair, the women fine chiselled faces, sharper features and paler skins than in the north. In their looks, their way of life, their *fado* songs and their *ferrapeira* dances, the people of Ponce to this day resemble their Portuguese ancestors from the Algarve. Will the bones of their brave forefathers who set sail from Sagres long ago to found this, the first European colony in the New World, one day be found beneath the cathedral of Our Lady of Guadeloupe?

The Portuguese had taken their first steps into the New World that the Chinese had discovered, but despite the evidence offered by copies of the charts drawn by the Chinese, one obstacle – as much psychological as physical – remained to be overcome before the Portuguese empire could spread across the globe. The fear of the unknown still dominated the minds of ordinary Portuguese seamen, and a lifetime of myth, legend and superstition could not be erased overnight. Magellan was still struggling to overcome the fears of his crewmen in the early years of the sixteenth century as he tried to coax them through the strait that was to bear his name.

In the summer of 1432, with Madeira, the Azores (discovered by La Salle) and Puerto Rico already colonized, Prince Henry called Gil Eannes, a skilled seaman and loyal retainer, to his court at Sagres. Eannes had been despatched on a mission the previous year to the Canary Islands. Now Henry insisted that, come what may, he must round Cape Bojador on the coast of modern Western Sahara, to the south of Morocco. The cape featured in many lurid seamen's myths about the unknown world. It was a place where vast cataracts crashed into the sea, fierce currents dragged ships to their doom and even the sea-water itself had been turned into 'red slime'.

Eannes followed Prince Henry's commands with understandable caution, standing well out to sea so as to approach the dreaded Cape Bojador from the south and thus avoid the legendary waterfall off the cape, but he found no serpents or giant sea monsters as he made his first landfall a few miles beyond the cape. The land appeared uninhabited; there were even a few flowers on the beach. Eannes plucked a bouquet for Prince Henry: 'My Lord, I thought that I ought to bring some token of the land since I was on it. I gathered these herbs which I here present to your gaze, the which we in this country call Roses of Saint Mary.'[15] Returning northwards to Bojador itself, Eannes found the 'eternally rushing water' was but vast shoals of grey mullet, the 'waterfalls tumbling off the earth' were cliffs, rising sheer from the sea, and the 'sea baked into red slime' was water discoloured by the red Sahara sand.

Eannes's achievement in rounding Cape Bojador completely changed European man's attitude to seafaring. At a stroke, he had shattered centuries of legend and superstition. If a ship could safely round Cape Bojador, man could sail anywhere. There was no need for irrational fears about falling off the edge of the earth. With the Chinese charts to guide them, there was nowhere the Portuguese sea-captains would not venture, once they had persuaded their men to follow where they led; exploring the limits of the world became merely a matter of time.

ON THE
SHOULDERS
OF
GIANTS

By 1460, THE YEAR HENRY THE NAVIGATOR DIED, PUERTO RICO was well known and Portuguese exploration of the three groups of islands in the Atlantic – the Azores, the Canaries and the Cape Verde Islands – was complete. The islands were stocked with animals and became bases for explorers making their way between North and South America and Africa. By a fortunate coincidence, all lay in the track of the circulatory wind systems; the Canaries and Cape Verde Islands on the way out to the Americas and the Azores on the way back. Gradually, Europeans reached the lands the Chinese admirals had discovered.

In parallel with his systematic and continual improvements to ocean navigation, Henry the Navigator had relentlessly pushed his captains further and further across the seas. By the time Portuguese ships set sail for the Cape of Good Hope, the measurement of latitude in the northern hemisphere was as accurate as the Chinese calculations had been years earlier.

Bartolomeu Dias (c. 1450–1500) led the way. In 1482, he was captain of one of the ships exploring the Gold Coast and Africa past the 'bulge', and in 1487 he was appointed to the command of a small squadron of three ships that was to attempt to round the southern tip of Africa. Neither Dias nor his masters knew how far south the Cape really stretched – the charting of West Africa by the Chinese fleet had been carried out before they had mastered the calculation of latitude in the southern hemisphere – but they had no doubts that it could be rounded. Dom Pedro's map of 1428 had showed the Cape's triangular shape, and before Dias set sail the Portuguese king gave his emissary, Pêro da Covilha, a map of the world (*Carta de Marear*) showing that the Cape could be rounded to reach India. When Dias duly reached the Cape, he

came in sight of that Great and Famous Cape *concealed for so many centuries*, which when it was seen made known not only itself but also another new world of countries. Bartolomeu Dias, and those of his company, because of the perils and storms they had endured in doubling it, called it the Stormy Cape, but on their return to the Kingdom, the King Dom João gave it another illustrious name, calling it the Cape of Good Hope [my italics].[1]

Dias was followed by Vasco da Gama (c. 1469–1525) who was ordered to continue round the Cape to India and the source of spice. Da Gama was provided with charts showing the Cape, and precise declination tables:

> Tables showing the declination of the sun were provided by the Astronomer Royal, Abraham Zacuto Bin Samuel. These . . . had been translated from Hebrew into Latin the previous year and printed at Leira under the title *Al Manach Perpetuum Celestium Motuum Cujus Radix Est 1473*. Other books, maps and charts were supplied . . . amongst these documents almost certainly . . . [were] the log and charts of Dias.[2]

After rounding the Cape, da Gama proceeded up the east coast of Africa, finding the famous ports of Sofala, Kilwa, Zanzibar, Mombasa and Malindi, developed by Chinese and Indian fleets over the centuries when the Indian Ocean trade was by far the most busy and lucrative in the world. By the late 1400s the Chinese had closed their trading routes with the outside world; nonetheless, the Portuguese explorers found evidence of the earlier Chinese visits in the mass of blue and white porcelain decorating many houses the length of East Africa. When da Gama returned from his second voyage, he knew the way to Malacca and the Spice Islands in the East. The world's spice trade was now within Portugal's grasp. Anyone who opposed them was mown down with grapeshot. In effect, da Gama stole the trade the Indians and Chinese had spent centuries developing. Skilful though he was, like Dias before him, da Gama discovered nothing new.

In parallel with da Gama's pursuit of the spice trade in the East, King João of Portugal had sent Pedro Álvares Cabral (1467–1520) to South America, to the lands shown on the 1428 World Map. In 1500, King João's successor, Manuel I, ordered Cabral to take possession of the western parts of the Indies. Like Dias and da Gama, Cabral used the Canaries and then the Cape Verde Islands as his bases before making landfall on the South American coast. At this time, a cluster of explorers reached South America within a year of one another: Vespucci, Pinzón and De Lepe in 1499, and Mendoza the next year. The first three made landfall on the Amazon delta, then sailed north-westwards.

This north-east coast of Brazil, discovered by the Chinese treasure fleets of Zhou Man and Hong Bao, had appeared on many maps drawn before any of those European explorers set sail. Andrea Bianco's map of 1448 referred to *Ixola Otinticha Xe Longa a Ponente 1500 mia* – 'a genuine island is 1,500 miles west of here [West Africa]' – and Master João de Barros, on the 1500 expedition to the Brazilian coast, confirmed that the land had appeared on earlier maps: 'The lands might the King see represented on the Mappa Mundi which Pêro daz Bisagudo had.'[3] Bisagudo was a nickname given to the famous explorer Pero da Cunha who had been sent with a Portuguese map of the world to colonize what is now Ghana in Africa. De Barros said the only real difference between what Cabral's expedition saw in 1500 and what appeared on Bisagudo's earlier 'Mappa Mundi' was that he, de Barros, could now certify Brazil was inhabited. Christopher Columbus also confirmed that Brazil was known to the Portuguese before any of their expeditions set sail for South America. He noted in his diaries that he wished to proceed further south of Trinidad 'to see what was the meaning of King John of Portugal who said there was terra firma to the south'.[4]

So, Andrea Bianco, Columbus and de Barros all state that a map of Brazil existed before the first European expedition sailed in 1500. The only possible sources of the information on that map, the 1428 World Map, were the cartographers with the Chinese fleets of 1421–3. The port of San Luis is instantly recognizable on the Piri Reis map (derived from the 1428 map) and the latitudes of the Orinoco and Amazon deltas are precisely correct. In addition, there is no shortage of other, permanent traces of the Chinese visit to

South America: Asiatic chickens were found in the Orinoco delta by the first European explorers, and Venezuelan Indians have blood groups that are otherwise unique to south-west China.

With the Cape of Good Hope rounded and South America discovered, the exploration of the rest of the world quickly followed. Ferdinand Magellan (c. 1480–1521) was orphaned when he was ten years old and became a page at the Portuguese court, where he was trained in navigation. He was sent to East Africa in 1505, and for the next seven years saw service in the Indian Ocean. He took part in the expedition to establish a Portuguese colony in India, and in 1511 he played a significant part in the conquest of Zheng He's former forward base, Malacca. He returned home in 1512 and sailed with the Portuguese expedition to Morocco, where he was severely wounded. After a disagreement with his commander, he left the army without permission. As a result he was disgraced and was refused a pension.

In disgust, he moved to Spain and in 1518 was appointed captain general of a fleet to explore a westward route to the Spice Islands, across the Pacific. He sailed from the Guadalquivir estuary the next year with five ships and 241 men. Magellan knew of the strait that bears his name before he set sail, for it was shown on a map in the King of Portugal's treasury that Magellan inspected and took with him.[5] On reaching the Spice Islands, Magellan showed the chart to the local king.[6] It depicted a way through the Strait of Magellan and across the Pacific; 'From Cape Frio until the Islands of the Maluccas throughout this navigation there are no lands laid down in the maps they [Magellan's expedition] carry with them.'[7]

Magellan never claimed to be the first man to have circumnavigated the world; nevertheless, his was still an amazing feat. He was in a tiny ship, a toy compared to the Chinese leviathans, and, unlike the Chinese, the Portuguese had very little experience of long transoceanic voyages and were unaware that certain foods could prevent scurvy. Magellan, Dias, da Gama and Cabral were very skilful navigators and seamen, they were also brave and resolute men with awesome qualities of leadership, but not one of them actually discovered 'new lands'. When they set sail, each one of them had a chart showing where he was going. All their 'discoveries' had been made nearly a century earlier by the Chinese.

Nor did Christopher Columbus 'discover' the Americas. Far from setting sail full of fear that his fleet might fall off the edge of the world, he knew exactly where he was going, as can be seen in excerpts from his logs when he was still in mid-Atlantic:

Wednesday September 19th [1492]

The Admiral did not wish to be delayed by beating to the windward in order to make sure whether there was land in that direction, but he was certain that to the north and to the south there were some islands, as in truth there were . . . [he said] 'and there is time enough, for, God willing, on the return voyage, all will be seen'. These are his words.

Wednesday October 24th

[describing how to reach Antilia] I should steer west-south-west to go there . . . and in the spheres which I have seen and in the drawings of mappae mundi it is in this region.

Wednesday November 14th

And he says that he believes that these islands are those without number which in the mappae mundi are placed at the end of the east.[8]

It is clear from these three entries that Columbus had seen spheres and mappae mundi showing islands in the Atlantic, and that these lay, in Columbus's opinion, to the north and south of his position on 19 September 1492. Puerto Rico (Antilia) appears on the 1424 Pizzigano chart, the coast of New England on the Cantino, Brazil on Andrea Bianco's map of 1448 and many West Indian islands on Cristobal Soligo's chart of 1489 – all drawn before Columbus reached them.

In 1479, Columbus had married Doña Felipa Perestrello, the

daughter of the governor of Porto Santo, the small island near Madeira settled by the Portuguese. His forthcoming marriage gave him sufficient confidence to correspond with the celebrated scientist Toscanelli, who replied at once: 'I have received thy letters with the things that thou didst send me and with them I received a great favour. I notice thy splendid and lofty desire to sail to the regions of the east by those of the west [i.e. reach China by sailing westwards], as is shown by the chart which I send you.'[9] The 'chart' that accompanied Toscanelli's letter to Columbus has been lost, but it can be reconstructed using another letter from Toscanelli to the King of Portugal, enclosing a chart of the Atlantic: 'But from the Island of Antilia known to you to the far famed island of Cipangu there are ten spaces ... so there is not a great space to be traversed over unknown waters.'[10]

Antilia was indeed very well known to the Portuguese. They had settled there in 1431, and were still there when Columbus set sail in 1492, but his knowledge of the Americas went far further. By his own evidence he knew of the 'Strait of Magellan' in the south and the coast of north-east Brazil.[11] He had seen mappae mundi and spheres showing the Atlantic. He also knew well that China and the Spice Islands could be reached by sailing eastwards round the Cape of Good Hope, for Christopher and his brother Bartholomew were both present when Dias reported to the king that he had rounded the Cape at that latitude.[12] Columbus was hell bent on gaining fame and glory by sailing westwards for China and the Spice Islands.

Columbus certainly saw the 1428 master chart of the world. This is corroborated in a number of ways: in notes on the 1513 Piri Reis map which credit Columbus with knowing that there were only two hours of daylight in the far south; in Columbus's letter to the King of Portugal in which he writes about lands in South America, a letter written before the Portuguese explorers had set sail for that continent; and in his notes inscribed on the inside flap of his own copy of Marco Polo's book about his voyage from China to India by sea. In short, Columbus knew that China could be reached by sailing westabout (Toscanelli's letter) or by sailing eastabout. He must have known from the 1428 World Map that the eastabout voyage was the shorter.

In these circumstances, it must have been horrifying for Columbus to realize that the Portuguese were well on their way to rounding the Cape of Good Hope and sailing into the Indian Ocean, whence they could sail with the monsoon winds to China. The Portuguese advances down the African coast must have been a matter of grave concern to him. By 1485, Dias had reached the African coast as far as 13°S. At that stage, not only did Columbus know of the route westwards, but he had sailed to Iceland (in 1477), which country he was told Chinese people had visited.

In 1485, Christopher Columbus left Portugal, where he had been on and off since his marriage. During that time he may well have sailed to Antilia on a secret voyage funded by the Pope, as Señor Ruggero Marino has stated. Marino bases his assumption largely on the inscription on the tomb of Pope Innocent VIII, who died in July 1492, i.e. before Columbus set out on his first 'voyage to the Bahamas'. On the Pope's tomb were the words 'novi orbis suo auro inventi gloria' – 'the glory of the new world having been found with his gold'.

Bartholomew Columbus remained in Portugal as a member of the team improving the Portuguese maps as and when new evidence came in from the voyages of discovery. In 1487–8, Dias pushed on further down the African coast and reached what we call the Cape of Good Hope. In 1473, the Portuguese had discovered how to calculate latitude from the sun's declination, so Dias was able to put the latitude of the Cape of Good Hope at 34°22′ South. Both Bartholomew and Christopher knew this correct latitude (see p. 384).

Columbus's plans for a voyage westwards were now in desperate trouble, for the Portuguese were on the verge of opening up the route to India round the Cape of Good Hope. Unless he acted quickly, his chances of glory were over. At this time, the Catholic monarchs Ferdinand and Isabella had begun their assault on the last

Moorish enclave in Spain, south of the Sierra Nevada mountains around Granada. Columbus had no chance of extracting funds from the Portuguese, who were concentrating on the easterly route to China, and knew that his only chance lay with the Catholic monarchs who did not have the 1428 chart and thus did not know that the shorter route lay eastabout. It was therefore in Columbus's interests to persuade Ferdinand and Isabella that the quickest route to China lay westwards. This, in my submission, is the motive for the forgery and theft Christopher and Bartholomew Columbus now perpetrated.

Their timing was extraordinarily fortunate, for in 1492 Granada had fallen and the Catholic monarchs wished to extend the pursuit of the Moors overseas. Columbus's plan to sail westabout for China would fall on receptive ears if he could persuade Ferdinand and Isabella that his plan was realistic and that it offered the chance of reaching the Spice Islands before the Portuguese.

In 1963, Alexander O. Vietor, the map curator at Yale University, reported a gift by an anonymous donor 'in the form of a magnificent painted world map signed by Henricus Martellus approximately six feet by four feet [180 × 120 cm]'. Vietor went on:

> It is painted in what seems to be tempera over a base of paper in sheets of different sizes, the whole backed up with a large framed canvas, much in the manner of a painting . . . It has graduations of latitude and of longitude in the margins, the first instance of longitudes being shown on the map . . . on this map Cipango is placed 90 degrees from the Canaries.[13]

Mr Vietor subsequently corresponded on the matter with Professor Arthur Davies, who at the time held the Reardon Smith Chair of Geography at the University of Exeter (1948–71). Vietor also provided Professor Davies with infrared photographs of the map for close study. This map, which I shall call the 'Yale Martellus', is four times the size of another map Martellus published in 1489. The experts, principally Davies and Vietor, are unanimous that the

Yale Martellus was the original and the 1489 Martellus a copy at one-quarter the scale. Ashleigh Skelton has also concluded that the Yale map is genuine, its author Martellus. My belief is that both maps, although genuine, contain forgeries, and the forger was Bartholomew Columbus.

The 1489 Martellus map extends from the Canaries to the east coast of China. Although no meridians or longitude scales are given, estimates based on the measurement of the map show that the distance from Lisbon to the east coast of China eastabout is not less than 230° and probably 240°. Westabout, the coast of China is shown approximately 130° west of Lisbon. This is a colossal exaggeration of the distance eastabout. The Catalan atlas of 1376 had the distance from Portugal to China eastabout at approximately 116°; the Genoese map of 1457 approximately 136°; and the Fra Mauro of 1459 about 120°. The true measurement is 141° from the Canaries to Shanghai, so the 1489 Martellus exaggerates the distance to China from Portugal eastabout by nearly 100°. The Columbus brothers of course knew the true distance eastwards from Lisbon to China because the Portuguese had the 1428 World Map.

The 1489 Martellus map could not have been completed before that year, for it featured complete details of the discoveries of Bartolomeu Dias's voyage of 1487 – when he doubled the Cape of Good Hope and reached the Indian Ocean. He returned to Portugal in December 1488. Within a year, then, full details of this trip, including Dias's rich nomenclature, had appeared on the map Martellus made in Italy, this despite strenuous efforts on the part of the King of Portugal to keep the map secret. The penalty for stealing maps was death. The Portuguese government's policy had been shattered in one fell swoop by someone in a unique position to know all the details.

The second forgery, on both Martellus maps, is that a huge dogleg of fictitious land has been appended to the Malayan peninsula from the equator south to 29° South, thereafter being widened to reach China. So enormous and wide was this peninsula that it seemed to render impossible any voyage between China and India. In short, anyone who had got into the Indian Ocean could not continue to the east. To a third party, such as the Catholic monarchs, who did not have the 1428 map, it showed that eastabout China could not be reached by rounding the Cape of Good Hope.

The third forgery is that Martellus's two maps extend southwards the latitude of the Cape of Good Hope, which Dias had fixed at 34°22' South, to 45° South. That Bartholomew Columbus was responsible for this addition is beyond doubt, for it was made in his own hand. In the volume of *Imago Mundi* found among the possessions of Christopher Columbus after his death are numerous notes written in the margins or below the printed matter. Number 23 has been identified by Professor Davies, who has spent a lifetime analysing the characteristics of the Columbus brothers' scripts, as being the handwriting of Bartholomew. It reads:

> Note in the year '88 in the month of December arrived in Lisbon Bartholomew Diaz [*sic*], captain of three caravelles which the most serene king of Portugal had sent to try out the land in Guinea. He reported to the same most serene king that he had sailed beyond Yan 600 leagues, namely 450 to the south and 250 to the north, up a promontory which he calls Capa de Buon Esperanza [Cape of Good Hope] which we believe to be in Abyssinia. He says that in this place he found by the astrolabe that he was 45 degrees below the equator and that this place is 3,100 leagues distant from Lisbon. He has described this voyage and plotted it league by league on a marine chart in order to place it under the eyes of the most serene king himself. I was present in all of this.[14]

Bartholomew Columbus's claim that Dias had put the Cape of Good Hope at 45° South was blatantly untrue. No-one in Lisbon at the time bar the Columbus brothers knew of this 45° assertion, for Bartholomew made it after he had left Portugal.

To date, no link has been shown between the Columbus brothers and Martellus; it could have been that Martellus was the forger. The link, however, can be deduced in two ways. The first is that Martellus's map contains information only the Portuguese knew (Martellus was Italian), moreover information guarded upon pain of death which had been acquired only months earlier. Someone with access to top-secret Portuguese maps must have provided the information to Martellus. That points the finger at Bartholomew Columbus, or others who were part of that trusted mapmaking circle, which includes Behain of Bohemia, for example.

The direct link between Bartholomew Columbus and the Martellus map, however, comes from the construction of the Yale Martellus. The sheets of paper on which the Yale map is drawn are of different sizes, which excludes the possibility that they were printed map sheets, for they would then have had to be the same size to fit within the map portfolio. In private letters between Alexander Vietor and Professor Davies, Vietor stated that an X-ray examination had revealed no evidence of printing on the paper sheets and that everything on the Yale map was hand-drawn, lettered and coloured. In short, it came from a tracing. The tracings have been identified by Professor Davies as being in the hand of Bartholomew Columbus. In making this devastating assertion, Professor Davies wrote:

When Columbus left Lisbon in 1485 for Spain, Bartholomew, with his highly trained skills as a cartographer in the Genoese style, stayed on in the map workshop of King John II. He was engaged in building up a large map of the world based on Donnus Nicolaus and on the Portuguese charts. It was, like all important maps at that time, drawn on sheets of parchment which could be joined together almost invisibly, and mounted on linen. This large map, 180cm by 120cm, formed a standard Portuguese world map, continually added to by new discoveries, including those of Cão and Dias. By the beginning of 1489, Columbus faced poverty and failure in Spain: his pension had been ended in 1488 and he no longer had free board and lodging from Medina Seli or the Marquess de Moya. Bartholomew prepared to join him in Spain and help his projects. They needed money, and in particular the vital and continued support of the Bank of St George in Genoa. They got both. Money could be obtained from the sale of maps kept secret in Portugal. Before leaving Lisbon, Bartholomew copied maps of convenient size. The large standard world map he had to copy in some secrecy and, because of its size, he needed eleven sheets of paper, cheaper, thinner and quieter than parchment. These sheets of the Yale Martellus were tracings in the hand of Bartholomew. Early in 1489 he left Lisbon. He went first to Seville to help his brother and there altered the Yale map by substituting another sheet of paper which showed Africa to 45° South rather than its true latitude of 34° 22' South. The Martellus map was rather like a picture with a picture frame. The frame ends at 41°S. To get the addition into the picture, it has to burst through the frame down to 45°S.[15]

A second lead comes from a legend shown on the east coast of Africa which reads 'Ultima navigatio Portuga A.D., 1489'. On the face of it, seeing the Martellus map extending down to 45°S, this inscription would appear to assert that Dias had proceeded north along the east coast of South Africa to beyond Natal. This he did not do on that voyage. The legend is shown between 33° and 34°S, which exactly accords with where Dias got to – the Rio de Infante, the Great Fish River at 34°S. It appears to be north of Natal only because Africa is shown as extending to 45°S. When Bartholomew altered the prototype map to 45°S, he was unable to remove the legend.

The three forgeries combined appeared to all but rule out the possibility of reaching China eastabout from Portugal. The purpose of the Martellus maps clearly was not to influence the Portuguese, who knew the true situation for they had the 1428 World Map; it was to influence the Catholic sovereigns who were completely in the dark. At that time, one degree of latitude was thought to be fifty nautical miles (ninety kilometres), according to Toscanelli's letter. To reach India round Africa, according to the forged Martellus maps, would involve sailing from 39°N to 45°S, and then north to India, another 45° + 15° – all told, the voyage to India would be some fifteen thousand miles. Moreover, and perhaps this was the decisive factor, ships would have had to sail below 45° South in order to round Africa through seas Dias had already described as the roughest he had encountered anywhere in the world.

In several ways, the forged Martellus maps depicted a monumental eastward journey, whereas by sailing westwards for Antilia to China, Spanish ships could pass through the Strait of Magellan and beat the Portuguese to it. This is the reason, I submit, why the Portuguese concentrated on the eastern route to China and the Spanish tried to reach the same destination via South America. Bartholomew Columbus stole the intellectual property of the Portuguese government. He then forged a chart he and Christopher knew was bogus, and both of them used that chart to extract money and backing under false pretences from the Bank of Genoa and the Catholic monarchs of Spain. Columbus's true legacy to posterity is not the discovery of the Americas, but of the circulatory wind systems of the Atlantic he so brilliantly analysed and exploited on his later voyages. Knowledge of these wind and current patterns proved invaluable in the preparation and execution of the voyages that led to the colonization of the Americas in the following centuries.

Finally, to that brilliant seaman, Captain James Cook, 'the ablest and most renowned navigator this or any country hath ever produced. He possessed all the qualities necessary for his profession and great undertakings.'[16] Cook made the first of his three great voyages in 1768, sailing to the Pacific to observe the transit of Venus. He then continued across the Pacific and 'discovered' New Zealand, finding it a suitable country for settlement 'should this ever be thought an object worthy of the attention of Englishmen'. He explored Australia's east coast, claimed the whole country in the name of the king, and sailed for home via New Guinea and the Cape.

On his second voyage, in 1772, 'to complete the discovery of the southern hemisphere', Cook put in at New Zealand and landed animals and planted vegetables to provide food supplies for future explorers and settlers. He then sailed south to the edge of the Antarctic continent. Cook's mission on his third voyage to the Pacific was to find a northern passage from the Pacific to the Atlantic. He again visited New Zealand and Australia, then sailed for North America, exploring the coast from Oregon northwards. He entered the Bering Strait, could find no ice-free route through and began the journey home. He was killed in Hawaii on 14 February 1779 after a dispute with the natives.

Cook was a great man, and the greatest navigator of all time, but he discovered neither New Zealand nor Australia. More than two centuries before he embarked on his voyages, a cluster of maps from the Dieppe School showed Australia with remarkable clarity. The Jean Rotz map was in the possession of the British government when Cook set sail, and Joseph Banks, who sailed with Cook, had acquired another of the finest, the Harleian (Dauphin), showing Australia with the same precision as the Rotz map. The Desliens and Desceliers charts from the Dieppe School were also known to the Admiralty. The Endeavour Reef, on which Cook later ran aground, is clearly shown on these earlier maps, together with what later became known as Cooktown Harbour. When Cook had extricated himself from the reef, he sailed directly for Cooktown, the only harbour in a thousand miles of coastline. 'This harbour will do excellently for our purposes, although it is not as large as I had been told.'[17] Desliens's map does indeed show it larger, for sea levels were lower when Admiral Zhou Man originally charted the coast in 1422–3.

When Cook returned, claiming to have discovered Australia, the head of the Map Department at the British Admiralty, Captain Dalrymple, wrote a furious protest. Captain James Cook had enormous courage, determination and integrity, but he had not discovered the continent. The Admiralty had maps showing Australia drawn 250 years earlier.

Brave and determined though they were, Columbus, Dias, da Gama, Magellan, Cook and the rest of the European explorers set sail with maps showing the way to their destinations. They owed

Cook's ship, the *Endeavour*, sketched by Sydney Parkinson in June 1770.

everything to the first explorers, the Chinese on their epic voyages of 1421–3. How lucky Europe was, and how unfortunate China, that fire had ravaged the Forbidden City on 9 May 1421. Europeans had now rediscovered almost the entire world, known at first hand until then only by the Chinese and Niccolò da Conti. The charts, ships and systems of ocean navigation used by the great European explorers owed much to Henry the Navigator and his brother, Dom Pedro, but more to the Chinese emperor, Zhu Di, and his brave and skilful eunuch admirals, Zheng He, Zhou Man, Hong Bao, Zhou Wen and Yang Qing.

The revelation that Vasco da Gama was not the first to sail to India round the Cape of Good Hope, that Christopher Columbus did not discover America, that Magellan was not the first to circumnavigate the world, and that Australia was surveyed three centuries before Captain Cook and Antarctica four centuries before the first European attempt may come as a disappointment, even a shock, to the champions of those brave and skilful explorers, but the Kangnido, Pizzigano, Piri Reis, Jean Rotz, Cantino and Waldseemüller charts are indisputably genuine. They contain information that can only have come from cartographers aboard the pioneering Chinese fleets. Niccolò da Conti was aboard the junks that reached Australia from India; Dom Pedro obtained this information from da Conti himself, and had it incorporated in the map that showed the whole world. Toscanelli persuaded Columbus that China could be reached by sailing west, and Magellan spoke no less than the truth when he told his near mutinous crew that he had seen the 'Strait of Magellan' on a map in the Portuguese treasury before he set sail. Truth, after all, is stranger than fiction.

And what epitaph is there at Sagres to commemorate the lifetime of sacrifice and achievement of Prince Henry the Navigator, the man who began this wave of European exploration that was to conquer the world? Nothing but a run-down sundial where the weeds grow among the stones. Zheng He's tomb on Bull's Head Hill in the west of Jiangsu province is also neglected, weed-choked and covered in graffiti, and his museum has been closed for lack of interest. These great men must have their reward in heaven.

EPILOGUE:
THE
CHINESE
LEGACY

THE LEGACY OF THOSE GOLDEN YEARS WHEN CHINA'S POWER and influence extended from Japan to Africa and beyond to encompass the whole world remains. Chinese Buddhist architecture graces the Asian skyline from Malacca to Kobe. Chinese silk of the Ming dynasty is found from Africa to Japan, glorious blue and white ceramics from Australia to Manchuria, and graves in many places across the globe bear witness to Chinese jade jewellery of that era. Even the most blasé traveller to south-east Asia must be struck by the pervasiveness of China's legacy. From Sumatra to Timor to Japan, communities are still united by trade, religion and a written language inherited from China. For four thousand kilometres west to east and an equal distance from north to south, China's imperial footprint remains, the imprint of a colossus.

The depth of Chinese culture is as awesome as its width. Three thousand years ago the Chinese had mastered brass moulding and carving with simple yet stunning designs. By the Qin dynasty (221–206 BC), pottery was being cast as sublime as anything our planet has seen, epitomized by the graceful horses and fluid soldiers of Emperor Qin's terracotta army. By the Tang dynasty (AD 618–907), at a time when our European ancestors were clothed in rags, rich Chinese were dining off gold plates adorned with phoenixes and dragons and drinking their wine from silver chalices engraved with dancing horses. Fruit was displayed in white jade bowls. Merchants' wives, sheathed in fine embroidered silk, wore subtle Persian scents. Exquisite jade and gold jewellery adorned their ears, throats and wrists.

The Chinese had millennia of experience and expertise in every sphere of human activity. By 305 BC conservation of land and rotation of crops had been the subject of letters to the emperor. Zhu Di's huge ships and incredible expeditions were the culmination of eight hundred years of voyages of discovery – Song dynasty (960–1279) ships had reached Australia. Chinese trade with India was six hundred years old when Admiral Zheng He set sail, and even his vast fleet was dwarfed by that of Kublai Khan two centuries earlier. Chinese science and technology were centuries ahead of the rest of the world, their military and civil engineering know-how epitomized by the Great Wall. The stability and protection that wall provided ensured that, of all the great civilizations of antiquity, China alone survived. Its most striking national symbol is a monument to the history, resilience and enduring power of China and its people.

Although much evidence of the Chinese voyages of discovery has been lost or destroyed over the centuries, one very tangible kind is visible everywhere today: the plants and animals the Chinese fleets carried with them to new lands, and those they brought back to China and south-east Asia. China's greatest contribution to civilization may well be the cultivation and propagation of plants.

For centuries it was believed that the global propagation of the world's plants began after Columbus 'discovered' the Americas in 1492, and accelerated when the British founded their great maritime empire after the Battle of Trafalgar. In fact, although the Victorians were certainly great plant collectors, almost all of the important agricultural plants had been spread across the world before Columbus set sail on his first voyage. Europeans not only had charts showing them the way to the New World, they found the most important crops already flourishing when they arrived there. No fewer than twenty-seven important cash crops are known to have been brought to the islands of Hawaii from India, Asia, Indonesia, the Americas and even Africa. The sweet potato, sugar cane, bamboo, coconut palm, arrowroot, yam, banana, turmeric, ginger, kavi, breadfruit, mulberry, bottle gourd, hibiscus and candlenut tree were all growing in Hawaii when the first Europeans arrived; none of them is indigenous to the islands.

This pattern was repeated throughout Polynesia and halfway across the world to Easter Island. There the first Europeans found totora reeds originating in Lake Titicaca, tomatoes, wild pineapples and sweet potatoes from South America, tobacco from Central and North America, gourds from Africa, papayas from Central

America, yams from south-east Asia and coconuts from the South Pacific. The first Europeans to reach the Caribbean also found coconuts; Magellan loaded maize in the Philippines that had originated in Central America; California was graced with Chinese roses; South America had Asiatic chickens. No fewer than ninety-four genera of plants were found to be common only to South America and Australasia;[1] another seventy-four genera, including 108 distinct species, are common only to tropical West Africa and tropical America.

It has been argued that this mass of plants could have been propagated naturally, by seeds carried by ocean current and wind, or by birds. Coconuts will float, and in theory they could have found their own way from the South Pacific across the Indian Ocean, the South Atlantic and the North Atlantic to end up in the Caribbean. Some certainly did float from island to island, and some seeds and spores were undoubtedly carried on the wind, but to suggest that all plants were propagated in this way is preposterous. The argument collapses with maize and sweet potatoes; they do not float, and sweet potatoes are far too heavy for birds to carry from country to country. In the last three decades, a number of distinguished botanists have carried out research into the places of origin of cultivated plants. Improved understanding of the classification of plants has radically altered views on their wild relatives and hence place of origin. An example is the coconut, which early European explorers found on Atlantic and Pacific coasts of Central America.

The coconut (*Cocos nucifera*) was once thought to have originated in the New World because this is where the other species of *Cocos* occurred. Now, however, *Cocos* is treated as a monotypic genus whose closest living relative is African. This, together with the fossil records of the coconut and its variability and range of uses in south-east Asia, suggests that the coconut originated in the western Pacific and spread west to east, not east to west, across the ocean.[2]

An analysis of the plants common to Africa and South America and of those common to South America and Australasia discloses that they were all carried in the direction of the prevailing winds and currents – in short, by ships crewed by men. No Polynesian ships are ever known to have left the Pacific to enter the Indian and South Atlantic oceans, and propagation predates the European voyages of discovery. Only one nation could have transported this array of plants and animals around the globe. The Chinese ships certainly carried plants and seeds – they were found in the Sacramento junk – and they not only circumnavigated the world but did so in precisely the direction propagation has been found to have occurred, from China through south-east Asia to India, thence to Africa, from there across the South Atlantic to South America, and finally on to Australasia.

Rice was by far the most important Chinese crop, perhaps the most diverse and adaptable crop on our planet. The Chinese developed varieties that could flourish on dry mountain slopes, while others needed to be submerged. Some species took months to ripen, others only two. Some were sensitive to temperature, others to sunlight. Some crossbred species became so tolerant of salt that they could be used to reclaim marshes along the sea shores. Rice is an ideal food crop – it tastes good and, flavoured with soy products, has high nutritious value. It stores well, and is easy and economical to cook. It yields more calories per unit of land than any other grain crop. Until the twentieth century, rice produced seven times as many calories per hectare of land as any other grain,[3] and China was the most efficient agricultural country in the world.

The entire way of life of over a billion people revolves around rice, the ideal crop for sustaining the dense populations of Asia, where it has even higher status than bread in Western societies. In China, a man who has lost his job has 'broken his rice bowl'. Marriages and business deals are sealed over cups of sake – rice wine. In the West, we throw confetti as a symbol of rice, to bring good luck at weddings. When Japanese children look at the night sky, rather than the man in the moon, they see a rabbit making rice cakes.

In the Ming era, China exported rice to the Pacific, principally through Makassar (Selat in modern Indonesia). Rice ships accompanied the treasure fleets, and rice was found in the hold of the Sacramento junk.[4] But the Chinese were also importers of plants, and they showed their inventive genius by utilizing the crops they found in distant lands. The south-east Asian climatic zone, stretching from China to Indonesia, was an important source of crop plants. A case can be made that the domestication of such crucial crops as millet, rice and yams originated in this zone. Later introductions to China included sugar cane, bananas, ginger and some species of citrus fruits, and cotton was imported from India, but perhaps the most spectacular example was the maize brought back by Zheng He's fleets from the Americas.

After rice, maize is the world's most prolific crop; compared to wheat, at least three times as much can be harvested from the same area. Furthermore, it can grow in arid deserts or in humid jungles, at sea level or up to 12,000 feet (3,600 metres). Maize originated in Central America, yet it was loaded in the Philippines by Magellan, the first European to reach there, and surviving Chinese records tell of 'extraordinarily large ears of grain' being carried back by Zheng He's fleets to China. Maize was ideal for China's mountain dwellers for it had deep roots, preventing the plant being washed away by heavy rain, and cultivation on the mountain slopes minimized the danger of frost damage. To the Miao people of southern China, the introduction of maize with its extremely high yield was an enormous benefit. Today, maize, the third most important crop in the world, has spread across Asia and is the staple food in many African countries.

The third group of foods carried by the Chinese were taros, yams and sweet potatoes. Sweet potatoes (*Ipomoea batatas*) thrive in the hot, moist climate of South America where they originated, and they have subsequently become an important root crop in warm, sub-tropical countries. By the time Captain Cook arrived in New

Zealand, sweet potatoes had become the principal food of the Maori. Their name for them, *kumara*, is almost identical to the name *kumar* still used in the Lima region of coastal Peru. True yams (the *Dioscorea* species) originated in Africa and south-east Asia, yet they were growing in Hawaii when the first Europeans landed there. Taros originated in south-east Asia but had also reached Hawaii before the Europeans. They are members of the Arum family (*Aracheae*) and, like potatoes, are rich in starch grains and also in the soluble starch amylase. Taros are widely cultivated throughout the Pacific from Tahiti in the south – taro ponds greet the visitor leaving Tahiti's airport – to Hawaii in the north.

It can be said that rice, maize, sweet potatoes, taros and yams, originating in entirely different parts of the world, provided the essential food for those living in the tropics and sub-tropics. Their transportation was of incalculable benefit to mankind, for man now had the capacity to grow and harvest crops in almost every soil and climatic condition.

The Chinese also played a vital part in propagating other cash crops. Apart from its role as the world's leading producer and exporter of silk, China also led the way in other fabrics. First used in the Indus valley several millennia ago, cotton is probably the world's most important cash crop, accounting for 5 per cent of the world's agricultural output. Scientists and scholars were initially baffled by the chromosomal structure of South American cotton, but after a series of painstaking experiments experts have now agreed that one parent of American cotton undoubtedly came from Asia. The wild American cotton the first Europeans found in the Americas had one gene that came from India. Cotton had been brought from India to Canton, where it was cultivated by the eighth century. It was widely grown during the Mongol Yuan dynasty that preceded the Ming, and Ming fleets carried huge amounts of cotton on their voyages.[5] The King of Cochin was rightly grateful to Emperor Zhu Di: 'How fortunate we are that the teachings of the sages of China have benefited us. For several years now, we have had abundant harvests in our country and our people have had houses to live in, have had the bounty of the sea to eat their fill of, and enough fabrics for clothes.'[6]

Coconut is far and away the most important nut crop in the world. Its native home was in the islands of Indonesia, yet coconuts were found by the first Europeans when they arrived in the Caribbean and on the Pacific coast of Central America, and there are now about 3.5 million hectares of coconut plantations in the Philippines, India, Indonesia, Sri Lanka and the Caribbean. Coconuts grow within the tropics, yet can withstand slight frost. Besides providing delicious meat and coconut milk, oil extracted from the dried white meat has been used for centuries for cooking and frying and in the manufacture of soaps, cosmetics and lubricants. After extracting the oil, dried copra cake can be ground to a meal high in protein, used for cattle and chicken feed. The trunk provides roof beams, and the fibres of the husk (coir) can be used to make ropes. Ming fleets traded coir extensively.

Bananas originated in south-east Asia, but were also found in Hawaii by the early European explorers and have subsequently spread to India, Africa and tropical America. Along with grapes, oranges and apples, bananas are the world's most important fruit crop; their cousins, starchy plantains, are eaten as a vegetable throughout the tropics. Pineapples originated on the hot, steamy Atlantic coast of South America, yet Columbus noted pineapples on his second voyage to the West Indies in 1493. The evidence of the great voyages by the Chinese treasure fleets is literally growing all around us today.

At the start of my long journey in the tracks of the great fifteenth-century Chinese explorers, I had learned of a monument, a carved stone erected by Zheng He overlooking a bay in the Yangtze estuary in China, and read the inscription incised on its surface. It was almost the only surviving physical evidence on the whole Chinese mainland of that epic sixth voyage of the treasure fleets. Little else had survived the purges of the mandarins. Translated, it read:

> The emperor ... has ordered us [Zheng He] and others [Zhou Man, Hong
> Bao, Zhou Wen and Yang Qing] at the head of several tens of thousands of
> officers and imperial troops to journey in more than a hundred ships ... to
> treat distant people with kindness ... We have gone to the western regions ...
> altogether more than three thousand countries large and small. We have
> traversed more than a hundred thousand *li* [forty thousand nautical miles] of
> immense water spaces.

I had puzzled over this inscription as I began the voyage of discovery that was to consume me for years. Now at the conclusion of my journey, I returned, believing that I had found the evidence to overturn the long-accepted history of the Western world. I had found a wealth of evidence that the Chinese fleets commanded by Admirals Zheng He, Yang Qing, Zhou Man, Hong Bao and Zhou Wen on that epic sixth expedition had surveyed every continent in the world. They had sailed through sixty-two island archipelagos comprising more than seventeen thousand islands and charted tens of thousands of miles of coastline. Admiral Zheng He's claim to have visited three thousand countries large and small appeared to be true. The Chinese fleets had voyaged across the Indian Ocean to East Africa, around the Cape of Good Hope to the Cape Verde Islands, through the Caribbean to North America and the Arctic, down to Cape Horn, the Antarctic, Australia, New Zealand and across the Pacific. Throughout the entire hundred thousand *li*, only in the Antarctic would the treasure ships have had to sail into the wind or an opposing current.

Before that great voyage of 1421 to 1423, Zhu Di had already brought all of south-east Asia, including Manchuria, Korea and Japan, into China's tribute system. The eastern end of the Silk Road had been reopened from China as far as Persia (modern Iran). Central Asia was in thrall to China, and the Indian Ocean was dominated by Chinese shipping. The treasure fleets of 1421 to 1423 added to this already vast trading empire. They created permanent colonies along the Pacific coast of North and South America, from California to Peru. Settlements were also initiated in Australia and throughout the Indian Ocean as far as East Africa. Supply bases were established right across the Pacific to link first the Americas with China, and then Australia and New Zealand with China. Vast distances were covered: there were bases from Easter Island to Pitcairn Island, through the Marquesas and the Tuamotu Archipelago, at Tahiti, Sarai in Western Samoa, Tonga, San Christobal in the Solomons, Nan Madol, Yap and Tobi in the Carolines, and Saipan in the Marianas. The remains of stone barracks, quays, houses, reservoirs and observation platforms may be seen on many of these islands to this day. Zheng He's great fleets and their supply trains were to link all these settlements and supply bases.

My claims about the Chinese voyages in the 'missing years' from 1421 to 1423 rest on the authenticity of the Kangnido, Piri Reis, Jean Rotz, Cantino, Waldseemüller and Pizzigano charts. No-one has ever questioned their veracity. The Vinland map has been questioned in the past, but as I have demonstrated (see chapter 14), I believe it passes the authenticity test. The Piri Reis, Jean Rotz and Cantino charts depict the whole of the southern hemisphere, covering tens of millions of square miles of ocean, thousands of islands, and tens of thousands of miles of coastline from the Antarctic to the equator. The lands they show can only have been surveyed by fleets that had sailed the southern hemisphere before the European voyages of discovery, and those fleets can only have been Chinese.

There is also a wealth of physical evidence for these great Chinese voyages. The Pandanan junk in the Philippines vividly demonstrates the extent of Chinese trade with the states of the Indian Ocean, the Americas and south-east Asia. Ming porcelain has been found down the East African coast, in the Persian Gulf and Australia, Ming silk as far north as Cairo. The wrecks of treasure ships lie off New Zealand and southern Australia, and there is also a

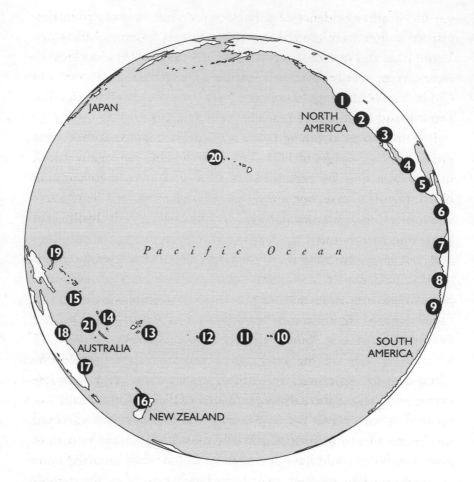

1 Sacramento	8 North Peru	15 Caroline Islands
2 Los Angeles	9 South Peru	16 New Zealand – Waikato River
3 Bahía California	10 Easter Island	17 New South Wales
4 Mexico – Michoacán	11 Pitcairn Island	18 Gympie
5 Guatemala	12 Tahiti	19 Micronesia
6 Venezuela	13 Kiribati	20 Hawaiian Islands
7 Ecuador	14 Samoa	21 Norfolk Island

Chinese bases across the Pacific Ocean.

wealth of other evidence of a Chinese presence in those countries. Carved stones were erected across the Indian Ocean, in the Cape Verde Islands, New Zealand and South America. Chinese chickens were carried to South America, maize brought from the Americas to China. Votive offerings have been found in the Lamu archipelago, at Darwin and on Ruapuke beach in New Zealand.

It is the spread, depth and variety of the evidence that makes the great Chinese voyages of 1421–3 so credible. One mahogany wreck in Australia may be explained away as an Indian merchantman blown far off course, but several wrecks, accompanied by Chinese votive offerings, ceramics and adze anchors, tell an entirely different story, one corroborated by Aboriginal folklore and cave paintings and clearly recognizable charts of the Barrier Reef drawn hundreds of years before the first Europeans reached Australia. The Chinese porcelain dating from the Ming era found throughout the Indian Ocean might have come from the cargoes of shipwrecked Portuguese caravels, but again, the evidence does not exist in isolation. There are the accounts of yellow-skinned people, the Chinese votive offerings, and silk found by the first Portuguese explorers. There is also a detailed chart of millions of square miles of ocean that was drawn before the Portuguese could have surveyed the Indian Ocean in such detail. The only explanations to date of how Antarctica could have appeared on a chart four hundred years before Europeans reached those parts have come from the pens of Erik von Daniken (aliens from outer space) and Charles Hapgood (Egyptian civilization before the Pharaohs).

Magellan saw the 'Strait of Magellan' and the Pacific depicted on a chart before he set sail; that can only mean that someone had passed through the strait and crossed the Pacific before he did, and had drawn animals native to Patagonia before any European knew of them. That the 'someone' was Chinese is confirmed by the pictures of animals (published 1430) and the Chinese artefacts along the route they followed, and the continents shown on the Chinese charts that have survived. That the Chinese had the ships, the expertise, the funds and the time to make such an extraordinary circumnavigation of the world is beyond question, just as it is beyond doubt that no-one else in that era could have done it.

These claims will doubtless be greeted with astonishment, yet if one takes a dispassionate view, there is nothing illogical about them. The Chinese enjoyed a far older and richer maritime tradition than the Europeans. When Zhu Di's fleets set sail in 1421, they had at least six centuries of ocean exploration and astro-navigation behind them; when Dias and Magellan set sail, the Portuguese had no means of accurately navigating south of the equator. Zheng He's fleets of treasure ships with their attendant supply ships were the products of a massive shipbuilding programme made possible by the economic strength of China; the tiny caravels of Cabral, Dias and Magellan would have looked like dinghies alongside the Chinese craft. Until Napoleon built his great flagship *L'Oriente* almost four centuries later, no wooden ship had ever approached the size of the giant treasure ships that epitomized Chinese naval supremacy and domination of the oceans. Even the European warships at Trafalgar could barely match the Chinese junks in size, range or firepower. Nelson's fleet of, at best, thirty ships carrying eighteen thousand men would have been dwarfed by Zheng He's armada of more than a hundred ships carrying twenty-eight thousand men. His treasure ships were twice the length and three times the beam of HMS *Victory*. They had far better damage control and logistical support, and could remain at sea far longer, for months on end if necessary.

The Chinese fleets had charted the world, they could determine longitude by means of lunar eclipses, and by comparing charts they were able to resolve any remaining longitudinal differences and complete the first map of the world as we know it today. But that knowledge was bought at a terrible cost. Only four of Hong Bao's ships and just one of Zhou Man's returned to China – a loss of at least fifty ships in those two fleets alone. The human toll was equally high: a mere nine hundred of the nine thousand men in Zhou Man's fleet were still with their admiral come October 1423. Up to three-quarters of the fleets' original complement must have died or been abandoned in the scattered settlements around the globe.

Twenty-four wrecks have already been located around the world; many more, carrying thousands of tons of treasure, remain to be found. The oceans will inevitably release more and more evidence as time goes by. The costs in both human and financial terms remain unparalleled – even the mightiest empire the world had ever seen was unable to sustain them – but the tasks Zhu Di had set his admirals had been achieved. It was a towering achievement, unequalled in the annals of mankind.

Zhu Di's master plan to discover and chart the entire world, and bring it into Confucian harmony through trade and foreign policy, could have succeeded, for the whole world now lay at China's feet – or so it must have seemed to his admirals when the handful of surviving ships of the treasure fleets limped home during the autumn of 1423, only to find that China, and the world, had changed for ever. Zhu Di was dying, a broken man, and the mandarins were dismantling the apparatus of the worldwide empire he had so nearly created. There would be no more tribute system, no more great scientific experiments, no more epic voyages of trade and discovery. China was entering its long night of isolation from the outside world. The eunuch admirals were dismissed, their ships broken up or left to rot at their moorings, the maps and charts and thousands of precious documents recording their exploits destroyed. Zhu Di's great achievements were disowned, ignored and, in time, forgotten.

One of the fascinating 'what ifs' of history is what would have happened had lightning not struck the Forbidden City on 9 May 1421, had fire not roared down the Imperial Way and turned the emperor's palaces and throne to cinders. Would the emperor's favourite concubine have survived? Would the emperor have kept his nerve? Would he have ordered Admiral Zheng He's squadrons to continue their voyages? Would they have carried on establishing permanent colonies in Africa, the Americas and Australia? Would

New York now be called New Beijing? Would Sydney have an 'English' rather than a 'Chinese' quarter? Would Buddhism rather than Christianity have become the religion of the New World?

Instead of the cultured Chinese, instructed to 'treat distant people with kindness', it was the cruel, almost barbaric Christians who were the colonizers. Francisco Pizarro gained Peru from the Incas by massacring five thousand Indians in cold blood. Today he would be considered a war criminal.

In effect the Portuguese used Chinese cartography to show them the way to the East. Then they stole the spice trade, which the Indians and Chinese had spent centuries building. Anyone who might stop them was mown down. When da Gama reached Calicut he told his men to parade Indian prisoners, then to hack off their hands, ears and noses. All the amputated pieces were piled up in a small boat. The historian Gaspar Correa describes da Gama's next move:

> When all the Indians had been thus executed [*sic*], he ordered their feet to be tied together, as they had no hands with which to untie them: and in order that they should not untie them with their teeth, he ordered them to strike upon their teeth with staves, and they knocked them down their throats . . .[7]

Then a Brahmin was sent from Calicut to plead for peace. The 'brave' da Gama had his lips and ears cut off and the ears of a dog sewn on instead.

It seems certain that a further voyage by Zheng He's fleets would have included the one section of the globe they had not yet reached and charted – Europe. The upheavals in Beijing ended any possibility of that, but who can say what the subsequent history of the world would have been had the Chinese treasure ships appeared over the European horizon in the 1420s? One thing seems certain: had the emperors who followed Zhu Di not retreated into xenophobia and isolation, China, not Europe, would have become the mistress of the world.

The Forbidden City still stands as a monument to the vision of the great Zhu Di, but what more fitting epitaph could there be to the 'Emperor on Horseback' than the valiant horseman mounted on the tip of Corvo's volcano in the Azores, high above the Atlantic rollers crashing onto the cliffs far below? He pointed dramatically to the west, towards Fusang, the Americas, the land his brave and skilful mariners had discovered. As China began to draw in on itself, abandoning Zhu Di's great ambitions, others, notably the Portuguese and Spanish, began to fill the vacuum they had left. For centuries they have basked in the glory that rightfully belonged to others; it is now time, at last, for us to redress the balance of history and give credit where it is due.

To assert the primacy of the Chinese exploration of the New World and of Australia is not to denigrate the achievements and memories of Dias, Columbus, Magellan and Cook. The exploits of these brave and skilful men will never be forgotten, but it is now time to honour other men who have been allowed to languish in obscurity for too long. These remarkable Chinese admirals rounded the Cape of Good Hope sixty-six years before Dias, passed through the Strait of Magellan ninety-eight years before Magellan, surveyed Australia three centuries before Captain Cook, Antarctica and the Arctic four centuries before the first Europeans, and America seventy years before Columbus. The great admirals Zheng He, Hong Bao, Zhou Man, Zhou Wen and Yang Qing deserve to be remembered and celebrated too, for they were the first, the bravest and most daring of all. Those who followed them, no matter how great their achievements, were sailing in their wake.

It had taken me years to complete the research into these great Chinese voyages, but finally, by Christmas 2001, my work was finished. I sent it out for comment to experts around the world, and when their corrections were incorporated I was ready to publicize my findings at the lecture I gave at the Royal Geographical Society on 15 March 2002. It was broadcast around the world to thirty-six countries populated by two billion people, and since then a further mass of corroborative evidence has come my way from people carrying out research on every continent. Some has been used in this book, and more continues to arrive every day. Many exciting discoveries such as the Sacramento junk, the sand mounds on Bimini and the tower at Rhode Island have yet to be fully examined and evaluated. The story is only just beginning, and it is one for all of us to share.

APPENDIX 1

CHINESE CIRCUMNAVIGATION OF THE WORLD 1421–3: SUPPORTING EVIDENCE

Part I: Europeans did not discover the New World

1. Evidence provided to the Royal Geographical Society, 15 March 2002
2. The whole world was accurately charted by 1428
3. The first European explorers set sail with maps showing their destinations

Part II: Only the Chinese fleets could have discovered the New World before the Europeans

4. China claims Zheng He did so
5. Key to the discoveries – the determination of latitude
6. Chinese determination of longitude
7. Areas of the world surveyed
8. Size of the Chinese fleet, their bases and voyages

Part III: Evidence

9. Surviving Chinese maps and star charts
10. Chinese or Asiatic people found by the first European explorers
11. Evidence in countries Chinese fleet visited
12. Plants indigenous to one continent carried to another
13. Animals indigenous to one continent found in another
14. Evidence of mining and other activities found by first Europeans
15. Wrecks of very old, large, unidentified ships found in wake of Chinese fleet
16. Artefacts and votive offerings
17. Stone buildings, observation platforms and carved stones
18. Linguistics/languages
19. Customs and games

Part IV: Mitochondrial DNA analysis

20. DNA analysis
21. Teeth of native peoples

Part V: Selected bibliography

Part 1: Europeans did not discover the New World

1. Evidence provided to the Royal Geographical Society, 15 March 2002

– on website www.1421.tv

2. The whole world was accurately charted by 1428

ASSERTIONS

- Four huge Chinese fleets circumnavigated the world between March 1421 and October 1423.
- Sailors and concubines from those great fleets settled in Malaysia, India, Africa, the Americas, Australia, New Zealand and islands across the Pacific.
- The first European explorers all had maps showing where they were going before they set sail; they met Chinese settlers when they arrived.
- China, not Europe, thus discovered and settled the New World. European 'discoveries' would not have been possible had China not led the way.

EVIDENCE

(i) The world was charted by whom?

- Pizzigano, Fra Mauro, Piri Reis, Cantino, Caverio, Waldseemüller and Jean Rotz charts between them show whole world charted before Europeans set sail.
- European explorers referred to earlier maps made before they set sail; the diaries of Columbus, Dias, Cabral, da Gama, Magellan and Cook are the evidence.
- Countries shown on maps before European explorers set sail:

    (a) North America – shown on Waldseemüller, Cantino and Caverio charts
    (b) Caribbean – Pizzigano, Cantino, Caverio and Waldseemüller
    (c) South America – Piri Reis
    (d) Africa, India and the East – Cantino (longitude of East Africa precisely correct before Europeans could measure longitude)
    (e) Antarctic – Piri Reis
    (f) Arctic and Siberia – Waldseemüller
    (g) Australia – Jean Rotz, Desliens, Vallard, Desceliers
    (h) China and Far East – Jean Rotz

(ii) The Portuguese claim

Antonio Galvão's description of the world map which the Portuguese dauphin
Dom Pedro took back with him from Venice in 1428: 'Dom Peter, the King of
Portugal's eldest sonne, was a great traveller . . . came home by Italie, taking
Rome and Venice in his way: from whence he brought a map of the world,
which had all the parts of the world and earth described. The Streight of
Magelan was called in it the dragon's taile: the Cape of Boa Esperança, the fore-
front of Afrike and so foorth.'

   Galvão again: 'It was told me by Francis de Sousa Tavares that in the yeere
1528, Don Fernando, the King's sonne and heire did show him a map which was
found in the studie of the Alcobaza which had been made 120 yeeres before
which map did set forth all the navigation of the East Indies with the Cape of
Boa Esperança according as our later maps have described it; whereby it
appeareth that in ancient time there was as much or more discovered than now
there is.'

   So who drew the 1428 chart? It is the author's claim that Dom Pedro
debriefed Niccolò da Conti in Florence in 1424. Da Conti had sailed with the
Chinese fleet from India to Australia and China (*Travels of Niccolò da Conti*).

3. The first European explorers set sail with maps showing their destinations

Accounts of first European explorers to reach land it is claimed they discovered:

• Columbus's 'discovery' of the Americas – letter from Toscanelli to
  Columbus: 'I notice thy splendid and lofty desire to sail to the regions of the
  east by those of the west [i.e. to sail to China westabout] . . . as is shown by
  the chart which I send you . . . [chart is excerpt of Portuguese 1428 chart of
  world showing Antilia]'

  Letter from Toscanelli to King of Portugal (before Christopher Columbus
  set sail): '. . . from the Island of Antilia known to you [Antilia is Puerto
  Rico, discovered by the Chinese in 1421] . . . to Cipangu [China] . . .'

  Columbus's log, Wednesday, 24 October 1492, when in western Atlantic: 'I
  should steer west-south-west to go there [to reach Antilia] . . . and in the
  spheres which I have seen and in the drawings and mappae mundi it is in
  this region.'

Thus, according to Columbus, Caribbean islands appeared on Portuguese maps of the world (mappae mundi) before he set sail.

• Cabral expedition to South America – João de Barros arriving on the first expedition to South America writes to King Manuel of Portugal: 'The lands might the King see represented on the Mappa Mundi which Pêro daz Bisagudo had.'

Thus, Brazil appeared on a Portuguese map of the world before the first European expedition set forth.

• Dias and da Gama rounding the Cape of Good Hope – Dias's chronicler describing their approach to Cape of Good Hope: 'They came in sight of that Great and Famous Cape concealed for so many centuries . . .' This is the Cape drawn on Fra Mauro's planisphere of 1459 (Fra Mauro was working for the Portuguese government at the time).

Thus, southern Africa appeared on Fra Mauro's map, prepared for the Portuguese, before the first European expedition reached the Cape.

• Magellan's 'first circumnavigation of the world' – on entering the 'Strait of Magellan' Magellan quelled a mutiny thus: 'The Captain General said there was another Strait which led out [to the Pacific] saying that he knew it well and had seen it in a marine chart of the King of Portugal . . .' Later, Magellan, having crossed the Pacific, met the King of Limasava. Note from Magellan's chronicler: 'And he [Magellan] shows him the marine chart . . . telling him how he had found the Strait to come hither . . .'

Thus, according to Magellan, the so-called Strait of Magellan appeared on a Portuguese chart before Magellan set sail, as did the Pacific.

• Cook's 'discovery' of Australia and New Zealand. The 'Dauphin' map (1536) showing Australia was owned by the First Lord of the British Admiralty, Edward Harley. Joseph Banks, who travelled with Captain Cook, bought it. Since Henry VIII's day the British government had owned the Jean Rotz chart, which also showed Australia.

Thus, Australia was known to the Admiralty from two sources before Captain Cook set sail.

- Cook ran aground on a reef shown on the Rotz and Dauphin maps. When he extricated the *Endeavour* he made straight for what is now called Cooktown (the only port on a thousand miles of coastline). He wrote in his diary on reaching this port: 'This harbour will do excellently for our purposes although it is not as large as I had been told.'

Part II: Only the Chinese fleets could have discovered the New World before the Europeans

4. China claims Zheng He did so

- The stone memorials erected in 1430–1 at Liu-Chia-Chang (31°7'N, 121°35'E) and Chiang-su (26°8'N, 119°35'E) claim he reached three thousand countries large and small (Duyvendak's translation).
- Further carved stone tablets were erected in Ceylon/Sri Lanka, the Indian Ocean, the Congo delta, Cape Verde Islands, North America, Brazil and New Zealand.
- A Chinese star chart which survived the purge, the *Wu Pei Chi*, shows which stars the Chinese were under, hence their terrestrial position. This chart may be dated by the declination of Polaris.
- Maps of the voyage which escaped destruction: the Kangnido (East, South and West Africa); Mao Kun (Indian Ocean); Taiwan porcelain map (Australia); jade pendant (Antarctic).
- Chinese and Persian records which escaped the purge, giving the dates on which the treasure fleets set sail in 1421 and returned in 1423: *Ming Shi*; *Ming Shi Lu*; *Hsi Yang Fan Kuo Chih*; *Kuo Ch, Veh*; *Hsin Chiao Ming T'ung-Chien*; *Ming Chih*; *Zubdatu't Tawarikh*.
- Chinese pictorial record, *The Illustrated Record of Strange Countries* (*I Yü Thu Chih*), published 1430, shows lions and elephants of India; zebras and giraffes of Africa; armadillos, jaguars and mylodons of South America.
- Chinese novel published 1597 describing Zheng He's fleet's adventures, the *Hsi-Yang-Chi*.
- The life work of the late Professor Wei (Nanjing), *The Chinese Discovery of America* (in Chinese – unpublished).
- *The Chinese Discovery of Australia* by Professor Wei Chu-Hsien (in Chinese – Eastern Art Library, Oxford).

5. Key to the discoveries – the determination of latitude

- The extraordinary precision of the southern portion of the Piri Reis map showing Patagonia's coast, the Falklands, South Shetlands and South Sandwich Islands
- Not only is the coast perfectly drawn, but animals unique to South America – huemils, guanacos and mylodons – appear (they also appear in the *I Yü Thu Chih*)
- The Piri Reis map was drawn four hundred years before Europeans reached the Antarctic; it also shows the Andes as far north as Ecuador
- The precision of the Piri Reis map coupled with the extent of the coastline from the equator to the Antarctic can only mean the cartography was carried out by people who could determine latitude even in the High Antarctic in dozens of ships surveying simultaneously

Who but the Chinese with six centuries' experience of ocean navigation could have reached the Antarctic? Chinese records claim their fleets reached both the North Pole (thirty claims) and the South Pole (five claims). Do Chinese navigational and star charts provide the answer? The most notable is the *Wu Pei Chi*, but it has been amended over the years and not all the amendments were dated. How can we date the amendments?

The sailing instructions in the *Wu Pei Chi* give the course to steer between Dondra Head (Ceylon/Sri Lanka) and Sumatra. By a very fortunate coincidence, this course is due east. The current latitude of their track is 6°N. However, Chinese navigators were advised to keep Polaris 1 *chi* above the horizon. This means there is a difference of 3°40' between the position of Polaris when the amendments were made and its position today. Using the Microsoft *Starry Nights* computer program (which enables the position of the stars in the night sky to be determined every night for the past two millennia), we can date the *Wu Pei Chi* to 1420–30 (Polaris's apparent position changes one degree every 175 years due to the earth's precession).

Knowing the *Wu Pei Chi* date, we can compare the stars on it with those on the *Starry Nights* program. This is the breakthrough, for we can now establish that at the compass-rose position shown on the Piri Reis map (south-west Falklands), Canopus is at 90° elevation. The reason the cartographers have taken such inordinate trouble to survey the coast of Patagonia is that they have established the declination and right ascension of Canopus, which is right above them. Chinese records reveal that the need to 'fix' the position of Canopus and the Southern Cross constellation had long preoccupied Chinese astronomers.

The emperor ordered the fleet south to achieve this. (A conference in Nanjing will emphasize this preoccupation with Canopus.)

Corroborative evidence should thus also be found where the leading stars of the Southern Cross are at 90° elevation. This is precisely what appears on the Piri Reis map. Deception Island and the position of the mountains of Livingstone Island are precisely correct. The Chinese surveyed them at position 62°49'S, 60°38'W, the declination of the Southern Cross's leading star, Crucis Alpha.

The Chinese may now determine the true position of the South Pole and eliminate magnetic variation (Canopus and the Southern Cross become circumpolar below 68°S). They can also determine latitude in the southern hemisphere by cross-referencing Canopus with Polaris in the northern hemisphere. The Chinese now have the capacity to chart the whole world, deploying several fleets. Where would they have been likely to do so?

(a) At 52°40'S, the declination of Canopus, all ships could keep the star right overhead, all thus surveying from the same base line. Evidence of the Chinese voyage is indeed found all the way across the world at 52°40'S, in Patagonia, Kerguelen and Campbell Island (which appears precisely drawn on the Jean Rotz chart).

(b) At 28°30'N, where Canopus disappears below the horizon. Evidence is found at this latitude around the world.

(c) At 3°20'N, where Polaris disappeared below the horizon in 1421. Evidence of the Chinese voyage is also found here.

OBSERVATION PLATFORMS USED BY THE CHINESE 1421–3
(Blueprint, Pyramids of Ihuatzio and Tingambato, Michoacán, Mexico)

South America to Australia

Marquesas (Temoe)	134°29'W	23°22'S
Society Islands (Tahiti)	149°0'W	17°50'S
Bora Bora	151°0'W	17°30'S
Western Samoa (Savai)	172°42'W	13°30'S
Tonga Tabu	175°4'W	19°43'S
Gympie (Australia)	152°42'E	26°12'S
Gosford (NSW)	151°13'E	33°26'S

South America to Indonesia

Tahiti	149°0'W	17°50'S
Malden (Kiribati)	157°43'E	1°55'N
Solomons (San Cristobal)	161°51'E	10°26'S
Carolines (Nan Madol)	158°21'E	6°51'N
Marianas (Saipan)	145°45'E	15°9'N
Carolines (Yap)	138°9'E	9°31'N
New Guinea	143°38'E	3°35'S
Nanjing	118°45'E	32°6'S
Beijing	116°25'E	39°55'N

6. Chinese determination of longitude

– see Appendix 4, 'The Determination of Longitude', which constitutes a key part of the evidence.

7. Areas of the world surveyed

- Indian Ocean (Cantino)
  Nine million square miles and thousands of islands. Assuming ships fifteen miles apart, sailing at 4.8 knots and surveying for ten hours a day, thirty ships would have had to be at sea for eighteen months.
- South America and the Antarctic (Piri Reis)
  Approximately six million square miles – about twenty ships required over an eighteen-month period.
- North America and North Atlantic (Cantino)
  Approximately twelve million square miles – about forty ships.
- Far East
  No fewer than twenty ships over an eighteen-month period.
- Australasia
  No fewer than twenty ships over an eighteen-month period.

In all, no fewer than 130 ships over a period of one and a half years would be required. The only nation that could put such a huge fleet to sea to provide the information for the cartographers of the Piri Reis, Cantino, Jean Rotz, Waldseemüller and Pizzigano charts was China.

8. Size of the Chinese fleet, their bases and voyages

(i) The fleet

'In its heyday, about 1420, the Ming navy probably outclassed that of any other Asian nation at any time in history, and would have been more than a match for that of any contemporary European state, or even a combination of them. Under the Yung-Lo emperor [Zhu Di] it consisted of some 3,800 ships in all, 1,350 patrol vessels and 1,350 combat ships attached to guard stations (*wei* and *so*) or island bases (*chai*). A main fleet of 400 large warships was stationed at Hsin-chiang-khou near Nanking and 400 grain-transport freighters. In addition, there were more than 250 long-distance "treasure ships", or galleons (*Pao chhuan*), the average complement of which ranged from 450 men in *c*. 1403 to over 690 in 1431, and certainly overstepped 1,000 in the largest vessels. A further 3,000 merchantmen were always ready as auxiliaries, and a host of small craft did duty as despatch-boats and police launches. But the peak of the development which had started in 1130 came in 1433, and after the great reversal of policy the navy declined much more rapidly than it had grown, so that by the middle of the sixteenth century almost nothing was left of its former grandeur' (Needham, 1954, Vol. 4, Pt 3, p. 484).

(ii) Bases

Hand in hand with the development of Zheng He's fleet went that of overseas bases. By 1421 the Chinese had bases around the Indian Ocean and down the East African coast to Sofala. They already had an extensive network across Indonesia and the South China Sea.

(iii) Experience

Since 1405 there had been five voyages becoming progressively more adventurous as the years went by. During the fourth voyage the Chinese had separated their fleets and sailed far down the East African coast.

Part III: Evidence

9. Surviving Chinese maps and star charts

Title & approx. date of amendments	Subject/relevance
Wu Pei Chi, c. 1422 (only a small part translated)	Chinese accept this contains information brought by Zheng He; it gives courses to steer between China and Africa and between other continents
Mao Kun, c. 1403–22	Kerguelen, Indian Ocean and islands, East African coast – courses to steer
Kangnido (1402–73)	Asia, East, South and West Africa including Atlantic Azores
Star Chart (Mao Kun), c. 1422	Polaris compared with Southern Cross and Alpha Centauri
Matteo Ricci (c. 1588) globe	Australia (drawn when Fr Ricci was in China)

10. Chinese or Asiatic people found by the first European explorers

- Caribbean
  Columbus (Cuba)
- California
  Stephen Powers (Sacramento/Russian River)
- North America
  Verrazzano (Narragansett Bay)
  Professor Delabarre (Narragansett Bay)
- Brazil
  Cabral (men with 'pale skins' and Mayoruna Indians)
- Venezuela
  Arends and Gallengo (1964) (Chinese transferrins)
- Peru
  Chinese-speaking people
- Indian Ocean
  Professor Wang Tao (graves of sailors from Zheng He's fleet)

- Pacific
  Professor Wang Tao (graves of sailors from Zheng He's fleet)
- Panama
  Marsh Darien Expedition, 1924
- Ireland
  Columbus (bodies)
- Greenland
  Columbus ('People from Cathay have visited here')
- Azores
  Columbus (bodies from Corvo, washed ashore on Flores)
- South America
  Arias – crossing Pacific
  Ludovico de Varthema
- South Pole
  Ludovico de Varthema
- Australia
  Warrnambool
- Pacific
  Bougainville
  Cartier
  Wallace
- Africa
  Fr Monclaro – Pate
- New Zealand
  Cook

11. Evidence in countries Chinese fleet visited

(i) Local people's accounts of Chinese, or 'Yellow Men', prior to European voyages of discovery

- Africa (Pate, east coast): Chinese people settled among them – evidence includes giraffe presented to China in 1416; Father Monclaro's accounts; Tomé Pires diaries.
- North America: Columbus meets people he believes are Chinese; Verrazzano (Rhode Island) meets Asiatic people; Indians (Newport) describe 'great ship like a house firing cannon sailing upriver'; Pope's letter describing barbarian ship arriving in Greenland from North America.

- California: 'ships like great houses' off coast.
- Mexico: Narayit tribe's accounts of Asian ship visiting them before Europeans arrived.
- South America: Father Arias to King of Spain, 'light-skinned people sailed from South America across the Pacific'.
- Antarctic: Ludovico de Varthema, ship from China followed Southern Cross to the Antarctic where days were short and it was very cold.
- Pacific: Bougainville and Carteret found pale, yellow-skinned people resembling Chinese on Pacific islands.
- Fiji (Yasawa Islands): 'Yellow men visited us.'
- Australia (accounts of Aborigines): Yangery tribe, Warrnambool – yellow people from shipwreck settle among them; Tweed River, Queensland – men in stone garments attempt to mine Mount Warning area; Byron Bay area, NSW – massacre of foreign sailors; Hawkesbury River – massacre of foreign sailors; Fraser Island, off Gympie – small boats leave big ship (J. Green, 1862); Glenelg River, Arnhem Land – 'Honey-coloured people settled Arnhem Land, women in pantaloons wore silk, men in long robes'; Gympie – 'culture heroes' sailed into Gympie harbour and took rocks away with them; Dhamuri people – strange people landed to build pyramids (observation platforms).
- New Zealand: two very large ships preceded Captain Cook: Maoris, North Island – light-coloured people settled among them and begat children; South Island – strange shipwreck (prior to Europeans).

(ii) Art showing pre-European foreigners

- Australia: Hawkesbury River – strange visitors in long robes; Glenelg River, Arnhem Land – Chinese junks and robed Chinese (Governor Grey's account); Qinrans – man thrown from horse; north of Cooktown – foreign ships.
- Mexico: *Lienzo de Jucutácato* showing foreigners arriving; Cueva Pintada – supernova of Crab Nebula of July 1054 together with wooden peg dated 1400–1512 and pictures of foreigners pierced by arrows.

(iii) Drawings and descriptions on European maps of Australia published prior to Van Diemen and Cook

- Jean Rotz: wealth of written and pictorial descriptions of Arnhem Land, its geography and minerals, trees and lakes. Shows east coast and west coast to Swan River.

- Vallard: horses being led across Arnhem Land, Aboriginal houses, fauna and flora.
- Toscanelli (1474): Australia with its rivers.

(iv) Petroglyphs (rock art) prior to Europeans

- Hawkesbury River: foreign ship; depiction of funeral of foreign people.
- Ruapuke beach: Tamil calligraphy.
- Cooktown: foreign ship.
- Glenelty River (SA): foreign seafarers.
- Mexico: Crab Nebula explosion (recorded by Chinese AD 1054).
- New England: foreign ship and shipwreck (Dighton Rock); foreign ship (Chelmsford, Massachusetts).
- North America: carvings/paintings of horses (wiped out there c. 10,000 BC); Mississippi plains, Colorado, Wisconsin, Louisiana, Oklahoma; Chichen Itza (Yucatán); Salem (New York).

(v) Accounts of contemporary historians

Author	Title/description	Date written/(published)
Chen Cheng (Chinese)	*Diary of Travel in the Western Regions*. Chinese emperor's overtures to Persia and description of reopening trade to Mediterranean.	1405–14 (1414)
Ma Huan (Chinese)	*Ying-yai Shenglan*. The overall survey of the ocean shores. Chinese fleet in south-east Asia and Indian Ocean.	1416–33 (1433)
Fei Xin (Chinese)	*Marvellous Visions from the Star Raft*. Chinese fleet reaching Africa and then Timor (East Indonesia), three hundred miles from Australia.	1405–31 (1436)
Ibn Taghri-Birdi (Egyptian)	*Nujum* (A History of Egypt). Chinese fleet reaching Red Sea and Jeddah.	1431

Ghiyash D Din Naqqash (dictated to Hafiz Abru – Persian)	*Zubdatu't Tawarikh* (Cream of Chronicles). Inauguration of the Forbidden City, 2 February 1421, delegates arriving and returning.	1419–22 (1424)
Niccolò da Conti (Venetian)	*The Travels of Niccolò da Conti*. Claims to have travelled to Australia. Describes Chinese fleet passing through Indian Ocean and his passage to Australia and China.	c. 1424 (1434)
Fra Mauro	Planisphere notes. Describe huge Chinese junks sailing across Indian Ocean non-stop (about end of 1420), rounding Cape of Good Hope to Cape Verde Islands and 'obscured islands'.	c. 1424 (1459)
Ibn Battuta	*The Travels of Ibn Battuta*. Describes huge Chinese ships in Indian Ocean.	c. 1325–54 (1356)
Hai Yao Pen Tshao (Chinese)	Doings of the Southern Countries beyond the Seas. *Classics of Shan Hai Jing*. *Chui Hiao* ('Atlas of Foreign Countries'). Describes medicines brought from India and south-east Asia; boomerangs of Aborigines; Pygmies of Queensland.	c. 330 BC (c. 265–316 BC)

12. Plants indigenous to one continent carried to another

(i) Before European voyages of exploration

From China to:
- Australia – lotus and papyrus
- North America – rice, poppy seeds, keteleria, roses (*R. laevigata*)
- Pacific islands – mulberries
- South America - rice

From tropical Asia to:
- Pacific Islands – taro, yam, banana, turmeric, bottle gourds

From Malaysia to:
- Pacific islands – arrowroot (pia)
- China – rubber, pepper

From India to:
- North Pacific islands – sugar cane, wild ginger
- North and Central America – cotton
- Pacific – cotton

From Africa to:
- Central Pacific – bottle gourds

From South America to:
- China – maize
- South-east Asia – maize
- New Zealand – kumera
- Pacific islands – yams, sweet potato
- Australia – 74 items
- Philippines – potatoes, maize

From South Pacific to:
- North Pacific (Hawaii) – bamboo, coconuts, kava, candlenut tree, hibiscus
- Central America – coconuts

From Norfolk Island to:
- Campbell Island – Norfolk pines

From Indonesia to:
- China – spice

From Philippines to:
- China – pepper

From North America to:
- China – maize, amaranth

From Mexico to:
- Philippines – tobacco, sweet potatoes, maize (seen by Magellan, first European); *possibly* pineapple, arrowroot, peanut, lima and yam beans, balimbing, cassava, chico, papaya, zapute, tomato and squash (Magellan does not record seeing these)

(ii) Found in Hawaii by first Europeans

From
- Tropical America – sweet potatoes
- India – wild ginger
- Pacific islands – bamboo, breadfruit, candlenut trees, hibiscus, kava
- Tropical Asia – taro, ti plants, yam (five-leafed), banana, turmeric
- Malayan archipelago – arrowroot
- East Asia – pepper, mulberry

(iii) Found on Easter Island before European voyages of exploration

From
- South America – totora reeds, tomato, tobacco, sweet potato
- South Pacific – coconuts
- South-east Asia – yam
- Mesoamerica – papaya

13. Animals indigenous to one continent found in another

(i) Asiatic chickens in South America. The chickens found by the Spanish and Portuguese arriving in South America were entirely different from those they had left at home. Amerind chickens laid blue-shelled eggs, had Asiatic names and were not used for food, rather for religious practices. They had different combs, feathers, spurs, sizes, shapes, legs, necks, heads and names; varieties found are Malays, melanotic silkies, frizzle fowls and Cochin Chinese. As late as 1600 Mediterranean peoples did not have and did not know of the galaxy of Asiatic chickens found in the Americas. Asiatic chickens cannot fly; someone took them to the Americas before Europeans got there.

(ii) Horses – North America. Bones and skulls – Mississippi drainage area and Canada. Pictures/carvings of horses in North America, Australia and in Mexico (Jucutácato shroud) and Yucatan.

(iii) Chinese ship dogs – Mexico, South America, South Africa, south-east Asia, Pacific, Falklands, New Zealand, Tahiti (Cook).

(iv) Sea otters found in New Zealand (from India)

(v) Lions, elephants and tigers from India; giraffes, rhinoceros, ostriches and zebras from Africa; and kangaroos from Australia to Chinese emperor's zoo.

14. Evidence of mining and other activities found by first Europeans

(i) Mining

- Australia
  Gympie – gold
  Arnhem Land – lead
- Fiji
  Copper (Lasawa)
- Arctic
  Smelted bronze, iron, copper – Devon Island and Bathurst Island
- North America
  Newport – coal
- Mexico
  Copper, gold

(ii) Pre-Columbian metallurgy, lacquerware and dye-stuffs in Mesoamerica

In one small area of Mexico (Michoacán–Rio Balsas) the following pre-Columbian items and activities are found (the area appears on the Waldseemüller chart):

(a) ancient shipwreck;
(b) Jucutácato shroud (picture of people arriving from ship);
(c) copper mining using sophisticated technology;
(d) manufacture of lacquer boxes using Chinese technology;
(e) dye-stuffs using Chinese technology to extract dyes from insects, shellfish, leaves and roots;
(f) *hachuelas* similar to traditional Buddhist designs;
(g) mirror identical to Lamaist designs.

15. Wrecks of very old, large, unidentified ships found in wake of Chinese fleet

- Indonesia
- Vietnam (2)
- Annam (1)
- Philippines (Pandanan)
- Caribbean (9)
- Australia: west coast – Perth (King Sound), Perth (swampland); south coast – Warrnambool (mahogany ship); east coast – Byron Bay, Woolongong, Double Island, Fraser Island; north coast – anchor
- New Zealand: Campbell Island; Ruapuke beach; Dusky Sound
- America: Pacific coast, Neahkanie beach; San Francisco, Sacramento junk; Los Angeles, anchor; Atlantic coast, Narragansett Bay
- Mexico: Bahía de Zihuatanejo (Playa la Ropa); Chinese clothes washed ashore at Zihuatanejo (Playa la Ropa)
- China: Nanjing
- Ecuador: anchor

16. Artefacts and votive offerings

(i) Porcelain

- East and South Africa: early Ming porcelain found by first European explorers in the palaces of rulers the length of the east coast of Africa
- Australia: early Ming porcelain found at Bradshaw, Elecho Island, Yirrkalla, Winchelsea Island, Cape York, Gympie, Tasmania
- America, Pacific coast: Ming porcelain
- Mexico (Zihuatanejo)
- Philippines and Indonesia: Magellan's descriptions of rulers dressed in silk possessing early Ming plates

(ii) Votive offerings

- East Africa (Pate): bronze lion
- Azores (Corvo): statue (of Zhu Di?) found by first Europeans to land there
- Australia (NSW): onyx scarabs, Shao Lin's head, stone heads; Queensland – jade Buddha, Ganesh, Hanuman, onyx scarab; Arnhem Land – jade figurine Shu Lao
- New Zealand: serpentine duck (Ruapuke beach); Chinese steatite figurine (Mauku, Auckland)
- Mexico (Guatemala border)

(iii) Other items

- Mexico, Pate (East Africa): lacquer boxes made according to Chinese tradition
- Caroline Islands: pink beads and obsidian from Mexico
- Hao Atoll (Tuamotu archipelago): emerald ring
- Joluca (Mexico): Roman bust
- El Salvador/Guatemala border: Egyptian figures
- Peru: bronzes and pottery with Chinese inscriptions
- Nasca (Chile): bronzes and pottery with Chinese inscriptions
- Teotihuacan (Mexico): Chinese jade medallion
- Chiapa de Corzo (Mexico): Chinese jade earpiece
- New Zealand: 'Colenso bell'

17. Stone buildings, observation platforms and carved stones

(i) Observation platforms and observatories

- Australia: Penrith, west of Blue Mountains; Gympie, central NSW coast; Atherton
- North Atlantic: Newport Round Tower; Canaries; Kane Basin (Arctic)
- Pacific: Tuamotu; Tahiti; Marquesas; Society Islands; Carolines – Lele, Ponape, Nan Madol, Yap, Tobi; Marianas – Saipan; Gilberts – Kiribati; Solomons – San Cristobal; Mala; New Guinea (5); Malden Island; Magnetic Island

NB These will be correlated to show they were built by a fleet which sailed with the wind.

(ii) Carved stones recording voyage

- China – Liu-Chia-Chang (Fukien province)
- Malaya – Malacca
- Ceylon/Sri Lanka – Dondra Head
- India – Calicut, Cochin
- Africa – Matadi Falls (Congo)
- Cape Verde Islands – Janela
- South America – Santa Catarina
- New Zealand – Ruapuke beach
- North America – Dighton Rock, 'Sacramento stone'

(iii) Stones to denote position

- North America – S. Peabody, Royaston, Barre, Shutesbury, Chelmsford, Upton, Concord, Waltham, Carlisle, Acton, Lynn, Cohasset, Newport, California

(iv) Miscellaneous stone dwellings

- North America – Narragansett Bay, east of San Francisco Bay (Chinese village)
- High Arctic – Newfoundland; Labrador; Kane Basin
- Australia – Bittangabee Bay, Newcastle, Sydney

(v) Stone markers to denote position

- Newfoundland
- Labrador
- Kane Basin
- Outer Hebrides

THE NEWPORT ROUND TOWER – ASTRONOMICAL ALIGNMENTS

Carbon dating of the tower now puts earliest date at 1410. Professor William S. Penhallow, Professor Emeritus of Physics, University of Rhode Island, has concluded the tower is a cylinder with arches sitting on eight pillars whose windows are cut so as to enable astronomical sightings (in 3D) of the sun, moon, Polaris and Dubhe (Ursa Major) at spring equinox and winter solstice. Everything required to determine longitude by an eclipse of the moon is found in the alignment of the windows. A structure north-east of the tower has been located (gnomon line?) and is being investigated. The author has requested an analysis of the mortar of the tower to see whether it contains rice flour or gypsum, ingredients used by the Chinese to add strength to mortar. Further requests to analyse mortar on 17(i) and 17(iv) above will be made and results posted on website.

18. Linguistics/languages

(i) Linguistics

Identical or very similar names used by Chinese and local peoples in East Africa (Bajun – honey-coloured people) and Australia (Bajuni – honey-coloured people); in New Zealand (*kumara*) and in Mexico (*kumar*) for sweet potato; and in South America a raft is *balsa* and a boat *sampan*, in Mesoamerica the chicken call is *kik-kiri-kee*, as in China.

(ii) Languages

Chinese spoken in California, Russian River (Powers) and Peruvian village.

19. Customs and games

(i) Mexico (Professor Needham's description)

- Complicated rain-making ceremonies, identical down to minute detail
- Teponatzli drums like *mu yü*
- Tripod pottery
- Double permutation calendars
- Far-reaching parallels in symbolic correlations of colours, animals, etc., viz. 'Rabbit in the Moon' tale identical to Aztecs and China
- Games (*parolli*)
- Computing devices (*quipu*) (Inca)
- Jade with its range of complex beliefs
- Papermaking (Aztec)
- Great walls and roads using mortar (Inca)
- Music – more than 50 per cent of American musical instruments occur in the Burmese hinterland
- Neck rest pillows
- Chinese carrying poles

(ii) California – between Russian and Sacramento Rivers (Major Powers' government report)

- Win Tun, Pomo, Yukil, Mai Du tribes: similarities with Chinese in language; gambling; theatrical performances; women's dresses and hair styles; snaring wildfowl with decoys; burial in ancestral soil; farmers, not hunters; men with beards; sophisticated pottery; elegant ornate jasper knives; irrigation ditches and stone villages.

Part IV: Mitochondrial DNA analysis (to be carried out)

20. DNA analysis

- California – Sacramento/Russian Rivers (Win Tun, Pomo, Yukil and Mai Du tribes)
- Mexico – Michoacan Indians (Pacific coast)
- Guatemala – Pacific coast Indians near border with El Salvador
- Darien peninsula – white Indians (Marsh Darien Expedition)

- West Venezuelan Indians (Trapa, Paraujano and Macoita peoples)
- Brazil – Mayoruana Indians
- Africa (Pate) – Bajuni people
- Australia, Arnhem Land – Aborigines
- Pacific – Tahiti, Bora Bora, Kiribati, Carolines, Marianas (graves of Chinese sailors – Professor Wang Tao)
- North America – Narragansett Bay Indians (Professor Delabarre)
- New Zealand – Maoris between Ruapuke and Auckland (Waikato River).

It is hoped results will be posted on web.

21. Teeth of native peoples

Advice is being sought from Professor Christy G. Turner II. It is hoped results will be posted on web.

Part V: Selected bibliography

By far the most comprehensive bibliography can be found in Sorenson, John L. and Raish, Martin H., *Pre-Columbian Contact with the Americas Across the Oceans: An Annotated Bibliography* (Provo Research Press, 1990). Several thousand books are listed.

APPENDIX 2

EYEWITNESS

DIARIES

A selection of contemporaneous accounts follows. In each case (where known/available), original title and details are followed with details of an English translation. Published London unless stated otherwise.

Forbidden City

Hafiz Abru, *Zubdatu't Tawarikh*
written in 1419–22, published 1424
trs. K.M. Maitra as *A Persian Embassy to China*, Lahore 1934

Marco Polo, *Travels of Marco Polo*
written in 1271–95, published c. 1297
trs. T. Waugh, 1984

The Silk Road

Ch'ang Ch'un, *Hsi Yu Ki*
written in 1405–14, published 1414
trs. A. Waley as *Journey from China*, 1931

Marco Polo, *Travels of Marco Polo*
as above

Hafiz Abru, *Zubdatu't Tawarikh*
as above

Chinese maritime empire

Ma Huan, *Ying-yai Shenglan*
written in 1416–33, published 1433
ed./trs. J.V.G. Mills as *The Overall Survey of the Ocean Shores*, 1970

Fei Xin, *Xingcha Shenglan*
written in 1405–31, published 1436
trs. J.V.G. Mills as *Marvellous Visions from the Star Raft*, Wiesbaden 1996

The Colossus falls

Hafiz Abru *Majma al-Tarawikh*
as above

Tamerlane's attack on China

Ibn Khaldun, *Al-Ta'rif*
written in 1405, published 1405
trs. W.J. Fischel as *Ibn Khaldun in Egypt*, Berkeley 1967

Ibn Arabshah, *Tamerlane*
written in 1395, published c. 1440
trs. J.H. Sanders, 1936

R. Gonzales de Clavijo, *Embassy to the Court of Tamburlane*
written in 1403–6, published 1406
trs. G. le Strange, 1928

Islamic trade routes

Ibn Khaldun, *Al-Ta'rif*
as above

Ibn Taghri-Birdi, *History of Egypt 1382–1469*
trs. W. Popper, Berkeley 1954

Ahmad al-Makrizi, *History of Egypt*
trs. E. Brochet (French), Paris 1908

India's trade with China

Abdul Razak, *Travels*
ed./trs. R.H. Major in *India in the Fifteenth Century*, 1857

Yahya Sirhindi, *Tarikh I-Mubarak*
written in 1400–21, published 1421, Calcutta 1931

Ibn Arabshah, *Tamerlane*
as above

Niccolò da Conti, *Travels*
written c. 1424, published c. 1434
ed./trs. R.H. Major as 'The Travels of Niccolò da Conti' in *India in the Fifteenth Century*, 1857

India's ocean trade

Ibn Battuta, *Travels*
written in 1325–54, published 1356
trs. S. Lee as *The Travels of Ibn Battuta*, 1829

Ludovico de Varthema, *Travels*
published c. 1506
trs. J.W. Jones as *The Travels of L. de Varthema*, 1863

Ma Huan, *Ying-yai Shenglan*
as above

Fei Xin *Xingcha Shenglan*
as above

Middle East trade routes severed

Ahmad al-Makrizi, *History of Egypt*
as above

Ibn Taghri-Birdi, *History of Egypt 1382–1469*
as above

Ibn Khaldun, *Al-Ta'rif*
as above

The Ottomans surround Byzantium

Bertrandon de la Broquière, *Voyage d'Outremer*
written in 1421–32, published 1455
trs./ed. G.R. Kline, New York 1988

H. Dukas, *Historia Turco-Byzantina*
published 1455
trs. H.J. Magoulias as *Decline and Fall of Byzantium to the Ottoman Turks*, Detroit
1975

Pedro Tafur, *Andanzas y Viajes*
written in 1435–9, published 1439

G. Phrantzes, *Chronicles*
written in 1460–77
ed. I. Bekker as *Chronicon Maius* (German), 1838

Russia

Anon., *Mediaeval Russian Epics, Chronicles and Tales*
written in 1380–1422
ed. S. Zenkovsky, New York 1974

Bertrandon de la Broquière, *Voyage d'Outremer*
as above

Anon., *The Secret History of the Mongols*
written in 1240, published post-1368
ed./trs. F.W. Cleaves, Harvard 1982

The Holy Roman Empire

Jan Huss, *De Ecclesia*
written in 1413, published 1413
trs. D.S. Schaff, New York 1915

Henry V

Anon., *Incerti Scriptoris Chronicon Angliae de Regnis Ricardus II . . . Henricus VI*
written in 1377–1470
ed. J.S. Davies as *English Chronicles of the Reigns of Richard II . . . Henry VI*, 1856

Anon., *Red Book of the Exchequer*
written in c. 1192
ed. H. Hall, 1896

J. Wycliffe, *The Lantern of Light*
written in 1405
ed. L.M. Swinburn, New York 1971

M. Kempe, *The Boke of Margery Kempe*
written in c. 1435, published c. 1450
ed. L. Staley, Kalamazoo, Michigan 1996

V. Lobeira, *Amadis de Gaul*
written in c. 1405
ed./trs. R. Southey, 1872

Renaissance and technical revolution

F. Datini, *Archivio Datini*
Prato – Archivio dello Stato, written in 1363–1410

A. Taccola, *De Ingeneis*
written in 1427–33, published 1433
trs./ed. F.D. Prager and G. Scaglia as *Mariamo Taccola and his Book De Ingeneis*,
1972

Venice

M. Contarini, *Papers*
in State Archive of Venice, written in 1421–4

French exploration before Columbus

Register of Confiscations in Normandy
written in 1420
Public Record Office

J. de Bethencourt, *Le Canarien, livre de la conquête et conversion des Canaries*
trs. R.H. Major, 1872

J. Rotz, *The Boke of Idrography*
ed. H. Wallis, Oxford 1981

Prince Henry the Navigator discovers the New World

A. Galvão, *The Discoveries of the World*
published 1568
trs. R. Hakluyt, New York 1969

Civilizations of the Americas

Bernardino de Sahagún, *Historia General de las Cosas de la Nueva España*
trs./ed. A.J.O. Anderson and C.E. Dibble as *General History of the Things of New Spain*, Salt Lake City 1970

B. Diaz del Castillo, *The True History of the Conquest of Mexico*
written in 1568
trs. A. Idell, New York 1957

Juan de Betanzos, *Suma y Narración de los Incas*
trs. R. Hamilton and D. Buchanan as *Narrative of the Incas*, Austin 1996

Ayala Felipe Huamán, *Nueva Crónica y Buen Gobierno*
written in 1613–15

P. Cieza de León, *Crónicas*
trs. H. de Onis as *The Incas of Pedro Cieza de Leon*, Oklahoma 1959

Garcilaso de la Vega, *Commentarios Reales de Los Incas*
published c. 1605
ed. R. Hamilton as *Royal Commentary of the Inca*, Austin, Texas 1996

Papers from the Franciscan Monastery, Arequipa

Tutul Xiu, *The Xiu Family Papers*
written in 1419–42, Mérida, Yucatán

Diego de Landa, *Relación de las Cosas de Yucatán*
written in 1566
trs. W. Gates as *Yucatan Before and After the Conquest*, Baltimore 1937

Miscellaneous

Codex Borbonicus
written in 1507
ed. G.C. Vaillant as *A Sacred Almanac of the Aztecs*, New York 1940

Codex Borgia
ed. G. Diaz, A. Rodgers and B.E. Byland, 1993

Codex Mendoza
written in 1541
ed. F.F. Berdan & P.R. Anawalt, Berkeley 1992

F. Diego Duran, *Historia de las Indias de Nueva-España y Islas de Terre Firme*
written in c. 1570
trs. D. Hayden as *History of the Indies of New Spain*, Oklahoma 1996

H. Cortés, *Documentos Cortesianos*
ed. J.L. Martinez, Mexico 1990

APPENDIX 3

KEY CHARTS
DESCRIBING THE FIRST
NAVIGATION OF
THE WORLD

Date	Name of chart	Original cartographers	Current location
1404–70	Kangnido	Chinese and Koreans	Copy (1470) in Ryukoku University, Kyoto, Japan
1513	Piri Reis (Turkish admiral)	Chinese, then Portuguese; based partly on 1428 World Map	Topkapi Serai Museum, Istanbul, Turkey
1540–2	Jean Rotz (Dieppe cartographer)	Chinese, then Portuguese; based partly on 1428 World Map	The British Library, London, England
1420	*Wu Pei Chi*	Chinese sailing directions	Chinese government in Beijing
1422	Mao Kun	Chinese; shows in pictorial form the tracks of Zheng He's fleet in Indian Ocean	Beijing
1502	Cantino		Biblioteca Estense, Modena, Italy
1505	Caverio	} Chinese, then Portuguese {	James Ford Bell Library, University of Minnesota, Minneapolis
1424	1424 chart Pizzigano Waldseemüller		Library of Congress, US

APPENDIX 4

THE DETERMINATION OF LONGITUDE BY THE CHINESE IN THE EARLY FIFTEENTH CENTURY

Authors: Professor John Oliver, co-chairman and Professor of the
Department of Astronomy, University of Florida (JO)

Mr Marshall Payn (MP)

Gavin Menzies, author of *1421 – The Year China Discovered the
World* (GM)

This paper is set out as follows:

Introduction
Chinese astronomical knowledge in 1421
The Chinese determination of elapsed time
Chinese observatories
Eclipses
Passage of events during a lunar eclipse
Longitude determined by elapsed time during a lunar eclipse
Proof of the theory
Practical implementation

Introduction (GM)

GM contends that during its sixth voyage (1421–3), the Chinese fleet perfected a method of determining longitude. This is illustrated by the longitude of the East African coast being accurately charted by the Chinese, then later shown on the Cantino map (1502) some three centuries before John Harrison invented the chronometer. Longitude on the East African coast between Cape Town and Djibouti, a distance of seven thousand nautical miles, is correct to within twenty nautical miles (twenty seconds of time). Detailed reasons for concluding that the Chinese were the original surveyors whose work was used to create the Cantino can be found in chapter 6 of this book.

Chinese astronomical knowledge in 1421 (GM)

By the time of their sixth voyage Zheng He's fleets had inherited expertise gained from six centuries of charting the stars in the night sky. The Chinese had recorded pulsars, quasars and neutron stars for centuries, and had predicted and noted the return of Halley's comet on every pass since the second century BC. They were aware that the earth was a globe and had divided it into 365 and a quarter degrees (the number of days in the year) of latitude and longitude. Longitude was determined by the position on the globe east or west of Beijing; latitude was determined not from the equator but from Polaris in the north and the mid-point of the circumpolar stars in the south. The end result was the same as achieved later by Europeans. Following the voyage of Grand Eunuch Hong Bao to the Antarctic in early 1422, the Chinese knew the correct position of the South Pole. They were thus able to eliminate magnetic variation and to calculate latitude in the southern hemisphere as they did with Polaris in the north. In the early Ming era, Beijing's astronomers charted no fewer than 1,400 stars each night as they traversed the sky, a practice Emperor Zhu Di had reinstated. The Chinese were able to predict both solar and lunar eclipses with considerable accuracy.

The Chinese determination of elapsed time (GM)

An essential requirement for determining longitude was a precise measurement of elapsed time. The Chinese measured the passage of time by the sun's shadow.

The most famous existing observatory is the Zhou Gong Tower, built seven centuries ago. It is a truncated pyramid measuring twenty-five feet square at the top. Stairways lead from ground level to the platform on the top, upon which stands a three-roomed building with a good view to the north of a forty-foot gnomon, or vertical pole. The observatory, too, has a thin vertical rod for observation of meridian transits, and one of the rooms is equipped with a clepsydra, or large water clock.

Lying on the ground to the north of the tower and extending for 120 feet is the device for measuring the sun's shadow. To ensure this device was level, two parallel troughs of water extended along its length, enabling its stones to be laid precisely parallel with the water.

The gnomon itself extended forty feet into the sky. This enabled the sun's shadow thrown by the pole to be measured. As an illustration, at the equinox on the equator the sun rises in the east and sets in the west. At midday it is exactly above the observer and hence casts no shadow – it is a dot. The longest shadows are cast at sunrise and sunset. The length of the shadow will tell the time on that particular day at that particular place.

Back in AD 721, the Chinese realized that the length of the sun's shadow varied not only according to the time of day but for every day of the year, and depended on the observer's latitude. They conducted an experiment between latitudes 17°20′N and 40°N. Along this meridian line, thousands of miles long, they measured simultaneously the length of shadows at the summer and winter solstices using a standard eight-foot gnomon. This showed that shadow lengths varied just over 3.56 inches for each four hundred miles of latitude. They could thus make corrections for their position.

They also appreciated that the length of shadow varied with the seasons. In one celebrated measurement, it was 12.3695 feet at the summer solstice and 76.7400 feet at the winter. This enabled them to make corrections for each day of the year as well as for different positions on the earth's surface.

The final adjustment was to correct the irregular motion of the earth around the sun occasioned by the eccentricity of the earth's orbit and the difference between the equator and the ecliptic – this is known as 'The Equation of Time'. It causes differences between absolute and solar time, reaching a maximum positive difference of fourteen minutes and thirty seconds in February and a maximum negative difference of sixteen minutes and thirty seconds in November. So accurately did the Chinese determine this equation of time that the great mathematician Laplace wrote: 'The [Chinese] observations made from 1277 to 1280 are valuable on account of their great precision and prove incontestably the diminution of the obliquity of the ecliptic and the eccentricity of the earth's orbit between then and now' (Needham, 1954, vol. 3, p. 398). This outstanding precision is illustrated by their estimate of the length of lunation at 29.530591 days – an error of less than one second in a month.

Chinese observatories (GM)

The Chinese replicated the Chou Kung Tower, first in Nanjing, then, when the capital was moved north in 1421, in Beijing. Later, as noted in chapters 4 and 8, they built observatories around the world. We know what equipment was in the observatories from an inventory listed in *History of the Yuan Dynasty* (1276–9) (Needham, 1954, vol. 3, p. 369). Here are the principal pieces of equipment:

Hun thien hsiang – celestial globe (Ricci's first instrument)
Yang i – hemispherical sundial
Kao piao – lofty gnomon, forty feet, as at Yang Cheng
Li yun i – theodolite
Cheng li – verification instrument to determine exact positions of sun and moon
    near eclipse
Ching-fu – shadow amplifier
Jih yueh shi yi – instrument for observation of solar and lunar eclipses
Hsing kuei – star dial
Ting shih – time-determining instrument
Hou chi – pole-observing instrument
Chiu piao hsuan – plumb lines
Chengi – rectifying instrument

As may be seen, the list has instruments for recognizing stars in the sky (celestial globe); for measuring the length of the sun's shadow (lofty gnomon); for determining exact positions of the sun and moon at eclipses (cheng li); for amplifying the sun's shadow (ching-fu); for observing lunar eclipses (jih yueh shi yi); and for observing the Pole Star (hou chi).

Some of the instruments need explanation. The Chinese had long known that the longer the sun's shadow (i.e. the bigger the gnomon), the more accurate the measurement of time. However, the longer the shadow got, the more attenuated and fainter it became. In the early Ming era they devised a 'camera obscura', a hole in the top of the roof of the observation chamber which resulted in a sharper shadow. They intensified this with a type of magnifying glass. The upshot was that a long shadow could now be measured to within one-hundredth of an inch.

The measurements of time so far described would only work when the sun was out. Measuring time in darkness was accomplished using various types of water clock – clepsydras – which themselves were calibrated by day against the gnomons. There were several types of clepsydra; one of the best known was a steelyard type (chheng lou) which had compensating mechanisms to take account of both air pressure in the atmosphere and the height of water in the clock itself. One of these was found in the Pandanan junk wreck. We can see and marvel at the ingenuity of these astonishing devices for the polyvascular type is illustrated and explained in the Chinese encyclopedia printed in 1478 (*Shi Lin Guang Ji*) now in the Cambridge University Library. We can summarize by saying that by the end of the voyage of 1421–3 the Chinese had the ability to measure time from their observation platforms which by then straddled the globe.

Eclipses (GM)

Eclipses of the earth's moon and the sun, that is solar and lunar eclipses, occur when the sun, moon and earth are in line with one another and when the moon's orbit around the earth is in the same plane as the earth's orbit around the sun. When these planes differ the result is a new or full moon rather than an eclipse.

Solar eclipse

In an eclipse of the sun, the line-up is like this:

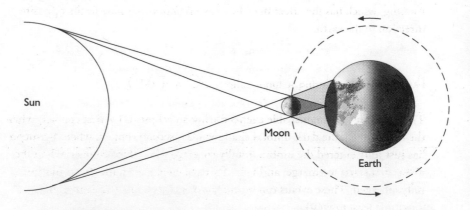

The moon's shadow blots out the sun over a small portion of the earth. It becomes night for a very short period. The spot of darkness, the umbra, travels across the earth as the moon rotates around the earth, and the earth itself rotates. Thus, observers in different locations see the solar eclipse at different times.

Lunar eclipse

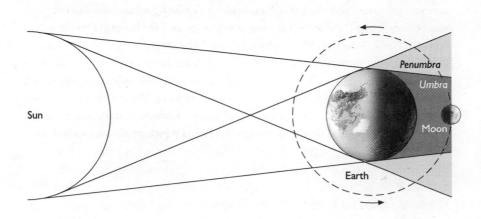

In a lunar eclipse, the earth is between sun and moon. Because the earth is so much bigger than the moon, the earth's shadow blots out the moon. The great difference, insofar as astronomical observations are concerned, is that in a lunar eclipse the event may be seen simultaneously by observers across half the earth, whereas in a solar eclipse the event occurs only above a small piece of earth at any one time.

The key to using a lunar eclipse to determine longitude is (i) that the event is seen across the world simultaneously; and (ii) while the event is seen, the earth is rotating, which has the effect that the heavens appear to rotate in the opposite direction to the earth.

Passage of events during a lunar eclipse (JO and MP)

There are four distinguishable events during an eclipse: U1 – first contact, when the moon enters the dark umbral shadow; U2 – second contact, when the moon has just fully entered the umbra (totally covered); U3 – third contact, when the moon first starts to emerge; and U4 – fourth contact, when the moon has just fully emerged. These events can be observed across almost 180 degrees of longitude (east to west).

Longitude determined by elapsed time during a lunar eclipse (JO and MP)

With their gnomons and water clocks, the Chinese were able to determine the passage of time, minute by minute, throughout the day and night. They could also forecast when a full lunar eclipse would occur – about every six months somewhere across the globe. The instruction to the navigators and astronomers was as follows: 'After landing in unknown territory, when the next total eclipse begins, wait until the third event [U3] occurs and the last bit of darkness disappears. Just when the first sliver of light appears as the moon starts to come out of its eclipse [U3], both the observer in the new territories and the astronomer in Beijing look into the night sky and determine which major star is transiting the local meridian.' The local meridian is an imaginary line on the celestial sphere which starts at the celestial pole north of the observer, extends directly over the observer's head (the observer's zenith), and ends at the celestial pole south of the observer. Along this imaginary line, the observer selects a known star crossing the line. This is both observers' key sighting at this point.

When the astronomer in the newly discovered territories has returned to Beijing, he and the astronomer at Beijing's observatory compare notes. The one who has returned from abroad relates that at event U3, star alpha was transiting his local meridian. The Beijing observer relates that at that U3 moment, star beta was transiting his local meridian, both well-known stars. They now get out their time-keeping device. This has been calibrated from the gnomons. They wait until star alpha crosses the zenith and then start counting with their time-measuring device until star beta crosses their zenith. The time elapsed between star alpha and star beta crossing the zenith is the distance the earth has rotated between the two observers – the one in Beijing, the other in the newly discovered lands. The earth rotates 360 degrees every twenty-four hours. Thus, if we assume that the time elapsed between the transit of star alpha and star beta was exactly six hours (i.e. a quarter of the time it takes the earth to rotate), then the difference in longitude between Beijing and the new territory is also a quarter of the total longitude around the world, i.e. one-quarter of 360 degrees, or 90 degrees.

Note by GM: Refinements can be introduced by conducting this procedure four times at U1, U2, U3 and U4 and then applying the averages to reduce errors.

Proof of the theory (JO and MP)

We decided to test our theory by observing the lunar eclipse of 16 and 17 July 2000. We positioned our team across the Pacific from Tahiti to Singapore. By a happy coincidence, we chose the same positions on which the Chinese had erected observation platforms.

Where	Long	Obs?	Observations				Local Sidereal Time				Uobs-LST				Error	
			U1	U2	U3	U4	LST1	LST2	LST3	LST4	U1	U2	U3	U4	Ave	rms
Papeele, Tahiti	-149°	yes		339°	0.8°			341.2°	08.0°			-2.2°	-0.0°		-1.1°	±1.5°
Singapore	103.8°	yes		235°		276°		234.0°		277.1°		-1.0°		-1.1°	0.0°	±1.5°
near Melbourne, Australia	145°	yes	258°	275°	301°		258.4°	274.7°	301.5°		-0.4°	0.3°	-0.5°		-0.2°	±0.5°
Tekapo, New Zealand	170.5°	yes	284°	301°	329°	343°	284.4°	300.7°	327.5°	343.8°	-0.4°	0.3°	1.5°	-0.8°	0.1°	±1.0°
Nelson, New Zealand	173.1°	yes	285°	305°	330°	345°	287.0°	303.3°	330.1°	346.4°	-2.0°	1.7°	-0.1°	-1.4°	-0.5°	±1.6°

Table 1: Observations of the 16/17 July 2000 lunar eclipse. As can be seen, the error of a single observation was typically ±1.5° or better. Since one degree is the equivalent of four minutes of time, this error is the equivalent of about six minutes of time. The error of the combination of two observations would be better by √2 and would thus be about ±1°.

The observations list the celestial longitude measured from the vernal equinox of whatever star was transiting the local meridian – that is, the straight line passing from north over the observer's head to south. The celestial longitude is measured along the equator of a star map. Thus, 339° (Tahiti) measures the position of a rotating cylindrical star map. The time elapsed between U2 and U3 enabled that cylindrical star map to rotate for 339° past 360° to 8° – about two hours. Average errors were: Tahiti 1.1 degrees, New Zealand 0.1 degree, Melbourne 0.1 degree, Singapore zero degrees. Our observers were amateurs; with more training and experience than we could provide the errors could be reduced.

Practical implementation (GM)

The result has startling implications, for longitude has been calculated from Tahiti in the east with sixty-six nautical miles' error to Singapore in the west with no longitudinal error. There is six nautical miles' longitudinal error between Singapore and New Zealand, none between New Zealand and Australia. Longitude has been calculated across nearly one-third of the world correct to within sixty-six miles.

The Chinese could have determined longitude just as accurately as Professor Oliver's team did. The brilliance of this method is that, unlike calculations for latitude, no sextant is required. Neither is a clock; the only instrument needed is one to accurately determine elapsed time, a role fulfilled by the gnomon.

Having accurately determined the longitude of Malacca (Singapore), the Chinese fleets could now use observation platforms and gnomons on their bases around the Indian Ocean – at Semudera (Sumatra), the Andamans, Dondra Head (Ceylon/Sri Lanka), Calicut on the Malabar coast of India, Zanzibar in East Africa, the Seychelles and Maldive archipelagos – all of which appear on the *Wu Pei Chi* charts which credit Zheng He with providing the information. There is no reason why longitudes across the whole Indian Ocean should not have been determined in one eclipse, provided a sufficiently large fleet was deployed. This, I think, happened with the results seen in the Cantino, where the coast of East Africa appears as if drawn with the aid of satellite navigation.

The brilliance of Zheng He's astro-navigation arises both from its simplicity and because each part contributes towards a composite whole greater than its parts.

Establishing the right ascension and declination of Canopus and of Crucis Alpha and Beta (Southern Cross) had enabled them to be cross-referenced to Polaris (see *Wu Pei Chi* chart for passage between Dondra Head and Sumatra). Measuring Polaris's altitude as they sailed north would have enabled Chinese navigators to calculate half the circumference of the earth. Sailing due north between the equator and 40°N was 2,400 nautical miles (10,000 *li*); thus, continuing to the North Pole would be a further 50° or 12,500 *li;* thus, the earth's circumference must be 100,000 *li*. Because they knew the position of Canopus and the Southern Cross, they could use the size of the earth to determine the true position of the South Pole (the centre of the circumpolar stars – Canopus becomes circumpolar below 68°S). Hence, they could determine the position of the South Magnetic Pole so as to establish true south and north.

The Chinese now had everything needed to accurately chart the world – latitude, longitude, size, direction. They went on to chart every continent with great accuracy. The fruits of their labours reached Europe via Niccolò da Conti and enabled Europeans to set sail on their voyages of discovery with maps based on Chinese cartography.

OBSERVATION PLATFORMS USED BY THE CHINESE 1421–3

Pacific, east to west

Marquesas	140°W	9°30'S
Tahiti	149°W	17°50'S
Society Islands (Bora Bora)	151°W	17°30'S
Kiribati (Gilberts, Phoenix) Islands	160°4'W	0°24'N
Ruapuke beach	174°47'E	37°56'S
Nan Madol	158°21'E	6°51'N
Gympie (New South Wales)	152°42'E	26°12'S
Gosford (central NSW)	151°13'E	33°26'S
New Guinea	143°38'E	3°35'S
Yap Island	138°9'E	9°31'N
Nanjing	118°45'E	32°6'N
Beijing	116°25'E	39°55'N

Indian Ocean

Malacca	102°15'E	2°11'N
Semudera (Bandar Aceh)	95°19'E	5°32'N
Nicobars (Polo Milo)	93°42'E	7°27'N
Andamans (Lapatte)	92°47'E	9°22'N
Ceylon/Sri Lanka (Dondra Head)	80°13'E	6°02'N
Calicut	75°49'E	11°16'N
Maldives (Male)	73°30'E	4°7'N
Seychelles	55°29'E	4°36'N
Madagascar (Mahajanga)	46°14'E	15°45'S
Zanzibar	39°11'E	6°11'N
Sofala	39°44'E	20°9'S

APPENDIX 5

FURTHER INFORMATION
ON WEBSITE

1. Reconstructed track of Chinese fleet through Caribbean – December 1421
2. Translation of names on Zuane Pizzigano's chart
3. Wording on Fra Mauro's Planisphere of 1459
4. Reconstructed track of Chinese fleets from Falklands to Antarctic
5. Translation of words on Piri Reis chart together with plants and animals of Patagonia
6. Reconstructed track of Chinese fleets from Antarctic to Australia
7. Translation of words on Jean Rotz chart together with places identified
8. Places identified on the Waldseemüller chart
9. Places identified on the Cantino chart
10. Excerpts from the Chinese star chart contained in the *Wu Pei Chi*
11. The Newport Round Tower – astronomical alignments and details of mortar
12. Notes and further bibliography on the Sacramento junk
13. Notes and further bibliography on the Bimini junk
14. Notes and further bibliography on the Ruapuke wreck
15. Notes and further bibliography on the Warrnambool mahogany ship
16. Notes and further bibliography on the Pandanan junk
17. Letters between the author and Professor Ptak
18. Programme of DNA analysis
19. Further notes on the Dondra Head, Matadi Falls, Cape Verde and San Julian stones
20. Updates on synopses of evidence
21. Bibliography on Eastern contacts with Pacific America

NOTES

Chapter 1: The Emperor's Grand Plan

1   Anlui province on the north bank of the Yangtze in eastern central China.
2   Chinese emperors were known not by their personal name but by their title, and, after death, a 'temple name', such as 'Sincere Emperor', reflecting the course of their life.
3   Mary M. Anderson, *Hidden Power: The Palace Eunuchs of Imperial China*, Prometheus, Buffalo, New York, 1990, pp. 15–18, 307–11.
4   R.H. Van Gulik, *Sexual Life in Ancient China*, Leiden, 1961, p. 256.
5   Anderson, op. cit.
6   Dorothy and Thomas Hoobler, *Images across the Ages: Chinese Portraits*, Raintree, Austin, Texas, 1993.
7   Confucius, as quoted by F. Braudel in *A History of Civilisations*, trs. R. Mayne, Penguin, Harmondsworth, 1994, p. 178.
8   The dragon was credited with miraculous powers and was used as a metaphor for people of great virtue and talent. Almost all the items and artefacts closely connected with the emperor – his throne, his robes, his bed, etc. – were prefixed with 'dragon' or 'phoenix', the phoenix being another mystical creature with extraordinary powers.
9   In early 2002 the Chinese government announced ambitious plans to restore the dry-docks and build a full-size replica of one of Zheng He's junks.
10   Ming Tong Jian, *Comprehensive Mirror of Ming History*, 1873, Ch. 14, quoted in Louise Levathes, *When China Ruled the Seas*, Simon & Schuster, 1994, pp. 73–4.
11   Ahmad ibn Arabshah, *Miracles of Destiny in Timur's History*, 1636.
12   *Shun Feng Hsiang Seng* ('Fair Winds for Escort'), anon., c. 1430, Bodleian Library.
13   Miles Menander Dawson, *The Wisdom of Confucius*, Boston, Mass., 1932, pp. 57–8.
14   Quoted by Edmund L. Dreyer in *Early Ming China: A Political History 1355–1435*, Stanford University Press, Calif., p. 204.
15   Hafiz Abru, *A Persian Embassy in China*, 1421, trs. K.M. Maitra, Lahore, 1934, p. 55.
16   Emperor Zhu Di's instructions to Zheng He, paraphrased from the two stone steles of 1431.
17   The number of voyages made by the treasure fleets is, and will continue to be, a matter of dispute. The inscriptions on commemorative stones erected by Zheng He before his final voyage claim that his fleets had, until then, made seven. Most authorities classify his fourth and fifth voyages as one. I have adhered to this classification; the voyages beginning in 1421 were therefore the sixth.
18   Hoobler, op. cit.
19   L. Carrington Goodrich (ed.), *The Dictionary of Ming Biography*, Columbia UP, New York, 1976, p. 1365.
20   N.I. Vavilov, 'The Origin, Variation, Immunity and Breeding of Cultivated Plants', trs. K.S. Chester, *Chronica Botanica*, Vol. 13, Waltham, Mass., 1949–50; and J. Needham, *Science and Civilisation in China*, Vol. VI, Pt 2, sec. 41, p. 428.

Chapter 2: A Thunderbolt Strikes

1   Hafiz Abru, *A Persian Embassy to China*, 1421, trs. K.M. Maitra, Lahore, 1934, pp. 113–15.

2 Ibid., p. 115.

3 Ibid., pp. 115–17.

4 Ibid., p. 117

5 Shang Chuan, *Yongle Huang Di*, Beijing, 1989, pp. 214–15, citing the Cochin tablet 'Taizong Shi Lu', ch. 236.

6 S.W. Mote and Denis Twitchett (eds), *The Cambridge History of China*, Vol. 7, *The Ming Dynasty*, Cambridge UP, Cambridge, 1988, p. 292.

7 Abru, op. cit., p. 108.

8 Quoted in Louise Levathes, *When China Ruled the Seas*, Oxford UP, Oxford, 1994, p. 157.

9 Ellen F. Soullière, *Palace Women in the Ming Dynasty*, Princeton University doctoral thesis, 1987, quoted in Levathes, op. cit., p. 226.

10 Levathes, op. cit., pp. 163 and 164.

11 P.B. Ebrey, *The Cambridge Illustrated History of China*, Cambridge UP, Cambridge, 1996, p. 278.

12 Quoted in L. Carrington Goodrich (ed.), *The Dictionary of Ming Biography*, Columbia UP, New York, 1976, p. 338.

13 See J. Needham, *Science and Civilisation in China*, Vol. 4, Pt 3, Cambridge UP, Cambridge, 1954, p. 525; and J.J.L. Duyvendak, *China's Discovery of Africa*, Probsthain, 1949, p. 27, and 'The True Dates of the Chinese Maritime Expeditions in the Early Fifteenth Century', *T'oung Pao*, XXXIV, pp. 395–8.

Chapter 3: The Fleets Set Sail

1 The originals are in Beijing, but the British Library holds copies.

2 J. Needham, *Science and Civilisation in China*, Vol. 3, sec. 20, Cambridge UP, Cambridge, 1954, p. 230.

3 Ibid., Vol. 4, Pt 3, pp. 565ff.

4 Ibid., Vol. 6, Pt 1, pp. 365ff.

5 Ibid., Vol. 6, Pt 5, pp. 19ff.

6 Ibid.

7 Antonio Pigafetta, *Magellan's Voyage*, trs. R.A. Skelton, Yale UP, New Haven, Conn., 1969, p. 56.

8 R.H. Van Gulik, *Sexual Life in Ancient China*, Leiden, 1961, pp. 308ff.

9 Ibid., p. 125.

10 Ibid., p. 265.

11 Ibid., p. 133.

12 Ibid.

13 Ibn Taghri-Birdi, *A History of Egypt, 1382–1469 AD,* Berkeley, California, 1954.

14 Ma Huan, *The Overall Survey of the Ocean Shores*, Beijing, 1433, trs. J.V.G. Mills, Cambridge UP (for Hakluyt Society), 1970, p. 108.

15 Ibid., p. 143.

16 Ma Huan, op. cit., trs. Paul Wheatley in *The Golden Khersonese*, University of Malaya Press, Kuala Lumpur, 1961, p. 143.

17 Ma Huan, op. cit., trs. Mills, p. 104.

18   Ibid. A slightly different translation is quoted by Richard Hall in *Empires of the Monsoon*. HarperCollins, 1996, p 89.
19   F. Braudel, *The Wheels of Commerce*, trs. Siân Reynolds, Fontana, 1985, p. 130.
20   Ibid., p. 131.
21   Zheng He, quoted in Dorothy and Thomas Hoobler, *Images across the Ages: Chinese Portraits*, Raintree, Austin, Texas, 1993.
22   The identity of the admiral in command of the third fleet is not known with absolute certainty, but after corresponding with Professor Roderich Ptak of the University of Munich I believe Chou Wen to be the most probable leader.

Chapter 4: Rounding the Cape

1   See ch. 3, n. 22.
2   Stone inscription in the Palace of the Celestial Spouse at Chiang-su, dated 1431, trs. J.J.L. Duyvendak, 'The True Dates of the Chinese Maritime Expeditions in the Early Fifteenth Century', *T'oung Pao*, XXXIV, p. 347.
3   Stone inscription in the Palace of the Celestial Spouse at Liu-Chia-Chang, dated 1431, trs. J.J.L. Duyvendak, *China's Discovery of Africa*, Probsthain, 1949, p. 29.
4   Professor Needham, Richard Hall and Louise Levathes.
5   Richard Hall, *Empires of the Monsoon*, HarperCollins, 1996, p. 550, has splendid illustrations.
6   Ma Huan, *The Overall Survey of the Ocean Shores*, Beijing, 1433, trs. J.V.G. Mills, Cambridge UP (for Hakluyt Society), 1970, p. 138. It can be seen that Muslim people are ruling Hindus.
7   Ibid., pp. 140 and 141.
8   Poggio Bracciolini, *The Travels of Niccolò da Conti*, 1434, partial translation in R.H. Major (ed.), *India in the Fifteenth Century*, Hakluyt Society, 1857.
9   *The Travels of Niccolò da Conti*, quoted in Hall, op. cit., p. 124.
10   J.H. Parry, *The Discovery of the Sea*, Elek, 1979, p. 45.
11   I understand that a book written by the late Professor Wei will be published at the conference, claiming that Zheng He's fleets discovered the Americas.
12   100,000 *li* equals 40,000 nautical miles. The circumference of the globe is 21,600 nautical miles.
13   As translated by J. Needham in *Science and Civilisation in China*, Vol. 4, Pt 3, Cambridge UP, Cambridge, 1954, p. 572.
14   Ibid.
15   Quoted by Eannes de Zuzara, *The Chronicle of the Discovery and Conquest of Guinea*, trs. C.R. Beazley, Hakluyt Society, 1896–9.
16   Hall, op. cit., pp. 124–6.
17   Vice-Admiral Sir Ian McIntosh, letter to the author, 2001.
18   Chuan Chin, one of the Koreans who organized the publication of the Kangnido.
19   The work of M. Chevalier and his colleagues.
20   Antonio Galvão, *Tratado Dos Diversos e Desayados Caminhos*, Lisbon, 1563. The translation I have used is that of Richard Hakluyt, 1601, pp. 23–4, quoted by F.M. Rogers in *The Travels of the Infante Dom Pedro*, Harvard UP, Cambridge, Mass., 1961, p. 48.

21   Ibid.
22   H. Harisse, *The Discovery of North America*, 1892, p. 272.
23   [British] Admiralty, *Ocean Passages of the World*, third edn, 1973.

Chapter 5: The New World

1   Bibliography in J. Needham, *Science and Civilisation in China*, Vol. 4, Pt 3, sec. 29, Cambridge UP, Cambridge, 1954, p. 542.
2   Note VII on the Piri Reis map, translated by G.C. McIntosh in *The Piri Reis Map of 1513*, University of Georgia Press, Athens, Georgia, 2000, p. 46.
3   Charles R. Darwin, *Journal of Researches into the Geology and Natural History of the Various Countries Visited by HMS Beagle, 1832–36*, Henry Colburn, 1839, pp. 54 and 124.
4   Antonio Pigafetta, *Magellan's Voyage*, trs. R.A. Skelton, Yale UP, New Haven, Conn., 1934, p. 54.
5   Note XXIII, in McIntosh, op. cit., p. 44.
6   Note XXIV, ibid.
7   Ibid.
8   Ma Huan, *The Overall Survey of the Ocean Shores*, Beijing, 1433, trs. J.V.G. Mills, Cambridge UP (for Hakluyt Society), 1970, p. 155.
9   See chapter 9.
10   A detailed and extensive bibliography of plants and animals brought to the Americas before the European voyages of exploration is contained in J.L. Sorenson and M.H. Raish, *Pre-Columbian Contact with the Americas across the Oceans: An Annotated Bibliography*, Provo Research Press, 1990.
11   Ferdinand Magellan, 13 December 1519, in *The First Voyage round the World by Magellan*, translated from the Accounts of Pigafetta by Lord Stanley of Alderley, Hakluyt Society, 1874, and Antonio Pigafetta, *Primer Viage Alrededor del Mundo*, Leoncio Cabrero Fernandez, Madrid, 1985.
12   J. de Acosta, 'Historia Natural y Moral de las Indias', No. 34, Cronic., Venice, 1596. Acosta used linguistic evidence to demonstrate the spread of pre-Columbian chickens in South America.
13   George F. Carter, 'The Chicken in America', in Donald Y. Gilmore and Linda S. McElroy (eds), *Across before Columbus?*, NEARA Publications, Edgecomb, Maine, 1998, p. 154.
14   Ibid., p. 158.
15   M.D.W. Jeffreys, 'Pre-Columbian Maize in Asia', in Carroll Riley et al. (eds), *Men across the Sea*, University of Texas Press, 1971, pp. 382ff.
16   Maize: Antonio Pigafetta, *Primo Viaggio intorno al Mondo*, MS version of c. 1524 translated in E.H. Blair and J.A. Robertson, *The Philippine Islands 1493–1893*, 1906, Vols 33 and 34, pp. 154, 164, 182 and 186; M.D.W. Jeffreys, 'Who Introduced Maize into Southern Africa?', *South Africa Journal of Science*, Vol. 63, Johannesburg, 1963, pp. 23–40; A. de Candolle, *Origin of Cultivated Plants*, 1967, p. 355. See also ch. 8, n. 20, and ch. 5, n. 18.
17   Ibid.
18   J.J.L. Duyvendak, *China's Discovery of Africa*, Probsthain, 1949, p. 32.

19   *Wu Pei Chi* and the *Shun Feng Hsiang Seng*, Beijing.
20   Chiu Thang Shu, quoted in J. Needham, *Science and Civilisation in China*, Vol. 4, sec. 20, Cambridge UP, Cambridge, 1954, p. 274.

Chapter 6: Voyage to Antarctica and Australia

1   Charles R. Darwin, *Journal of Researches into the Geology and Natural History of the Various Countries Visited by HMS Beagle, 1832–36*, 1839.
2   Ibid.
3   Antonio Pigafetta, *Magellan's Voyage*, trs. R.A. Skelton, Folio Society, 1975, p. 49.
4   Ibid.
5   Ibid., p. 50.
6   Ibid., p. 57.
7   Professor C.H. Hapgood, *Maps of the Ancient Sea Kings*, Chilton Books, New York, 1966, pp. 193ff.
8   Erich von Daniken, *Chariots of the Gods*, trans. M. Heron, Souvenir, 1969, p. 20.
9   British Admiralty Chart 554.
10   Ludovico Varthema, *Travels of L. de Varthema* (1510), trs. J.W. Jones, Hakluyt Society, 1863, p. 249. 'He told us that on the other side of the said island [Java] . . . there are some other races who navigate by the said four or five stars opposite to ours [the Southern Cross] and moreover . . . beyond the said island the day does not last more than four hours, and that it was colder than in any other part of the world.'
11   Ibid.
12   Longitude 70°W.
13   Latitude 60°S.
14   Latitude 64°S.
15   The Scott Polar Research Institute of Cambridge has kindly provided ice charts for the Antarctic.
16   As may be verified with the Microsoft computer program *Starry Nights*.
17   See Note VI on the Piri Reis map, translated by G.C. McIntosh in *The Piri Reis Map of 1513*, University of Georgia Press, Athens, Georgia, 2000, pp. 16 and 17.
18   L. Carrington Goodrich (ed.), *The Dictionary of Ming Biography*, Columbia UP, New York, 1976, p. 1365.
19   Ibid., p. 199.
20   Zvi Dor-Ner, *Columbus and the Age of Discovery*, Grafton, 1992, p. 10, and Richard Hall, *Empires of the Monsoon*, HarperCollins, 1996, p. 92.
21   Vanessa Collingridge, *Captain Cook, Obsession and Betrayal in the New World*, Ebury, 2002.
22   K.G. McIntyre, *The Secret Discovery of Australia*, Souvenir, Melbourne, 1977, p. 268.
23   Ibid., p. 269.
24   Ibid., pp. 271ff.
25   Ibid., p. 275. The wood is now said to be in the Australian National Library, Canberra.
26   Ibid., p. 289.
27   Professor Wei Chuh-Hsien, *The Chinese Discovery of Australia*, Hong Kong, 1961.

Chapter 7: Australia

1   The southern portion of the map was based on a chart found on the person of a Spanish seaman captured by the Ottomans in 1501.
2   *Hsi-Yang-Chi*, quoted by J.J.L. Duyvendak in 'Desultory Notes on the *Hsi-Yang-Chi*', *T'oung Pao*, XLII, 1953, pp. 20ff.
3   Don Luis Arias, letter to the King of Spain, quoted in A.W. Miller, *The Straits of Magellan*, Portsmouth, 1884, p. 7.
4   F. Fernández-Armesto (ed.), *Times Atlas of World Exploration*, Times, 1991, p. 167.
5   Lin Dao, *Sui Shu* (official history of the Sui dynasty), AD 636, ch. 82.
6   32°40'S; 152°11'E.
7   43°42'S; 146°32'E.
8   Rex Gilroy, *Pyramids in the Pacific*, Gympie, Australia, 1999.
9   Chinese star charts of 1422 show Polaris 3°40' away from its position today; the North Pole has also moved by that amount over the intervening centuries, at a rate of 1° precession every 175 years.
10 Robyn Gossett, *New Zealand Mysteries*, Auckland, 1996, p. 31.
11 Gilroy, op. cit.; Brett J. Green, *The Gympie Pyramid Story*, Gympie, Australia, 2000, and Gossett, op. cit., p. 148.
12 B. Hilder, 'The Story of the Tamil Bell', in *Journal of the Polynesian Society*, Vol. 84, 1975.
13 Eldon Best, 'Note on a Curious Steatite Figurine Found at Mauku, Auckland', in *NZ Journal of Science and Technology*, Vol. II, 1919, p. 77.
14 Gossett, op. cit.

Chapter 8: The Barrier Reef and the Spice Islands

1   K.G. McIntyre, *The Secret Discovery of Australia*, Souvenir, 1977, and 'Early European Exploration of Australia', unpublished paper, p. 11.
2   China 29%, India 16% – Angus Maddison, *Class Structure and Economic Growth in India and Pakistan since the Moghuls*, Allen & Unwin, 1971.
3   Those records seen by Fr Ricci and early Jesuit missionaries to China: *Chui Hiao* ('Atlas of Foreign Countries') and sixth-century scrolls telling of voyages of massive junks to Australia, and *The Classics of Shan Hai Jing*. Rex Gilroy, *Pyramids in the Pacific*, Gympie, Australia, 1999.
4   Saltpetre, copper, carbonates, haematites, quartz, amethyst, alum and cinnabar formed the first; the second comprised sulphur, mercury, feldspar, copper sulphate, magnetite, azurite and realgar; and the third group included stalagmites, iron, iron oxides, lead carbonate, lead tetroxide, tin, agate and fuller's earth. J. Needham, *Science and Civilisation in China*, Vol. 3, sec. 25, Cambridge UP, Cambridge, 1954, p. 643.
5   Ibid., pp. 653ff.
6   Warren, Delavault, Hawksworth and others. Ibid., p. 678.
7   Ibid., pp. 653ff.

8   For this information I am indebted to Brett Green, whose family recorded the
     Aboriginal songs and folklore of this coast. See Brett J. Green, *The Gympie Pyramid
     Story*, Gympie, Australia, 1998, and Gilroy, op. cit.

9   Needham, op. cit.

10   Gilroy, op. cit., and Green, op. cit.

11   Green, op. cit.

12   A. Grenfell Pike (ed.), *The Explorations of Captain James Cook in the Pacific*, Limited
     Editions Club, New York, 1957, p. 77.

13   Other cartographers of the Dieppe School depicted the Gulf differently: Desliens
     showed it narrower than it should be while Desceliers depicted it close to its actual
     size, suggesting that the Dieppe cartographers were using more than one Portuguese
     chart – a note on the Piri Reis map referred to four Portuguese mappae mundi.

14   Governor Grey, quoted in McIntyre, *Secret Discovery*, p. 79.

15   The date of this figurine has recently been disputed. Professor Needham, in *Science
     and Civilisation in China*, Vol. 4, Pt 3, p. 537 and at Fig. 991, states, 'The statuette is
     in style Ming or early Ching, quite reasonably contemporary with Cheng Ho.' He
     writes at p. 537, 'Wei Chu-Hsien (4), p. 99, concurs.' (This reference is to *The Chinese
     Discovery of Australia*, Hong Kong, 1960). Professor Needham further cites H. Doré,
     Recherches sur les superstitions en Chine, Vol. XI, p. 966, and P.M. Worsley, 'Early
     Asian Contacts with Australia', in *Past and Present*, No. 7, 1955. The current curator
     of the Technological Museum in Sydney, where the statuette is housed, states, 'The
     Museum's preferred dating of this object is the early nineteenth century.'

16   Admiralty sailing instructions, Cook, op. cit.

17   Cdr A.W. Miller, RN, *The Straits of Magellan*, Griffin, Portsmouth, 1884, p. 7.

18   Don Luis Arias, letter to the King of Spain, quoted, ibid.

19   John Merson, *Roads to Xanadu*, Weidenfeld and Nicolson, 1989, p. 75.

20   On maize found in the Philippines: M.D.W. Jeffreys, 'Pre-Columbian Maize in
     Asia', in Carroll Riley et al. (eds), *Men across the Sea*, University of Texas Press, 1971,
     pp. 382ff.; E.L. Sturtevant, 'Notes on Edible Plants', New York State Department of
     Agriculture 27th Annual Report, 1919, p. 616 ('In 1521 maize was found by
     Magellan at the island of Limasava'); H.W. Krueger, 'Peoples of the Philippines',
     Smithsonian Institution War Background Studies No. 4, Washington DC, 1942, p.
     23 (Pigafetta observing maize cultivation on Limasava); W. Richardson, *General
     Collection of Voyages and Discoveries Made by the Portuguese and Spaniards during the
     15th and 16th Centuries*, 1789, p. 496 ('The islanders invited the General into their
     boats in which were their merchandise viz cloves . . . and maize'; C.O. Saver, 'Maize
     into Europe', in *Accounts 34th Int. Cong. Amer.*, Vienna, 1960, pp. 777–88 (Pigafetta's
     'miglio' translated as maize); Antonio Pigafetta, *Primo Viaggio intorno al Mondo*, MS
     version of c. 1524 translated in E.H. Blair and J.A. Robertson, *The Philippine Islands
     1493–1893*, 1906, pp. 164 and 182 (cakes of 'riso e miglio' on island of Zubu (Cebu));
     Pigafetta, op. cit., p. 154 ('ears like Indian corn . . . shelled off like lada'); J.J.L.
     Duyvendak, *China's Discovery of Africa*, Probsthain, 1949, p. 32.

Chapter 9: The First Colony in the Americas

1   11°N.
2   Peter Whitfield, *New Found Lands: Maps in the History of Exploration*, British Library, 1998, pp. 54–5.
3   Article by Dr Tan Koonlin in *The Rose* (journal of the American Rose Society), Vol. 92, Pt 4; R.E. Shepherd, *History of the Rose*, Macmillan, New York, 1954; E. Wilson, *Plant Hunting*, Vol. 2, Stratford, Boston, Mass., 1927.
4   *Sacramento Bee*, 26 January 2001, and *Enterprise Record of Chico*, 23 January 2001.
5   Carey McWilliams, *Factories in the Field*, University of California Press, Berkeley, 2000, pp. 68–80.
6   Stephen Powers, 'Aborigines of California: An Indo-Chinese Study' in *Atlantic*, Vol. 33, 1874, and Stephen Powers, *Contributions to North American Ethnology*, Vol. 3, Department of the Interior, Washington DC, 1877.
7   Powers, *Ethnology*, p. 417.
8   All ibid., introduction and pp. 146–434.
9   Referring to California's East Bay walls in John Fryer, *Ancients in America*.
10 Fra Bernardino de Sahagún, *The Florentine Codex: General History of the Things of New Spain 1325–1550*, School of American Research, Santa Fe, 11 vols, 1950–69.
11 Bernardino Diaz del Castillo, *The Conquest of New Spain*, New York, 1956.
12 Barbara Pickersgill, 'Origin and Evolution of Cultivated Plants in the New World', *Nature*, 268 (18), pp. 591–4.
13 Alberto Ruz Lhuillier, 'The Mystery of the Temple of the Inscriptions', *Archaeology*, Vol. 6, No. 1, 1953, as quoted by Charles Gallenkamp in *Maya: The Riddle and Rediscovery of a Lost Civilisation*, Penguin, Harmondsworth, 1987, pp. 93–104.

Chapter 10: Colonies in Central America

1   Lacquering is described by Fra Bernadino de Sahagún in *The Florentine Codex: General History of the Affairs of New Spain 1325–1550*, trs. A.J.O. Anderson and C.E. Dibble, Salt Lake City, 1970.
2   Ma Huan, *The Overall Survey of the Ocean Shores*, trs. J.V.G. Mills, Cambridge UP (for Hakluyt Society), Cambridge, 1970.
3   H. Mertz, *Gods from the Far East: How the Chinese Discovered America*, New York, 1972, pp. 72–3.
4   Stephen C. Jett, 'Dyestuffs and Possible Early Contacts between South Western Asia and Nuclear America', in *Across before Columbus?*, NEARA Publications, Edgecomb, Maine, 1998, pp. 141ff.
5   Ibid., p. 146.
6   De Sahagún, op. cit.
7   An attempt is being made to compare DNA of Michoacán dogs with that of shar-peis. The results will be posted on the website.
8   Nicolás León, 'Studies in the Archaeology of Michoacán: The Lienzo of Jucutácato', in *Smithsonian Institution Annual Report*, Washington DC, 1889.

9   J. Needham, *Science and Civilisation in China*, Vol. 4, Pt. 3, Cambridge UP, Cambridge, 1954, pp. 540–3.
10 The Peruvian historian Pablo Padron, 'Un Huaco con Caracteres Chinos', Sociedad Geográfica de Lima, Vol. 23, pp. 24–5.
11 Carl Johannessen and M. Fogg, 'Melanotic Chicken Use and Chinese Traits in Guatemala', in *Revista de Historia de América*, Vol. 93, 1962, p. 75.
12 W.C. Parker and A.G. Bearn, *Annals of Human Genetics* 25, 1961 (227).
13 Padron, op. cit.
14 This is the only part of the *I Yü Thu Chih* to have been translated – by Viviana Wong, to whom I am most grateful.
15 In the *Atlas of Foreign Countries*, anon., AD 265–316, China.
16 K.G. McIntyre, *The Secret Discovery of Australia*, Souvenir, Melbourne, 1977.
17 J.L. Sorenson and M.H. Raish, *Pre-Columbian Contact with the Americas across the Oceans: An Annotated Bibliography*, Provo Research Press, 1990.
18 George F. Carter, 'Fusang: Chinese Contact with America', in *Anthropological Journal of Canada*, 14, No. 1, 1976.

Chapter 11: Satan's Island

1   [British] Admiralty, *Ocean Passages of the World*, third edn, 1973.
2   Armando Cortesão, *The Nautical Chart of 1424*, University of Coimbra, Portugal, 1954, pp. 105 and 110.
3   Bartolomeu las Casas, *Historia de las Indias*, Lisbon, 1552.
4   Antonio Galvão, *Tratado Dos Diversos e Desayados Caminhos*, Lisbon, 1563, and Cortesão, op. cit., p. 73.
5   Dr Chanca, quoted in J.H. Longille, *Christopher Columbus*, Inscribers, Washington DC, 1903, p. 184.
6   Chanca, ibid., p. 187.
7   Ibid., p. 184.
8   Syllacius, quoted, ibid., pp. 184ff.
9   Chanca, quoted, ibid., pp. 181 and 182.
10 See the website for more detailed information.
11 Letters between Smithsonian Institution, Washington DC, and author, 6 and 7 July 2002.
12 Syllacius, quoted in Longille, op. cit., pp. 184ff.
13 Ibid., p. 185.
14 This is explained in more detail on the website.
15 Inscription translated by J.J.L. Duyvendak, *China's Discovery of Africa*, Probsthain, 1949, p. 28.
16 4403, 3912 and 2710 (see the website for more detailed information).
17 3912.
18 77°30'W between 23°10' and 23°50'N.

Chapter 12: The Treasure Fleet Runs Aground

1   2710, 3810 and 3912.
2   F.L. Coffman, *Atlas of Treasure Maps*, New York, 1957.
3   26, 61, 63 and 64 in Coffman's numbering system.
4   27, 28, 29 and 30 in Coffman's numbering system.
5   Peter Martyr, quoted in E.W. Lawson, *The Discovery of Florida and Its Discoverer Juan Ponce de León*, 1946, p. 8.
6   Martyr, quoted, ibid., p. 11.
7   *The Undersea World of Jacques Cousteau* and the TV series *In Search Of . . . Atlantis*, narrated by Leonard Nimoy, Channel 4 (UK) and National Geographical Channel (USA).
8   Dr David Zink's discoveries are featured in two books, *The Ancient Stones Speak*, Dutton, 1979, and *The Stones of Atlantis*, W.H. Allen, 1978.
9   J. Needham, *Science and Civilisation in China*, Vol. 4, Pt 3, Cambridge UP, Cambridge, 1954, p. 669.
10   This was confirmed by the Old Dominion University of Virginia, to which Dr Zink sent samples.
11   Alemanide, rhaotide and celtide.
12   At Christie's.
13   Washington Irving, *Life and Voyages of Christopher Columbus*, quoted in Loren Coleman, *Mysterious America*, Faber, 1983, p. 218.
14   Ferdinand Columbus, *La Historia della Vita di Cristoforo Columbus*, Milan, 1930.

Chapter 13: Settlement in North America

1   Francis I, King of France, to Verrazzano, quoted in D.B. Quinn (ed.), *North American Discovery*, Harper & Row, 1971.
2   The account of Verrazzano's voyage is given in his letter of 8 July 1524 to Francis I, quoted, ibid., p. 65.
3   Ibid.
4   Suzanne O. Carlson's finds were published in an article on the internet on 4 March 2002: www.neara.org/carlson/atlantic.html.
5   Professor F.J. Pohl, *Atlantic Crossings before Columbus*, W.W. Norton, New York, 1961, pp. 185ff.
6   Marco Polo, *The Travels of Marco Polo*, trs. R. Latham, Penguin, Harmondsworth, 1958, p. 237.
7   William S. Penhallow, 'Astronomical Alignments in the Newport Tower', in *Across before Columbus?*, NEARA Publications, Edgecombe, Maine, 1998, pp. 85ff.
8   This is explained more fully in chapter 15.
9   E.R. Snow, *Tales of the Atlantic Coast*, Redman, 1962, p. 19.
10   Ibid., pp. 26ff.
11   David Borden, of Marblehead, Massachusetts, and his friend Fred Chester, who grew up near the Dighton Rock State Park, gave me this information.
12   Borden to author.
13   Borden to author.
14   A full list, together with a photograph, is shown on the website.

Chapter 14: Expedition to the North Pole

1   Manuel Faria de Souza, *Epítome de las Historias Portuguesas*, Madrid, 1638 (my translation of his Medieval Castilian).
2   Rebecca Catz, 'Spain and Portugal and the Navigators', unpublished paper presented 25 September 1990, Washington DC.
3   About 51°40′W.
4   Quoted in Farley Mowat, *The Farfarers: Before the Norse*, Seal Books, Toronto, 1998, p. 176.
5   Pope Nicholas V, quoted ibid., p. 308.
6   Peter Schlederman, *Voices in Stone*, Calgary, Canada, 1996, and Mowat, op. cit. Although my conclusions differ from those drawn by Peter Schlederman and Farley Mowat, I rely heavily on their research, without which this chapter could not have been written.
7   Schlederman, op. cit., p. 127.
8   Canadian Government maps of the Canadian Arctic (Hydrographic and Map Service of Canada, Map X1734); *Eskimo Maps of the Canadian Eastern Arctic* by John Spink and D.W. Moodie (1972); the *Sea Ice Atlas of Arctic Canada*, published by the Ottawa Department of Energy, Mines and Resources, 1982, and the map of Greenland drawn by the Geo Daetisk Institut of Copenhagen, 2000.
9   Ferdinand Columbus, *La Historia della Vita di Cristoforo Columbus*, Milan, 1930, quoting a now lost memorandum by his father, seeking to prove that the Arctic was habitable.
10 Catz, translation of Columbus's note in a copy of Pope Pius II, *History of Remarkable Things that Happened in My Time*, in op. cit.
11 J. Needham, *Science and Civilisation in China*, Cambridge UP, Cambridge, 1954.

Chapter 15: Solving the Riddle

1   Antonio Galvão, *The Discoveries of the World*, Hakluyt Society, 1862, p. 369.
2   The Portuguese historian Castaneda.
3   Eric Axelson (ed.), *Dias and His Successors*, Saayman & Weber, Cape Town, 1988, p. 66.
4   The Jesuit Father Monclaro, 1569, quoted in Louise Levathes, *When China Ruled the Seas*, Simon & Schuster, 1994, p. 198.
5   N. Puccioni, *Giuba e OltreGiuba* ('The River Juba and Beyond'), Florence, 1937, p. 110.
6   Levathes, op. cit., p. 199.
7   H.D. Howse, *Greenwich Time and the Discovery of Longitude*, National Maritime Museum, Greenwich, 1980, p. 2.
8   J. Needham, citing *History of the Yan Dynasty*, in *Science and Civilisation in China*, Vol. 3, Pt 2, sec. 20, Cambridge UP, Cambridge, 1954, p. 398, and La Place calculations, p. 299.
9   Ibid., p. 369.
10 Ibid., p. 392.
11 Those wishing to marvel at the ingenuity of these astonishing devices will find an illustration of the polyvascular type in a Chinese encyclopedia, the *Shi Lin Kuang Chi* of 1478, held by Cambridge University Library, England.
12 Marco Polo, *The Travels of Marco Polo*, trs. R. Latham, Penguin, Harmondsworth, 1958, p. 288.

Chapter 16: Where the Earth Ends

1   Francisco Alcaforado, report of proceedings to Prince Henry the Navigator.

2   Gomes Eannes de Zuzara, *The Chronicle of the Discovery and Conquest of Guinea*, trs. C.R. Beazley, Hakluyt Society, 1896–9.

3   E.D.S. Bradford, *Southward the Caravels*, Hutchinson, 1961, p. 8.

4   Vasco Lobeira, *Amadis de Gaul*, ed. and trs. R. Southey, 1872.

5   Malcolm Letts (ed. and trans.), *Mandeville's Travels*, Hakluyt Society, 1953, p. 116 (Egerton text), p. 321 (Paris text). Mandeville was an English squire with a vivid imagination that allowed him to describe far-off lands without visiting them.

6   Ibid.

7   Camoes, *Os Luciades* ('The Luciads'), Lisbon, 1572.

8   This is a simplified explanation; there are refinements to take into account the earth's tilt and curvature.

9   Quoted in F.M. Rogers, *The Travels of the Infante Dom Pedro of Portugal*, Harvard UP, Cambridge, Mass., 1961.

10 Ibid.

11 I have used the chronology of Oliveira Martins, but the precise details of Dom Pedro's itinerary are disputed by different historians. The confusion arises because many countries used different calendars, and because Dom Pedro made not one but many journeys between 1416 and 1428. It is most probable that he left Portugal again in 1419 to visit the Emperor Sigismund and served the Emperor in the wars against the Ottomans. He then settled in Treviso and visited Venice in the summer of 1421, as soon as another war, between the Emperor and Venice, was over. He then went to Egypt in 1424, returning via England (1426) and Venice again (1428) to Portugal.

12 Antonio Galvão, *The Discoveries of the World*, Hakluyt Society, 1862. See p. 107.

13 For the connection between Niccolò da Conti and 'Bartholomew the Florentine', see F.M. Rogers, op. cit., pp. 42 and 264; Gustavo Uzielli, *La Vita e i Tempi di Paolo dal Pozzo Toscanelli*, Rome, 1894, and W. Sensburg, *Poggio Bracciolini und Niccolò da Conti*, Vienna, 1906. For the connection between Toscanelli and 'Bartholomew the Florentine', see Gustavo Uzielli, *Paolo dal Pozzo Toscanelli: Iniziatore della Scoperta d'America*, Florence, 1892; Sidney Welch, *Europe's Discovery of South Africa*; Arnold J. Pomerans, *The Great Age of Discovery*, New York, 1958, p. 18, and P. Kermann, *Zeigt Mir Adams Testament*. For the connection between Toscanelli and Dom Pedro, see Uzielli, *Toscanelli: Iniziatore*, p. 76. For the connection between 'Bartholomew the Florentine' and Martin Behaim, see F.M. Rogers, *The Quest for Eastern Christians*, University of Minnesota Press, 1962, pp. 42 and 95.

14 For Niccolò da Conti, see: (i) G. Uzielli, *La Vita e i Tempi di Paolo dal Pozzo Toscanelli*, Rome, 1894, pp. 10, 11, 63, 90, 122, 141, 154–75, 189–92, 228, 246, 386, 566–7; (ii) 'The Travels of Niccolò da Conti', partial translation in R.H. Major (ed.), *India in the Fifteenth Century*, Hakluyt Society, 1857; (iii) W. Heyd, *Histoire*, Vol. 1, 1885, pp. 378, 380; (iv) V. Bellemo, *Nicolo da Conti*, 1882, pp. 331–47; C. Desimoni, *Pero Tafur*, 1882, pp. 331–47; (vi) F. Kunstman, *Afrika vor den Entdeckungen der Portugiesen*, Aufrosten der Academie, Munich, 1853.

For 'Bartholomew the Florentine', see: (i) Uzielli, *La Vita e i Tempi*, pp. 63, 165–6; (ii) T. de Mura, *M. Behaim*, Treutel et Wurz, Strasbourg, 1802, pp. 33–5; (iii) p. Amat (ed.), *Studi Bibliografichi in Italia*, Pt 1, Ed. 2, Rome, 1882, p. 123.

For Pope Eugenius IV (Gabriele Condulmaro), see Uzielli, *La Vita e i Tempi*, p. 166:

'Gabriele Condulmaro poteva essere a Venezia nel 1424, ma non era ancora Papa, essendo stato assunto alla tiara soltanto nel 1431.'

For Bartholomew of Florence's journey, see Uzielli, *La Vita e i Tempi*, p. 63: 'Ecco ciò che ne dice maestro Bartolomeo Florentino che tornò dalle Indie nel 1424 e che accompagnò a Venezia il Papa Eugenio IV, e al quale raffontò ciò aveva veduto e osservato in un soggiorno di ventiquattro anni in oriente.'

15 See n. 13.
16 Paolo Toscanelli, letter to Columbus, in H. Vignaud, *Toscanelli and Columbus*, Sands, 1902, pp. 322 and 323.
17 Also known as 'Behaim' and 'Martin of Bohemia'. See note 13.
18 Antonio Pigafetta, *Magellan's Voyage*, trs. R.A. Skelton, New Haven, Conn., 1969, pp. 58ff.
19 See ns 13 and 14.
20 See ns 13 and 14, and p. 107.
21 See n. 13.

Chapter 17: Colonizing the New World

1 Antonio Galvão, *Tratado Dos Diversos e Desayados Caminhos*, Lisbon, 1563, and Antonio Cordeyro, *Historia Insulana*, Lisbon, 1717, quoted in H. Harrisse, *The Discovery of North America*, 1892, p. 51.
2 J.H. Longille, *Christopher Columbus*, Inscribers, Washington DC, 1903, p. 191.
3 Extract from Columbus's notebook, quoted in Bartolomeu las Casas, *Historia de las Indias*, Lisbon, 1552.
4 Galvão, op. cit., p. 370.
5 Those of Andrea Bianco in 1448; Grazioso Benincasa in 1463, 1470 and 1482; Andrea Benincasa in 1476, and Albino Canepa in 1480 and 1489.
6 Cf. Armando Cortesão, *The Nautical Chart of 1424*, Coimbra, 1954, p. 106.
7 Carol Urness, *Portolan Charts*, James Ford Bell Library, University of Minnesota, 1999.
8 Published by the Lisbon Academy of Sciences.
9 For coffee in Puerto Rico before European voyages, see D. Maclellan, 'Coffee Varieties in Puerto Rico', *Puerto Rico Agriculture Station Bulletin* No. 30, Mayaguez, Puerto Rico, 1924; P.C. Stanley, *The Rubiaceae of Central America*, Chicago, 1930 (Field Museum of Natural History, Botanical Series Vol. 7, no. 1); E.C. Hill, *Coffee Planting*, Higginbotham, Madias, 1877, pp. 1–3 and 17–19; E.R. Thurber, *Coffee from Plantation to Cup*, American Grocer Publishing Association, New York, 1881, intro. and pp. 4–5.
10 Produce photographed at Mayaguez Agricultural Station.
11 Albino Canepa: the domain of *saluagio viúadi (nom vulgar des Alguns brasilieros)*, the common name for people coming from Brazil, the Caribs.
12 Using the average flows described in the Admiralty's *Ocean Passages of the World* and the relevant Admiralty pilots.
13 To date I have only studied the catalogue of Prince Youssuf Kamal to see how many corrections or additions were made to Antilia. This discloses fourteen before Columbus set sail: by the Beccarios (1435 and 1436), Andrea Bianco (1436 and 1448), Parreto (1455), the Benincasas (1463, 1470, 1476 and 1482), Toscanelli (1474), the Canepas (1480 and 1489), Jaime Bertram (1482) and Christofal Soligo (1489).
14 Prince Youssuf Kamal, *Monumenta Cartographica Africae et Aegypti*, 16 vols, Cairo, 1926–51. This catalogue lists an enormously valuable collection of surviving charts and maps showing European and Chinese exploration of West Africa.
15 Quoted in E.D.S. Bradford, *Southward the Caravels*, Hutchinson, 1961, p. 107.

Chapter 18: On the Shoulders of Giants

1   João de Barros, letter to the future King Manuel of Portugal, quoted in Eric Axelson, *Dias and His Successors*, Cape Town, 1988, p. 3.
2   K.G. Jayne, *Vasco da Gama and His Successors 1460–1580*, Methuen, 1970, p. 36.
3   João de Barros, letter to the King of Portugal, 1 May 1500, quoted in Jaime Batalha Reis, *Estudios Géográficos y Históricos*, Ministry of Colonial Affairs, Lisbon, 1941, p. 286.
4   S.E. Morison, *Portuguese Voyages to America in the Fifteenth Century*, Harvard UP, Cambridge, Mass., 1940, p. 131.
5   See chs 5 and 6, where these matters are considered in detail.
6   As above, and ch. 8.
7   Sebastian Alvarez, the King of Castile's factor, quoted in Cdr A.W. Miller, RN, *The Straits of Magellan*, Griffin, Portsmouth, 1884, p. 7.
8   *The Journal of Columbus*, trs. Cecil Jane, revised and annotated by L.A. Vigneras, Anthony Blond and Orion Press, 1960, pp. 12, 43 and 62.
9   H. Vignaud, *Toscanelli and Columbus*, Sands, 1902, p. 323.
10 Toscanelli, letter to the King of Spain, 1474, quoted in J.H. Parry, *The Discovery of South America*, Elek, 1979, p. 48.
11 Note VII on the Piri Reis map, translated by G.C. McIntosh in *The Piri Reis Map of 1513*, University of Georgia Press, Athens, Georgia, 2000, p. 46.
12 Arthur Davies, 'Behain, Marcellus and Columbus', *Geographical Journal*, Vol. 143, p. 454.
13 A.O. Vietor, 'A Pre-Columbian Map of the World circa 1489', *Imago Mundi* xvii, 1963.
14 Davies, op. cit., p. 458.
15 Davies, op. cit.
16 Lord Palliser, Captain Cook's commander.
17 K.G. McIntyre, *Early European Exploration of Australia*, unpublished paper, p. 12.

Epilogue: The Chinese Legacy

1   Barbara Pickersgill, 'Origin and Evolution of Cultivated Plants in the New World', *Nature* 268 (18), pp. 591–4.
2   R.A. Whitehead, *Evolution of Crop Plants*, Longman, 1996, pp. 221–5.
3   F. Braudel, *A History of Civilisations*, trs. R. Mayne, Penguin, 1994, pp. 158–9.
4   Judith A. Carney, Professor of Geography at the University of California, Los Angeles, has written a fascinating book, *Black Rice: The African Origins of Rice Cultivation in the Americas* (Harvard UP, Cambridge, Mass., 2001), which tells the story of the true origins of rice in the Americas and argues that the standard belief that Europeans introduced rice to West Africa and then brought the knowledge of its cultivation to the Americas is a fundamental fallacy.
5   Roderich Ptak, 'China and Calicut in the Early Ming Period: Envoys and Tribute Emissaries', in *Journal of the Royal Asiatic Society*, 1989, St 447, and private letters between Professor Ptak and the author.
6   Cochin tablet, 'Taizong Shi Lu', ch. 183, quoted in Louise Levathes, *When China Ruled the Seas*, Oxford UP, Oxford, 1996, p. 145.
7   Gaspar Correa, *The Three Voyages of Vasco da Gama*, trs. H.E.J. Stanley from *Lendas da India*, 1869.

SELECT
BIBLIOGRAPHY

Chapters 1: The Emperor's Grand Plan and 2: A Thunderbolt Strikes

Abru, Hafiz (trs. K.M. Maitra), *A Persian Embassy to China*. Lahore, 1934.

Battuta, Ibn (trs. S. Lee), *The Travels of Ibn Battuta*. 1829.

Bonavia, J., *Collins Illustrated Guide to The Silk Road*. The Guide Book Co. Ltd, Hong Kong, 1988.

Boulnois, L. (trs. D. Chamberlin), *The Silk Road*. Allen & Unwin, 1966.

Braudel, F. (trs. R. Mayne), *A History of Civilizations*. Penguin, 1994.

Chaudhuri, K.N., 'A Note on Ibn Taghri Birdi's description of Chinese Ships in Aden and Jeddah'. *Journal of the Royal Asiatic Society*, no. 1, 1989, 112.

—— *Trade and Civilisation in the Indian Ocean*. Cambridge University Press, 1985.

Dreyer, E.L., *Early Ming China: A Political History 1355–1435*. California, Stanford University Press, 1982.

Dunn, R.E., *The Adventures of Ibn Battuta a Muslim Traveller of the 14th Century*. Croom Helm, 1986.

Duyvendak, J.J.L., *China's Discovery of Africa*. London, Probsthain, 1949.

—— *Ma Huan Re-examined*. Amsterdam, 1933.

—— 'Sailing Directions of Chinese Voyages'. *T'oung Pao*, vol. XXXIV, Leiden, 1939.

—— 'The True Dates of the Chinese Maritime Expeditions in the Early 15th Century'. *T'oung Pao*, vol. XXXIV, Leiden, 1939.

Ebrey, P.B., *The Cambridge Illustrated History of China*. Cambridge University Press, 1996.

Fairbank, J.K., *China and Central Asia, 1368–1884*. The Fairbank Press.

Fei Xin (trs. J.V.G. Mills), *Marvellous Visions from the Star Raft*. Wiesbaden, 1996.

Fitzgerald, C.P., *A Chinese Discovery of Australia*. Australia Writes, 1953.

Gibb, H.A.R., *The Travels of Ibn Battuta*. Hakluyt Society, 1994.

Groslier, B.P., *Art of the World: Indochina*. Methuen, 1967.

Hucker, C.O., 'Governmental Organisation of the Ming Dynasty'. *Harvard Journal of Asiatic Studies*, 1958.

Kirkup, J.F., *Streets of Asia*. J.M. Dent and Sons Ltd, 1969.

—— *Tropic Temper*. Collins, 1963.

Levathes, L., *When China Ruled the Seas*. Simon & Schuster, 1994.

Ma Huan (trs. J.V.G. Mills), *The Overall Survey of the Ocean Shores*. Cambridge University Press (for Hakluyt Society), 1970.

Mayers, W.F., 'Chinese Explorations in the Indian Ocean during the Fifteenth Century'. *Chi. Rev. III* 1875, *IV* 1875–6.

Merson, J., *Roads to Xanadu*. Weidenfeld & Nicolson, 1989.

Michaelson, C., *Gilded Dragons: Buried Treasures from China's Golden Ages*. British Museum Press, 1999.

Mills, J.V.G., 'Notes on Early Chinese Voyages'. *Journal of the Royal Asiatic Society*, April 1951.

Morgan, D., *The Mongols*. Oxford, Blackwell, 1986.

Mote, F.W., *Imperial China 900–1800*. Cambridge, Massachusetts, 1999.

—— and Twitchett, D., *The Cambridge History of China* (vol. 7, 1368–1644). Cambridge University Press, 1988.

Mulder, W.Z., 'The Wu Pei Chi Charts'. *T'oung Pao*, vol. XXXVI, 1944.

Needham, J., *Science and Civilisation in China*, vols 2, 4 & 5. Cambridge University Press, 1954.

Polo, Marco (trs. R. Latham), *The Travels of Marco Polo*. Penguin, 1958.

Ptak, R., 'China and Calicut in the Early Ming Period: Envoys and Tribute Embassies'. *Journal of the Royal Asiatic Society*, no. 1, 1989, 81–111.

Rossabi, M., 'Chen Cheng: Diary of Travelling in the Western Regions'. *Ming Studies* 17, Fall 1983, 49–59.

—— 'Cheng Ho and Timur – Any Relation?'. *Oriens Extremis* 20, 1973.

—— *Ming China and Inner Asia*. New York, Pica Press, 1975.

—— 'Ming China and Turfan 1406–1517'. *Central Asian Journal* 16, 1972.

—— 'The Tea and Horse Trade with Inner Asia during the Ming'. *Journal of Asian History* 4, 1970, 136–168.

—— 'Two Ming Envoys to Central Asia'. *T'oung Pao* 62:1–3, 1–34, 1976.

Seckel, D. (trs. A.E. Keep), *The Art of Buddhism*. Methuen, 1964.

Sivin, N. et al. (eds), *The Contemporary Atlas of China*. Weidenfeld & Nicolson, 1988.

Soullière, E., *Palace Women in the Ming Dynasty*. Princeton University doctoral thesis, 1987.

Sun, Guanji, 'Zheng He's Expeditions to the Western Ocean'. *Journal of Navigation* 45, 1992.

Sykes, P., *The Quest for Cathay*. A & C Black, 1936.

Taghri-Birdi, Y.I. (trs. W. Popper), *History of Egypt 1382–1469*. California, Berkeley, 1954.

Tien, Ju-kang, 'Zheng He's Voyages and the Distribution of Pepper in China'. *Journal of the Royal Asiatic Society*, no. 2, 1981.

Van Gulik, R.H., *Sexual Life in Ancient China*. Leiden, 1961.

Walker, A., *Aurel Stein, Pioneer of the Silk Road*. John Murray, 1995.

Wheatley, P., *The Golden Khersonese*. Kuala Lumpur, University of Malaya Press, 1961.

Willetts, W., 'The Maritime Adventures of Grand Eunuch Ho'. *Journal of Southeast Asian History* 5, no. 2, 1964.

Yamamoto, T., 'Chinese Activities in the Indian Ocean before the Coming of the Portuguese'. *Diogenes* 3, 1980.

Zhang, J.Y., 'Relations between China and the Arabs from Early Times'. *Journal of Oman Studies*, vol. 2, pt 1, 1983.

Zhou Xun, *Five Thousand Years of Chinese Costumes*. China Books & Periodicals, San Francisco, 1987.

Tamerlane

Bartold, V.V. (trs. T. Minorsky), *Four Studies on the History of Central Asia*. Leiden, E.J. Brill, 1962.

Commissariat, M.S., *A History of Gujarat*. Bombay, Longmans, 1938.

Du Bec-Crespin, J., *The Historie of the Great Emperor Tamerlan*. 1597.

Gonzales de Clavijo, R. (trs. G. le Strange), *Embassy to the Court of Tamburlane 1403–1406*. New York, Harper & Brothers, 1928.

Hookham, H., *Tamburlaine the Conqueror*. Hodder & Stoughton, 1962.

Knobloch, E., *Beyond the Oxus*. Benn, 1972.

Lamb, H.A., *Tamerlane, the Earth Shaker*. New York, 1928.

Majumdar, R.C. (gen. ed.), *History and Culture of the Indian People* (11 vols). George Allen & Unwin, 1951–71.

Mainz, B.F., *The Rise and Fall of Tamerlane*. Cambridge University Press, 1989.
Marlowe, C. (ed. J.S. Cunningham), *Tamburlaine the Great*. Manchester University Press, 1981.
Tamerlane (trs. H.M. Eliot, ed. H.M. Dowson), *Tuzaki-I Timuri* (autobiography). Lahore, 1871.

Chapter 3: The Fleets Set Sail

Adler, E.N., *Jewish Travellers in the Middle Ages*. Routledge, 1930.
Akrish, J., *Kol Mebasser*. Constantinople, 1577.
Al-Harizi, *Sefer Tahkemoni* (Tracks to the East). Warsaw, 1899.
Arasaratnam, S., *Maritime Trade, Society and European Influence in Southern Asia 1600–1800*. Aldershot, 1995.
Benjamin of Tudela (trs. M.N. Adler), *The Itinerary of Rabbi Benjamin of Tudela*. 1907.
Bianquis, T. et al. (eds), *Encyclopaedia of Islam*. Leiden, E.J. Brill, 1999.
Blair, E.H. and Robertson, J.A., *The Philippine Islands 1493–1803*. Cleveland, 1903–9.
Bovill, E.W., *Missions to the Niger*. Cambridge, 1964.
Bretschneider, E., *History of European Botanical Discoveries in China*. 1898.
—— *Notes of Chinese Botany from Native and Western Sources*. Shanghai, 1882.
Burton, R.F., *First Footsteps in East Africa*. Longmans, 1856.
—— *Works*, Vols 1 & 2: *Personal Narrative of a Pilgrimage to Al Madinah and Meccah*. Tylston and Edwards, 1893.
Caillié, R.A., *Journal d'un Voyage à Temboctou*. Paris, 1830.
Chardin, J., *Sir John Chardin's Travels in Persia*. Argonaut Press, 1927.
Cooley, W.D., *The Negroland of the Arabs Examined and Explained*. J. Arrowsmith, 1841.
Cowell, E.B. et al., *Buddhist Mahayana Texts*. Oxford, 1894.
Crawfurd. J., *A Descriptive Dictionary of the Indian Islands and Adjacent Countries*. Bradbury and Evans, 1856.
Das Gupta, A., *Merchants of Maritime India 1500–1800*. Aldershot, Variorum, 1994.
Doughty, C.M., *Travels in Arabia Deserta*. Cambridge, 1888.
Dunn, R.E., *The Adventures of Ibn Battuta a Muslim traveller of the 14th century*. Croom Helm, 1986.
Eisenstein, J.D., *Ozar Massuoth* (Treasure of Travel): *Jewish Travellers 1165 to 1839*. New York, 1926.
Enthoven, R.E., *The Tribes and Castes of Bombay*. Bombay, 1920.
Faria e Sousa, M., *The Portugués Asia: or The History of the Discovery and Conquest of India by the Portugués*. C. Brome, 1695.
Fatimi, S.Q., *Islam Comes to Malaysia*. Singapore, 1963.
Forbes, A.D.W., 'The Mosque in the Maldive Islands'. *Archipel* XXIII, 1981.
Franke, H. and Hok-Iam Chan, *Studies on the Jurchens and the Chin Dynasty*. Variorum, 1997.
Gamble, J.S., *A Manual of Indian Timbers*. Calcutta, 1881.
Gonzales De Mendoza, J. (trs. J. Parke), *The Historie of the Great and Mightie Kingdome of China*. 1588.
Haurani, G.F., *Arab Seafaring in the Indian Ocean in Ancient and Early Medieval Times*. Princeton, 1951.
Hegel, G.W.F. (trs. J. Sibree), *The Philosophy of History*. New York, 1900.
Hiern, W.P., *A Monograph on Ebenaceae*. Cambridge, 1873.

Hill, A.H., 'The Coming of Islam to North Sumatra'. *Journal of Southeast Asian History* 4, no. 1, March 1963, 6–21.

Hiskett, M., *The Development of Islam in West Africa*. Longman, 1984.

Hunwick, J.O., 'The Mid-Fourteenth Century Capital of Mali'. *Journal of African History*, 14, 1973, 195ff.

Langlois, J.D. (ed.), *China under Mongol Rule*. Princeton, 1981.

Lee, S., *The Travels of Ibn Battuta 1325–1354*. 1829.

Levtzion, N., *Ancient Ghana and Mali*. Methuen, 1973.

Loewy, A. (ed.), *Publications of the Society of Hebrew Literature. Miscellany of Hebrew Literature*. 1872–7.

Mahan, A.T., *The Influence of Sea Power upon History 1660–1783*. New York, 1957.

Mahesvari, P. and Singh, U., *Dictionary of Economic Plants in India*. New Delhi, 1965.

Maimonides, M. (trs. S. Pires), *The Guide of the Perplexed*. 1974.

Majumdar, R.C. (gen. ed.), *History and Culture of the Indian People*, vol. VI: *The Delhi Sultanate*. Bombay, 1960.

Merrill, E.D., 'An Enumeration of Hainan Plants'. *Lingnan Sci*, J.5:1–186.

Norris, H.T., *The Tuaregs*. Warminster, 1975.

Pelliot, P. 'Les Grands Voyages Maritimes Chinois au Début du XV Siècle'. *T'oung Pao*, vol. XXX, 237–452.

—— *Notes on Marco Polo*. Paris, 1959–73.

Piccus, R., *Wood from the Scholar's Table: Chinese Hardwood Carvings and Scholar's Articles*. Hong Kong, 1984.

Pires, T. (trs. A. Cortesão), *The Suma Oriental of Tome Pires*. 1944.

Polo, Marco (trs. H. Yule), *The Book of Ser Marco Polo*. 1871.

Pyrard, F. (trs. A. Gray), *The Voyages of François Pyrard of Laval*. Paris, 1998.

Rabbi Jacob Ben Nathaniel, Ha Cohen, *Journey to the East*. Cambridge University Library (unpublished).

Rabbi Petachia of Ratisbon, *Sibbub* (Circular Voyage). Prague, 1595.

Ray, H., *Trade and Diplomacy in India–China Relations: A Study of Bengal during the Fifteenth Century*. New Delhi, Radiant, 1993.

Read, B.E., *Chinese Medicinal Plants*. Peiping, 1936.

Rockhill, W.W., 'Notes on the Relations and Trade of China with the Eastern Archipelago and the Coasts of the Indian Ocean during the Fourteenth Century'. *T'oung Pao*, XIV, 1913; XV, 1914; XVI, 1915.

Rodd, F.J.R., *People of the Veil*. Anthropological Publications, 1926.

Schafer, E., 'Rosewood, Dragons Blood and Lac'. *Journal of the American Oriental Society* 77, 1975.

Segal, J.B., *A History of the Jews of Cochin*. Vallentine Mitchell, 1993.

Sinor, D., *Studies in Medieval Inner Asia*. Aldershot, Ashgate, 1997.

Smith, G.R. and Porter, V., 'The Rasulids in Dhofar in the VIIth–VIIIth/XIIIth–XIVth Centuries'. *Journal of the Royal Asiatic Society*, no. 1, 1988, pp. 26–44.

Souza, G.B., *The Survival of Empire: Portuguese Trade and Society in China and the South China Sea 1630–1754*. Cambridge University Press, 1986.

Tibbetts, G.R., *A Study of the Arabic Texts Containing Material in South East Asia*. Brill, 1979.

Wang, G., *A Study of the Early History of Chinese Trade in the South China Sea*. Kuala Lumpur, 1958.

Wheatley, P., *The Golden Khersonese*. Kuala Lumpur, 1961.
Williams, L., *Forests of Southeast Asia, Puerto Rico and Texas*. 1967.
Yule, H., *Cathay and the Way Thither*. Hakluyt Society, 1866.

Chapter 4: Rounding the Cape

Aldridge, J., *Cairo*. Macmillan, 1970.
Al-Makrizi, Ahmad (trs. E. Brochet), *History of Egypt*. Paris, 1908.
Anon., *Cambridge History of Africa*. Cambridge University Press, 1975–86.
Anon., *Cambridge History of India*. Cambridge University Press, 1922–64.
Arabshah, I. (trs. J.H. Sanders), *Tamerlane*. 1936.
Atiyah, E., *The Arabs*. Pelican, 1955.
Bahn, P.G., *Lost Cities*. Weidenfeld & Nicolson, 1997.
Barthold, V.V. (trs. T. Minorsky), *Turkestan Down to the Mongol Invasion*. Luzac & Co., 1968.
—— (trs. V. & T. Minorsky), *Ulugh Begh (Four Studies on the History of Central Asia)*. Leiden, E.J. Brill, 1962.
Bianquis, T. et al. (eds), *Encyclopaedia of Islam*. Leiden, E.J. Brill, 1999.
Bovill, E.W., *The Golden Trade of the Moors*. Oxford University Press, 1958.
Boyle, J.A. (ed.), *The Cambridge History of Iran* Vol. 5. Cambridge University Press, 1968.
Bracciolini, P. (trs. P.W.G. Gordan), *Two Renaissance Book Hunters*. Columbia University Press, 1974.
Braudel, F. (trs. S. Reynolds), *The Mediterranean and the Mediterranean World in the Age of Philip II*. 1992.
Carpini, G. de P., *The Story of the Mongols – Whom We Call the Tartars*. Branden Books, Boston, 1996.
Chang, K.S., 'Africa and the Indian Ocean in Chinese Maps of the 14th and 15th Centuries'. *Imago Mundi* 24, 21–30.
Chaudhuri, K.N., *Trade and Civilisation in the Indian Ocean*. Cambridge University Press, 1985.
Cleaves, F.W., *The Secret History of the Mongols*. Harvard University Press, 1982.
Coedes, G. (trs. S.B. Lowing), *The Indianised States of South East Asia*. Honolulu, 1968.
Commissariat, M.S., *A History of Gujarat*. Bombay, Longmans, 1938.
Connah, G., *African Civilisations*. Cambridge University Press, 1987.
Coomaraswamy, A.K., *History of Indian and Indonesian Art*. E. Goldston, 1927.
Cowan, J., *A Mapmaker's Dream: The Meditations of Fra Mauro*. Vintage, 1997.
Davidson, B., *A History of West Africa 1000–1800*. Longman, 1977.
Fernandez-Armesto, F. (ed.), *The Times Atlas of World Exploration*. Times Books, 1991.
Fischel, W.J., 'The Spice Trade in Mamluk Egypt'. *Journal of Economic and Social History of the Orient* 1, 1958, 157–74.
Fuchs, W., *The Mongol Atlas of China*. Peking, 1946.
—— 'Was South Africa already known in the 13th century?' *Imago Mundi* 10, 50.
Gibbon, E., *The Decline and Fall of the Roman Empire*. 1910.
Gillon, W., *A Short History of African Art*. Penguin, 1986.
Gonzales de Clavijo, R. (trs. G. le Strange), *Embassy to the Court of Tamburlane 1403–1406*. Harper & Brothers, New York, 1928.
Hall, R., *Empires of the Monsoon*. HarperCollins, 1996.

Hallade, M.M. (trs. D. Imber), *The Gandhara Style*. Thames & Hudson, 1968.

Harley, J.B. and Woodward, D., *The History of Cartography*, Vol. 2. University of Chicago Press, 1992–4.

Hitti, P.K., *A History of the Arabs*. London, Macmillan, 1956.

Holt, P.M., Lambton, A.K.S. and Lewis, B. (eds), *The Cambridge History of Islam*. Cambridge University Press, 1970.

Hourani, A., *A History of the Arab Peoples*. Faber, 1991.

Hourani, G.F., 'Direct Sailing Between the Persian Gulf and China in Pre-Islamic Times'. *Journal of the Royal Asiatic Society*, 1947, 157–60.

Kamal, Prince Youssuf, *Monumenta Cartographica*, p. 1,410 (Fra Mauro's Planisphere).

Keay, J., *India: A History*. HarperCollins, 2000.

Keohane, A., *The Berbers of Morocco*. Hamish Hamilton, 1991.

Khaldun, I., *An Arab Philosophy of History*. London, 1950.

Lamb, H.A., *Genghis Khan: The Emperor of All Men*. New York, R.M. McBride, 1928.

Lane, E.W., *Arabian Society in the Middle Ages*. New York, Barnes and Noble, 1883.

Lane-Poole, S., *A History of Egypt in the Middle Ages*. Karachi, 1977.

Ledyard, G., 'The Kangnido: A Korean World Map (1402)', in Levenson, Jay A. (ed.), *Circa 1492: Art in the Age of Exploration*. New Haven, 1991.

Lee, S., *The Travels of Ibn Battuta 1325–1354*. 1829.

Lewis, A., 'Maritime Skills in the Indian Ocean 1368–1500'. *Journal of Economic and Social History of the Orient* 16, 1973.

Lewis, B., *The Arabs in History*. Oxford University Press, 1993.

Lobban, R., *Historical Dictionary of the Republic of Cape Verde*. Scarecrow, 1988.

Lyster, W., *The Citadel of Cairo*. Palm Press, Cairo, 1993.

Ma Huan (trs. J.V.G. Mills), *The Overall Survey of the Ocean Shores*. Cambridge University Press (for Hakluyt Society), 1970.

Majumdar, R.C. (gen. ed.), *History and Culture of the Indian People* (11 vols). George Allen & Unwin, 1951–71.

Mansfield, P., *The Arabs*. Allen Lane, 1976.

Marshall, R., *Storm from the East*. BBC Books, 1993.

Morris, J., Wood, G. and Wright, D., *Persia*. Thames & Hudson, 1969.

Needham, J., *Science and Civilisation in China*, vol. 3. Cambridge University Press, 1959.

Oliver, R. and Atmore, A., *The African Middle Ages*. Cambridge University Press, 1981.

Oliver, R.A. and Mathew, G., *A History of East Africa*. Oxford University Press, 1963–76.

Parker, G., *The Times Atlas of World History*. Times Books, 1997.

Raychaudhuri, T. (ed.), *Cambridge Economic History of India*, Vol. 1. Cambridge University Press, 1982.

Rosser, W.H., *North Atlantic Directory*. 1869.

—— and Imray, J.F., *South Atlantic Directory*. 1870.

Seckel, D. (trs. A. Keep), *The Art of Buddhism*. New York, Crown, 1964.

Switzer, G., *Diamonds in Pictures*. Oak Tree Press, 1967.

Taghri-Birdi, Y.I., *An Nujum, Az-Zahira, Fi. Muluk. Misr Wal-Kahira*. Berkeley, 1909.

Tibbetts, G.R., *Arab Navigation in the Indian Ocean Before the Coming of the Portuguese*. 1971.

—— 'Early Muslim Traders in SE Africa'. *Journal of the Malaysian Branch of the Royal Asiatic Society*, XXX, 1957.

Varthema, L. (trs. J.W. Jones), *The Travels of L. de Varthema*. London, 1863.

Vernadsky, G., *The Mongols and Russia*. Moscow, 1997.

Waley, A.D., *Secret History of the Mongols*. Allen & Unwin, 1963.

Willett, F., *African Art*. Thames & Hudson, 1971.

Williams, J., *Money – A History*. British Museum Press, 1997.

Wright, J., 'Sijilmasa, a Saharan Entrepot'. *Journal of the Society for Moroccan Studies*, 1991.

Zhang, J.Y., 'Relations between China and the Arabs from Early Times'. *Journal of Oman Studies*, vol. 2, pt 1, 1983.

West Africa

Axelson, E., *Congo to Cape: Early Portuguese Explorers*. Faber, 1973.

Bentley, W.H., *Pioneering on the Congo*. New York, Fleming H. Revell, 1900.

Burton, R.F., *Two Trips to Gorilla Land and the Cataracts of the Congo*. 1876.

Crone, G.R., *The Voyages of Cadamosto and Other Documents on Western Africa in the Second Half of the Fifteenth Century*. Hakluyt Society, 1937.

Forbath, P., *The River Congo*. Secker & Warburg, 1978.

Lopez, D., *History of the Kingdom of the Congo and Surrounding Countries*. 1591.

Mauny, R., *Les Navigations Mediaevales sur les Côtes Sahariennes Anterieures à la Découverte Portugaeis [sic] (1434)*. Lisbon, 1960.

Chapter 5: The New World

South America

Bridges, E.L., *Uttermost Part of the Earth: Indians of Tierra del Fuego*. 1948.

Carvajal, G. de Medina (trs. G. Lee), *The Discovery of the Amazon*. New York, 1934.

Darwin, C.R., *Journal of Researches into the Geology and Natural History of the Various Countries Visited by the HMS Beagle, 1832–36*. 1839.

Galvão, A. (trs. R. Hakluyt), *The Discoveries of the World*. New York, 1969.

Gonzales, A.R., *Arte pre-Columbino de la Argentina*. Buenos Aires, 1997.

Hapgood, C.H., *Maps of the Ancient Sea Kings*. New York, Chilton Books, 1966.

Inan, A.A., *Life and Works of the Turkish Admiral Piri Reis. The Oldest Map of America*. Ankara, 1954.

Miller, A.W., *The Straits of Magellan*. Portsmouth, 1884.

Musters, G.C., *At Home with the Patagonians*. 1871.

Parry, J.H., *The Discovery of South America*. Elek, 1979.

Pigafetta, A. (trs. R.A. Skelton), *Magellan's Voyage*. New Haven, 1969.

Shipton, E.E., *Land of Tempest: Travels in Patagonia 1958–62*. New York, Dutton, 1963.

—— *Tierra del Fuego: The Fatal Lodestone*. C. Knight, 1973.

Simpson, G.G., *Attending Marvels*. New York, 1934.

Tschiffely, A.F., *This Way Southward: the Account of a Journey Through Patagonia and Tierra del Fuego*. New York, W.W. Norton, 1940.

Willey, G.R., *An Introduction to American Archaeology*, Vol. 2 – *South America*. New Jersey, 1971.

In relation to the mylodon

Bird, J.B., *Travels and Archaeology in South Chile*. Iowa, 1988.
Chatwin, B., *In Patagonia*. Jonathan Cape, 1977.
Grays Garay, N., *Fauna of Torres del Paine*. Punta Arenas, 1993.
Grizmek, B., *Grizmek's Animal Life Encyclopaedia*. New York, 1972–5.
Moreno, F.P. and Woodward, A.S., *On a Portion of Mammalian Skin, named* Neomylodon listai, *from a Cavern near Consuelo Cove, Last Hope Inlet, Patagonia*. Zoological Society of London, 1899.
Owen, R., *Description of the Skeleton of an Extinct Gigantic Sloth,* Mylodon robustus. 1862.

The Piri Reis chart

Kahane, H. & R. and Tietze, A., *The Lingua Franca in the Levant*. Illinois, 1958.
Khalili, N.D., *The Empire of the Sultans Ottoman Art*. Topkapi Serai, Istanbul, 1995. (This is not a book, but a collection of maps normally on display in Istanbul which recently formed a touring exhibition entitled 'Empire of the Sultans'.)
Lunde, P., 'Piri Reis and the Columbian Theory'. *Aramco Magazine*, Jan–Feb 1980.
McIntosh, G.C., *The Piri Reis Map of 1513*. University of Georgia Press, 2000.
Ozen, M.E. (ed. N. Refliogu), *Piri Reis and his Charts*. Istanbul, 1994.
Soucek, S., 'Islamic Charting in the Mediterranean', in *History of Cartography* Vol. 2 (1). Chicago, 1992, 263–87.

Chapters 6: Voyage to Antarctica and Australia and 7: Australia

Admiralty South Polar charts 1927 and 1942.
Anon., *Chui Hiao* ('Atlas of Foreign Countries'). China, AD 265-316.
Anon., *The Classics of Shan Hai Jing*. China, c.338 BC.
Anon., *Hsi-Yang-Chi* (popular account of Zheng He's voyages). China, 1597.
Anon., *I Yü Thu Chih* ('Illustrated Record of Strange Countries'). Nanjing, 1430.
Bagnell, A.K., *The Tamil Bell*. Wellington, 1948.
Bass, G.F., *A History of Seafaring Based on Underwater Archaeology*. 1972.
Beaglehole, J.C., 'Birthplace of Our History'. *Australasian Post,* 17 March 1955.
—— *The Exploration of the Pacific*. A and C Black, 1934.
—— *The Life of Captain James Cook*. A and C Black, 1974.
Berndt, R.M. and C.H., *Arnhemland, its History and People*. Melbourne, 1954.
Clark, C.M.H., *A History of Australia*. Cambridge University Press, 1962.
Crawfurd, J., *Notes on an Ancient Hindu Sacrificial Bell*. Ethnological Society of London, 1867.
Dalrymple, A., *An Account of the Discoveries in the South Pacifick* [*sic*] *Ocean*. Sydney, 1996.
Deem, G., *Ancient and Mysterious Discoveries in Australia*. Australia, c. 1999.
Elkin, A.P. and Berndt, R.M., *Art in Arnhemland*. Chicago, 1951.
Finlay, H., *Australia*. Lonely Planet, 1994.
Gilroy, R., *Pyramids in the Pacific*. Gympie, Australia, 1999.

—— *Were the Chinese the First to Discover Australia?* Australia, 1986.

Gossett, R., *New Zealand Mysteries*. Auckland, 1996.

Gray, G., *Ark of the Covenant*. Australia.

Green, B., *The Gympie Pyramid Story*. Gympie, Australia, 1998.

Green, J., *Journals and Private Papers 1862–63* (relating to Aboriginal people and their legends and sightings of shipwrecks at Gympie).

Harst, J. von, presidential address, Trans NZ Institute, 10. Wellington, 1877.

Kingsley, H., *The Recollections of Geoffrey Hamlyn*. Cambridge, 1859.

Lewis, M. and Clark, W., *A History of the Expedition under the Command of Lewis and Clark*. New York, 1893.

McIntyre, K.G., 'Portuguese Discoveries on the Australian Coast'. *Victoria Historical Magazine* 45 (4), 1974.

—— *The Secret Discovery of Australia*. Melbourne, Souvenir, 1977.

McKiggan, I., 'The Portuguese Expedition to Bass Strait in AD 1522'. *Journal of Australian Studies* 61, June 1977.

Major, R.H. (ed.), 'The Travels of Niccolò da Conti', in *India in the Fifteenth Century* (1857).

Martin, A.J. and James, P.E., *All Possible Worlds: A History of Geographical Ideas*. John Wiley & Sons, USA, 1993.

Mulvaney, J. and Kamminga, J., *The Prehistory of Australia*. Smithsonian Institution Press, 1999.

Needham, J., *Science and Civilisation of China*, vols 1 to 4. Cambridge University Press, 1954–9.

New South Wales Department of Mineral Resources, *Mineral Resources of New South Wales 1996–2002*.

Reid, Donald, *Private papers 1980–90* (relating to wrecks at Tin Can Bay).

Rotz, J. (ed. H. Wallis), *The Boke of Idrography*. Oxford, 1981.

Schilder, G. (trs. O. Richter), *Australia Unveiled*. Amsterdam, 1976.

Scott, E., *Australian Discovery by Sea*. Ernest Dent, 1929.

Simpson, C., *The New Australia*. Sydney, 1971.

Skelton, R.A., *Explorers' Maps*. New York, Spring Books, 1970.

Spate, O.H.K., 'Terra Australis – Cognita', in *Let Me Enjoy*. ANU, Canberra, 1965.

Wei, Chu-Hsien, *The Chinese Discovery of Australia* (Mitchell Library, Sydney). Hong Kong, 1961.

Whitehouse, E.B., *Australia in Old Maps 820–1770*. Boolarong Press, 1994.

Williams, G. and Frost, A., *Terra Australis to Australia*. Oxford University Press, 1988.

Wiseman, R., *Pre Tasman Explorers*. Auckland, 1996.

Wrecks (ch. 7)

RUAPUKE BEACH

Best, E., 'Notes on a Curious Steatite Figurine found at Mauku, Auckland'. *New Zealand Journal of Science and Technology*, vol. II, 1919, 77.

Gossett, R., *New Zealand Mysteries*. Auckland, 1996.

Hilder, B., 'The Story of the Tamil Bell'. *Journal of the Polynesian Society*, vol. 84, 1975.

McFadgen-Richardson, B.I., *The Tamil Bell*, unpublished MS.

NEAHKAHNIE BEACH (ch. 9)

Anon., *Tales of the Neahkahnie Treasure*. Nehalem Valley Historical Society, Tillamook, Oregon.

Bawlf, S., *Sir Francis Drake's Secret Voyage to the Northwest Coast of America AD 1579*. British Columbia, Sir Francis Drake Publications, 2001.

Cotton, S.J., *Stories of Nehalem*. Ann Arbor, UMI, 1989.

Head, L.M., *Neahkahnie Mount*. Portland, Oregon, 1910.

Hult, R.E., *Lost Mines and Treasures of the Pacific Northwest*. Binford and Mort, 1957.

—— *Treasure Hunting Northwest*. Binford and Mort, 1971.

Keller, A.S. et al., *Creation of Rights of Sovereignty Through Symbolic Acts – 1400–1800*. New York, 1938.

McKee, A., *The Queen's Corsair*. Souvenir Press, 1978.

Nuttall, Z., *New Light on Drake*. Liechtenstein, Kraus Reprint, 1967.

Robertson, J.W., *Francis Drake and Other Early Explorers Along the Pacific Coast*. San Francisco, 1927.

Viles, D.M., *North America's Hidden Legacy at Neah-Kah-Nie Mountain, 1579*. Oregon, 1982.

PANDANAN (PHILIPPINES) (chs 10 and 13)

Dizon, E.J., *Underwater Archaeology of the Pandanan Wreck: a mid 15th Century Vessel*. Paper to South East Asia Archaeology Conference, Berlin, 1998.

Green, J. and Harper, R., 'The Excavation of the Pattaya Wrecksite and Survey of three other Thailand sites, Thailand 1982'. *Australian Institute of Maritime Archaeology*, 1982.

—— and Prishanchittara, S., 'The Excavation of the Ko Kradat Wrecksite, Thailand 1979/80'. *Australian Institute of Maritime Archaeology*, 1982.

Lovigny, C. (ed.), *The Pearl Road: Tales of Treasure Ships in the Philippines*. Makati Co. Ltd, 1996.

AUSTRALIA (chs 7 and 8)

Bateson, C., *Australian Shipwrecks*. Sydney, Reed, 1972.

Clark, P., 'Shipwreck Sites in the South-East of South Australia'. *Australian Institute of Maritime Archaeology*, 1990.

Coroneos, C. and McKinnon, R., 'Shipwrecks of Investigator Strait and the Lower York Peninsula'. *Australian Institute of Maritime Archaeology*, 1997.

Gill, E.D., 'Constraints imposed by the earth sciences on the interpretation of the Warrnambool mahogany shipwreck site'. *The Artefact*, vol. 2, 1997.

Gray, J., *Ark of the Covenant*. Australia.

Green, J. and Harper, R., 'The Maritime Archaeology of Shipwrecks and Ceramics in South East Asia'. *Australian Institute of Maritime Archaeology*, 1987.

Halls, C., 'Mystery of the mahogany ship'. *The Victorian – Tasmanian Water Sport*, 1975.

Hilder, B., 'Mahogany Ship Mystery'. *Parade*, June 1975.

Holroyd, J., 'In search of the mahogany ship'. *Travel Victoria*, no. 5, 1980–1.

Kingsley, H., *The Recollections of Geoffrey Hamlyn*. Cambridge, 1859.

Loney, J., *The Mahogany Ship*. Marine History Publications (Aus.), 1998.

McIntyre, K.G., *The Secret Discovery of Australia*. Melbourne, Souvenir, 1977.

Wicking, T.A., *The Mahogany Ship*, 5 vols. Warrnambool, 1979.

Williams, G. and Frost, A., *Terra Australis to Australia*. Oxford University Press, 1988.

Chapter 8: The Barrier Reef and the Spice Islands

Anon., *Hsi-Yang-Chi* (popular account of Zheng He's voyages). China, 1597.
Bosworth, M.L., *The Rise and Fall of 15th Century Seapower*. Maritime History, 1999.
Diamond, J., *Guns, Germs and Steel: The Fates of Human Societies*. New York, W.W. Norton, 1997.
Gould, R.A., *Archaeology and the Social History of Ships*. Cambridge University Press, 2000.
Landes, D.S., *Revolution in Time: Clocks and the Making of the Modern World*. Harvard, 1983.
Latourette, K.S., *A Short History of the Far East*. New York, Macmillan, 1957.
Mackenzie, D.A., *Myths and Traditions of the South Sea Islands*. 1930.
Needham, J., *Science and Civilisation in China*, vols 1 and 4. Cambridge University Press, 1954–9.
Swanson, B., *Eighth Voyage of the Dragon: A History of China's Quest for Seapower*. Annapolis, Maryland, 1982.

Periodicals

Chinese Culture 19, 3 (September 1968), 'The Revamping of Oceangoing Sea Routes'.
Oriens Extremis 5 (1958), 'Decline of Early Ming Navy'.

Chapter 9: The First Colony in the Americas

Adams, R.E.W., *Prehistoria Mesoamerica*. Boston, 1977.
Beals, R.L., 'The Aboriginal Culture of the Cahita Indians'. *Ibero-Americana* 19, University of California, 1943.
Bray, W., *Everyday Life of the Aztecs*. Batsford, 1968.
Cabrera Castro, R., *Teotihuacan: Art from the City of the Gods (Human Sacrifice at the Temple of the Feathered Serpent)*. Thames & Hudson, 1993.
Carrasco, D., *Quetzalcoatl and the Irony of Empire*. University of Chicago Press, 1982.
Clendinnen, I., *Aztecs*. Cambridge University Press, 1991.
Davies, N., *The Aztecs*. Norman, University of Oklahoma, 1973.
—— *The Toltec Heritage*. Norman, University of Oklahoma, 1980.
Diaz, G., Rodgers, A. and Byland, B.E., *The Codex Borgia*. Constable, 1993.
Diaz del Castillo, B. (trs. A. Maudslay), *The Discovery and Conquest of Mexico*. 1928.
Diehl, R.A., *Tula, the Toltec Capital of Ancient Mexico*. Thames & Hudson, 1983.
Duran, D. (trs. D. Heyden), *The History of the Indies of New Spain*. University of Oklahoma Press, 1994.
Dutton, B.P., 'Mesoamerican Culture Traits which appear in the American South West'. *International Congress of Americanists* 35, 1962.
Elgar, M.A. and Crespi, B.J. (eds), *Cannibalism: Ecology and Evolution Among Diverse Taxa*. Oxford, 1992.
Flinn, L., Turner, C.G. and Brew, A., 'Additional Evidence for Cannibalism in the South West'. *American Antiquity* 41, 308–18.

Gajdusek, D.C. and Zigas, V., 'Kuru'. *American Medical Journal* 26, 1959, 442–69.

Hartman, D., 'Preliminary Assessment of Mass Burials in the South West'. *American Journal of Physical Anthropology* 42 (2), 1975.

Hassig, R., *Aztec Warfare: Imperial Expansion and Political Control*. University of Oklahoma Press, 1988.

Hogg, G.L., *Cannibalism and Human Sacrifice*. Hale, 1958.

Keegan, J., *A History of Warfare*. Hutchinson, 1993.

Kelly, E.A., *The Temple of Skulls at Alta Vista*. Carondale, Southern Illinois University Press, 1978.

Kirkpatrick, F.A., *The Spanish Conquistadores*. A and C Black, 1946.

Landa, D. (trs. W. Gates), *Yucatan Before and After the Conquest*. Baltimore, 1937.

Leon Portilla, M., *Aztec Thought and Culture*. Oklahoma, 1963.

Millon, R., *Teotihuacan: City State and Civilisation*. Austin, University of Texas Press, 1981.

Nickens, P.R., 'Prehistoric Cannibalism in the Mancos Canyon'. *The Kiva* 40, 1975, 283–93.

Pickering, R.B., *Human Osteological Remains from Altavista*. Boulder, Westview Press, 1985.

—— and Foster, M.S., 'A Survey of Prehistoric Disease and Trauma in Northwest and West Mexico'. *Proceedings of Denver Museum of Natural History*, 1994.

Pijoan Aguarde, C.M., *Evidencias de Sacrificio Humano y Canabalismo*. Doctoral thesis, Mexico University, 1997.

Reed, E.K., 'Fractional Burials, Trophy Skulls and Cannibalism'. *Region 3, Anthropology* 5, 79, Santa Fe, 1949.

Sahagún, B. de (trs. F.R. Bandelier), *A History of Ancient Mexico*. Nashville, 1932.

Sturtevant, W.C. (ed.), *Handbook of North American Indians*. Smithsonian Institution Press, Washington DC, 1983.

Sugiyama, S., *Mass Human Sacrifice and Symbolism of the Feathered Serpent Pyramid in Teotihuacan, Mexico*. Ph.D. dissertation, Arizona State University, 1995.

Thomas, H., *The Conquest of Mexico*. Hutchinson, 1993.

Turner, C.G. and J.A., *Man Corn: Cannibalism and Violence in the Prehistoric American Southwest*. University of Utah Press, 1999.

Vaillant, G.C., *Aztecs of Mexico*. Penguin, 1975.

Vergara, L.M.A., *Chichen Itza: Astronomical Light and Shadow Phenomenon*. Mexico (undated).

Webb, W.S. and Snow, C.E., *The Adena People*. University of Tennessee Press, 1957.

Wright, R., *Stolen Continents – The Indian Story*. John Murray, 1992.

Chapter 10: Colonies in Central America

Chinese in the Americas

Jairazbhoy, R.A., *Asians in Pre-Columbian Mexico*. Northwood, author, 1976.

Jett, C., 'Asian Contacts with the Americans in pre-Columbus Times'. *NEARA Journal* 26, 1992.

Jett, S.C., 'Diffusion Versus Independent Development: the basis of controversy', in Riley, C.L. (ed.), *Man Across the Sea*. Texas, 1971, 1–53.

—— 'Pre Columbian trans oceanic contacts', in Jennings, J.D. (ed.), *Ancient South Americans*. San Francisco, 1983, 337–93.

Johnston, T.C., *Did the Phoenicians Discover America?*. J. Nisbet, 1913.

Lumholtz, C., *Unknown Mexico*. New York, AMS Press, 1973.

Marschall, W., *Influencias Asiaticas en las Culturas de La América Antigua*. Mexico, 1979.

Meggers, B.J., 'The Transpacific Origin of Meso American Civilisation'. *American Anthropologist* 77, 1975, 1–27.

Mertz, H., *Gods from the Far East: How the Chinese Discovered America*. New York, 1972.

Morton, J.F., 'The Ocean-going Noni or Indian Mulberry'. *Economic Botany* 46 (3), 241–56.

Needham, J. and Lu, G.D., 'Transpacific Echoes and Resonances: Listening Once Again'. *World Scientific*, Singapore, 1976.

Nuttall, Z.A., *Curious Survival in Mexico of the use of Purpura Shellfish for Dyeing*. Cedar Rapids, Iowa, 1909.

Sauer, C.O., *Agricultural Origins and Dispersals*. Cambridge, Mass., MIT Press, 1969.

Solheim, W.G., 'New Light on a Forgotten Past'. *National Geographic* 139 (3), 1971, 332–8.

Sorenson, J.L. and Raish, M.H., *Pre-Columbian Contact with the Americas Across the Oceans: an Annotated Bibliography*. Provo Research Press, 1990.

Spinden, H.J., 'New World Correlations'. International Congress of Americanists, 1924.

Dye-stuffs

Carter, G.F., 'Shells as Evidence of the Migrations of Early Culture'. *The New Diffusionists*, 23 (6), 1976, 50–7.

Gade, D.W., 'Red Dye from Peruvian Bugs'. *Geographical Magazine* 45 (1), 1972.

Gerhard, P., 'Shellfish Dye in America'. Congresso Internacional de Americanists, 1964.

Gordon, C.H., *Before Columbus: Links Between the Old World and Ancient America*. Turnstone, 1971.

Heyerdahl, T., *The Maldive Mystery*. Bethesda, Maryland, Adler, 1986.

Krochmal, A. and C., *The Complete Illustrated Book of Dyes from Natural Sources*. New York, Doubleday, 1974.

Sahagún, B. de (ed. A.M. Garibay), *Historia General de las Cosas de la Nueva España*. Mexico, Editorial Porrua, 1975.

Chickens

Acosta, J. de, *Historia Natural y Moral de las Indias*. No. 34 Cronic, Venice, 1596.

Bay-Peterson, J., *Catalogue of the Native Poultry of South East Asia*. Taiwan, 1991.

Capa, P.R., *Estudios Criticos Aserca de la Dominación Española en América*. 3, Madrid, 1915.

Carter, G.F., 'Pre-Columbian Chickens in America', in Riley, C.L. (ed.), *Man Across the Sea*. Texas, 1971.

Crawford, R.D., 'Domestic Fowl', in Mason, I.L. (ed.), *The Evolution of Domestic Animals*. Longmans, 1984, 293–311.

Finsterbusch, C.A., *Cock Fighting All Over the World*. Hindhead, Saiga, 1980.
Johannessen, C.L., 'Folk Medicine Uses of Melanotic Asiatic Chickens as Evidence of Early Diffusion to the New World'. *Social Science & Medicine* 150, 1981, 427–34.
Langdon, R., 'When the Blue Egg Chickens Come Home to Roost'. *The Journal of Pacific History* 25, 1981, 164–92.

Metallurgy and lacquer boxes

Cabrera Castro, R., *Arqueología en el Bajo Balsas, Guerrero y Michoacán*. Mexico, 1976.
Heil, C., 'The Pre-Columbian Lacquer of West Mexico'. *NEARA Journal* 30, 32–9.
Hosler, D., 'Copper, Sources, Metal Production and Metals Trade in Late Postclassic Mesoamerica'. *Science* 273, 1996.
—— 'Pre-Columbian American Metallurgy'. 45th International Congress of Americanists, 1985.
Leon, N., 'Studies in the Archaeology of Michoacán: The Lienzo of Jucutácato'. *Smithsonian Institution Annual Report*, 1889.

Civilization and peoples of the Americas

Abel-Victor, S., *Between Continents, Between Seas: Pre-Columbian Art of Costa Rica*. Harry Abrams, Detroit, 1981.
Ades, D., *Art in Latin America*. Madrid, 1989.
Ascher, M. and R., *Code of the Quipu*. Michigan, 1981.
Bahn, P.G., *Lost Cities*. Weidenfeld & Nicolson, 1997.
Bakewell, P.J., *A History of Latin America*. Oxford, Blackwell, 1997.
Bankes, G., *Peru Before Pizarro*. Oxford, Phaidon, 1977.
Barbier, J.P., *A Guide to Pre-Columbian Art*. Thames & Hudson, 1997.
Bastian, F.O., 'Creuzfeldt-Jakob Disease and Other Transmissible Spongiform Encephalopathies'. St Louis, USA, 1991.
Benson, E.P., *The Mochica*. Thames & Hudson, 1972.
Bethell, L. (ed.), *The Cambridge History of Latin America*. Cambridge University Press, 1984.
Bingham, H., *Machu Picchu: A Citadel of the Incas*. New Haven, 1930.
Brundage, B.C., *A Rain of Darts – The Mexican Aztecs*. University of Texas Press, 1972.
—— *Two Earths, Two Heavens – An Essay Contrasting the Aztecs and Incas*. Albuquerque, University of New Mexico Press, 1975.
Burger, R.L., *Chavin and the Origins of Andean Civilisation*. Thames & Hudson, 1995.
Calvert, A.S. and P.P., *A Year of Costa Rican Natural History*. New York, 1917.
Carrasco, D., *Montezuma's Mexico, Visions of the Aztec World*. University Press of Colorado, 1972.
Catherwood, F., *Views of Ancient Monuments in Central America, Chiapas & Yucatán*. New York, Bartlett and Welford, 1844.
Cieza de León, P. (trs. H. de Onis), *The Incas of Pedro de Cieza de León*. Oklahoma Press, 1959.

Clendinnen, I., *Aztecs: An Interpretation*. Cambridge University Press, 1991.

Coe, M.D., *The Maya*. Thames & Hudson, 1984.

—— *The Olmec World: Ritual and Rulership*. Princeton University, 1995.

—— and S.D., *The True History of Chocolate*. Thames & Hudson, 1996.

Collier, G.A., *The Inca and Aztec States 1400–1800*. Academic Press, 1982.

Conrad, G.W. and Demarest, A.A., *Religion and Empire. The Dynamics of Aztec and Inca Expansionism*. Cambridge University Press, 1984.

Cortés, H. (trs. A.R. Pagden), *Letters from Mexico*. Oxford University Press, 1972.

Davies, N., *The Ancient Kingdoms of Mexico*. Allen Lane, 1990.

—— *The Aztecs: A History*. Macmillan, 1973.

—— *The Toltecs Until the Fall of Tula*. University of Oklahoma Press, 1977.

Diaz, B.J., *The Mayans' Magnificent White Roads*. Merida, 1992.

Diaz del Castillo, B. (trs. J.M. Cohen), *The Conquest of New Spain*. Penguin, 1963.

Emerson T.E. and Lewis, R.B., *Cahokia and the Hinterlands*. University of Illinois Press, 1991.

Fagan, B.M., *The Aztecs*. New York, Freeman, 1984.

—— *Kingdoms of Gold, Kingdoms of Jade*. Thames & Hudson, 1991.

Fowler, M.L., *Cahokia, Ancient Capital of the Midwest*. Addison Wesley Module in Anthropology 48, 1974.

Gajdusek, D.C. and Zigas, V., 'Kuru'. *American Medical Journal* 26, 1959, 442–69.

Gallenkamp, C., *Maya*. Penguin, 1987.

Garcilaso de la Vega, El Inca, *Royal Commentaries of the Inca*. Ayacucho, Peru, 1976.

Goetz, D., *Popol Vuh*. Norman, University of Oklahoma, 1951.

Hammond, N., *Ancient Maya Civilisation*. Cambridge University Press, 1982.

Hemming, J., *The Conquest of the Incas*. Penguin, 1983.

Huff, S., *The Mayan Calendar Made Easy*. Florida, 1984.

Hyslop, J., *The Inca Road System*. Academic Press, New York, 1984.

Kendall, A., *Everyday Life of the Incas*. Batsford, 1973.

Kirkpatrick, F.A., *The Spanish Conquistadores*. A. and C. Black, 1946.

Kolata, A.L., *Tiwanaku: Portrait of an Andean Civilisation*. Cambridge, 1993.

Landa, D. (trs. W. Gates), *Yucatan Before and After the Conquest*. Yucatan, Baltimore, 1937.

Laughton, T., *The Maya, Life, Myth and Art*. 1998.

Lonsbury, F.G., *The Inscription on the Sarcophagus Lid at Palenque*. Texas, 1974.

Lopez de Gomara, F., *Cortes, The Life of the Conqueror by His Secretary*. University of California Press, 1964.

Macedo, J.C., *The Ancient Moche Society of Peru*. Nueva Arqueología, Lima, 1996.

Markham, C.R., *The Incas of Peru*. Smith, Elder, 1910.

Matthews, P. and Schele, L., *Lords of Palenque – The Glyphic Evidence*. University of Texas, 1974.

Miller, M.E., *The Art of Mesoamerica from Olmec to Aztec*. Thames & Hudson, 1986.

Millon, R., *Teotihuacan: City State and Civilisation*. Austin, University of Texas Press, 1981.

Mintz, S.W., *Sweetness and Power: The Place of Sugar in Modern History*. Penguin, 1986.

Morris, C. and Thomson, D.E., *Húanuco Pampa*. Thames & Hudson, 1985.

Mortimer, W.G., *The History of Coca: The Divine Plant of the Incas*. San Francisco, And/Or Press, 1974.

Moseley, M.E., *The Incas and their Ancestors*. Thames & Hudson, 1992.

Murray, A., *The Economic Organisation of the Inca State*. Ph.D. dissertation, Department of Anthropology, University of Chicago, 1956.

Nylander, C. (trs. J. Tate), *The Deep Well*. Pelican, 1971.

O'Callaghan, J., *A History of Medieval Spain*. Cornell University Press, 1975.

O'Neill, J.P., *Mexico, Splendors of Thirty Centuries*. Metropolitan Museum of Art (exhibition), Little Brown, 1990.

Patterson, T.C., *The Inca Empire. The Formation and Disintegration of a Pre-capitalist State*. Oxford, Berg, 1991.

Reinhard, J., *Nazca Lines. A New Perspective on their Origin and Meaning*. Lima, Los Pinos, 1986.

—— 'Peru's Ice Maidens'. *National Geographic*, June 1996, 62–81.

—— *The Sacred Centre Machu Picchu*. Lima, Nuevas Imágines, 1991.

Richardson, J.B., *People of the Andes*. Washington, 1994.

Rowe, J.H., *Inca Culture at the Time of the Spanish Conquest*. Washington, 1946.

—— *What Kind of Settlement was Inca Cuzco?*. Nawpa Pacha 5, Berkeley, 1967, 59–76.

Sahagún, B. de, *General History of the Things of New Spain*. University of Utah Press, 1975.

Savoy, G., *Antisuyo: The Search for the Lost Cities of the Amazon*. New York, 1970.

Schele, L. and Friedel, D., *A Forest of Kings*. New York, Morrow, 1992.

Soustelle, J., *Arts of Ancient Mexico*. Stanford, 1967.

Stannard, D.E., *American Holocaust*. New York, Oxford University Press, 1993.

Stirling, S., *The Last Conquistador*. Stroud, Sutton, 1999.

Tedlock, D., *Popul Vuh*. New York, Simon & Schuster, 1985.

Teeple, J.E., *Maya Astronomy*. Carnegie Institute, 1931.

Thompson, E.H., *People of the Serpent*. New York, Houghton Mifflin, 1932.

Thompson, J.E.S., *Mexico Before Cortez*. New York, 1963.

Von Hagen, A. and Morris, C., *The Cities of the Ancient Andes*. Thames & Hudson, 1998.

Zuidema, R.T. (trs. E.M. Hooykyns), 'The Ceque System of Cuzco'. Leiden, E.J. Brill, 1964.

Chapter 12: The Treasure Fleet Runs Aground

Coffman, F.L., *Atlas of Treasure Maps*. New York, 1957.

Hsü, K.J. and Chen, H.H., *Geologic Atlas of China*. Oxford, Elsevier, 1999.

Seong-Joo, L., and Golubic, S., 'Microfossil populations etc.'. *Precambrian Research* 96 (3–4), 1999, 183–208.

Sweeting, M.M., *Karst in China*. Berlin, Springer, 1995.

Terry, T.P., *World Treasure Atlas*. La Crosse, Wisconsin, 1978.

Wilson, D., *The World Atlas of Treasure*. Collins, 1981.

Zink, D.D., *The Ancient Stones Speak*. Dutton, 1979.

—— *The Stones of Atlantis*. W.H. Allen, 1978.

Chapter 13: Settlement in North America

Bass, G.F. (ed.), *Ships and Shipwrecks of the Americas*. Thames & Hudson, 1988.

Burgess, R., *Snorkelers and Divers Guide to Old Shipwrecks of Florida's SE Coast*. Florida, 2000.

Byam, M., *Discovery of North America*. Feltham, Hamlyn, 1970.

Cahill, R.E., *New England's Ancient Mysteries*. Boston, 1993.

Campbell, T., *Early Maps*. New York, 1981.

Coleman, L., *Mysterious America*. Massachusetts, 1983.

Conant, K.H., 'Newport Tower or Mill'. *Rhode Island History* 7 (1), January 1948, 2–7.

Cumming, W.P., Skelton, R.A. and Quinn, D.B., *The Discovery of North America*. Elek, 1971.

Danish National Museum, *Newport Tower Photogrammetric Measurement*. Copenhagen, 1992.

Davis, A., *Discovery of New England by the Northmen 500 Years Before Columbus*. Boston, 1844.

Faria e Sousa, M., *Epítome de las Histórias Portuguesas*. Madrid, 1628.

Folsom, F. and M.E., *America's Ancient Treasures*. Albuquerque, University of New Mexico Press, 1993.

Harisse, H., *Discovery of North Americas*. H. Stevens, 1892.

Harris, E., 'The Waldseemüller World Map: a Typographic Appraisal'. *Imago Mundi* 37, 1985, 30–53.

Irving, W., *Life and Voyages of Christopher Columbus*. New York, 1851.

Juricek, J.T., 'John Cabot's First Voyage'. *Smithsonian Journal of History* 2, 1967–8.

Lawson, E.W., *The Discovery of Florida and its Discoverer Juan Ponce de León*. Florida, 1946.

Leland, C.G., *Fusang or The Discovery of America by Chinese Buddhist Monks in the Fifth Century*. Curzon Press, 1973.

Mallery, G., *Picture Writing of the American Indians*. New York, 1972.

Morison, S.E., *Admiral of the Ocean Sea*. Boston, 1942.

—— *The Great Explorers: The European Discovery of America*. Oxford University Press, 1978.

Parry, J.H., *The Discovery of the Sea*. New York, Dial Press, 1974.

Peirce, C.S., 'The Old Stone Mill at Newport'. *Science*, vol. 4, December 1884, 512–14.

Penhallow, W.S., Brennan, M.J., Ray, C.J., Upgrew, A. and Stock, J., 'The Archaeology of the Old Stone Tower, Newport, Rhode Island'. American Astronomical Society, 1992.

Pohl, F.J., *Amerigo Vespucci*. New York, Columbia, 1945.

—— *Atlantic Crossings Before Columbus*. New York, 1961.

Prytz, K., *Westward Before Columbus*. Oslo, 1991.

Pulford, A.O., *Mysteries of Yesteryear*. Alliance Press, 1945.

Quinn, D.B. (ed.), *America from Concept to Discovery*. New York, Arno Press, 1979.

—— *North American Discovery*. Columbia, University of S. Carolina, 1971.

St Rain, T., *Mysteries of America: A Comprehensive Guide to Ancient Mysteries of North America*. 2001.

Snow, E.R., *Tales of the Atlantic Coast*. 1962.

Swarup, G.A.K. et al., *History of Oriental Astronomy*. Cambridge University Press, 1987.

Williams, S., *Fantastic Archaeology: the Wild Side of North American Prehistory*. Philadelphia, 1991.

Wroth, L.C., *The Voyages of Giovanni da Verrazzano 1524–1528*. New Haven, Yale University Press, 1970.

Chapter 14: Expedition to the North Pole

Ashe, G., *Land to the West*. New York, Viking, 1962.

Bjornbo, A.A., *Cartographia Groenlandica*. Danish Polar Centre, Copenhagen, 1912.

Bloomkvist, N., *When the Biggest Kingdom in Europe Was Formed in Kalmar*. Nordic Council of Ministers, 1996.

Campbell, E., 'Verdict on the Vinland Map'. *Geographical Magazine* 46, 1974.

Christiansen, E., *The Northern Crusade*. Penguin, 1997.

Cranz, D., *History of Greenland*. 1767.

Fischer, J. (trs. B.H. Soulsby), *The Discoveries of the Norsemen in America*. New York, Franklin, 1970.

Foote, P., 'On the Legends of the Vinland Map'. *Viking Society for Northern Research* XVII (1), London, 1966, 73–89.

Gad, F. (trs. E. Dupont), *The History of Greenland*. C. Hurst, 1970.

Galvão, A., *The Discoveries of the World*. New York, 1969.

Geo Daetisk Institut, Copenhagen, *Greenland Eskimo Maps*.

Goss, J., *The Mapmaker's Art*. Skokia, Illinois, Rand McNally, 1993.

Government of Canada, *Geological Survey of Canada Maps – Canadian Arctic*. ISBN/Control no. M/C 0846636, 1969.

Hardy, G.M.G., *The Norse Discoverers of America*. Oxford, 1921.

Harris, J.N., *The Last Viking: West by Northwest*. 1999.

Hennig, R., *Terrae Incognitae*. Leiden, 1944–56.

Heyerdahl, T. and Lilliestrom, P., *Ingen Grenser*. Oslo, 2000.

Hobbs, W.H., 'Zeno and the Cartography of Greenland'. *Imago Mundi* 6, 1949, 5–19.

Ingstad, H.M. (trs. N. Walford), *Land Under the Pole Star*. 1966.

—— (trs. E.J. Fris), *Westward to Vinland*. 1969.

Latouche, R. (trs. E.M. Wilkinson), *The Birth of Western Economy: Economic Aspects of the Dark Ages*. Methuen, 1961.

Lauring, P.A. (trs. D. Mohnen), *History of the Kingdom of Denmark*. Host & Son, Copenhagen, 1960.

Lindsay, D., *Sea-ice Atlas of Arctic Canada 1961–69*. Ottawa, 1975.

Major, R.H., *The Voyages of the Venetian Brothers Antonio and Nicolo Zeno to the Northern Seas in the XIVth Century*. Boston, 1875.

Mallet, P.H., *Northern Antiquities*. T. Carman, 1770.

Mowat, F., *The Farfarers*. Toronto, Key Porter, 1998.

—— *Westviking – The Ancient Norse in Greenland and North America*. 1996.

Nakamura, H., 'Old Chinese World Maps preserved by the Koreans'. *Imago Mundi* 4, 1947.

Norland, P., 'Buried Norsemen', in Seaver, K.A. (ed.), *The Frozen Echo*. Stanford University Press, 1996.

Oakley, S., *The Story of Sweden*. Faber & Faber, 1996.

Oleson, T.J., *Early Voyages and Northern Approaches 1000–1632*. Oxford University Press, 1964.

Quinn, D.B., *North America from Earliest Discoveries to First Settlements*. New York, Harper & Row, 1971.

Santarém, Vicomte de, *Atlas*. Paris, 1849.

Seaver, K.A., *The Frozen Echo: Greenland and the Exploration of North America AD 1000–1500*. Stanford University Press, 1996.

—— 'The Vinland Map – New Light on an Old Controversy – Who Made It and Why'. *Map Collector* 70, Spring 1995, 32–40.

Schlederman, Peter, *The Vikings Saga*. Weidenfeld & Nicolson, 1992.

—— *Voices in Stone*. Calgary, 1996.

Skelton, R.A., Marston, T.E. and Painter, G.D., *Proceedings of the Vinland Map Conference*. Chicago, 1971.

—— *The Vinland Map and the Tartar Relation*. New Haven, Yale University Press, 1965.

Spink, J. and Moodie, D.W., *Eskimo Maps from the Canadian Eastern Arctic*. Toronto, York University, 1972.

Stevens, H.N., *Ptolemy's Geography*. H. Stevens, 1908.

Storm, G. (trs. H. Jones), *North Atlantic Saga*. Christiana, 1888.

Thomas, A.H. and Oakley, S.P., *Historical Dictionary of Denmark*. Scarecrow Press, 1998.

Thomson, D.W., *Men and Meridian*. Ottawa, 1966.

Vernadsky, G., *The Mongols and Russia*. Moscow, 1997.

Wallis, H., 'The Strange Case of the Vinland Map'. *Geographical Journal* 40, Pt 2, 1974.

—— 'The Vinland Map: Fake, Forgery or Jeu d'esprit?'. *Map Collector* 53, 1990, 2–6.

—— Maddison, F.R. et al., *Chemical Analysis of the Vinland Map*. Report by McCrone Associates to Yale University Library, 22 January 1974.

Wylie, J.H., *The Council of Constance to the Death of John Hus*. 1900.

Chapter 15: Solving the Riddle

Ayres, W.S., 'Mystery Islets of Micronesia'. *Archaeology*, Jan/Feb 1990, 58–63.

—— 'Nan Madol, Pohnpei'. *Society for American Archaeology Bulletin*, vol. 10, November 1992.

Buck, P.H., *Vikings of the Sunrise*. New York, 1938.

Chapter 16: Where the Earth Ends

Admiralty, *Africa Pilot* Part I, 5th Edition. Admiralty, London, 1890.

Bellefond, V. de, *Relations des Côtes d'Afrique Appelées Guinea*. D. Thiers, Paris, 1669.

Bethencourt, J. (ed. and trs. R.H. Major), *Le Canarien. Livre de la conquête et conversion des Canaries 1402–1422*. 1872.

Boxer, C.R., *The Portuguese Seaborne Empire*. Hutchinson, 1969.

Bracciolini, P., *The Travels of Nicolo da Conti*. Milan, 1929.

Coleman, L., *Mysterious America*. Faber, 1983.

Colombo, C. (trs. L.C. Jane), *The Journal of Christopher Columbus*. A. Blond, 1960.

D'Avezac, M., *Notice de Découvertes Faites au Moyen-âge dans l'Océan Atlantique Anterieurement aux Grands Explorations Portugaises du Quinzième Siècle*. Paris, 1845.

Devigne, R.T., *Jean de Bethencourt Roi des Canaries*. Toulouse, 1944.

Eannes de Zuzara, G. (trs. C.R. Beazley), *The Chronicle of the Discovery and Conquest of Guinea*. New York, Franklin, 1963.

Fréville, *Mémoire sur la Commerce Maritime de Rouen Depuis les Temps, le Plus Reculéstes*. Le Brument, 1857.

Galvão, A., *The Discoveries of the World*. New York, 1969.

—— *Tratado*. Lisbon, 1563.

Gravier, G., *Les Normands sur le Route des Indes*. Rouen, 1880.

Hermann, P. (trs. A.J. Pomerans), *The Great Age of Discovery*. New York, 1958.

Lafiteau, *Histoire des Découvertes et Conquêtes des Portugais dans le Nouveau Monde*. Paris, 1733.

las Casas, B., *Historia de las Indias*. Lisbon, 1552.

Leland, C.G., *Fusang or the Discovery of America by Chinese Buddhist Monks in the Fifth Century*. Curzon Press, 1973.

Magry, M.P., *Les Navigateurs Français et la Révolution Maritime de XIV au XVI Siècles*. Paris, 1867.

Major, M., *The Life of Prince Henry the Navigator*. London, Asher, 1868.

Major, R.H. (ed.), *India in the Fifteenth Century*. New York, Franklin, 1964.

Mauny, R., *Les Navigations Mediaevales sur les Côtes Sahariennes Antérieures à la Découverte Portugaise (1434)*. Lisbon, 1960.

Monstrelet, E., *La Chronique d'Enguerran de Monstrelet (1400–1444)*. Paris, L. Douet d'Arc, 1859.

Parry, J.H., *The Discovery of South America*. 1979.

Ravenstein, E.G., *Martin Behaim: His Life and His Globe*. G. Philip, 1908.

Rogers, F.M., *The Quest for Eastern Christians*. Minneapolis, 1962.

—— *The Travels of the Infante Dom Pedro of Portugal*. Harvard, 1961.

Rotz, J., *The Boke of Idrography Presented in 1542 by Jean Rotz to King Henry VIII*. Rare Books, British Library.

Sensburg, W., *Poggio Bracciolini und Nicolò de Conti*. Vienna, 1906.

Uzielli, G., *Paolo dal Pozzo Toscanelli*. Florence, 1892.

—— *La Vita e i Tempi di Paolo dal Pozzo Toscanelli*. Rome, 1894.

Vautier, C., *Extrait de Régistre des dons, confiscations, maintenues et autres actes faits dans le duché de Normandie pendant les années 1418, 1419, 1420 par Henry V*. Paris, 1828.

Viera Y. Clavijo, *Noticias de la Historia-General de las Islas de Canaria*. Madrid, 1774.

Vignaud, H., *Toscanelli and Columbus*. Sands, 1902.

Chapter 17: Colonizing the New World

Ajayi, J.F.A. and Espie, I., *A Thousand Years of West African History*. Ibadan University Press, 1965.

Bagrow, L. and Skelton, R.A. (trs. D.L. Paisey), *History of Cartography*. Cambridge, Mass., Harvard, 1964.

Beazley, C.R., *Prince Henry the Navigator: The hero of Portugal and of modern discovery 1394–1460*. Cass & Co, 1968.

Bovill, E.W., *The Golden Trade of the Moors*. Oxford University Press, 1958.

Boxer, C.R., *The Portuguese Seaborne Empire*. Hutchinson, 1969.

Bradford, E.D.S., *Southward the Caravels*. Hutchinson, 1961.

Campbell, A., 'Verdict on the Vinland Map'. *Geographica Magazine* 46, 1974, 310–11.

Canto, E. do, *Archivo dos Açores*. Lisbon, 1878–1906.

Chu Ssu-Pen, *The Mongol Atlas of China* (c. 1555). Peiping, 1946.

Cipolla, C.M., *Guns and Sails in the Early Phase of European Expansion*. Collins, 1965.

Collingridge, G., *The Discovery of Australia*. Sydney, 1895.

Cortesão, A., *History of Portuguese Cartography*. Coimbra, 1969.

—— *The Nautical Chart of 1424*. University of Coimbra, 1954.

Crone, G.R., *Maps and their Makers*. Hutchinson, 1968.

—— *The Mythical Islands of the Atlantic Ocean*. Amsterdam, 1939.

Cumming, W.P., Skelton, R.A. and Quinn, D.B., *The Discovery of North America*. Elek, 1971.

Davis, R., *The Rise of the Atlantic Economies*. Weidenfeld & Nicolson, 1973.

Diffie, B.W. and Winius, G.D., *Foundation of the Portuguese Empire 1415–1580*. St. Paul, University of Minnesota Press, 1977.

Eannes de Zuzara, G. (trs. C.R. Beazley), *The Chronicle of the Discovery and Conquest of Guinea*. New York, Franklin, 1963.

Falchetta, P., 'Marinai, Mercanti, Cartografi, Pittori'. *Ateneo Veneto*, vol. 33, 1995.

Fernandez-Armesto, F., *Before Columbus: Exploration and Colonisation from the Mediterranean to the Atlantic, 1229–1492*. Pennsylvania, 1987.

—— *The Times Atlas of World Exploration*. Times Books (HarperCollins), 1991.

Fischer, J. (trs. B.H. Soulsby), *The Discoveries of the Norsemen in America*. New York, Franklin, 1970.

Fischer, S.J., *Claudius Clavius the First Cartographer of America*. Historical Records of American Catholic Historical Society, vol. VI.

Foote, P.G., *On the Legends of the Vinland Map*. London, Viking Society for Northern Research XVII (1), 1996, 73–89.

Galvão, A., *The Discoveries of the World*. New York, 1969.

—— *Tratado*. Lisbon, 1563.

Harisse, H., *Discovery of North Americas*. H. Stevens, 1892.

Harley, J.B. and Woodward, D., *History of Cartography*. University of Chicago Press, 1992–4.

Heyerdahl, T. and Lilliestrom, P., *Ingen Grenser*. Oslo, 2000.

Las Casas, B., *Historia de los Indias*. 1550.

Longille, J.H., *Christopher Columbus*. Washington DC, Inscribers, 1903.

McIntyre, K.G., *The Secret Discovery of Australia*. Melbourne, Souvenir, 1977.

Major, R.H., *The Life of Prince Henry of Portugal surnamed the Navigator*. A. Asher, 1868.

Mascarenhas, J., *Historia de la Ciudad de Ceuta*. Academy of Sciences, Lisbon, 1918.

Morison, S.E., *Portuguese Voyages to America in the Fifteenth Century*. Harvard, 1940.

Neugebauer, O., 'Ptolemy's Geography'. *Isis* 50, 1959, 22–9.

Nordenskild, A.E., *Facsimile Atlas to the Early History of Cartography*. Pennsylvania, 1973.

Parry, J.H., *The Discovery of South America*. New York, Taplinger, 1979.

Phillips, J.R.S., *The Medieval Expansion of Europe*. Oxford University Press, 1988.

Ptolemy (trs. G. Treshel), *Geographica Errationis Libri Octo*. Vienna, 1541.

Rogers, F.M., *The Travels of the Infante Dom Pedro of Portugal*. Harvard, 1961.

Rotz, J., *The Boke of Idrography Presented in 1542 by Jean Rotz to King Henry VIII*. 1542.

Russell, P., *Prince Henry 'the Navigator', a Life*. Yale University Press, 2000.

Salgado, C., *El Cantar Folklórico de Puerto Rico*. San Juan, 1986.

Santarém, Vicomte de, *Atlas*. Paris, 1849–52.

Scammell, G.V., *The World Encompassed: The First European Maritime Empires c.800–1650*. Berkeley, University of California, 1981.

Seaver, K.A., 'The Vinland Map – New Light on an Old Controversy – Who Made It and Why'. *Map Collector* 70, Spring 1995, 32–40.

Skelton, R.A., *Explorers' Maps*. New York, Spring Books, 1970.

—— Marston, T.E. and Painter, G.D., *Proceedings of the Vinland Map Conference*. Chicago, 1971.

—— *The Vinland Map and the Tartar Relation*. New Haven, Yale University Press, 1965.

Stevens, H.N., *Ptolemy's Geography*. H. Stevens, 1908.

Tooley, R.V., *Maps and Mapmakers*. Batsford, 1970.

Ure, J., *Prince Henry the Navigator*. Constable, 1977.

Verge-Franceschi, M., *Henri, le Navigateur*. Paris, 1994.

Vilarinho, L., *Guide to the Maritime Museum, Lisbon*. Museu de Marinha, Lisbon (undated).

Wallis, H., 'The Vinland Map: Fake, Forgery or Jeu d'esprit?'. *Map Collector* 53, 1990, 2–6.

—— Maddison, F.R. et al., *Chemical Analysis of the Vinland Map*. Report by McCrone Associates to Yale University Library, 22 January 1974.

Wylie, J.H., *The Council of Constance to the Death of John Hus*. Longmans, 1900.

Chapter 18: On the Shoulders of Giants

Columbus

Colombo, C. (trs. L.C. Jane), *The Journal of Christopher Columbus*. A. Blond, 1960.

Columbus, F., *La Historia della Vita di Cristoforo Columbus*. Milan, 1930.

Crone, G.R., *The Discovery of America*. Hamish Hamilton, 1969.

—— *Maps and their Makers*. Hutchinson, 1968.

Davies, A., 'Behaim, Martellus and Columbus'. *Geographic Journal* 143, November 1977, 451–9.

Davies, H., *In Search of Columbus*. Sinclair Stevenson, 1991.

Dor-Ner, Zvi, *Columbus and the Age of Discovery*. Grafton Books, 1992.

Harisse, H., *Discovery of North Americas*. H. Stevens, 1892.

las Casas, B. (trs. and ed. A. Collard), *History of the Indies*. New York, 1971.

Morison, S.E., *Portuguese Voyages to America in the Fifteenth Century*. Harvard, 1940.

Parry, J.H., *The Discovery of the Sea*. Berkeley, University of California, 1981.

—— *The Discovery of South America*. New York, Taplinger, 1979.

Ravenstein, E.C., *Martin Behaim – His Life and His Globe*. 1908.

Vignaud, H., *Toscanelli and Columbus*. Sands, 1902.

North America

Byam, M., *Discovery of North America*. 1970.
Davies, A., 'Behaim, Martellus and Columbus'. *Geographic Journal* 143, November 1977, 451–9.
Davis, A., *Discovery of New England by the Northmen 500 years before Columbus*. Boston, 1844.
Lawson, E.W., *The Discovery of Florida and its Discoverer Juan Ponce de León*. Florida, 1946.

Dias, Cabral and De Castro

Alvarez, F., *Verdadeira Informação das Terras do Preste João das Indias*. Lisbon, 1889.
Axelson, E. (ed.), *Dias and His Successors*. Cape Town, 1988.
Batalha Reis, J., 'The Supposed Discovery of South America before 1448'. *Acta Cartographica* V, 1–26.
Cortesão, A., *The Mystery of Vasco da Gama*. Coimbra, 1973.
Liesegang, G.J., 'Archaeological Sites in the Bay of Sofala'. *Azania* VII, 1972, 147–59.
Poignant, R., *Discovery Under the Southern Cross*. Sydney, Collins, 1976.
Theal, G.M., *Records of South-Eastern Africa*. 1898.
Welch, S.R., *Europe's Discovery of South Africa*. Cape Town, 1935.

Da Gama

Batalha Reis, J., *Estudios Geográficos e Históricos*. Lisbon, 1941.
Boxer, C.R., *The Portuguese Seaborne Empire*. Hutchinson, 1969.
Cortesão, A., *The Mystery of Vasco da Gama*. Coimbra, 1973.
Galvão, A., *The Discoveries of the World*. New York, 1969.
Jayne, K.G., *Vasco da Gama and His Successors 1460–1580*. Methuen, 1970.
Latino-Coelho, J. M., *Vasco da Gama*. Lisbon, Corrazzi, 1882.
Liesegang, G.J., 'Archaeological Sites in the Bay of Sofala'. *Azania* VII, 1972, 147–59.
Ravenstein, E.G. (trs. and ed.), A *Journal of the First Voyage of Vasco da Gama 1497–1499*. Hakluyt Society, 1898.
Theal, G.M., *Records of South-Eastern Africa*. 1898.

Magellan

Lord Stanley of Alderley, *The First Voyage Round the World by Magellan*. 1874.
Miller, A.W., *The Straits of Magellan and Eastern Shores of the Pacific Ocean*. Portsmouth, 1884.
Parry, J.H., *The Discovery of South America*. 1979.
Pigafetta, A. (trs. and ed. R.A. Skelton), *Magellan's Voyage*. Yale, 1969.

Cabot

Williamson, J.A., *The Voyages of John and Sebastian Cabot*. 1937.

Cook

Cook, James, *The Explorations of Captain James Cook in the Pacific*. New York, 1957.
(see also chapter 7)

Epilogue: The Chinese Legacy

Armstrong, W.P., 'Morning Glories', in *Pacific Horticulture* 58 (1), 1997, 15–21.
Bray, F., 'The Chinese Contribution to Europe's Agricultural Revolution', in *Explorations in the History of Science and Technology in China*. Shanghai, 1982.
Carney, J.A., *Black Rice. The African Origins of Rice Cultivation in the Americas*. Harvard University Press, 2001.
Carter, G.F., 'Movement of People and Ideas Across the Pacific', in *Plants and the Migration of Pacific Peoples, A Symposium*. Bishop Museum Press, 1963.
Chiba, T., *The Dispersal of Maize in Continental China*. 21st International Geographic Conference, Calcutta, 1968.
Huggill, P.J. and Dickson, B.D., *Transfer and Transformation of Ideas and Material Culture*. Texas, 1988.
Jeffreys, M.D.W., 'Pre-Columbian Maize in Africa'. *Nature* 4386, 1953, 965–6.
—— 'Pre-Columbian Maize in Asia', in Riley, C.L. (ed.), *Man Across the Sea*. Texas, 1971.
—— 'Pre-Columbian Maize in the Old World: An examination of Portuguese sources', in *Gastronomy, the Anthropology of Food*. The Hague, 1975.
—— 'Pre-Columbian Maize in the Philippines'. *South African Journal of Science* 61, 1967, 5–10.
—— 'Who Introduced Maize into Southern Africa?'. *Suid Afrikaanse Triskrif vir Wetenskar* 63, 1967, 24–40.
John, H.S. and Jendrusch, K., 'Plants Introduced to Hawaii by the Ancestors of the Hawaiian People'. Unpublished paper.
McMahon, M. (ed.), *Hartmann's Plant Science*. 2001.
Mangelsdorf, P.C., *Corn, Its Origin, Evolution and Improvement*. Cambridge, Massachusetts, 1974.
Merrill, E.D., 'The Botany of Cook's Voyages'. *Chronica Botanica* 14 (5/6), 1954, 1–373.
Needham, J., *Science and Civilisation in China*. Cambridge University Press, 1954.
Pickersgill, B., 'Origin and evolution of cultivated plants in the New World'. *Nature* 268 (18), 591–4.
Ptak, R., *China's Seaborne Trade with South and South East Asia 1200–1750*. Aldershot, Ashgate, 1999.
Sauer, C.O., *Plant and Animal Exchanges between Old and New Worlds*. California State University (unpublished), 1963.
Singhal, D.P., *India and World Civilisation*. Michigan State University, 1969.
Stonor, C.R., 'Maize Among the Hill Peoples of Assam'. *Annals, Missouri Botanical Garden* 36, 1949, 355–404.

Permanent colonies

AUSTRALIA
Wei Chu-Hsien, *The Chinese Discovery of Australia*. Hong Kong, 1961.

CALIFORNIA
Powers, S., 'Aborigines of California'. *Atlantic*, vol. 33, 1874.
—— *Tribes of California*. San Francisco, 1877.

GREENLAND
Sorenson, J.L. and Raish, M.H., *Pre-Columbian Contact with the Americas Across the Oceans: An Annotated Bibliography*. Provo, Utah, 1990.

GUATEMALA
Johannessen, C. and Fogg, M., 'Melanotic Chicken Use and Chinese Traits in Guatemala'. *Revista Historia de America* 93, 1981, 73–89.

MEXICO
Estrada, E. and Meggers, B.J., 'A Complex of Traits of Probable Transpacific Origin in the Coast of Ecuador'. *American Anthropologist* 63, 1961.
Mertz, H., *Pale Ink: Two Ancient Records of Chinese Exploration in America*. Chicago, 1972.
Needham, J., *Science and Civilisation in China*. Cambridge University Press, 1954.
Padron, P., 'Un Huaco con Caracteres Chinos'. *Sociedad Geográfica de Lima*, vol. 23.

NORTH PACIFIC
Christian, F.W., *The Caroline Islands*. 1899.

PACIFIC ISLANDS
Buck, P.H., *Vikings of the Sunrise*. New York, 1938.
Childress, D.H., *Ancient Micronesia*. Illinois, 1998.
Handy, E.S, and Craighill, H., *Polynesian Religion*. Honolulu, 1927.

PERU
Chang, K.C., *Manual de la Colonia China en el Perú*. Unpublished, undated.

VENEZUELA
Arends, T. and Gallengo, M.L., 'Transferrins in Venezuelan Indians'. *Science* 143, 1964.

Key Charts

The Cantino (1502)

Bagrow, L. and Skelton, R.A. (trs. D.L. Paisey), *History of Cartography*. Cambridge, Mass., Harvard, 1964.
Cumming, W.P., Skelton, R.A. and Quinn, D.B., *The Discovery of North America*. Elek, 1971.

Schwartz, S.I. and Ehrenberg, R.E., *The Mapping of North America*. New York, 1980.
Whitfield, P., *New Found Lands: Maps in the History of Exploration*. Routledge, 1998.
Wolff, H., 'America – Early Images', in *America – Early Maps of the New World*. Munich, 1992.

The Caverio (1505)

Larsen, S., *La Découverte de l'Amérique Vingt Ans Avant Christophe Colombe*. Paris, 1926.
Ulloa, L., *El Pre-descubrimiento Hispano-Catalán de América en 1477*. Paris, 1928.

Waldseemuller (1507)

Harris, E., 'The Waldseemüller World Map: a typographic appraisal'. *Imago Mundi* 37, 1985, 30–53.
Heawood, E., 'The Waldseemüller facsimiles'. *Geographical Journal* 23, 1904, 760–70.
Karpinski, L.C., 'The First Map with Name America'. *Geographical Review* 20, 1930, 664–8.
Parker, J., *Antilia and America: a Description of the 1424 Nautical Chart and the Waldseemüller Globe Map of 1507*. Minneapolis, 1955.
Whitfield, P., *New Found Lands: Maps in the History of Exploration*. Routledge, 1998.
Wills, G.F., *Letters from a New World: Amerigo Vespucci's Discovery of America*. New York, 1992.
Wolff, H. (ed.), *Early Maps of the New World*. Thames & Hudson, 1992.

INDEX